ReNEUAL MODEL RULES ON EU ADMINISTRATIVE PROCEDURE

ReNEUAL MODEL RULES ON EU ADMINISTRATIVE PROCEDURE

Edited by
Paul Craig,
Herwig C. H. Hofmann,
Jens-Peter Schneider, and
Jacques Ziller

OXFORD
UNIVERSITY PRESS

OXFORD
UNIVERSITY PRESS

Great Clarendon Street, Oxford, OX2 6DP,
United Kingdom

Oxford University Press is a department of the University of Oxford. It furthers the University's objective of excellence in research, scholarship, and education by publishing worldwide. Oxford is a registered trade mark of Oxford University Press in the UK and in certain other countries

First Edition published in 2017

Published in the United States of America by Oxford University Press
198 Madison Avenue, New York, NY 10016, United States of America

British Library Cataloguing in Publication Data
Data available

Library of Congress Control Number: 2016963300

ISBN 978–0–19–879530–8

FOREWORD BY THE EUROPEAN OMBUDSMAN

When I gave the oath of office as European Ombudsman at the Court of Justice in October 2013, I said that my ambition is to help the EU institutions to live up to their own best selves. That is in the interest of the institutions and their staff. It is in the interest of persons who have direct dealings with the institutions. But above all, it is in the interest of European citizens generally.

As European Ombudsman, the gap between the governing institutions of the European Union and its citizens is my particular concern. Those of us who work in the institutions need to understand that we face a crisis of European citizenship. And one key aspect of that crisis is that many citizens see the EU and its institutions as remote and alien.

The enormous work the Research Network in European Union Administrative Law (ReNEUAL) undertook and successfully accomplished in drafting Model Rules of administrative procedure helps makes more visible, and more understandable, the administrative framework through which the EU institutions carry out their functions.

No set of rules can possibly hope to cover every conceivable issue or situation. There must always be room for the exercise of good judgment in applying principles. The law should not become a shield for the administration to hide behind by saying that a particular action is not expressly allowed or forbidden. It is therefore of fundamental importance that ReNEUAL succeeded in avoiding rules that are excessively detailed. The Model Rules do not invite a box ticking approach, nor do they create an obstacle course that inhibits sound judgment or defies common sense.

The Model Rules make sense both as a basis for possible future legislation and as a persuasive synthesis of principles to be found in the existing law. I am convinced that they could have a significant long-term impact in helping the EU institutions to live up to their own best selves. They will certainly provide a valuable source of inspiration in carrying out the Ombudsman's mission to serve democracy by working with the institutions of the European Union to create a more effective, accountable, transparent, and ethical administration.

Emily O'Reilly
European Ombudsman

JOINT STATEMENT OF THE EUROPEAN LAW INSTITUTE (ELI) AND THE RESEARCH NETWORK ON EU ADMINISTRATIVE LAW (ReNEUAL)

ReNEUAL was set up in 2009. Its mission was to develop a set of model rules on EU administrative procedure. These model rules are meant to reinforce general principles of EU law and to codify best practices identified in existing EU legislation or national legal orders. One of the objectives of the ELI—founded in 2011—is to strengthen the dialogue between academia and legal practitioners in order to make an informed contribution to European law-making on issues of a truly European dimension. In order for the proposed EU administrative procedural law to reach the broadest possible audience and achieve the best possible results ReNEUAL and ELI decided in 2012 to cooperate on the development of the Model Rules on EU Procedure, which were drafted and developed by ReNEUAL. In 2012 ELI agreed to cooperate on the ReNEUAL project 'Towards Restatements and Best Practice Guidelines on EU Administrative Procedural Law'.

For the ELI, this type of cooperation was an experiment with an unconventional format. The fact that ReNEUAL had already worked for several years on developing the project, meant that it was possible for ReNEUAL to move to the final stages before the ELI could fully follow its own internal procedures to substantively review and adopt all the detailed provisions of the Model Rules.

Publication of the Model Rules therefore takes place without the Model Rules being put formally in the format of an ELI instrument. Nevertheless, important substantive elements of the ELI method, such as diversity and inclusion of academics and practitioners, were included.

The ELI and ReNEUAL recognize this process as mutually beneficial and enriching. The joint process meant that various bodies established by the ELI, including a membership consultative committee, were included in the discussion. Amongst the joint activities special mention is made of a conference organized in cooperation with the European University Institute's Centre for Judicial Cooperation in Florence in February 2014. This enabled discussion with high-level national and European judges and contributed constructively to the development of the Model Rules.

The ReNEUAL Model Rules 2014 have greatly benefited from the ELI/ReNEUAL joint efforts. This cooperation is now the basis for further joint activities to improve EU administrative procedure law.

Both the ELI and ReNEUAL are convinced of the benefits of their future cooperation and collaboration.

Diana Wallis
President of the European Law Institute

Herwig C.H. Hofmann, Jens-Peter Schneider, Jacques Ziller
ReNEUAL Coordinators

EDITORIAL NOTE AND ACKNOWLEDGEMENTS

This publication of the Research Network on EU Administrative Law (ReNEUAL) is the result of a cooperative effort by many people and institutions. The printed version of the ReNEUAL Model Rules (2015) contains minor amendments by comparison to the online version published on September 1st 2014. These amendments result from clarifications introduced in the process of the translation of the original text drafted in English into French, German, Italian, Polish and Spanish.

ReNEUAL was set up in 2009 upon the initiative of Professors Herwig C.H. Hofmann and Jens-Peter Schneider who coordinate the network together with Professor Jacques Ziller. ReNEUAL has grown to a membership of well over one hundred scholars and practitioners active in the field of EU and comparative public law.

The objectives of ReNEUAL are oriented towards developing an understanding of EU public law as a field which ensures that the constitutional values of the Union are present and complied with in all instances of exercise of public authority. It aims at contributing to a legal framework for implementation of EU law by non-legislative means through a set of accessible, functional and transparent rules which make visible the rights and duties of individuals and administrations alike. The Model Rules on EU Administrative Procedure are proof that it is possible to draft an EU regulation of administrative procedures adapted to the sometimes complex realities of implementing EU law by Union bodies and Member States in cooperation.

In order to develop the Model Rules, ReNEUAL established four working groups addressing the main aspects of EU administrative procedure. These working groups were concerned primarily with executive rule-making (chaired by Deirdre Curtin, Herwig C.H. Hofmann and Joana Mendes (Book II)); single-case decision-making (chaired by Paul Craig, Giacinto della Cananea, Oriol Mir, and Jens-Peter Schneider (Book III)); public contracts (chaired by Jean-Bernard Auby, Ulrich Stelkens and Jacques Ziller (Book IV)); and information management (chaired by Diana-Urania Galetta, Herwig C.H. Hofmann and Jens-Peter Schneider (Books V/VI)). The design of these working groups reflected the scope of the ReNEUAL project on Model Rules on EU Administrative Procedure. In order to draft the various books, the chairpersons of the working groups established drafting teams. In addition to the chairpersons, the following scholars acted as drafting team members: Micaela

Lottini (Book VI); Nikolaus Marsch (Book VI); Michael Mirschberger (Book IV); Hanna Schröder (Book IV); Morgane Tidghi (Book VI); Vanessa M. Tünsmeyer (Books III, V); Marek Wierzbowski (Book III). Edoardo Chiti, Paul Craig, and Carol Harlow actively collaborated in the initial drafting of Book II. Detailed information about the chairpersons and the additional members of the drafting teams are provided in the respective list following this note and acknowledgements.

A steering committee composed of the chairs and most active members of the working groups undertook the task of managing the project and ensuring the consistency of content and drafting and finally acted as the editorial board for these ReNEUAL Model Rules. It was joined by Professor George Berman (Columbia University, New York) as external member.

The working groups' research and drafting activities benefitted from the insights and critical input in terms of time and expertise by many ReNEUAL members as well as civil servants from the EU institutions and bodies, and also other experts from Europe and other parts of the world during presentations at workshops and conferences, as well as from reactions to earlier publications.

ReNEUAL would like to express its particular gratitude for the support from the European Ombudsman and the European Parliament. In 2011 the European Parliament established a sub-committee to the JURI committee under the presidency of MEP Luigi Berlinguer. The committee heard *inter alia* ReNEUAL steering committee members Paul Craig, Oriol Mir and Jacques Ziller as experts. The EP sub-committee prepared the January 2013 EP resolution requesting the Commission to submit a proposal for an EU Administrative Procedures Act. Following this invitation, the European Commission has undertaken hearings to which ReNEUAL steering committee members have contributed.

Since 2011 ReNEUAL has closely cooperated with the European Ombudsman: initially with Ombudsman Nikiforos Diamandouros and since 2014 with Ombudsman Emily O'Reilly. Both have publicly supported ReNEUAL's efforts to improve EU administrative procedure law. We are especially grateful for the opportunities they offered to discuss the ReNEUAL project in 2012 and 2014 at conferences in the European Parliament organized by the Ombudsman. We would also like to thank Ian Harden, Secretary General, European Ombudsman's office, for his interest in and support for the ReNEUAL project.

ReNEUAL would also like to acknowledge the cooperation with ACA-Europe, an association composed of the Court of Justice of the European Union and the Councils of State or the supreme administrative jurisdictions of each of the members of the European Union. ACA-Europe's first joint conference with ReNEUAL was organized in April 2013 at the European Food Safety Authority in Parma, Italy, at which judges from nearly all EU member states of the EU participated and contributed to the discussion of composite decision-making procedures. The meeting had been prepared by a preparatory workshop of members of the French Conseil d'Etat with Herwig Hofmann under the chairmanship of the vice-President of the Conseil, Jean-Marc Sauvé. The second conference in which ACA-Europe cooperated with ReNEUAL was held in The Hague (Netherlands) in November 2013 under the Dutch presidency of ACA-Europe, in collaboration with the Council of State of the Netherlands and with participation of Paul Craig and Jean-Bernard Auby of ReNEUAL.

The European Law Institute (ELI) joined the ReNEUAL project in 2012. In this context, we received many thoughtful comments by members of the ELI Membership Consultative Committee, chaired by Marc Clément (Lyon) and Christiaan Timmermans (The Hague) and by participants of two ELI annual general meetings. We would like to thank all individual commentators for contributing their time, energy, and knowledge to this joint project as well as ELI for lending its institutional support. A conference organized by the Centre for Judicial Cooperation, Department of Law of the European University Institute in Florence under the directorship of Loïc Azoulai in cooperation with ELI and ReNEUAL in February 2014 allowed for further in-depth discussion. Next to the organizers, we would like especially to thank the participating judges from Member States' high jurisdictions.

ReNEUAL is grateful for financial and material support from various sources including contributions from the host universities of the professors involved. We would like to especially acknowledge the contributions from the following:

- Deutsche Forschungsgemeinschaft, Germany (GZ: SCHN 364/1-1);
- Fonds National de Recherche du Luxembourg, Luxembourg (INTER/DFG/11/09);
- Ministerio de Ciencia e Innovación, Administración General del Estado, Spain (Proyecto DER2011-22754);
- Ministero dell'Istruzione, dell'Università e della Ricerca, Italy (PRIN 2012—prot. 2012SAM3KM);
- Nederlands Wetenschappelijk Organisatie, the Netherlands.

ReNEUAL further would like to mention the welcome support *inter alia* for the organization of events by universities and other academic bodies including (in alphabetical order):

- Amsterdam: Amsterdam Centre for European Law and Governance ACELG, University of Amsterdam;
- Barcelona: Comissió Jurídica Assessora of Catalonia; University of Barcelona (UB);
- Florence: Florence Centre for Judicial Cooperation, Law Department, European University Institute (EUI)

- Freiburg i.Br.: Institute for Media and Information Law, University of Freiburg;
- Luxembourg: Centre for European Law, Faculty of Law, Economics and Finance, University of Luxembourg;
- Institut Universitaire International du Luxembourg, Jean Monnet Chair in European Public Law at the University of Luxembourg (financial support by the European Commission, Life Long Learning Project);
- Madrid: Instituto Nacional de Administración Pública;
- Milan: Facoltà di Giurisprudenza, Università degli Studi di Milano;
- Osnabrück: European Legal Studies Institute;
- Paris: Chaire Mutations de l'Action Publique et du Droit Public (MDAP), Sciences Po, Paris;
- Pavia: Dipartimento di Scienze Politiche e Sociali, Università degli Studi di Pavia;
- Speyer: German University of Administrative Sciences Speyer.

The ReNEUAL steering committee is most grateful for the many valuable contributions made to the discussions on earlier drafts of these model rules on EU administrative procedure, especially in the context of the conferences mentioned above, the ReNEUAL Conference 2013 in Luxembourg as well as during various workshops organized by the different working groups. The sheer amount of contributions makes it impossible to acknowledge each individual one appropriately, but we would nonetheless like to especially mention the contributions in the form of comments, contributions to drafting and critical review (in alphabetical order) by:

Henk Addink, Professor, University of Utrecht
Michael Asimow, Professor, Stanford University Law School
Joseph Azizi, Professeur Associé, University of Luxembourg, Former Judge and President of Chamber, General Court, Court of Justice of the European Union
Dimitry Berberoff Ayuda, Judge at the Administrative Chamber of the High Court of Justice of Catalonia
Luigi Berlinguer, Former Member of the European Parliament
Raffaele Di Giovanni Bezzi, DG Connect, European Commission
Stanislaw Biernat, Constitutional Tribunal of Poland
Jean-Claude Bonichot, Judge, Court of Justice of the European Union
Kieran Bradley, Judge at the Civil Service Tribunal, Court of Justice of the European Union
Alex Brenninkmeijer, Member of the European Court of Auditors
Anna Buchta, Head of Litigation and Legislative Policy, European Data Protection Supervisor
Dolors Canals, Professor of Law, University of Girona
Roberto Caranta, Professor of Law, University of Torino

Francisco Cardona, Senior Adviser for Civil Service Reform, OECD, Sigma
Edoardo Chiti, Professor of Law, Università degli Studi della Tuscia
Sarah Clegg, Research Assistant, University of Freiburg
Marc Clément, Judge at Administrative Court of Appeal of Lyon, France
Anne Davies, Professor of Law and Public Policy, University of Oxford
Lena-Sophie Deißler, Research Fellow, University of Freiburg
Dirk Detken, Head of Legal and Regulatory Affairs Unit, European Food Safety Authority
Paul de Hert, Professor of Law, Vrije Universiteit Brussels
Angelo de Zotti, Judge at the Administrative Tribunal of Lombardia—Italy
Piet Hein Donner, Vice-President of the Dutch Council of State
Anna Fleischer, Research Assistant, University of Freiburg
Eduardo Gamero, Professor of Administrative Law, University Pablo de Olavide, Seville
David Gaudillère, Judge at the French Conseil d'État
Gerhard Grill, Director, European Ombudsman
Marian Grubben, Head of Unit, DG Single Market Service Centre, European Commission
Ian Harden, Professor, Secretary General, European Ombudsman
Carol Harlow, Professor Emeritus of Public Law, London School of Economics and Political Science, London
Dirk Hudig, Secretary General, European Risk Forum
Pim Huisman, Assistant Professor, Vrije Universiteit Amsterdam
Peter Hustinx, European Data Protection Supervisor
Sir Francis Jacobs, Former President of the European Law Institute, former Judge at the ECJ
Marc Jaeger, President of the General Court, Court of Justice of the European Union
Oswald Jansen, Professor, University of Uthrecht, Legal Counsel City of The Hague
Heikki Kanninen, Vice-President of the General Court, Court of Justice of the European Union
Charles Koch, Former Woodbridge Professor of Law, College of William and Mary Law School, Williamsburg, Virginia
Beate Kohler-Koch, Professor emerita, Mannheim Centre for European Social Research (MZES), University of Mannheim
Nevena Kostova, Research Assistant, University of Freiburg (now University of Edinburgh)
Andrzej Kraczkowski, Research Assistant, University of Warsaw
Ingo Kraft, Judge, German Federal Administrative Court (Bundesverwaltungsgericht)
Hubert Legal, Director-General, Legal Service, Council of the European Union
Christian Lindner, Chef de Cabinet of Vice President Maroš Šefčovič, European Commission

Irena Lipowicz, Polish Public Rights Defender/Professor of Administrative Law, Cardinal Stefan Wyszyński University, Warsaw
Marilena-Silvia Lungu, Administrator, European Commission; University of Luxembourg
Lars Volck Madsen, Deputy-Head of Department, EU Law, Ministry of Foreign Affairs, Denmark
Olli Mäenpää, Professor of Administrative Law, University of Helsinki
María José Martínez Iglesias, Director, Directorate for Legislative Affairs, Legal Service, European Parliament
Richard Meads, Rapporteur, European Risk Forum
Arjen Meij, Visiting Professor, University of Luxembourg; former Chamber President at the General Court, Court of Justice of the European Union
Bucura Mihaescu-Evans, Researcher, University of Luxembourg
Alessandro Morini, Lawyer, former assistant University of Luxembourg
Paul Nemitz, Director, DG Justice, European Commission, Brussels
Jens Nymand-Christensen, Deputy Director, General Secretariat, European Commission
Nicolas Paine, Judge, High Court, UK
Timothée Paris, Judge, Cour administrative d'appel de Paris
Alexandre Peñalver, Professor of Administrative Law, University of Barcelona
Sara Pernus, Ph.D. Researcher, University of Amsterdam
Alain Pilette, Legal Service, Council of the European Union
Hans-Joachim Prieß, Lawyer, Freshfields Bruckhaus Deringer LLP
Georges Ravarani, President of the Administrative Court and Member of the Constitutional Court of Luxembourg
João Sant'Anna, Director, European Ombudsman
Ioannis Sarmas, Court of Auditors of the European Union
Jean-Marc Sauvé, Vice-President of the French Conseil d'Etat
Magdalena Śliwa, Research Assistant, Warsaw University
Ben Smulders, Director, Legal Service, European Commission
Jerzy Supernat, Professor at the Institute of Administrative Studies, University of Wrocław
Eljalill Tauschinski, Ph.D. Researcher, University of Amsterdam
Mario Tenreiro, Head of Unit, General Secretariat, European Commission
Christiaan Timmermans, ELI, former Dutch judge at the Court of Justice of the European Union
Frank van Ommeren, Professor, University of Amsterdam
Thomas van Rijn, Director, Legal Service, European Commission
Pieter van Nuffel, Legal adviser, Legal Service, European Commission
Diana Wallis, ELI President, former MEP
Wolfgang Weiß, Professor of Public Law, European Law and Public International Law, German University of Administrative Sciences Speyer

Rob Widdershoven, Professor, Utrecht University
Johan Wolswinkel, Assistant Professor, Vrije Universiteit Amsterdam
Bostjan Zalar, High Court judge of the Administrative Court of the Republic of Slovenia
Zheni Zhekova, Ph.D. Researcher, University of Luxembourg

CONTENTS

TABLE OF CASES

EUROPEAN COURT OF JUSTICE

TABLE OF LEGISLATION

Regulations

TABLE OF TREATIES AND CONVENTIONS

LIST OF ABBREVIATIONS

APA(s)	Administrative Procedure Act(s)
Austrian APA	Allgemeines Verwaltungsverfahrensgesetz 1991 (BGBl. Nr. 51/1991) das zuletzt durch Artikel 1 des Bundesgesetzes vom 31. Juli 2013 (BGBl. I Nr. 161/2013) geändert worden ist
CFR	Charter of Fundamental Rights of the European Union [2007] OJ C 303/1
CJEU	Court of Justice of the European Union
CJ	Court of Justice
CoE	Council of Europe
CoE Recommendation CM/Rec(2007)7	Council of Europe Recommendation of the Committee of Ministers to member states on good administration CM/Rec(2007)7
Commission Communication on contract awards	Commission Interpretative Communication on the Community law applicable to contract awards not or not fully subject to the provisions of the Public Procurement directives (2006/C 179/02)
DCFR	Draft Common Frame of Reference: Principles, Definitions and Model Rules of European Private Law—Draft Common Frame of Reference (DCFR)—Outline Edition, prepared by the Study Group on a European Civil Code and the Research Group on EC Private Law (Acquis Group), based in part on a revised version of the Principles of European Contract Law, available at http://ec.europa.eu/justice/policies/civil/docs/dcfr_outline_edition_en.pdf.
DG	Directorate-General
Dutch GALA	Wet van 4 juni 1992 houdende algemene regels van bestuursrecht (Stb. 1992, 315), in werking getreden op 1 juli 1994, laatstelijk gewijzigd bij Wet van 25 juni 2014, in werking getreden op 1 augustus 2014
ECHR	European Convention on Human Rights and Fundamental Freedoms
ECJ	European Court of Justice
ECSC	European Coal and Steel Community
EDPS	European Data Protection Supervisor
EO	European Ombudsman
EO Code	European Ombudsman—The European Code of Good Administrative Behaviour
EP	European Parliament

EP Resolution	European Parliament resolution of 15 January 2013 with recommendations to the Commission on a Law of Administrative Procedure of the European Union (2012/2024(INI))
EU	European Union
EURODAC	European Data Comparison system for the comparison of fingerprints for the effective application of the Dublin Convention established by Council Regulation (EC) No 2725/2000 of 11 December 2000
GALA	General Administrative Law Act
GC	General Court of the Court of Justice of the European Union
German APA	Verwaltungsverfahrensgesetz in der Fassung der Bekanntmachung vom 23. Januar 2003 (BGBl. I S. 102), das zuletzt durch Artikel 3 des Gesetzes vom 25. Juli 2013 (BGBl. I S. 2749) geändert worden ist
Italian APA	Legge 7 agosto 1990 n. 241, Nuove norme in materia di procedimento amministrativo e di diritto di accesso ai documenti amministrativi (pubblicata nella Gazzetta Ufficiale del 18 agosto 1990 n. 192)
MoU	Memorandum of Understanding
Polish APA	Ustawa z 14 czerwca 1960 r. Kodeks postępowania administracyjnego (Dziennik Ustaw Nr 30, poz. 168), tekst jednolity z dnia 30 stycznia 2013 r. (Dziennik Ustaw z 2013 r. poz. 267), zmiana z dnia 10 stycznia 2014 r. (Dziennik Ustaw z 2014 r. poz. 183)
RAPEX	Rapid Alert System for Non-Food Dangerous Products
RASFF	Rapid Alert System for Food and Feed
SIRENE	Supplementary Information Request at the National Entry [Regulation (EC) no 1987/2006 of the European Parliament and of the Council of 20 December 2006 on the establishment, operation and use of the second generation Schengen Information System (SIS II)]
SIS	Schengen Information System
Spanish APA	Ley 30/1992, de 26 de noviembre, de Régimen Jurídico de las Administraciones Públicas y del Procedimiento Administrativo Común (BOE núm. 285, de 27.11.1992), modificada por última vez por la Ley 27/2013, de 27 de diciembre, de racionalización y sostenibilidad de la Administración Local (BOE núm. 312, de 30.12.2013)
Swedish APA	Förvaltningslag (1986:223) Utfärdad: 1986-05-07, last amended by Lag (2014:630) om ändring i förvaltningslagen (1986:223)
TEU	Treaty on European Union
TFEU	Treaty on the Functioning of the European Union
TFP	European Civil Service Tribunal of the Court of Justice of the Union
US APA	Administrative Procedure Act of 1946, Pub.L 79-404, §§ 500-96, 60 Stat. 237 (1946)

MEMBERS OF THE DRAFTING TEAMS

Jean-Bernard Auby, Professor of Public Law, Chaire MDAP, Sciences-Po Paris

Paul Craig, Professor of English Law, St John's College, Oxford

Deirdre Curtin, Professor of European Law, University of Amsterdam

Giacinto della Cananea, Professor of Law, University Rome II

Diana-Urania Galetta, Professor of Italian and European Administrative Law, University of Milan (Università Statale di Milano)

Herwig C. H. Hofmann, Professor of European and Transnational Public Law, Jean Monnet Chair, University of Luxembourg

Micaela Lottini, Assistant Professor of Administrative Law, University Rome III

Nikolaus Marsch, Lecturer, University of Freiburg

Joana Mendes, Associate Professor of European Law, University of Amsterdam

Oriol Mir, Professor of Administrative Law, University of Barcelona

Michael Mirschberger, Research Fellow, German Research Institute for Public Administration Speyer

Jens-Peter Schneider, Legal Advisor of the Rector Chair for Public Law, University of Freiburg and a Visiting Professor at Colombia Law School

Hanna Schröder, former Research Fellow, German Research Institute for Public Administration Speyer (now: Legal Secretary, General Court of Justice of the European Union; any opinion expressed is strictly personal)

Ulrich Stelkens, Professor of Public Law, German and European Administrative Law, German University of Administrative Sciences Speyer

Morgane Tidghi, Former Marie Curie Fellow, University of Luxembourg

Vanessa M. Tünsmeyer, Research Fellow, University of Freiburg

Marek Wierzbowski, Professor of Administrative Law and Administrative Procedure, University of Warsaw

Jacques Ziller, Professor of European Union Law, University of Pavia

ADMINISTRATIVE PROCEDURE ACTS: HISTORY, FEATURES, AND RECEPTION

Paul Craig, Giacinto della Cananea, Diana-Urania Galetta, Oriol Mir, Jens-Peter Schneider, Ulrich Stelkens, Marek Wierzbowski, Jacques Ziller

1. Introduction

This book contains the Model Rules of Administrative Procedure, which were drafted by the Research Network on Administrative Law, ReNEUAL.[1] The rules and the commentary thereon are set out below. It may nonetheless be helpful to place this material in a broader perspective, since this will facilitate understanding of the rationale for the project.

This is more especially so in relation to the UK, where general codes that establish the applicable rules to govern an area are not part of the traditional landscape. This is coupled with the belief that the UK way of doing things is the norm, and that such codes are therefore both exceptional in empirical terms and to be regarded as of questionable value viewed from a more normative perspective. The empirical reality is quite to the contrary, and the normative evaluation of the worth of such enterprises is equally wide of the mark. Consider in this respect the data gained contained in a valuable study of codification of administrative procedure brought together by Jean-Bernard Auby, which reveals that a great many countries have adopted codes of administrative procedure.[2]

> [H]ere are the dates when the GAPAs were adopted: Austria in 1925; Bulgaria in 1979 with a new version in 2006; Chile in 2008; Croatia in 1931—when it was part of Yugoslavia—with new versions in 1956 and 2009; the Czech Republic in 1928, with a new version in 2004; Denmark in 1987; Estonia in 1936 with a new one in 2001; Finland in 1982 with a new version in 2003; Germany in 1976; Greece in 1999; Hungary, Italy in 1990; Japan in 1996; Luxembourg in 1978; the Netherlands in 1994; Norway in 1967; Peru in 1967; Poland in 1928 with a new version in 1961; Portugal in 1991; Serbia in 1997; South Korea in 1996; Spain in 1889 with

---

[1] http://www.reneual.eu/.

[2] J.-B. Auby, 'General Report', in J.-B. Auby (ed.), *Codification of Administrative Procedure* (Bruylant, 2014) 4.

a new one in 1992; Sweden in 1986; Switzerland in 1968; Taiwan in 1999; the United States in 1946.

It would be impossible within the confines of this chapter to consider all such instances of codification, and nor is it the objective, more especially given that the task has already been done by the volume just referred to. The objective is rather to consider three, more particular, issues concerning the historical rationale for the introduction of a code of administrative procedure, the defining features of such documents, and their reception. This inquiry is conducted in relation to five countries, Spain, Germany, Italy, Poland, and France, which created such codes at different times, and which reveal interesting commonalities and differences in relation to the three lines of inquiry just articulated.

2. Historical Perspective

(a) Introduction

Jean-Bernard Auby identifies three periods in the development of codes of administrative procedure.[3] The first period is represented by the Spanish code, and also that produced by Austria, the latter inspiring analogous developments in several other central European countries. The second period was post-war, and was characterized by creation of what became the two most influential models, those of the US and Germany. The third period dates from the 1990s onwards, during which a large number of new general administrative procedure acts were created, especially in post-communist countries, where codification of administrative procedure was seen as an important tool to combat administrative abuse of the kind that had been prevalent in the communist era. There were marked differences in the time taken by different countries to elaborate such a code. Thus, in the USA, it took approximately seven years, whilst, by way of contrast, the gestation period for the German code was closer to twenty years. It is helpful to focus more closely on the rationale and history that underpin the development of particular codes of procedure.

(b) Spain

It is fitting to begin with Spain, given that its code is the oldest. Spain has a very long codifying tradition in the field of administrative procedure. The first Spanish general codification of administrative procedure was enacted in 1889,[4] the same year in which the Spanish Civil Code was adopted. It was the first such European

[3] Ibid 4.

[4] *Ley de bases del procedimiento administrativo* of 19.10.1889.

codification,[5] and was passed almost forty years before Austria enacted its famous *Allgemeines Verwaltungsverfahrensgesetz* of 1925, although the Spanish code was far less influential. The later Spanish Administrative Procedure Act, *Ley de Procedimiento Administrativo* (LPA), of 17 July 1958, was a key piece of Administrative law legislation. It was adopted, somewhat paradoxically, under General Franco's dictatorship, but was technically much better and much more effective than the Act of 1889 and had a marked influence in other countries, particularly in Latin America. It embodied sophisticated regulation of the subject matter and the general approach has been maintained by later Spanish Administrative Procedure Acts.

The Act 30/1992 of 26 November1992, *Ley 30/1992, de 26 de noviembre, de Régimen Jurídico de las Administraciones Públicas y del Procedimiento Administrativo Común* (LRJPAC) adapted the codification of the administrative procedure to the democratic Spanish Constitution of 1978, and to the highly decentralized State the latter created. The LRJPAC has recently been repealed and replaced by a new APA, which entered into force on 2 October 2016: the Act 39/2015 of 1 October 2015 on the common administrative procedure, *Ley 39/2015, de 1 de octubre, del Procedimiento Administrativo Común de las Administraciones Públicas* (LPAC).

The new LPAC includes many, albeit minor, changes as compared to the previous LRJPAC,[6] the most important being regulation of electronic procedure and the inclusion of a final part on administrative rule-making. Electronic administrative procedures were hitherto regulated in separate legislation,[7] and are now intended to be the standard administrative procedure to be followed by all Spanish public administrations. Administrative rule-making was not regulated in the LRJPAC, but in the national and regional Acts on the respective Governments and other legislation. The APA now contains some general provisions applicable to all of them.

(c) **Germany**

Germany took considerably longer to adopt a code of administrative procedure, but it has proven to be particularly influential. German administrative procedure law was codified in the '*Verwaltungsverfahrensgesetz*' (Administrative Procedure Act;

[5] E. García de Enterría, 'Introducción: un punto de vista sobre la nueva Ley de Régimen Jurídico de las Administraciones Públicas y del Procedimiento Administrativo Común de 1992', in J. Leguina Villa and M. Sánchez Morón (eds), *La nueva Ley de Régimen Jurídico de las Administraciones Públicas y del Procedimiento Administrativo Común* (Tecnos, 1993) 11; W. Kahl, 'Das Verwaltungsverfahrensgesetz zwischen Kodifikationsidee und Sonderrechtsentwicklungen', in W. Hoffmann-Riem and E. Schmidt-Aßmann (eds), *Verwaltungsverfahren und Verwaltungsverfahrensgesetz* (2002) 94, fn, 167.

[6] The LPAC was passed in record time without the necessary political and academic debate, and was strongly questioned in Spanish Administrative law scholarship.

[7] The Act 11/2007 of 22.6.2007 on electronic access of the citizens to public services (*Ley 11/2007, de 22 de junio, de acceso electrónico de los ciudadanos a los Servicios Públicos*), which has also been repealed and replaced by the LPAC.

VwVfG in the following)[8] in 1976 after twenty years of intense debate and a number of drafts. The idea of codifying Administrative law was however advocated much earlier by Lorenz von Stein in 1866,[9] but his position remained isolated for a long time.[10] The general perception was that executive power required a margin for manoeuvre in order to fulfil its tasks of concretising the public interest in changing and dynamic circumstances.[11] An important first step was the enactment of sectoral codifications of administrative procedures in the field of social security law in 1911,[12] and in tax law in 1919.[13] Under the influence of the Austrian '*Allgemeinen Verwaltungsgesetz*' 1925, a first (limited) general codification of administrative procedural law emerged in 1926 in the state of Thuringia,[14] but this promising development was stopped by the Nazi dictatorship.[15]

The central issue for German Administrative law in the first years after World War II was the establishment of effective judicial review procedures and of an independent Administrative court system according to the far-reaching guarantees under the new, democratic constitution, the German Basic Law (*Grundgesetz—GG*).[16] However, administrative procedures were regulated in sector specific federal acts and increasingly by general codifications of a growing number of the *Länder* (states) during the 1950s and 1960s.[17] Consequently, the legislative landscape was fragmented and case law played an important role in supplementing it.

Important lawyers like Fritz Weber, the then-president of the Federal Administrative Supreme Court, preferred this fragmented status quo to codification because they envisaged that it would lead to less flexibility, impractical legislative or political

[8] VwVfG in the version of the promulgation of 23 January 2003 (Bundesgesetzblatt I 2003 p 102), most recently amended by Art 1 of the Law of 20 November 2015 (Bundesgesetzblatt I 2015, p 2010). An English translation of the most important paragraphs of the VwVfG can be found in M. P. Singh, *German Administrative Law in Common Law Perspective* (Springer, 2001) 286 et seq.

[9] G.-Chr. von Unruh, 'Kodifiziertes Verwaltungsrecht' (1988) Neue Zeitschrift für Verwaltungsrecht 690, 692.

[10] P. Stelkens and M. Sachs, in P. Stelkens, H J. Bonk and M. Sachs (eds), *Verwaltungsverfahrensgesetz—Kommentar* (Beck, 6th edn, 2001) Einleitung para 6 concerning acts in Prussia (1883) and Baden (1884).

[11] von Unruh (n 9); E. Forsthoff, *Allgemeines Verwaltungsrecht* (Beck, 3rd edn, 1953) 72–3, 137–8.

[12] Reichsversicherungsordnung of 19 July 1911 (Reichsgesetzblatt. 1911, p 509). A consolidated version was promulgated on 25 December 1924 (Reichsgesetzblatt. I 1924, p 779).

[13] Reichsabgabenordnung of 13 December 1919 (Reichsgesetzblatt. 1919, p 1993). A consolidated version was promulgated on 22 May 1931 (RGBl. I 1931, p 161); Stelkens and Sachs (n. 10) Einleitung para 7.

[14] Landesverwaltungsordnung of 10 June 1926 (Gesetzessammlung für Thüringen 1926, p 177), amended by the act of 22 July 1930 (Gesetzessammlung für Thüringen 1930, p 123). See von Unruh (n. 9) 690, 693–4; Stelkens and Sachs (n. 10) Einleitung para 7, also discussing a draft bill for a codification in the state of Württemberg; W Jellinek, 'Zum Entwurf einer Verwaltungsrechtsordnung für Württemberg' (1932) 60 Archiv für öffentliches Recht 1.

[15] Stelkens and Sachs (n. 10) Einleitung para 8.

[16] See especially, Art 19 (4), 92 of the Basic Law; Stelkens and Sachs (n. 10) Einleitung para 10.

[17] Stelkens and Sachs (n. 10) Einleitung para 11.

compromises, and have limited effects because of the federal division of legislative competences. In addition, they feared ossification of administrative procedural law, which was still not as mature as private law at the time of its codification.[18] By way of contrast, other high-ranking judges favoured general codification over uncoordinated regulation of aspects of general Administrative law in sector specific acts.[19] Academia was equally divided.[20] The driving forces for codification were administrative practitioners such as Klaus von der Groeben, who convinced the Deutsche Juristentag, a leading association of practicing as well as academic lawyers, to vote in support of codification in 1960.[21] The main arguments were increased legal certainty and legal protection for the citizen, increased effectiveness and efficiency of public administration, a uniform basis for legal education of lawyers and civil servants and some relief for the courts.

It nonetheless took another 16 years, a commission of administrative practitioners from all *Länder*, as well as from the federal level, and several draft bills to finalize the codification process in 1976.[22] The process gained decisive momentum after the general election of 1972 with the idea of fostering participation in administrative procedures.[23] Furthermore, representatives of the *Länder* authorities came to the view that a general codification of administrative procedure law would not only serve to protect the rights of the citizen vis-à-vis the administration, but that it would also facilitate day-to-day administration. This changed attitude of the *Länder* was decisive as the *Länder* authorities are generally competent to execute not only the laws of their respective *Land*, but also federal laws.[24] Therefore, the *Länder* authorities have far more practical experience of the realities of administration than

[18] F. Werner, in Verhandlungen des 43. Deutschen Juristentags 1960 'Empfiehlt es sich, den allgemeinen Teil des Verwaltungsrechts zu kodifizieren?' Band I (Gutachten) 2. Teil Heft B (Mohr Siebeck, 1960) pp 1 ff, especially pp 21 ff, and ibid Band II (Sitzungsberichte) (Mohr Siebeck, 1962) D 129 ff. See also, Baring, 'Bloß kein Gesetz' (1960) Juristische Rundschau 241.

[19] F Haueisen, 'Unnötige Normierung von Grundsätzen des allgemeinen Verwaltungsrechts im besonderen Verwaltungsrecht' (1959) Die öffentliche Verwaltung 5.

[20] See especially the proceedings of the major academic association for public law in 1958: Veröffentlichungen der Vereinigung der Deutschen Staatsrechtslehrer 17 (De Gruyter, 1959) 118 with antithetic reports by Bettermann and Melichar and a lively, mostly sceptical debate following.

[21] K von der Groeben, in Verhandlungen des 43. Deutschen Juristentags 1960 'Empfiehlt es sich, den allgemeinen Teil des Verwaltungsrechts zu kodifizieren?' Band II (Sitzungsberichte) (Mohr Siebeck, 1962) D 5 and D 100; on the vote in favour of a (limited) codification see ibid. D 141. See also, K von der Groeben, 'Über die Notwendigkeit eines allgemeinen Verwaltungsgesetzes', Deutsches Verwaltungsblatt 1966, 289.

[22] For comprehensive documentation, W Klappstein and G.-Chr. von Unruh, *Rechtsstaatliche Verwaltung durch Gesetzgebung: Entstehung und Bedeutung des Schleswig-holsteinischen Landesverwaltungsverfahrensgesetzes für das rechtsstaatliche Verwaltungsrecht* (Decker, 1987). For a short account, J.-P. Schneider, 'Strukturen und Typen von Verwaltungsverfahren', in W. Hoffmann-Riem, E. Schmidt-Aßmann and A. Voßkuhle (eds), *Grundlagen des Verwaltungsrechts Band II: Informationsordnung, Verwaltungsverfahrensarten, Handlungsformen* (Beck, 2nd edn, 2012) § 28 paras 9–10.

[23] H. H. Rupp, 'Freiheit und Partizipation' (1972) Neue Juristische Wochenschrift 1537–43.

[24] G. Robbers, *An Introduction to German Law* (Nomos, 5th edn, 2012) para 165.

the federal ministries. Codification was felt to enhance efficiency since it could serve as a step-by-step instruction, or checklist, for the responsible civil servant. It could in addition provide a clear framework for administrators to determine the relevant facts and conduct procedure in an objective and effective way. Thus, one of the most important characteristics of the VwVfG is described in the following citation of the aforementioned commission of administrative practitioners,[25]

> The Commission's aim was to avoid being too perfectionist. Therefore, exceptional cases of only theoretical importance have not been taken into account. However, the other extreme, the proliferation of general clauses, was to be avoided too. An administrative procedure code has to offer 'robust and solid' rules on administrative procedure for all interested bodies and persons and, not least, for the specialized administrative authorities.[26]

(d) Italy

The history of the codification process in Italy differed in certain respects from that in Germany. While an Italian code of administrative procedure is relatively recent, dating from 1990, the concept of administrative procedure dates back to the 1930s. Initially, academic literature focused on the administrative act, similarly to Otto Mayer's emphasis on the *Verwaltungsakt*.[27] But in the 1930s, together with the growth of government functions, the concept of administrative procedure, as distinct from process, emerged.[28] It was precisely because a concept of procedure existed that the Italian administrative judge could define and refine some standards of review, with regard to the right of defence of individuals and consultation. However, due to the concern that codification could 'ossify' the regulation of procedure, it was only at the end of the twentieth century that a code was enacted by parliament in the law of August 7th, 1990, n. 241,[29] on the basis of the preliminary work carried out by a group of scholars and administrative judges, who took into

[25] U. Stelkens, 'Kodifikationssinn, Kodifikationseignung und Kodifikationsgefahren im Verwaltungsverfahrensrecht', in H. Hill, K.-P. Sommermann, U. Stelkens and J Ziekow (eds), *35 Jahre Verwaltungsverfahrensgesetz—Bilanz und Perspektiven* (Duncker & Humblot, 2011), 270, 282.

[26] Musterentwurf eines Verwaltungsverfahrensgesetzes (EVwVerG 1963) 71 (translated into English by the authors).

[27] For further discussion, see G. della Cananea, 'Beyond the State: the Europeanization and Globalization of Procedural Administrative Law' (2003) 9 EPL 563 and, on the development of this concept, D. U. Galetta, 'Il procedimento amministrativo nella scienza del diritto amministrativo in Italia, dalle origini ad oggi: linee generali di sviluppo e critica di alcune recenti involuzioni', Il Foro amministrativo—TAR, 2011/11, 3779–90.

[28] After the pioneer works of F. Cammeo and U. Forti, the first systematic study on administrative procedure is A. M. Sandulli, *Il procedimento amministrativo* (Giuffrè, 1940).

[29] The Law was published in the Official Gazette of 18 August 1990, No. 192. An unofficial English translation is available at http://www.ijpl.eu/assets/files/pdf/leggi/Law%20no%20241-1990%20-%20for%20publication%20-%2025.03.2011.pdf.

account both existing case law and foreign legal materials,[30] with the aim of generalizing and improving existing standards of administrative action.

(e) Poland

The diversity in the historical origin of administrative codes is apparent once again in the case of Poland. The initial codification took place in 1928 by adoption of the Ordinance on Administrative Procedure. It covered only decisions concerning individual cases, and followed the pattern of Austrian codification from 1925. It is difficult to divine the precise reason for the adoption of the Ordinance, but it is likely that it was influenced by similar developments in other countries that had, prior to the First World War, been part of the Austro-Hungarian Empire. Thus, notwithstanding the collapse of the Empire, it still had an impact on the development of the legal systems of newly independent states, and influenced the nature of the statutes that they adopted. It was, moreover, the case that the adoption of a uniform regulation for the whole country facilitated the development of a unified system of public administration, which was especially significant given that Poland was a country composed of parts of former German, Russian, and Austrian empires.

The Ordinance was amended on a number of occasions, but remained in force till 1960, when it was replaced by the Code of Administrative Procedure,[31] which still remains in force, although it has been amended a number of times. The Code follows the Austrian tradition and concerns single case adjudication only. There is however a small part of the Code that relates to complaints and petitions. This part has broader application than the rest of the Code, and is not understood as 'administrative procedure' in spite of the fact that it has been included in the Code. Polish lawyers treat this Code as one of the country's 'legal monuments', in the same manner as German scholars treat the BGB and French scholars regard the Code Civil. It seems to be one of the oldest if not the oldest code of administrative procedure still in force, and has proven its value during the past 55 years.

(f) France

French Administrative law is one of the cornerstones of the family of civil law regimes in continental Europe. While it is therefore one of the earliest developed continental legal regimes of Administrative law, it is nonetheless a relative newcomer to codification of the kind that is considered in this chapter.

[30] G. Pastori, 'The Origins of Law n. 241/1990 and Foreign Models' (2010) 2 Italian Journal of Public Law.

[31] ustawa z 14 czerwca 1960 Kodeks postępowania administracyjnego. The English translation of the Code together with the Polish original was published in by C.H. Beck Polska (The Code of Administrative Proceedings C.H. Beck, 2010). There have been several rather minor amendments of the Code since then.

French administrative procedural law typically developed on a judge-made basis for more than a century. Principles such as the right to access one's own file or on the withdrawal of decisions, to name but two examples, were developed by the State Council (Conseil d'Etat), which is also the highest French administrative court. It established a jurisprudence with a very wide scope, as French administrative courts are ordinary judges for lawsuits regarding single-case decisions and rule-making as well as the contractual relationships of all public law bodies including State administration, local and regional government, independent bodies and quangos. They also have jurisdiction over private law bodies to which a 'public service' mission has been conferred. A number of statutory acts were later adopted, mainly at the end of the 1970s and beginning of the 1980s. Thus, French administrative procedure law, while reasonably comprehensive in substance, was until very recently a complex patchwork as regards the sources from which principles and rules could be identified.

The work programme 1996–2000 of the French High Committee for codification (*Commission supérieure de codification*) included for the first time the project of an administrative code (*Code de l'Administration*), in order to collect general administrative procedure rules and principles that were covered by specific statutes. The High Committee was founded in 1989 by Cabinet decree in order to codify existing legislation and regulations. It is chaired by a member of the State Council and is composed of civil servants from different sectors, with an education in law. More than seventy-five codified law books (*codes*) have been drafted and enacted in approximately twenty-five years.

The *codification a droit constant*—i.e. codification without change in the substance of existing law—brought about by those codes does not correspond to the great codifications of the Napoleonic period. The purpose is to codify the existing law as much as feasible, but without burdening the legislator with supplementary work. Therefore, a proposal is prepared by civil servants, which is then submitted by the Cabinet to Parliament for ratification without debate. Ratification without debate is possible only insofar as the existing content, and to a very large extent the wording of written statutes (*lois* which are by definition acts of Parliament) and Cabinet decrees (*décrets*), are not being changed. Those codes are usually composed of two parts: the first part contains the provisions with the rank of statute, the second part with the regulatory provisions. At least twelve of the initial codes—which predated the new general administrative procedure code of 2015, are particularly relevant to the issue of administrative procedures. They are the sectoral codes on customs, defence, environment, expropriation, family and social benefits, immigration and asylum, urban planning, post- and electronic communications, public procurement of State property as well as the general code for local authorities.

A general code on administrative procedure was, however, lacking. For a very long time most members of the Conseil d'Etat were opposed to such a general codification.

They feared that codification would freeze existing law and impede its further development in accordance with changes in society and technology. Indeed, the code that had been envisaged in 1996 was abandoned only a few years after it was placed on the agenda. In addition to resistance from the Conseil d'Etat and from ministries as regards a general law on administrative procedure, there was a more technical reason why the High Committee for codification had to back down: many of the most useful rules and principles were not set down in written statutory or regulatory provisions but in case law, and thus the usual codification method could not be applied. In the meantime, however, a number of distinguished members of the Conseil d'Etat, including the President of the judicial sections, Bernard Stirn—himself the editor of a *Code de l'Administration* published by Lexis-Nexis[32] for more than a decade—and the President of the *Conseil,* Jean-Marc Sauvé, had been able to convince their colleagues that there were more advantages than disadvantages to codification. The arguments included the idea that France could not afford to be seen as lagging behind other Member States or even the EU in this regard.

The reality is that most important reforms regarding Administrative law in France have been highly dependent upon the support of the Conseil d'Etat: the creation of an ombudsman (*Médiateur de la République*) by a law of January 3, 1973; the law of 6 January 1978 on data protection; the law of 17 July 1978 on access to administrative documents; the law of 11 July 1979 on reason giving for administrative decisions; the decree of 28 November 1983 on relations between public administration and its users; the law of 12 April 2000 on the rights of citizens in their relations with the administration; and the law of 2 July 2003 on simplification of the law. The rationale for the central role played by the Conseil d'Etat is in part because many of its members spend part of their career seconded to important positions in state administration, and, in addition, a number of French politicians have also been members of the Conseil d'Etat for some time. It was thus largely unsurprising for those apprised of the internal debates in the Conseil d'Etat when the Cabinet sought Parliamentary authorization to enact a code 'centred on procedures and relations between the citizens and public administration' by delegated legislation after a decision of the inter-ministerial committee for the modernization of public action (CIMAP) of 18 December 2012.

It was decided to set up a specific working party, which would discuss the issue with a 'circle of experts' composed of: members of the Conseil d'Etat and the administrative courts; a representative of the *Défenseur des droits* (successor to the *Médiateur de la République*); professors of public law, including Jean-Bernard Auby and Herwig Hofmann, both members of the ReNEUAL steering committee; representatives of

[32] Bernard Stirn and Simon Formery, *Le code de l'administration* (Litec, 3rd edn, 2008).

State administration; and a barrister (*avocat*). This working party cooperated from the outset with the High Committee for codification, which advised on the structure and wording of the code.

The outcome of this work is the *Code des relations entre le public et l'administration*,[33] which entered into force on 1 January 2016.[34] At the time of writing, the literature on the new code is still rather limited,[35] and there is no literature yet in the English language. The title 'Code of the relations between the public and public administration' has been preferred to a more technical one, such as code of administrative procedure. One reason, strongly emphasized by the authors of the drafts and by most commentators, is that this title would be more user friendly for members of the public. The word 'public' has been preferred to other less inclusive and/or more technical concepts, such as 'citizen' or 'user of public service' (*usager du service public*), which were used earlier by scholarship and practice. A second reason is that in French law *procédure administrative* traditionally needs further qualification, i.e. as *non-contentieuse* in order not to generate confusion with administrative court procedure and this wording would be even less user-friendly than those mentioned above. Nevertheless, there is no doubt that the new code is a proper 'administrative procedure act', which can be compared to most of the APAs discussed in this chapter.

3. Defining Features

(a) Introduction

There are, as Jean-Bernard Auby reminds us, significant differences in the defining features of administrative procedure acts.[36] These differences relate to the varying dimensions of such documents.

Thus, there are considerable variations in their size and degree of detail. The spectrum ranges from relatively slim models, such as the Swedish GAPA, which has only 33 articles, to far more detailed codes such as the Croatian, which has 292 articles. Codes of administrative procedure can also differ along the state/federal divide, such that it is common in federal systems for there to be two such codes. However, the most important criterion for differentiation between such codes concerns the type of subject matter that they deal with. The paradigm or core

[33] Available on the official French internet site for legal information Legifrance: https://www.legifrance.gouv.fr/affichCode.do?cidTexte=LEGITEXT000031366350&idSectionTA= . There is not yet an English language version of the code.

[34] With the exception of the provisions applicable overseas, which enter into force on 1 July 2016.

[35] See, 'Dossier: Le code des relations entre le public et l'administration', *Les Cahiers de la Fonction Publique*, n° 361, december 2015, 22–45; 'Dossier: Le code des relations entre le public et l'administration', *Revue Française de Droit administratif*, 2016 N° 4, 1–74.

[36] Auby (n. 2) 5–6.

subject matter of such codes is the administrative decision or individualized act that is directed towards a single person, or a small group of individuals. Beyond this, significant differences appear, with the major fault lines being between those codes that also cover the procedure governing rule-making and/or public contracts.

There is, moreover, an important conceptual issue, which is the relationship between the general code and other norms that touch on the same subject matter. Jean-Bernard Auby identifies three types of possible relationship.[37] The defining characteristic of the first model is that the general administrative code and the specific laws apply separately, each being applicable in its proper scope of application. The second model is predicated on the subsidiarity of the general administrative code, such that if there is a conflict with other legislation then the latter prevails. The third model by way of contrast is premised on the general administrative code and more specific laws being complementary, such that the former operates as a default rule to fill in gaps and deal with issues that are not dealt with by the latter.

These preceding defining features, and the different ways in which they are dealt with, are apparent from a closer look at the five codes considered in the previous section, the Spanish, German, Italian, Polish, and French.

(b) Spain

We can begin with the principal defining features of the Spanish codification.[38] The LPAC is an act of the national Parliament applicable to all Spanish administrative authorities, also those at regional and local level. According to Article 149(1)(18) of the Spanish Constitution, the national Parliament is competent to legislate on the 'common' administrative procedure to be followed by all Spanish authorities. This means that the general provisions of the LPAC coexist with the more detailed rules on specific procedures laid down by sector-specific legislation enacted by the national and the regional Parliaments.

The LPAC has 133 articles and 18 final provisions. It regulates not only administrative procedure *stricto sensu*, but also related questions such as the validity, effects, enforcement and withdrawal of (single case) administrative acts as well as administrative appeals. The regulation of administrative procedure envisages, furthermore,

[37] Auby (n. 2) 11–12.

[38] O. Mir, '§ 84 Grundzüge des Verwaltungsrechts in gemeineuropäischer Perspektive: Spanien', in A. von Bogdandy, S. Cassese and P. Huber (eds), *Handbuch Ius Publicum Europaeum, V* (C. F. Müller, 2014) paragraphs 49–108 and 128–34 (with Spanish translation: O. Mir, 'El Derecho administrativo español en el actual espacio jurídico europeo', in A. von Bogdandy and O. Mir (eds), *Ius Publicum Europaeum. El Derecho administrativo en el espacio jurídico europeo* (Tirant lo Blanch, 2013), paragraphs 49–108 and 129–35); L. Ortega, L. Arroyo and C. Plaza (eds), *Spanish Administrative Law under European Influence* (Europa Law Publishing, 2010).

the particularities of procedures leading to administrative sanctions and to state liability.

The LPAC also contains seven articles on administrative rule-making. Administrative rule-making has been long regulated in Spain. The participation of affected groups in the rule-making procedure is even imposed by Article 105(a) of the Spanish Constitution of 1978. Article 133 LPAC goes a step further and establishes a compulsory notice and comment procedure open to the public.

Contracts concluded by public administrations are only briefly addressed in Article 86 LPAC. From a general perspective, they are more deeply regulated in Articles 47–53 *Ley 40/2015, de 1 de octubre, de Régimen Jurídico del Sector Público* LRJSP and, especially, with regard to public procurement contracts, in the Spanish Act on public procurement of 4 November 2011, *Real Decreto Legislativo 3/2011, de 14 de noviembre, por el que se aprueba el texto refundido de la Ley de Contratos del Sector Público*, which has 334 articles. Spain has also a long tradition of codifying public procurement rules. Codifications in this field, which is subject to Administrative law, have existed since 1965.[39]

The LPAC is predicated on continuity with the principal features that have characterized the Spanish model since the LPA of 1958. Thus, the administrative procedure is conceived as the process by which a public authority prepares and formulates action with legal effects (a single case decision—*acto administrativo*—an administrative rule—*reglamento*—or a contract—*contrato*, *acuerdo*, and *convenio*.[40])

The regulation of administrative procedure follows a sequential structure: initiation ex-officio or by an application; the gathering of all the information needed to take a sound and lawful decision, including the hearing and consultation of the public and of other public authorities; and the conclusion of the administrative procedure.

The administrative procedure has an investigatory, non-adversarial nature, imposing on the public administration the responsibility for investigating the facts and concluding the matter within a certain time limit, this being three months if no specific time limit is established by sector-specific legislation.

Some essential procedural rights are granted to all the parties to the procedure: the right to be represented by a lawyer or some other person; the right to use any of the official languages; the right to request the exclusion of non-impartial officials; the right to propose evidence; the right to access one's file; the right to be heard; the right to be given reasons for the final decision; the right to be informed of the avail-

[39] *Ley de Contratos del Estado, texto articulado aprobado por Decreto 923/1965, de 8 de abril.*

[40] The term *contrato* ('contract') is only used for public procurement agreements, which have always been in Spanish practice and legislation much more important than other public contracts, usually referred to as *acuerdos* and *convenios* ('agreements'; Arts 86 LPAC and 47(1) LRJSP).

able remedies; and the right to be notified of the final decision are the most important ones.

The LPAC does not include any definition of the central notion of 'administrative act' and uses a broad concept that includes not only the legally binding single-case final decision, (the so called *resolución (que pone fin al procedimiento administrativo)* contained in Article 88 LPAC, which is the administrative act par excellence in Spain), but non-binding acts such as opinions and recommendations, preparatory measures, and acts having purely internal effects.

The LPAC uses also a broad notion of party (*interesado*, Article 4 LPAC) which includes holders of subjective rights and of individual or collective legitimate interests that might be affected by the procedure. In practice, according to Spanish jurisprudence, all persons who might benefit or be adversely affected by the decision may request to be involved in the procedure and acquire the status of *interesado*.

The LPAC still uses the traditional Spanish formal notion of public authority (*Administración pública*) restricted to bodies having legal personality in public law (Article 2(3) LPAC). However, it is the first Spanish APA that is also applicable to private law bodies belonging to the public sector where they have administrative powers (Article 2(2)(b) LPAC).

Two different degrees of invalidity of administrative acts are foreseen, so that illegal administrative acts might be either void (*nulos de pleno derecho* or just *nulos—nulidad de pleno derecho*) or voidable (*anulables—anulabilidad*). Administrative acts are only void where their illegality is particularly serious. However, the difference between voidness and voidability is not as important as in private law or in other Administrative law systems, because in Spain administrative acts are always binding unless their voidness is formally declared. Public administration has very strong enforcement powers. Thus, binding administrative acts can be enforced by the public administration itself, with only few exceptions where judicial authorization is needed.

Administrative appeals are always possible and in some cases are mandatory before challenging the administrative act before the courts. Administrative activities are subject to a specialized branch of jurisdiction, the so called Administrative jurisdiction (*jurisdicción contencioso-administrativa*), which is formed of fully independent judges and regulated by the Act 29/1998 of 13 July1998, *Ley 29/1998, de 13 de julio, reguladora de la Jurisdicción Contencioso-administrativa*.

(c) Germany

A specific feature of the German codification process is its complex federal nature. This is explained by the divided legislative powers under the German constitution for substantive law on the one hand, and procedural law on the other.[41] Thus, not only one (federal) VwVfG exists, but one federal VwVfG and sixteen VwVfG for the sixteen *Länder*.[42] Under this complex legal situation, the scope of application of the federal VwVfG and the *Länder VwVfGs* proved to be one of the most controversial topics of the codification process. At the end of this debate, the federal legislator integrated a derogation rule into the federal VwVfG. According to this rule, the VwVfG of a *Land* also governs the procedure if *Länder* authorities implement federal substantive law.[43] The 'federal conflict' is further limited in its consequences as all relevant actors at federal as well as at *Länder* level agreed (informally) to provide a uniform codification by way of simultaneous codification at national level and in all *Länder* (*Bund-Länder-Simultangesetzgebung*).[44] Consequently, it is common to refer *pars pro toto* only to the federal VwVfG when speaking of the German codification of administrative procedure law. The concordance between the federal VwVfG and the *Länder* VwVfGs is an important pre-condition for the reviewability of decisions based on the *Länder* VwVfGs by the Federal Administrative Supreme Court.[45] Critics highlight the obstacles to innovation and increased dangers of ossification resulting from the need for consensus.[46]

The scope of application of the VwVfG is limited *inter alia* because the VwVfG applies only to administrative activities under public law; the public-private law divide has been a characteristic of the German legal order since the nineteenth century and its complexity cannot be considered in detail here.[47] The VwVfG contains

---

[41] See Art 72 ff of the Basic Law. The reader may see a certain resemblance in the distribution of legislative powers concerning administrative procedure between the federation and the *Länder* in Germany on the one hand and between the EU and the Member States on the other hand. In fact, this parallel is often used to explain the phenomena of comitology and the structure of Art 291 TFEU, U. Stelkens, 'Art. 291 AEUV, das Unionsverwaltungsrecht und die Verwaltungsautonomie der Mitgliedstaaten' (2012) Europarecht 511, 539–40.

[42] To consult the VwVfG of the *Länder* see the catalogue at http://www.saarheim.de/Gesetze_Laender/vwvfg_laender.htm.

[43] See § 1(3) Federal VwVfG.

[44] H. Schmitz, 'Simultangesetzgebung von Bund und Ländern in Verwaltungsverfahrensrecht: Notwendigkeit und Umsetzungsmechanismen', in Hill, Sommermann, Stelkens and Ziekow (n. 25) 253 et seq. For a critical account, W. Klappstein, 'Möglichkeiten und Grenzen einer Simultangesetzgebung: Darstellung am Beispiel der Verwaltungsverfahrensgesetze' (1997) Zeitschrift für Gesetzgebung 126.

[45] See § 137 (1) no. 2 Code of Administrative Court Procedure.

[46] M. Burgi, 'Verwaltungsverfahrensrecht zwischen europäischem Umsetzungsdruck und nationalem Gestaltungswillen', Juristenzeitung 2010, 105, 111–12.

[47] For an overview, J.-P. Schneider, 'The Public-Private Law Divide in Germany', in M. Ruffert (ed.), *The Public-Private Law Divide: Potential for Transformation?* (British Institute of International and Comparative Law, 2009) 85; U. Stelkens, 'The Public-Private Law Divide—Annual Report 2010—Germany' (available at http://www.ius-publicum.com/repository/uploads/23_11_2011_10_39_Stelkens.pdf). For more detailed consideration, D. Ehlers and J.-P. Schneider in F. Schoch, J.-P. Schneider and W. Bier (eds), *Verwaltungsgerichtsordnung, loose-leafe* (Beck, 29th Supplement, 2015) § 40 paras 18–25; E. Schmidt-Aßmann and W. Hoffmann-Riem (eds), *Öffentliches Recht und Privatrecht als wechselseitige Auffangordnungen* (Nomos-Verl.-Ges., 1996).

subsidiarity clauses with regard to the parallel 'area codifications' of tax procedures and social security law as well as for special procedural rules in existing as well as in future sector-specific legislative acts. Thus, the German VwVfG may be classified as an incomplete codification, which does not (and for constitutional reasons cannot) prohibit later de-codification tendencies.[48]

Internal administrative appeal procedures[49] as a requirement for filing a court action against an administrative act are mainly regulated by the Code of Administrative Court Procedure (*Verwaltungsgerichtsordnung*).[50]

Even with regard to administrative activities under public law § 9, VwVfG restricts the scope of application of the main part of the act to procedures preparing decisions about the issuance of legally binding administrative acts in concrete and individual cases (*Verwaltungsakte*) as defined in § 35 VwVfG,[51] as well as about concluding public law contracts (*öffentlich-rechtliche Verträge*) pursuant to § 54 VwVfG.[52] This excludes procedures of administrative rule-making[53] or planning[54] (with the exception of planning approval proceedings as regulated by §§ 72–78 VwVfG concerning the approval of 'major infrastructures'), negotiating private law contracts by public authorities[55] (and therefore—in most cases—public procurement issues), as well as

[48] W. Kahl, 'Das Verwaltungsverfahrensgesetz zwischen Kodifikationsidee und Sonderrechtsentwicklungen', in W. Hoffmann-Riem and E. Schmidt-Aßmann (eds), *Verwaltungsverfahren und Verwaltungsverfahrensgesetz* (Nomos-Verl-Ges, 2002) 71, but also highlighting the integration of innovative rules transposing the EU Service Directive. See also, J.-P. Schneider, 'Strukturen und Typen von Verwaltungsverfahren', in W. Hoffmann-Riem, E. Schmidt-Aßmann and A Voßkuhle (eds), *Grundlagen des Verwaltungsrechts Band II: Informationsordnung, Verwaltungsverfahrensarten, Handlungsformen* (Beck, 2nd edn, 2001) 2, § 28 paras 23a–23b, 97a.

[49] See on internal administrative appeal procedures in Germany, U. Stelkens, 'Administrative Appeals in Germany', in D. C. Dragos and B. Neamtu (eds), *Alternative Dispute Resolution in European Administrative Law* (Springer, 2014) 3–55.

[50] See, §§ 68 f of the *Verwaltungsgerichtsordnung* in the version of the promulgation of 19 March 1991 (Bundesgesetzblatt I p 686), most recently amended by Art 3 of the act of 21 December 2015 (Bundesgesetzbatt I p. 1577)—a translation by *Neil Musset* can be found at http://www.gesetze-im-internet.de/englisch_vwgo/index.html.

[51] § 35 VwVfG defines the *Verwaltungsakt* as a unilateral decision taken by an authority to regulate an individual case in the sphere of public law and intended to have a direct, external legal effect. See for more details on the concept of '*Verwaltungsakt*' in German Administrative Law, Singh (n. 8) 63; Stelkens, (n. 49) 3, 7–17.

[52] See for more details on the concept of '*öffentlich-rechtlicher Vertrag*' in German Administrative Law, Singh (n. 8) 94; U. Stelkens and H. Schröder, 'Allemagne/Germany', in R. Noguellou and U. Stelkens (eds), *Droit Comparé des Contrats Publics/Comparative Law on Public Contracts* (Bruylant, 2010) 307, 315.

[53] H. Pünder, 'German administrative procedure in a comparative perspective: Observations on the path to a transnational ius commune proceduralis in Administrative law' (2013) 11 I-Con 940, 946–49.

[54] For details, W. Köck, 'Pläne', in Hoffmann-Riem, Schmidt-Aßmann and Voßkuhle (n 48) § 37 para 1 ff.

[55] H. Bauer, 'Verwaltungsverträge', in Hoffmann-Riem, Schmidt-Aßmann, and Voßkuhle (n. 48) § 36 paras 70–2, 110; A. Gromitsaris, 'Where is the Public Law Element in Public Sector Contracts?', in Ruffert (n. 47) 245, 251–6.

procedures concerning factual administrative actions,[56] administrative warnings and recommendations,[57] or non-legally binding forms of consensual administrative action.[58] The reason for this legislative self-constraint was to exclude fields of law from the codification that had not been sufficiently conceptualized in 1976. This restrictive tendency towards the inclusion of innovative instruments has continued since 1976. As a result, new transparency mechanisms like open access to administrative documents without the need of a subjective interest have not been integrated into the VwVfG.[59] On the other hand, the VwVfG regulates not only purely procedural matters, but also matters such as the definition of administrative acts and public law contracts as well as their validity and the VwVfG provides rules on withdrawal of administrative acts, on discretion, and on public certifications.

Conceptually, the VwVfG's underlying procedural principle can be described as classical rule-based and hierarchical administration.[60] The rules follow the typical workflow of an administrative procedure (leading to the issuing of an administrative act) and are therefore—in general—written from the perspective of the administrative authority in charge. However, the administrative procedure is *not* conceived as a contradictory procedure. § 24 (2) VwVfG spells this out clearly by saying, 'the authority shall take account of all circumstances of importance in an individual case, *including those favourable to the participants*'. It is moreover important to emphasize that §§ 9 ff VwVfG provide for a 'standard procedure', which can be characterized as being relatively informal. Nevertheless, the VwVfG does not provide the authorities with an unlimited procedural discretion. It sets a framework for guaranteeing a well-informed decision by the authority that will execute and develop the law in question, and safeguards the subjective rights of the private participant.[61] Important procedural rights of the private participant in an administrative procedure comprise, according to the VwVfG,[62] the rights to be heard (§ 28), to inspect documents (§ 29), to authorize a representative (§§ 14–15), and

[56] G. Hermes, 'Schlichtes Verwaltungshandeln', in Hoffmann-Riem, Schmidt-Aßmann and Voßkuhle (n. 48) § 39 para 1 ff.

[57] Chr. Gusy, 'Die Informationsbeziehungen zwischen Staat und Bürger' in Hoffmann-Riem, Schmidt-Aßmann and Voßkuhle (n. 48) § 23 para 95 ff.

[58] M. Fehling, 'Informelles Verwaltungshandeln', in Hoffmann-Riem, Schmidt-Aßmann and Voßkuhle (n. 48) § 38 para 1 ff.

[59] For an outline of the traditional approach to administrative secrecy: M. Fehling and J.-P. Schneider, 'Access to Information held by the State and Privacy', in R. Bernhardt and U. Beyerlin (eds), *Reports on German Public Law—XIIIth International Congress of Comparative Law* (Müller, 1990) 167–87.

[60] See on this Weberian conceptualization of public administration, J.-P. Schneider, 'Regulation and Europeanisation as Key Patterns of Change in Administrative Law', in M. Ruffert (ed.), *The Transformation of Administrative Law in Europe* (Sellier, 2006) 309–10.

[61] J.-P. Schneider, 'The Development of German VwVfG's Standard Procedure: Towards a Comprehensive Procedural Concept', in J. Barnes (ed.), *Transforming Administrative Procedure* (Global Law Press, 2008) 313, 317–22.

[62] J.-P. Schneider, 'Strukturen und Typen von Verwaltungsverfahren', in Hoffmann-Riem, Schmidt-Aßmann and Voßkuhle (n. 48) § 28 para 15 ff.

to use means of electronic communication under certain conditions (§§ 3a, 71e). Moreover, the VwVfG imposes important procedural obligations on the authority to proceed in an uncomplicated, appropriate, and timely manner (§§ 9, 42a), to investigate the facts in an unbiased manner (§ 24),[63] to give advice (§ 25), to respect confidential information disclosed to the authority by the participant (§ 30), and to give reasons for its final decision (§ 39). The 'standard procedure' also applies to the conclusion of public law contracts as defined in § 54 VwVfG. The benefits of codification are, however, limited insofar as §§ 54–62 VwVfG only regulates contracts under public law.

In addition to the 'standard procedure', the VwVfG provides for more advanced or complex types of procedure: a formal procedure with an obligatory oral hearing for issuing single-case decisions (§§ 63–71);[64] a procedure supported by a single administrative body as required by the service directive (§§ 71a–71e); and procedures for decision making by committees (§§ 71, 88-93). However, the most important modifications of the standard procedure concern the aforementioned planning approval proceedings as regulated by §§ 72–78 VwVfG with additional modifications in various sector-specific laws concerning the planning of public infrastructures.

The legal consequences of procedural defects concerning administrative acts are spelled out in §§ 45, 46 VwVfG. Such defects shall be ignored (only) in judicial review either if they are subsequently fixed pursuant to § 45 VwVfG, or where it is evident that the infringement of provisions governing procedure, form, or local competence has not influenced the decision on the matter (§ 46 VwVfG). The application of these precepts is complicated, more especially in situations where the public authority has discretion, and the issue has generated a considerable body of case law and academic commentary.

(d) Italy

Comparative analysis reveals some common and some distinctive features as regards other codes of administrative procedure. In common with other codes, whilst essentially laying down principles governing administrative procedure, the Italian APA defines some rules. Unlike the German Law on Administrative Procedure (1976), the Italian APA does not lay down a 'model' procedure. Nor, unlike the US APA (1946), does it lay down rules for both adjudication and rule-making. Indeed, it focuses on adjudication. As a result, rule-making and public contracts are subject

[63] Schneider (n. 61) 313, 329–30.

[64] For a critical analysis, R. Wahl, 'Fehlende Kodifizierung der förmlichen Verwaltungsverfahren im Verwaltungsverfahrensgesetz' (2002) Neue Zeitschrift für Verwaltungsrecht 1192. For a new scholarly proposal to integrate some formal proceedings into the VwVfG, see M. Burgi and W. Durner, *Modernisierung des Verwaltungsverfahrensrechts durch Stärkung des VwVfG* (Nomos, 2012).

to sector-specific rules. It is worth noting that, in addition to mentioning some general principles (legality, efficiency and effectiveness, impartiality, publicity, and transparency), Article 1 of the APA contains a renvoi to general principles of EU law, such as due process, proportionality, and legitimate expectations. The Italian APA aims at achieving four main goals.

First, it seeks to improve efficiency, by imposing duties of legality, accuracy in fact-finding, and consistency on all public authorities and bodies carrying out administrative procedure. Second, it obliges public administrators to make correct use of their discretion, by imposing deadlines for concluding procedures and methods for coordinating exercise of power by a plurality of public authorities, which is particularly important for administrative decisions concerning the environment and cultural 'goods'. Third, it aims at protecting individuals and groups, through notice and comment. As a result of this, all interests that may be adversely affected by the final decision must be involved in the procedure. Last but not least, the APA seeks to promote transparency by laying out a requirement to give reasons and by recognizing a right of access to documents.

As regards the APA's scope of application, three features deserve specific attention. First, while the APA applies entirely to state authorities and national public bodies, only some of its provisions apply to all public authorities. These include, in particular, the APA's provisions concerning disregard of deadlines, agreements between administration and individuals, and the invalidity of administrative acts. Second, some provisions of the APA apply to wholly or prevalently publicly-owned companies when they carry out administrative functions. Third, although it is undisputed, on the basis of parliamentary records, that the Act was meant to achieve relative uniformity in the business of government, there is a limit to its scope derived from recognition of the regions' autonomy. When constitutional reform strengthened their legislative competence, the question arose whether the provisions of the APA could bind the regions. The solution was found through a constitutional provision, Article 117 (2) (m), which reserves to the State the power to define standards for the protection of civil and social rights, with the consequence that these standards cannot be derogated *in peius*. They include the provisions 'concerning the public administration's duties to guarantee the participation of affected parties in procedures, to identify an officer responsible for such procedures, to conclude them within the pre-established timeframe and to guarantee access to administrative documentation, as well as those relating to the maximum duration of procedures' (Article 29 (2-bis)).

As far as the relationship between the APA and sector-specific legislation is concerned, the normal criterion of succession of laws over time applies. The APA is nonetheless a law of general principles. Three consequences follow from this. First, in some cases if there is no particular standard of conduct, the APA's default standard must be applied, for example with regard to the timeframe for concluding an administrative procedure. Second, if sector-specific legislation does exist, it must be interpreted consistently with the APA, and this is particularly important with regard to administrative rule-making and planning. Finally, if later legislation is intended to depart from the general provisions of the APA, it needs to do so expressly.

(e) **Poland**

The Polish Code is not the only source of rules concerning administrative procedure. There are also procedural rules contained in other sector-specific legislation. The Code itself covers the entire proceedings in individual matters before administrative authorities, both central and in local government. The Code contains at the outset a chapter on 'Principles of Administrative Proceedings' which includes the following principles: legality; taking into account the public interest and the just interest of citizens in deciding administrative cases; seeking the objective truth; enhancing the confidence of citizens in public administration; the duty of administrative authorities to inform the parties and take care that they do not suffer due to ignorance of the law or facts of the case; the right to be heard; duty to give reasons; the principle of prompt and simple proceedings; amicable resolution of the matters of conflicting interests; right to appeal the case within the public administration; and a principle that limits the ability to amend the decision once issued. The principles have played an important role in the decisions of administrative courts when establishing standards of fair proceedings before administrative authorities.

The Code defines the party to the proceedings by use of the notion of an entity possessing a 'legal interest' in the matter, in other words an entity whose rights or duties are at stake. This is the essential notion, since procedural rights are vested by the Code only in the parties, generally leaving others without procedural rights, unless they can show that they too are parties. The only exceptions are so called social organizations, viz associations of individuals having an interest in the matter, such as environmental organizations, who have special rights in some cases.

The party must be notified about the commencement of the proceedings, have access to the file, have the right to participate in hearings, and the right to be notified about closure of the evidentiary stage of the proceedings and comment on it. The decision must be delivered to the party, who has a right to appeal it to the superior administrative authority. Decisions taken upon appeal may be still reviewed by the administrative courts. Judicial review is regulated by a separate statute.[65]

The Code of Administrative procedure does not regulate rule-making, nor contracts entered by public administration. According to the Polish Constitution, administrative authorities do not have rule-making power. Some central authorities

[65] ustawa z 30 sierpnia 2002 prawo postępowaniu przed sądami administracyjnymi.

have the power to make delegated legislation, these being the Council of Ministers, Prime Minister, and Ministers. Local authorities may, moreover, issue regulations concerning local matters that are binding within the locality. Other administrative authorities, even regulatory authorities, do not have autonomous rule-making power. They can draft a regulation, but must then apply to the authorized minister to issue the regulation, and then only where statutes provide for delegated legislation. Statutes contain specific authorizations for particular ministers, as exemplified by the fact that the power to issue regulations concerning securities markets is vested in the Minister of Finance, with analogous power accorded to the Minister of Energy in relation to regulations concerning energy production. Participation in rule-making is secured by a special statute,[66] which imposes duties on the Council of Ministers, Prime Minister, and Ministers to set up programmes concerning the drafting of regulations, which allow for notice and comment.

Contracts entered into by public administration are considered to be governed by civil law. However Administrative law regulates the procedure concerning the making of contracts by the administration for purchase of goods and services.[67] Compliance with the procedural rules is supervised by the Public Procurement Office, which applies the Code of Administrative Procedure, with some exceptions that are regulated by Public Procurement law.

(f) France

The new French *Code des relations entre le public et l'administration*[68] consists of five books, which are preceded by three introductory articles defining the scope of the code and recalling that 'public administration is acting in the general interest and respects the principle of legality. It is bound by the obligation of neutrality and respect for the principle of secularism. It conforms to the principle of equality and guarantees everyone fair treatment'.[69]

Book I addresses 'dealings with public administration' (*les échanges avec l'administration*), i.e. 'requests of the public and their management' (title I); the 'right to present observations before specific decisions' (title II—which basically applies to single-case decisions); the 'association of the public to decisions of public administration' (title III—a series of norms on notice and comment and public enquiries). Book II

[66] Ustawa z dnia 6 września 2001 r. o dostępie do informacji publicznej (as amended) and ustawa z dnia 8 sierpnia 1996 r. o Radzie Ministrów (as amended).

[67] ustawa z dnia 29 stycznia 2004 r. Prawo zamówień publicznych (as amended).

[68] Available on the official French internet site for legal information Legifrance: https://www.legifrance.gouv.fr/affichCode.do?cidTexte=LEGITEXT000031366350&idSectionTA=. There is not yet an English language version of the code.

[69] 'L'administration agit dans l'intérêt général et respecte le principe de légalité. Elle est tenue à l'obligation de neutralité et au respect du principe de laïcité. Elle se conforme au principe d'égalité et garantit à chacun un traitement impartial'.

deals with unilateral acts, (which in French law traditionally include both adjudicatory and rule-making decisions), and contains rules and principles on giving reasons (title I), entry into force (title II), implicit decisions (title III), 'egress' out of force (*sortie de vigueur*—as opposed to *entrée en vigueur*—title IV, which deals basically with repeal and withdrawal). Book III deals with access to documents and 'reuse' (*réutilisation*) of public information. Book IV deals with dispute resolution, in three titles: I on administrative appeals, II on other non-judicial modes of dispute resolution, and III on judicial review—the latter basically refers to the code of administrative justice.[70] Book VI contains specific provisions applicable to overseas regions and territories.

As already mentioned, the new *Code des relations entre le public et l'administration* differs from the other recent French codes because it contains not only a reorganization of existing statutory provisions, but also a number of restatements of classical case law. It also contains a number of innovations that go beyond the language, which attempt as far as possible to avoid specialized jargon. Three major innovations are noteworthy in this respect.

First, the title on implicit decisions is based on the recent modified principle whereby the rule is now that 'silence maintained for two months by public administration after a request means acceptance', whereas, until a law of 12 November 2013, silence usually meant rejection of a request. The latter principle was a jurisprudential construct of the Conseil d'Etat developed in order allow for judicial review of failure to act by the public administration. According to Article D231-2 of the code '[t]he list of procedures for which the silence on request means acceptance is published on a website under the responsibility of the Prime Minister. The list mentions the authority to which the request must be sent and the deadline after which acceptance is acquired'. Second, the code extends the rules that had been established concerning time in the context of expropriation and environmental impact assessment to other situations, such as for example enquiries in view of assigning a designation of origin, which scholarship and practice termed 'nameless public enquiries', in order to establish a default regime for enquiries. Third, the regime of repeal and withdrawal of decisions, whether single-case decisions or rules of general application, which had been constructed by case law, has been considerably simplified, and modified to a certain extent.

The new code has a very broad scope and is intended to be a set of general default rules that apply not only to the relations between public administration (defined as State administrations, local and regional government, public bodies with legal personality and private persons in charge of a public service, including social security)

[70] Code de justice administrative, available on https://www.legifrance.gouv.fr/affichCode.do?cidTexte=LEGITEXT000006070933&dateTexte=&categorieLien=cid.

and the public (defined as natural persons and legal persons), but also as a rule to the relations between public administration and its own staff. There is no provision in the code on the relationship between it and other statutory or regulatory provisions. It should however be stressed that the Constitutional Council's case law on access to legislation and on the coherence of statutory acts as well as the Conseil d'Etat's case law on the same topics, (which is relevant for all those provisions that have the status of regulatory rules), can limit unnecessary deviations in sector-specific legislation and regulations, with the usual caveat for case law, which is that it can only develop on the basis of applications for judicial review. It should also be noted that the code does not contain provisions on the consequences of infringement of its rules, which means that the Conseil d'Etat as a supreme administrative court remains master of those issues. The Conseil has indeed developed a quite comprehensive jurisprudence in this regard, to the effect that infringements of rules and principles of a statutory nature, (which are identifiable through the letter L that precedes the number of the relevant article), or which are the expression of a subjective right, lead to annulment of the infringing decision or provision, whereas infringements of rules that have a regulatory nature, (which are identifiable through the letter D that precedes the number of the relevant article), are submitted to a more flexible regime that tries to balance legitimate expectations and the efficiency of public administration.

It is also worthwhile, in view of a comparison with the ReNEUAL model rules and especially with Books V and VI of the latter, to underline the fact that the provisions of the *Code des relations entre le public et l'administration* are written in order to apply to administrative procedures that are largely immersed in and driven by e-government, such as the rules on access to documents and 'reuse' of public information, or Article D231-2 on the list of procedures for which silence on request means acceptance.

4. Reception of Codes by the Public and Administrators

(a) Introduction

It would be impossible within the confines of this chapter to consider in detail the reception of the codes of administrative procedure in the countries discussed in this chapter. A thoroughgoing analysis could occupy a book in itself, and would entail an admixture of empirical and normative inquiry. It would, however, be regrettable to omit this issue entirely from the present inquiry and thus what follows gives some flavour of how such codes have been received in the countries on which this chapter has focused.

It is important to stress at the outset that such codes can benefit both the citizens affected by administration and the administration itself. This is not a zero-sum game. A well-written code can provide a clear guide for a citizen affected by administration on how such decisions might be challenged and the stages involved in such a process. From the perspective of the administration the codes can clarify the ascription of responsibility, and facilitate the drafting of legislation with procedural rules which are boilerplates and obviate the need to rethink the issue from scratch whenever a new statute is drafted.

(b) Spain

The successive Spanish APAs (the LPA, the LRJPAC and currently the LPAC) have played and continue to play a central role in Spanish Administrative law. They are considered to be the most important piece of legislation in the field of Administrative law, along with the Act on the Administrative jurisdiction. They form an essential part of Administrative law courses in law faculties, they are significant in competitions for civil service positions and in the daily activity of administrators, administrative judges, and administrative lawyers. The approval of any new APA is a major event giving rise to many publications, conferences, and training activities for public servants.[71]

There are doubtless features of successive APAs that could be improved,[72] but there is nonetheless a wide consensus among Spanish scholars on the benefits of such a general codification. The benefits in terms of legal certainty and clarity, as compared to the regulation of procedure being left to sector-specific legislation, court rulings and soft-law instruments, have never been questioned. This is further attested to by the fact that Spanish Administrative law scholars have strongly supported the idea of enacting an APA for the EU institutions.[73]

(c) Germany

Notwithstanding their limited scope of application and additional gaps with respect to certain aspects of administrative procedures mentioned above, the VwVfGs of the

[71] Thus, one of the many training activities that was organized on the new LPAC was attended by more than 800 public servants. Such a broad audience is unimaginable for any other Administrative law act.

[72] See, for example, O. Mir, 'The Book III of the ReNEUAL Model Rules from a Spanish perspective—When procedural law becomes substantive', in M. Ruffert (ed.), *The Model Rules on EU administrative procedures: Adjudication* (Europa Law Publishing, 2016), sections C and D with further references.

[73] See, for example, E. Nieto Garrido and I. Martín Delgado, *European Administrative Law in the Constitutional Treaty* (Hart, 2007), 115, 137; O. Mir, 'La codificación del procedimiento administrativo en la unión administrativa europea', in F. Velasco and J.-P. Schneider (eds), *La unión administrativa europea* (Marcial Pons, 2008) 73–85; O. Mir, 'Arguments in favour of a general codification of the procedure applicable to EU administration', in European Parliament, *Workshop on EU Administrative law: state of play and future prospects*, PE453.215, Brussels, European Parliament, 2011, 67–74; M. Fuertes, 'The importance of keeping it simple: Reflections on a Law on Administrative Procedure for EU Institutions', PE462.419, Brussels, European Parliament, 2011, 4–10; J. Soriano (ed.), *Procedimiento Administrativo Europeo* (Civitas-Thomson Reuters, 2012); S. Viñuales Ferreiro, *El procedimiento administrativo de la Administración europea* (Aranzadi-Thomson Reuters, 2015).

federation and of the *Länder* have been a milestone in the consolidation of German Administrative law and they constitute today a point of reference for scholarly work on general Administrative law in Germany.[74] The German administrative authorities and the administrative courts implement the VwVfG in their day to day business without any major problems. Thus, the codification serves effectively its goal of providing a harmonized and workable framework for efficient legal practice.

However, German Administrative law may be very roughly characterized by a focus on the protection of subjective rights through intense substantive judicial review and a rather restrictive concept of administrative discretion. By contrast, procedural Administrative law has remained to some extent underdeveloped. Certainly, the codification process for the VwVfG of 1976 attracted more academic interest on questions of administrative procedures. On the other hand, the VwVfG of 1976 reflected the underdeveloped procedural thinking of that time.

Nevertheless, the overall account of the German codification, the VwVfG, is positive. Most provisions of the VwVfG seem to be flexible enough to also allow for a more procedural approach in their application, as can be exemplified by the reaction of the German courts to rulings of the CJEU in the case of reclaiming unlawful state aids. In addition, the legislator has enacted several amendments since 2009, which have assimilated the VwVfG, at least to some extent, to recent needs for European inter-administrative cooperation,[75] broader public participation, and e-government policies.[76]

(d) Italy

In 1990, the Italian APA was welcomed, both by citizens and by judges and public administrations, as a turning point in Italian public law. It was regarded as a body of principles and rules that could eventually ensure the full respect for the principles of impartiality and sound governance laid down by the Constitution.[77] However, the implementation of the APA was slow, especially with regard to some of its standards. Other standards were diluted by later legislation, for instance the default standard concerning the timeframe for concluding procedure was extended from 30 days to 90. Moreover, new, controversial rules were enacted by Parliament in 2005, with either the aim or the effect of attenuating the consequences of disregard of standards of procedural fairness and propriety. A judicial policy of ensuring respect for standards is nonetheless clearly discernible in the last twenty-five years. Furthermore, some recent legislation, such as the law of August 4th, 2015, n. 214,

[74] J.-P. Schneider (n 22); Stelkens (n. 25) 270, 290–4.
[75] See §§ 8a–8e VwVfG.
[76] See §§ 3a, 27a, 33(7), 71e VwVfG.
[77] See the special issue of the Italian Journal of Public Law, Vol. 2, No 2/2010.

has the express intent of improving administrative efficiency and protecting citizens' rights at the same time.[78]

5. Conclusion

There will be no attempt to summarize the entirety of the preceding analysis. Suffice it to say that it is readily apparent from the foregoing that there is considerable variation in national administrative codes. This is evident both in relation to their precise historical provenance and their central defining features. This heterogeneity should not be hidden, nor is it a cause for concern. On the contrary, it reflects contestable differences of view as to what should be the reach of such documents, and this in turn reflects national differences concerning, for example, the nature and status of rule-making by the administration within that particular country. This divergence should not, however, conceal the commonality between the systems. It is evident most notably in the value attached to the creation of codes of administrative procedure, which can benefit both citizen and administration alike in the manner adumbrated above. This provides a fitting point from which to turn the focus to the Model Rules that form the subject matter of this book.

[78] It is published in the Official Gazette 13 August 2015, No 187.

BOOK I—GENERAL PROVISIONS

A. Introduction to the ReNEUAL Model Rules

Executive Summary of the Introduction

1 The project on ReNEUAL Model Rules on EU administrative procedure undertaken by the Research Network on EU Administrative Law (ReNEUAL) aims to determine how the **constitutional values of the Union** can be best **translated into rules on administrative procedure** covering non-legislative implementation of EU law and policies. Well-designed rules for implementation of EU law and policies could improve the quality of the EU's legal system. They have the potential to add to compliance with the general principles of EU law, to help simplify the legal system, enhance legal certainty, and fill gaps in the legal system.

2 The **ReNEUAL Model Rules are organized in six 'Books'**. These Books are designed to reinforce general principles of EU law and identify—on the basis of comparative research—best practices for different specific policies of the EU. The **process of drafting the model rules was conducted as follows.** First, policy areas of the EU and national legal systems were screened in a comparative fashion. Second, a preliminary version of possible rules which had been identified was

drafted and accompanied with explanations of the choices made and the sources consulted. Third, these ReNEUAL 'model' rules were subjected to a process of discussion and review in iterative consultations with a wide variety of practitioners and academics.

The ReNEUAL Model Rules are presented in a form that would suit **possible adoption as an EU Regulation**—with an appropriate legal basis *de lege lata* or *de lege ferenda*. Nevertheless, the term 'Model Rules' highlights the **academic character of the ReNEUAL project.** 3

The ReNEUAL Model Rules follow an approach of '**innovative codification**'. This involves a new law bringing together in one document existing principles, which are scattered across different laws and regulations and in the case law of courts. If necessary, the innovative codification also modifies these existing principles and rules and it may add new ones as well. 4

The **rules and principles of EU Administrative law** are on the whole the product of the incremental introduction of legislation in specific policy areas, some of which may have had an experimental design. EU Administrative law is thus characterized by **significant fragmentation** into sector-specific and issue-specific rules and procedures with highly complex, overlapping rules and principles. At the same time, there are also gaps in regulation. 5

EU law applies a mixture of tools in specific and evolving contexts of the implementation of EU law and policies. Each of these tools—single-case decisions, non-legislative acts of general application, agreements, and contracts—has its own specific requirements for ensuring procedural justice. EU law on administrative procedures is also characterized by the **multi-jurisdictional nature** of many of its procedures and a pluralization of the actors involved. 6

Rules for EU administrative procedures **do not exist in a vacuum; nor are they unique.** Legal systems around the world face similar difficulties when it comes to organizing the administrative implementation of law. Inspiration can be drawn from many of the Member States' laws on administrative procedure, but no one single model is transferable wholesale. 7

The main objective of the ReNEUAL project has been to produce ways of improving the implementation of EU law as a whole. From the beginning of the project, the possibility of transforming all or part of the project into draft EU legislation has been actively considered. Within the EU system of the conferral of powers, possible future EU legislation on administrative procedures requires the identification of treaty provisions granting a legal basis for the adoption of such legislation. The **legal basis for a codification of EU administrative procedures** is a delicate question. ReNEUAL has taken these difficulties into account in a variety of ways. 8

9 ReNEUAL's Model Rules on Administrative Procedures do not follow the same definition of the **scope of applicability** in all Books. Some specific considerations have to be taken into account, which lead to differentiation between the general scope of Books II, III and IV, which focus on EU institutions, bodies, offices, and agencies, whereas Books V and VI have been drafted having both EU authorities and Member State authorities in mind.

10 In line with the approach presented in this introduction, the drafting of the rules have repeatedly undergone—since the very beginning—**internal and external processes of consultation and debate**, the details of which are indicated in the explanations of the respective Books and in the Editorial Note.

I. Background and Mission of the ReNEUAL Project: EU Administrative Procedures and Constitutional Principles

11 Constitutional principles constitute decisive normative standards for the design of administrative procedures in the EU. The existence or non-existence of administrative procedural rules in the EU is not merely a 'technical' question, free of constitutional value choices. The realization of constitutional principles has a considerable potential impact on substantive outcomes. Administrative procedures for the implementation of EU law and policies entail administrative action in all its phases. **Rules on administrative procedures need to be designed to equally maximize the twin objectives of public law:** to ensure that the instruments in question foster the **effective discharge of public duties** and, at the same time, that the **rights of individuals are protected.**

12 **Constitutional values and principles are the central normative standards** for judging the design of procedures for implementation of EU law. Those values and principles include the protection of the **rule of law** and its emanations in sub-principles such as legality, legal certainty, proportionality of public action and the protection of legitimate expectations. Those values and principles further include the concepts of a **democratic Union** on the basis of a transparent system requiring not only the definition and protection of rights of participation and access to information but also, under Article 9 TEU, equality of citizens in their access to Union administration. Prominently, Articles 1(2) and 10(3) TEU require that, in the Union, in line with the principles of openness and of subsidiarity, 'decisions shall be taken as openly and closely as possible to the citizen'.

13 **Other individual rights and obligations** underpinning the design of procedures **arise from the principle of good administration** as partially restated in Article 41 CFR. Good administration requires that decisions be taken pursuant to procedures which guarantee fairness, impartiality, and timeliness. Good administration includes the right to be given reasons—a requirement also protected by the right to an effective remedy restated by Article 47 CFR—and the possibility of claiming

damages against public authorities who have caused harm in the exercise of their functions. Good administration also requires the protection of the rights of defence, language rights, and, more generally, protection of the notion of due process. In addition, good administration extends to information rights which include privacy and business secrets as well as access to information.

The Model Rules on EU administrative procedure produced by ReNEUAL **seek to address how the constitutional values of the Union can be best translated into rules on administrative procedure** covering the non-legislative implementation of EU law and policies. It is the understanding of the drafters of these ReNEUAL Model Rules that well-designed rules for the implementation of EU law and policies could improve the quality of the EU's legal system. Such ReNEUAL Model Rules have the potential to foster compliance with the general principles of EU law. This result would contribute not only to the clarity of the legal rights and obligations of individuals and participating administrations, but also to the transparency and effectiveness of the legal system as a whole. A codification of administrative procedures could help simplify the legal system, enhance legal certainty, fill gaps in the legal system and thereby further contribute to compliance with the rule of law. Establishing enforceable rights for individuals in procedures that affect them contributes to compliance with principles of due process and fosters procedural justice. Moreover, the existence of one basic set of rules for administrative procedures might reasonably be expected to reduce overall litigation. The **current rules and procedures for administrative procedures are fragmented and mostly policy specific.** There are gaps and it is not always possible to have a coherent interpretation of the rules that apply in different sectors even though they are intended to be similar. The current rules and procedures for administrative procedures often need to be complemented with procedural provisions concerning certain transversal issues. **14**

The **ReNEUAL Model Rules of administrative procedure are organized in six 'Books'.** These Books are designed to reinforce general principles of EU law and identify—on the basis of comparative research—best practices in different specific policies of the EU. Book I addresses the general scope of application of the model rules, their relation to sector-specific rules and Member States' law and the definitions of wordings applied in all the Books. The Preamble to Book I contains a summary of principles, which guide administrative behaviour, and the interpretation of all subsequent norms in Books II to VI. The latter Books cover more in-depth administrative procedures in the EU that have the potential to directly affect the interests and rights of individuals. The Books address non-legislative implementation of EU law and policies by means of rule-making (Book II), single case decision-making (Book III), contracts (Book IV), and, very important for the composite nature of EU administration, procedures of mutual assistance (Book V) and information management (Book VI). **15**

16 ReNEUAL's Model Rules on Administrative Procedures **do not follow the same definition of their scope of applicability in all Books.** The procedures covered by Books II, III and IV are those conducted by EU institutions, bodies, offices, and agencies. The procedures covered by Books V and VI address issues which cannot be solved without taking into account the relationship between EU institutions, bodies, offices, and agencies, on the one hand, and Member State authorities, on the other hand. Given the reality of Member States being more often than not involved in the implementation of EU law and policies, the Model Rules of Books V and VI are designed to be applicable also to implementation activity by Member States. Generally speaking, the ReNEUAL Model Rules were also drafted in order to be useful to Member State authorities who might choose to apply them to their activities when implementing EU law and policies.

17 The **process of drafting the model rules** was conducted by, first, screening policy areas of the EU and national legal systems in a comparative manner in order to identify joint problems and common or innovative solutions to these problems. A variety of fields, including, for instance, State aids, environmental protection, telecommunications, and research and innovation were thus studied. A second step consisted of the preliminary drafting of possible rules identified in these models, accompanied by the necessary explanations on the choices made and the sources consulted. In a third phase, these ReNEUAL Model Rules have been continuously submitted to discussion and review in various fora of practitioners and academics.[1] This process has led to repeated redrafting to improve and clarify the text. In ReNEUAL's view, the evolution of the European legal system has reached a point where such codification is not only possible but also necessary for the EU's future development as a regulatory system. ReNEUAL members concluded at an early stage of the project that Model Rules for EU law of administrative procedure are best designed following a process of **'innovative codification'**. 'Innovative codification' occurs when a new law establishes one source of existing principles which are usually scattered across different laws and regulations and in the case law of courts. It may also modify these existing principles and rules, if needed, as well as add new ones. This method allows contradictions in existing laws to be resolved and gaps to be filled. It also fosters the further dynamic development of EU law, taking into account particularly the evolution of case law as well as the changing needs of diverse policies. By contrast, what is known as '*codification à droit constant*'—a technique which amounts to establishing a legally binding consolidated version of existing legislation—would not be well suited to address the different challenges that are endemic to the EU system.

18 The ReNEUAL Model Rules on Administrative Procedure are presented in a **form adapted to their possible adoption as an EU Regulation**—with an appropriate

[1] See the Editorial Note and Acknowledgements for details of the many consultation processes.

legal basis *de lege lata* or *de lege ferenda*, as discussed in Section IV of this Introduction. Nevertheless, the term 'Model Rules' highlights the **academic** character of the ReNEUAL project. The Model Rules provide European legal scholarship and legal practitioners with a structured framework for debating and further developing EU Administrative law. The ReNEUAL Model Rules also aim to inform legislative bodies and courts about legal options and best practices. It has to be stressed that the codification we are elaborating is a **codification of binding law and also of *soft law* rules that thus become binding**: this means that **non-compliance with those rules should have consequences.** However, at this stage, the ReNEUAL Model Rules do not go further and actually indicate the consequences of non-compliance. The reasons are two-fold. First, while some national administrative procedure laws give binding indications as to the sanctions for non-compliance—annulment, damages, or other—many others do not and are nevertheless enforced by courts in the way they deem most appropriate. Second, the EU courts have managed very well until now when adjudicating the appropriate sanction for non-compliance with EU law. The choice that has been made in this version of the ReNEUAL Model Rules does not, however, mean that a codification of EU administrative procedure law should not in the future try and find an appropriate formulation of the sanctions to be applied in the event of non-compliance.

II. Law of Administrative Procedure in the EU—Characteristics and Challenges

EU administrative procedure law, covering forms of non-legislative implementation of EU law and policies, not only has to comply with the constitutional values and principles on which the EU is based, it also has **to address the main challenges of implementing EU law** in the real world and be adapted to some of the main characteristics—and shortcomings—of EU Administrative law as it stands. 19

Rules and principles on EU Administrative law have largely emerged from the evolutionary development and experimental design of legislation in specific policy areas. As a result, the rules applicable are **characterized by significant fragmentation** into sector-specific and issue-specific rules and procedures. Today, this fragmentation leads to an overburdening complexity of often overlapping rules and principles. One example is to be found in the codification of procedures for the application of competition rules by Regulation 1/2003.[2] Even though, according to recital 23, 'When complying with a decision of the Commission, undertakings cannot be forced to admit that they have committed an infringement...' the binding provisions of the regulation do not restate this principle, which is based 20

[2] Council Regulation (EC) No 1/2003 of 16 December 2002 on the implementation of the rules on competition laid down in Articles 81 and 82 of the Treaty [2003] OJ L 1/1 last amended by Council Regulation (EC) No 487/2009 of 25 May 2009 on the application of Article 81(3) of the Treaty to certain categories of agreements and concerted practices in the air transport sector (Codified version) [2009] OJ L 148/1.

on the CJEU's jurisprudence. The regulation, furthermore, does not mention the legal professional privilege protecting communications between a lawyer and client, which is guaranteed by the CJEU's jurisprudence.[3] It takes a skilled lawyer to be aware of the existence of those procedural guarantees, which are not to be found in the relevant regulation but are the consequence of the presumption of innocence and right of defence, guaranteed by Article 48 CFR. There is, in many respects, a growing gap between, on the one hand, the proliferation of new forms of administrative action in the EU and their regulatory framework and, on the other hand, their integration into a coherent system of protection that translates the overarching constitutional values and the various control and legitimacy mechanisms.

21 **Gaps in regulation** further result from the fact that some procedural elements are addressed within policy-specific rules only partially, which means that often unspecified **general principles of law must fill the void.** One example is the right to a fair hearing. According to the case law of the CJEU, an authority implementing EU law can be in violation of the EU general principle on the right to a fair hearing even in cases where the legal basis which establishes the procedures to be followed by that authority does not oblige it to organize a hearing.[4] Fragmentation often leads to a **lack of transparency, predictability, intelligibility, and trust** in EU administrative and regulatory procedures and their outcome, especially from the point of view of citizens and other non-specialists.

22 Despite the fact that most legal problems are not specific to single policy areas, relatively **few matters** of EU administrative procedure law **are the subject of a more systematic approach** beyond a single policy area in existing legislation. Most transversal issues such as the adoption and implementation of binding decisions with identified addressees (single-case decision), binding acts of general application (rule-making), binding agreements (contracts) or the handling of the collection and use of information as input into decision-making are not addressed in a transversal manner. The **absence of a systematic transversal** approach is not just a formal problem. It is one of the main reasons why lacunae in the protection of procedural rights continue to exist. It also limits the mobility of EU officials from one EU authority to the other, in contrast to the modernization goals of the EU civil service that have been implemented in the past decades.

23 A very **limited partial codification** of some principles in **Article 41 CFR** on good administration has been adopted for those 'administrative acts' affecting the single interests of individuals, groups, or businesses adopted by EU institutions, bodies, offices, and agencies. Partial guidance is also given by the **EO Code**[5] and by the

[3] Case 155/79 *AM&S Europe Limited v Commission* [1982] ECR 1575.

[4] C-135/92 *Fiskano AB v Commission* [1994] ECR I-2885, para 39.

[5] European Ombudsman—The European Code of Good Administrative Behaviour.

relevant institutions' internal rules of procedure. The **general principles of EU Administrative law** as developed by the CJEU, on the other hand, have a broader scope than such partial codifications or soft law codifications. Case law develops on the real-life canvas of specific conflicts involving EU law and the need to protect rights in that context. General principles of law can in theory cover rights and obligations arising in the context of rule-making, contracts, planning procedures, information exchange systems, and enforcement networks. Yet the reality is that the development of general principles dealing with many of these issues is hampered by the limited standing rights of individuals, especially when it comes to rule-making, contracts, and information management activities.

Rules on administrative procedures for the implementation of EU law have been **24**
developed very dynamically and often rather experimentally. An example of this is the use of information networks as a flexible model to ensure decentralized implementation of EU law, whilst creating common rules for a single market. ReNEUAL Model Rules should not reduce the dynamic, experimental nature of the system. They should instead allow for building blocks of standard models for decision-making procedures without limiting the possibility of further experimentalist developments in certain policy areas. The approach of defining these Model Rules as *lex generalis*, which could cover the general questions of the protection of rights in the design of effective decision-making procedures, allows for a simplified dynamic adaptation of elements in *lex specialis* which require policy specific adaptations. We are aware that this approach requires careful drafting of the rules governing the relationship between the *lex generalis* and *lex specialis*.

EU law applies a **mixture of instruments** to achieve the objectives of the Union in **25**
the specific and mostly fast evolving contexts of implementation of EU law and policies. Each of these instruments—single case decisions, acts of general application, agreements and contracts, etc.—have specific requirements for ensuring procedural justice as well as effectiveness. The ReNEUAL Model Rules have tried to assemble an appropriate set of rules for each of these instruments.

EU law on administrative procedures is characterized by the **multi-jurisdictional** **26**
nature of many of its procedures and a pluralization of the actors involved. Despite 'Europeanization' of the policy areas, there is no fully fledged EU administration. Instead, implementation of EU law within the joint legal space is generally undertaken by national bodies which are in some cases supported by EU bodies. The multi-jurisdictional nature and pluralization of actors involved in the implementation of EU policies reinforces fragmentation between sector-specific procedures. The lack of general rules of procedure at the level of EU institutions, bodies, offices, and agencies has therefore a negative impact on the coherence of the approach to procedural issues of a Member State's authorities. This creates barriers to administrative coordination within Member States.

27 The multi-jurisdictional nature and pluralization of actors **requires a high degree of procedural cooperation** between the actors in many areas in practice: this is achieved by composite procedures. Under these complex forms of integrated administrative procedures, the procedural steps leading up to the decision result from a mix of applicable laws by different actors. This is irrespective of whether the final decision is taken by an EU or a Member State authority. Composite procedures require joint gathering and use of information as the raw material of decentralized decision-making. In many policy areas, EU authorities establish shared databases for the collection and exchange of information in those procedures. Today, the design of composite procedures is geared predominantly towards achieving efficiency and the optimal use of pre-existing resources, but their multi-jurisdictional nature may diminish the protection of individual rights and the possibilities of effective judicial review. Rules of administrative procedure are, therefore, necessary to prevent the rights and interests of addressees and third parties in the implementation of EU law falling between two stools: situations covered by the EU-level review and accountability mechanisms and those of Member States. This second set of issues, arising from the multi-jurisdictional nature and pluralization of actors, is mainly addressed by Books V and VI of the ReNEUAL Model Rules.

III. Models for the Codification of EU Law on Administrative Procedure

28 Rules for EU administrative procedures do not exist in a vacuum. Legal systems around the world face similar difficulties when it comes to organizing the administrative implementation of law. Particularly during the last century, in line with the development of the 'administrative state', **many legal systems have turned to the codification of administrative procedures.** It is clear to the drafters of the ReNEUAL Model Rules on administrative procedure that the challenges to the implementation of EU law and policy might in many cases be characterized by a greater complexity than the issues encountered within states when implementing their own national law, even in federally organized states. Nevertheless, although national codification experiences are not generally transferable one-to-one to the EU level, they do contain valuable case studies and inspiration to be taken into account when analysing the possibilities of codifying EU administrative procedures.

29 Additional inspiration for codification on the EU level comes from the fact that the scope of Administrative law is not only national and supranational but also global. **Regulatory powers are increasingly transferred to international organizations at the global level.** The study of the conditions of regulation and decision-making at that level (sometimes referred to as 'global Administrative law'), shows that general principles such as consultation and participation, access to information rights, and

reason-giving are increasingly seen as central to the legitimacy of administrative action beyond the state.

Many of the present EU Member States have adopted codifications of administrative procedures—after a first attempt in Spain in 1889—over the course of the twentieth century beginning with Austria in 1925. A similar tendency is visible outside the EU, for example, in the US with the 1946 Administrative Procedure Act (**APA**). The movement towards codification has gained momentum in the second half of the twentieth century and the issue is now on the agenda, for instance, in France. This being said, **national codifications differ with regard to their scope and purpose**. In some countries there are either different laws of administrative procedure for different levels of government, or their entry into force has been staggered. For example, in Denmark the law was introduced in 1986 for central government and in 1987 for local government. Also, some Member States have a regional level of government with their own legislative powers (for example, Austria, Belgium, Germany, Italy, and Spain, as well as for certain parts of their territory, Finland, Portugal and the United Kingdom), which complicates the discussion of the codification of administrative procedure at the different levels. Germany, for example, has a parallel existence for the federal law of administrative procedure applicable to federal authorities and, alongside it, the laws of each *Land*, which are in turn applicable to the latter's authorities. In Germany, this was achieved in the context of a common and coherent legal and administrative culture. In Spain and in Italy, a single general law is applicable to all levels of administration, central as well as regional and local, but there is room for complementary legislation at the level of the regions and autonomous communities. **30**

The **depth of regulation may also differ across the national systems**. Whilst some codifications, such as the administrative procedure law of Italy, are to a large extent built on principles to be fleshed out in specific policy legislation, other procedural acts regulate the matters they cover in great detail. **31**

Differences exist, moreover, with regard to **administrative actions which are codified**. For example, many national procedures acts apply only to so-called administrative decisions (or adjudication), i.e. to unilateral decisions affecting single interests of individuals, groups, or businesses, even if they sometimes contain a few rules applicable to contracts, as in the German law of 1976. There are only a few laws on administrative procedure that have also included general provisions on agreements and contracts between administrative authorities and other private or public bodies or individuals. This was, for instance, the case with the initial Portuguese codification of 1992. Later these provisions on contracts were brought within a separate law in order to facilitate compliance with the frequently changing EU directives on public procurement, but a recent bill proposes to incorporate them again. In France, contracts and agreements entered into by the public administration are also **32** considered as 'administrative acts' and should, therefore, normally be subject to a general administrative procedure law. National approaches also differ as to whether rule-making is covered. The US APA[6] applies generally to 'rule-making', i.e. the exercise of regulatory power by federal administrations establishing famously a 'notice and comment' procedure, which aims to facilitate the participation of stakeholders in rule-making. In some Member States, like France, 'administrative acts' also include regulatory acts (decrees, ministerial regulations, etc.) and, therefore, it is logical that a codification of administrative procedure also applies to the latter. Furthermore, most Member States, like the EU itself, have adopted specific legislation on data protection and on access to documents. But only a few Member States have a more extensive set of principles on information management. For the implementation of EU law, information management is central to a growing number of networks which involve EU institutions, bodies, offices, and agencies on the one hand, and Member State authorities, on the other.

33 It follows from what has just been described that, although inspiration can be drawn from many of the Member States' laws on administrative procedure, **no one single model is transferable as such.** Our Model Rules on EU administrative procedure are designed to fit the special nature and the specific needs of implementing EU law. They inevitably differ from what is found within the Member States, or other national codifications beyond the EU, but nonetheless draw inspiration from national solutions.

IV. Legal Bases for EU Codification

34 The main objective of the ReNEUAL project on EU administrative procedure is to develop academic ideas for improving the implementation of EU law. As a consequence, ReNEUAL took the view that **the project should not be constricted by the existing framework of legislative competences.** Nonetheless, the possibility of the (future) adoption of the whole or parts of the project as EU legislation has been considered and factored in from the beginning of the project. Within the EU's system of conferral of powers, possible future EU legislation on administrative procedures requires the identification of treaty provisions providing a legal basis for the adoption of such an Act. ReNEUAL is fully aware of the **importance of addressing the issue of legal basis** for four reasons.

35 i) **If no proper legal basis can be found for codification**, the transformation of the results of the ReNEUAL project into legislation is **dependent on general treaty reform.** The chances that treaty reform in the short or medium term will be limited to the introduction of an appropriate legal basis for the codification of administrative procedures (or even include it) are not large.

[6] Administrative Procedure Act of 1946, Pub.L 79–404, §§ 500–96, 60 Stat. 237 (1946).

ii) The scope and impact of many rules will vary according to the legal basis that is chosen. It is not sufficient to identify an enabling legal basis, it is also necessary to check whether there are any limitations on the use of such legal bases as a result of other treaty provisions. 36

In practice, and in the scholarly literature, the **discussion** about a legal basis for codification of EU administrative procedures **has mainly centred on Article 298 TFEU**. However, other treaty provisions also need to be examined. Without trying to give a definite answer to the existence and limits of a legal basis for codification of EU administrative procedures, we highlight the relevant issues and indicate possible options. Article 298 TFEU states in paragraph 1 that '*[i]n carrying out their missions, the institutions, bodies, offices and agencies of the Union shall have the support of an open, efficient and independent European administration.*' The notions of independence, openness, and efficiency evoked in Article 298 TFEU are central to a Union based on the rule of law, given the need to comply with the overarching list of constitutional principles already referred to. Possible issues of legal basis are raised by the wording 'European administration' in its paragraph 1 as well as in the wording of Article 298 TFEU's paragraph 2, which requires that '*[i]n compliance with the Staff Regulations and the Conditions of Employment adopted on the basis of Article 336, the European Parliament and the Council, acting by means of regulations in accordance with the ordinary legislative procedure, shall establish provisions to that end.*' There is a lively debate amongst scholars and policy makers about the interpretation and scope of the latter provision but, so far, no case law of the CJEU is at hand to guide interpretation. **At this stage of the debate, it appears necessary only to exclude the narrowest of possible interpretations of Article 298 TFEU** that would allow use of the legal basis only for the regulation of the internal procedures of EU institutions, bodies, offices, and agencies. Such a narrow interpretation would appear neither compatible with the preparatory work of the 2002–2003 European Convention, nor is it sustainable in light of the necessary *effet utile* of Article 298 TFEU. The narrow interpretation would have the effect of reducing the scope of this article to a mere reference announcing the possibility of staff regulations being adopted under Article 336 TFEU, or a simple restatement of the principle of institutional self-organization. **ReNEUAL's initial view is that Article 298 TFEU constitutes the most appropriate legal basis** for a codification of general rules and principles of administrative procedures of the EU. 37

A specific issue, which has not been much discussed in the existing literature, has to do with the **existence of specific legal bases for certain transversal issues**. For example, this is the case for Article 322 TFEU for the adoption of financial regulations, for Article 15 TFEU for regulations on access to documents and for Article 16 TFEU for data protection. The question is whether the existence of those legal bases would prevent relevant topics being included in the framework of a general codification, such as the one envisaged in the present ReNEUAL Model Rules. ReNEUAL acknowledges 38 the existence of this problem, but is convinced that it can be solved. As the relevant legal bases quoted here provide for the use of the ordinary legislative procedure, **it should be possible to use a joint legal basis** combining the relevant provisions with Article 298 TFEU. This view is supported by well-established case law of the CJEU.

39 There is also another treaty provision to consider: **Article 295 TFEU regulating interinstitutional agreements.** The scope of this provision is limited to the European Parliament, the Council, and the Commission, and cannot, therefore, serve as a general basis for the codification of EU administrative procedures that would apply to all institutions, bodies, offices, and agencies. It seems difficult to argue that Article 295 TFEU pre-empts the use of Article 298 TFEU for all EU institutions, including the European Parliament, Council, and Commission. On the contrary, Article 295 TFEU indicates that Article 298 TFEU cannot be limited to internal arrangements, as otherwise a conflict between both articles would arise.

40 Another issue derives from the existence of **legal bases for sector-specific regulation that provide for the use of a special legislative procedure**. Such is the case, for instance, with Article 86 TFEU on establishing Eurojust, Article 87 TFEU on police cooperation, Article 118 TFEU on the protection of intellectual property rights, Article 182 TFEU on the adoption of specific programmes for research and technological development, or Article 192 TFEU for certain measures in the field of the environment. In such circumstances a joint legal basis, in combination with Article 298 TFEU, is not available. According to the well-established case law of the CJEU, the legislator would need to use the legal basis that corresponds to the central issues of the relevant Act. While acknowledging that the problem is not easy to solve, the EU legislator could, for instance, render the Model Rules applicable to such a sector by a sector-specific act applying the legislative procedure established in the relevant legal basis. Such a sector-specific act might take advantage, if needed, of the flexibility provided by the *lex generalis—lex specialis* relationship.

41 Even in the case where legal bases for sector specific regulation imply the use of the ordinary legislative procedure, a problem might arise if those **sector-specific legal bases include specific objectives**—as, for instance, in the fields of consumer protection or environment. Here again, we acknowledge the existence of a problem, but we do not think this should prevent us from trying to design generally applicable rules. At any rate, the provisions of Book I on the relationship between the Model Rules and other EU legislative acts are designed to provide a solution to this problem, by adopting, if necessary, sector-specific complementary or alternative procedural rules.

42 **iii)** A central political and legal issue is whether in the present wording of the treaties there is a legal basis for a transversal **codification of administrative procedures that would impact beyond the EU institutions, bodies, offices, and agencies and also impose duties on Member State authorities** in the same way that a number of sector-specific regulations or directives already do.

The concept of **'European administration'**, which appears in the treaties only in Article 298(1) TFEU, is not defined; there is very little discussion of this concept in the scholarly literature. Article 298(1) TFEU replaces Article 9(3) of the Amsterdam Treaty and Article 24(1) first indent of the Merger Treaty of 1965, which referred to a 'single' administration of the different Community institutions. It can, therefore, be argued that European administration means the administration of EU institutions, bodies, offices, and agencies. It is also possible to argue, however, that 'European' is not identical to 'single' and that it might therefore indicate a broader scope. The latter interpretation would enable Article 298 TFEU to provide a legal basis for a general codification extending to Member State authorities when they implement EU law. If this interpretation is not followed, Article 298 TFEU needs to be combined with other treaty provisions in order to extend the scope of the Model Rules to Member State authorities. A joint legal basis can only be used if those provisions provide for the use of the ordinary legislative procedure as indicated in the second paragraph of Article 298. Even though the use of joint legal bases for EU legislative acts has in practice become less frequent, they are accepted in the case law of the CJEU, especially where the various legal bases use the same legislative procedure. This is the case for various provisions allowing for the adoption of 'measures' for the harmonization of the legislative and administrative provisions of the Member States for the realization of EU policy goals. **43**

The lack of clarification of the scope of 'European administration' leads to the situation where there are **alternative interpretations of Article 298 TFEU**, both of which appear reasonable from a strictly legal point of view. **44**

One interpretation would allow for provisions in the form of regulations adopted through the ordinary legislative procedure to cover the internal administrative organization of EU institutions, bodies, offices, and agencies and also the cooperation between those various administrative actors. In addition, it would cover procedures leading to externally binding **acts of the institutions, bodies, offices, and agencies of the Union** and the external relations between those EU authorities and citizens or other private or public addressees of EU administrative actions. This interpretation is the basis of the European Parliament's Resolution of 15 January 2013 containing recommendations to the Commission on a Law of Administrative Procedure of the European Union. The EP started the debate at the political level and introduced the issue onto the legislative agenda for the coming years. Its approach is, however, limited, suggesting that it applies only to EU-level implementation and single-case decision-making with one party being a citizen.[7] The EP **45**

[7] European Parliament Resolution of 15 January 2013 with recommendations to the Commission on a Law of Administrative Procedure of the European Union (2012/2024(INI)), Recommendation 1 of the Annex. The Annex to the Resolution contains six 'detailed recommendations as to the content of the proposal requested'.

draft leaves aside the salient issues of composite procedures, questions of contracts, information systems, and even rule-making.[8] As much as ReNEUAL strongly welcomes the EP's resolution of 15 January 2013, ReNEUAL considers that the EP took a limited approach that does not fully develop the potential of the future legislation at this stage. Article 298 TFEU, even in its limited interpretation, allows for the adoption of procedural rules **dealing not only with single-case decisions, but also with rule-making and contracts and, to a certain extent, composite procedures.**

46 A **broader interpretation** of the second paragraph of Article 298 TFEU is also possible. The distinction between 'European administration' in Article 298 TFEU and 'institutions, bodies, offices and agencies of the Union' in other treaty provisions must be viewed **in the context of the pluralization of the administrative bodies involved in the implementation of EU law** on the national and EU levels. 'European administration' is used, on this understanding, to describe the entire corpus of administrative actors implementing EU law which, given the principle of primacy and the possibility of the direct effect of EU law, includes Member State administrations and courts. 'Institutions, bodies, offices and agencies of the Union' are, by contrast, only those administrations organized on the EU level. This broader interpretation is well adapted to the complexities of implementation of EU law, taking into account the importance of composite procedures in the practice of EU administration. Furthermore, this broad interpretation is also more compatible with the case law of the CJEU requiring all administrative actors in the Union to comply with EU law and, where necessary, to dis-apply conflicting national law. However, as explained both in this introduction and in the explanations to the Model Rules of Book I, for pragmatic reasons, ReNEUAL chose a general scope of application that would not extend to Member State authorities for all Books.

47 iv) **Two other treaty provisions with a general scope** need to be taken into account in the search for a legal basis for the general codification of the law of administrative procedures.

48 The first of these treaty provisions is **Article 352 TFEU**, which establishes the '**flexibility clause**'; it can be seen as an alternative to the use of Article 298 TFEU. Article

[8] European Parliament Resolution of 15 January 2013 with recommendations to the Commission on a Law of Administrative Procedure of the European Union (2012/2024(INI)), Recommendation 3 of the Annex lists principles including lawfulness; non-discrimination and equal treatment; proportionality; impartiality; consistency and legitimate expectations; respect for privacy; fairness; transparency; and efficiency and service. Recommendation 4 (on the rules governing administrative decisions) contains indications on: the initiation of the administrative procedure; the acknowledgment of receipt; the impartiality of administrative decisions; the right to be heard; the right to have access to one's file; time-limits; the form of administrative decisions; the duty to state reasons; the notification of administrative decisions; and the indication of remedies available.

352 TFEU could only be an alternative because, contrary to Article 298 TFEU, it provides for a special legislative procedure, requiring unanimity by the Council. A delicate issue is that, according to the CJEU's well-established case law, the flexibility clause may not be used in order to substitute another legal basis, but only in the event of a lack of a legal basis to attain one of the Treaty objectives. This being said, if it is argued that Article 298 TFEU does not provide a legal basis for a general codification of EU administrative procedures, it follows that Article 352 TFEU may be used. A second problem with Article 352 TFEU is that paragraph 3 thereof forbids harmonization of Member States' laws or regulations in cases where the Treaties exclude such harmonization. If Article 352 TFEU were to be used as a legal basis for a codification, the scope of which would include the Member State authorities, the resulting EU Act could not lead to harmonization in the sectors where the EU only has a competence for supporting, coordinating, or supplementing action. Further study is needed to establish the extent to which this presents a problem in practice.

The second treaty provision to be taken into account in this context is **Article 197 TFEU on administrative cooperation.** Article 197 TFEU is to be taken into consideration in relation to the extension of the scope of application to the Member State authorities. However, paragraph 2, which insists on the facultative character of measures adopted on the basis of Article 197 TFEU and excludes harmonization of the laws and regulations of the Member States, makes it clear that Article 197 TFEU could only be a basis for a non-binding EU act. The question whether Article 197 TFEU would exclude the adoption of a binding act based on another treaty provision such as Article 298 TFEU is answered by paragraph 3, according to which Article 197 TFEU 'shall also be without prejudice to other provisions of the Treaties providing for administrative cooperation among the Member States and between them and the Union'. **49**

It should be recalled that, irrespective of the interpretation of the exact meaning of Article 298 TFEU, any act with this legal basis or another one would additionally be scrutinized for compliance with the **principles of subsidiarity and proportionality.** **50**

This outline of the main issues regarding the legal basis for codification of EU administrative procedures shows the delicacy of the question. **ReNEUAL has taken these difficulties into account in several ways.** The scope of application of Books II, III and IV is, in principle, limited to EU institutions, bodies, offices, and agencies; the question whether the same legal basis can be used for different types of administrative actions has been taken into account in drafting the rules in Book I; and the wording of the Model Rules has been scrutinized for its relationship with possible legal bases in the Treaty. **51**

ReNEUAL concludes that solving the problem of the appropriate legal basis is **not a precondition to the academic drafting** of procedural rules and that discussion of the content of those rules should not be pre-empted by discussion of the legal basis. **52**

It is only after having assessed the content of those rules that a political decision can be made on how to proceed further. Three possibilities are envisaged: i) finding further arguments to sustain the use of existing legal bases, ii) putting the issue on the agenda of the next treaty revision conference in order to establish a new fully-fledged legal basis, or iii) enacting the rules of some of the six Books through different legal instruments, each based on an appropriate existing or future legal basis. This last solution—although inelegant and difficult to apply coherently—should not be considered incompatible with the concept of a single codification. As long as the Model Rules are written as a coherent whole, they may be contained in several different instruments.

53 **Irrespective of any discussion on the legal basis**, provisions laid down in the ReNEUAL Model Rules on administrative procedure could also be used as a type of 'stand by codification' or as 'boilerplate' to be supplemented with sector-specific norms in policy-specific legal acts that benefit from a single legal basis such as, for example, Article 114 TFEU for the internal market. A key issue in this respect is the relationship between the Model Rules and other norms of EU legislation, existing or forthcoming. That issue is addressed in Book I by Article I-2 and the relevant explanation. ReNEUAL's option is indeed to have Model Rules worded such that they are applicable without further detail in sector-specific legislation, or other transversal instruments, in order to be able to fill existing lacunae. In principle, the ReNEUAL Model Rules should also be considered as standard protection that may be expanded in sector-specific legislation. Deviation from the Model Rules in sector-specific legislation is not excluded, but it will need to be solidly grounded, both with regard to the specificities of the field that is being regulated, as well as paying due regard to the principle of proportionality.

54 The ReNEUAL Model Rules project is of course not limited to a legal basis discussion. This academic project is much more fundamentally conceived as a way of showing the usefulness of one single Law by means of an elaborate and much discussed and debated set of Model Rules, which can easily be used in whatever form the Union legislature might deem appropriate and politically expedient.

V. The Six Books of the ReNEUAL Model Rules on EU Administrative Procedures

55 ReNEUAL's **Model Rules on Administrative Procedures do not follow the same definition of the scope of applicability across the various books.** Some specific considerations have been taken into account, which lead to differentiation between the general scope of the proposed Model Rules as reflected in Book I and the more specific scope of some of the other Books. Generally speaking, Books II, III and IV are drafted for the EU institutions, bodies, offices, and agencies, whereas Books V and VI have been drafted for EU authorities and Member State authorities.

As far as **rule-making in Book II** is concerned, the most important part of this activity, from a qualitative point of view—and maybe to a certain extent also from a quantitative one—is by the EU institutions. At any rate, Article 291(2) TFEU applies: 'Where uniform conditions for implementing legally binding Union acts are needed, those acts shall confer implementing powers on the Commission, or, in duly justified specific cases and in the cases provided for in Articles 24 and 26 of the Treaty on European Union, on the Council'. Furthermore, the institutional context, as framed by Articles 289, 290 and 291 TFEU, calls for many specific rules. The drafting exercise has thus from the beginning been focused on rule-making by EU institutions, bodies, offices and agencies. **56**

As for **single-case decision-making in Book III,** the situation is somewhat different. In the implementation of EU law, a significant number of the relevant single case decisions are taken by Member State authorities. There is a need for coherence in the principles of administrative procedure and the relevant rules. Nevertheless, we are fully aware of the technical and political difficulties in applying the scope of Book III to all aspects of composite procedures and shared administration. We, therefore, also limit the scope of application of Book III to EU institutions, bodies, offices, and agencies even in the case of composite procedures. The Model Rules in Book III are conceived to be compatible with Member States' rules on administrative procedures. If a Member State so chooses, it may use Book III as a template for the reform of existing procedural rules or for the adoption of new procedural rules. **57**

Book IV on contracts deals with a particularly complex legal situation. The relevant Treaty provisions do not limit the choices of EU institutions, bodies, offices, and agencies when it comes to the law applicable to a contract. In practice, there are often good reasons to choose not to apply EU law as the law of the contract, but rather a specific Member State's law, or even the law of a non-EU State. Drafting clauses of administrative procedure applicable to all these situations would imply a degree of technicality and detail that go well beyond that of the Model Rules for single case decision-making and rule-making. The scope of Book IV is thus limited to contracts of EU institutions, bodies, offices, and agencies. Here again, however, nothing prevents Member State legislators from adopting the Model Rules—with the necessary adaptations—in their national legislation. Nor does it impede EU legislative acts on specific policies from referring to provisions of a general EU administrative procedure act. **58**

The **existence of composite procedures and shared administration** is one of the main reasons why the EU is—much more than a State administration—in need of rules of administrative procedure to ensure that the rights and interests of addressees and third parties in the implementation of EU law do not fall between two stools, namely situations which occur between those covered by the EU-level review and accountability mechanisms and those covered by review and accountability **59** mechanisms of Member States. It is therefore necessary for Books V and VI—regulating mutual assistance and inter-administrative information management—to extend to composite procedures and shared administration. The issue of an appropriate legal basis for the rules of Books V and VI is particularly delicate as it relates to rules that apply to Member State authorities and EU authorities at the same time, and as there is a specific legal basis for data protection. The pressing need for procedural rules in the field of Books V and VI is, however, more important in our view than the immediate solution of the existence of a legal basis *de lege lata* or *de lege ferenda*: this view has guided the drafting of Books V and VI.

60 ReNEUAL's work on information management has highlighted the fact that, beyond the issue of legal basis, it is necessary to develop rules on **mutual assistance between the EU and the Member State authorities** in order to ensure coherence and to keep pace with on-going developments in the implementation of EU legislation and policies. This issue is **covered in Book V** and its relevance for individual rights and interests lies not only in the fact that personal data or business secrets will be affected by such activity. It also arises from the need to better structure and design inter-administrative cooperation, which will generally benefit from the application of such rules.

61 **Information management covered in Book VI** is central to a growing number of networks which involve EU institutions, bodies, offices, and agencies, on the one hand, and Member State authorities, on the other. Even if in many cases such networks do not formally participate in a procedure that may lead to the adoption of a decision, acts of general application and contracts, the information they collect, collate and distribute to EU-level and Member State-level actors is often a central factor in decision-making. The current legal framework applicable to the exchange and use of information through EU information systems is insufficient and does not ensure compliance with the general principles of EU constitutional law. The novelty of many of those areas and the specific nature of the cooperation in these areas require creative approaches for the use of information systems in adjudication, rule-making, and contracts.

VI. The Approach

62 **In summary**, we believe that well-designed rules of administrative procedure for the implementation of EU law and policies will help to foster compliance with principles of the rule of law and of good administration for the benefit of individuals and the system of EU law as a whole. A well-designed codification can also contribute to compliance with the principle of subsidiarity, reducing the need for centralized EU level decision-making and thus ensuring that decision-making can effectively take place closer to the citizen. A codification of administrative procedures, preferably in the form of a binding legislative act applying, in the first place, to EU institutions, bodies, offices, and agencies will serve both central objectives of public law: it will provide instruments for an effective discharge of public duties while at the same time, and no less importantly, protect the rights of individuals. Inspiration for this codification can be drawn from solutions developed regarding specific EU policies which, after careful review, appear suitable to be generalized, as well as from Member State codifications and the success they have already had in many EU Member States in enhancing the compliance of the legal system with the rule of law. However, no single approach from Member States' codifications, international organizations or EU policies is applicable as such to the EU and all of its policies.

The **sources of inspiration for the proposed rules** consist of primary and secondary **63**
EU law, the case law of the CJEU, the practice of EU institutions, bodies, offices, and agencies, on the one hand, and the comparative law of the EU Member States and other relevant national and international experiences of full or partial codification of administrative procedure, on the other hand. Furthermore, some proposed rules are the result of comparative studies as well as studies of the so-called 'ombudsprudence' of the EO.

In addition, the drafting teams consulted academic literature. In order to present **64**
the Model Rules in the style of a legislative proposal, the editorial board decided to refrain from references to academic literature. Those interested in information on such literature are invited to consult the scholarly works of drafting team members which were produced during the project and which serve as supplementary material to these Model Rules and their introductions and explanations. This material includes:

- P. Craig, 'A General Law on Administrative Procedure, Legislative Competence and Judicial Competence', European Public Law 19 (2013), pp 503–24.
- D. Curtin/H.C.H. Hofmann/J. Mendes (eds), European Law Journal 19 (2013) pp 1–142 including the following articles:
  - D. Curtin/H.C.H. Hofmann/J. Mendes, 'Constitutionalising EU Executive Rule-Making Procedures: A Research Agenda', pp 1–21
  - J. Mendes, 'Delegated and Implementing Rule Making: Proceduralisation and Constitutional Design', pp 22–41
  - Th. Christiansen/M. Dobbels, 'Non-Legislative Rule Making after the Lisbon Treaty: Implementing the New System of Comitology and Delegated Acts', pp 42–56
  - L. Senden, 'Soft Post-Legislative Rulemaking: A Time for More Stringent Control', pp 57–75
  - A. Alemanno/A. Meuwese, 'Impact Assessment of EU Non-Legislative Rulemaking: The Missing Link in "New Comitology"', pp 76–92
  - E. Chiti, 'European Agencies' Rulemaking: Powers, Procedures and Assessment', pp 93–110

- M. Busuioc, 'Rule-Making by the European Financial Supervisory Authorities: Walking a Tight Rope', pp 111–25
- A. H. Türk, 'Oversight of Administrative Rulemaking: Judicial Review', pp 126–42.

– D.-U. Galetta/H.C.H. Hofmann/J.-P. Schneider (eds), Special edition: 'Information Exchange in the European Administrative Union', European Public Law 20 (2014), Issue I, pp 63–163 including:
- D.-U. Galetta/H.C.H. Hofmann/J.-P. Schneider, 'Information Exchange in the European Administrative Union: An Introduction', pp 65–9
- D.-U. Galetta, 'Informal Information Processing in Dispute Resolution Networks: Informality versus the Protection of Individual's Rights?' pp 71–88
- J.-P. Schneider, 'Basic Structures of Information Management in the European Administrative Union', pp 89–106
- M. Lottini, 'An Instrument of Intensified Informal Mutual Assistance: The Internal Market Information System (IMI) and the Protection of Personal Data', pp 107–25
- N. Marsch, 'Networks of Supervisory Bodies for Information Management in the European Administrative Union', pp 127–45
- H.C.H. Hofmann/M. Tidghi, 'Rights and Remedies in Implementation of EU Policies by Multi-Jurisdictional Networks', pp 147–63.

– D.-U. Galetta, 'Coamministrazione, reti di amministrazioni, Verwaltungsverbund: modelli organizzativi nuovi o alternative semantiche alla nozione di "cooperazione amministrativa" dell'art. 10 TCE, per definire il fenomeno dell'amministrazione intrecciata?', in A. Contieri/F. Francario/M. Immordino/A. Zito (a cura di), L'interesse pubblico tra politica e amministrazione, Editoriale Scientifica (Napoli, 2010), Vol. I, pp 191–202 e in Rivista italiana di diritto pubblico comunitario, 2009/6, pp 1689–98.

– D.-U. Galetta, 'Diritto ad una buona amministrazione e ruolo del nostro giudice amministrativo dopo l'entrata in vigore del Trattato di Lisbona', in Diritto Amministrativo, 2010/3, pp 601–38.

– D.-U. Galetta, 'Das Verwaltungsverfahrensgesetz im europäischen Kontext: Der Fall Italiens', in H. Hill/K.-P. Sommermann/U. Stelkens/J. Ziekow (a cura di), *35 Jahre Verwaltungsverfahrensgesetz—Bilanz und Perspektiven* (Duncker & Humblot, Berlin 2011), pp 155–70.

– D-U. Galetta, La giurisprudenza della Corte di giustizia in materia di autonomia procedurale degli Stati membri dell'Unione europea (Report annuale—2011)—The Jurisprudence of the European Court of Justice on the Procedural Autonomy of EU Member States (Annual Report—2011), in IUS Publicum Network Review (http://www.ius-publicum.com/repository/uploads/22_02_2012_12_08_Galetta_IT.pdf; http://www.ius-publicum.com/repository/uploads/22_02_2012_12_08_Galetta_UK.pdf, pp 1–37.

- D,-U. Galetta, 'La Ley Italiana 241/90 de Procedimiento Administrativo', in P. Aberastury/H-J. Blanke (a cura di), *Tendencias actuales del procedimiento administrativo en Latino América y Europa*, Editorial Universitaria de Buenos Aires (EUDEBA), Buenos Aires e Fundación Konrad Adenauer (Oficina México, México, 2012), pp 231–68 (disponibile in: http://www.kas.de/rspla/es/publications/34506/).
- D-U. Galetta, 'Die 'Nebeneffekte' unionsrechtlicher Vorschriften in Bereichen, in denen keine normative Kompetenz der EU besteht. Eine der aktuellsten Fragen zum Verhältnis von nationalem Recht und Europarecht', in J. Schwarze (a cura di), *Das Verhältnis von nationalem Recht und Europarecht im Wandel der Zeit* (Nomos Verlag, Baden-Baden, 2012), pp 179–88.
- D.-U. Galetta, 'Begriff und Grenzen der Verfahrensautonomie der Mitgliedstaaten der Europäischen Union', in J. Schwarze (a cura di), 'Der Rechtsschutz vor dem Gerichtshof der EU nach dem Vertrag von Lissabon—Europarecht—Beiheft' 1/2012 (Nomos Verlag, Baden-Baden, 2012), pp 37–47.
- D-U. Galetta, 'Le champ d'application de l'article 41 de la Charte des droits fondamentaux de l'Union européenne sur le droit à une bonne administration, à propos des arrêts Cicala et M.', in Revue trimestrielle de droit européen, 2013/1, pp 77–85.
- M. Lottini, 'Correct application of EU law by national public administrations and effective individual protection: the SOLVIT network', in Review of European Administrative Law, 3, 2, 2010, pp 5–26.
- M. Lottini, 'From "administrative cooperation" in the application of European Union law to "administrative cooperation" in the protection of European rights and liberties', in European Public Law, 1, 2012, pp 127–47.
- M. Lottini, 'Rapid Alert Systems as mechanisms of mutual administrative assistance', in Studi sull'Integrazione Europea, 1, 2014, pp 103–15.
- M. Lottini, 'The SOLVIT network and unlawful decisions of national administrations: "governing" the new challenges and problems of the internal market integration', in J. M. Beneito—J. Maillo (Directors) and J. Corti and P. Milla (Coordinators) *Fostering growth in Europe: Reinforcing the internal market*, University CEU (San Pablo Ediciones, Madrid, 2014), pp 463–82.
- H.C.H. Hofmann, G. C. Rowe and A. Türk, *Administrative Law and Policy of the European Union* (Oxford: Oxford University Press, 2011).
- H.C.H. Hofmann, A. Türk (eds), *Legal Challenges in EU Administrative Law: The Move to an Integrated Administration* (Cheltenham: Elgar Publishing, 2009).
- Herwig C.H. Hofmann, Jens-Peter Schneider and Jacques Ziller 'The Research Network on European Administrative Law's Project on EU Administrative Procedure', 7 Review of European Administrative Law [2014], pp 45–64.
- Herwig C.H. Hofmann, Morgane Tidghi, 'Rights and Remedies in Implementation of EU Policies by Multi-Jurisdictional Networks', 20 European Public Law [2014], Issue 1, pp 147–64.

- O. Mir, 'Die Kodifikation des Verwaltungsverfahrensrechts im Europäischen Verwaltungsverbund', in J.-P. Schneider/F. Velasco Caballero (eds), Strukturen des Europäischen Verwaltungsverbunds, 2009, pp 177–210 (with Spanish translation: La codificación del procedimiento administrativo en la unión administrativa europea, in F. Velasco/J.-P. Schneider (eds), La unión administrativa europea, 2008, pp 51–85).
- O. Mir, 'Arguments in favour of a general codification of the procedure applicable to EU administration', in: European Parliament, Workshop on EU Administrative law: state of play and future prospects, PE_432.776, 2011 (with Spanish translation: 'Razones para una codificación general del procedimiento de la Administración de la Unión', in M. Fuertes (Coord.), Un Procedimiento Administrativo para Europa (Cizur Menor, 2012), pp 131–65).
- R. Noguellou/U. Stelkens (eds), *Comparative Law on Public Contracts: Comparative analysis of the public contract law of 28 states (within and outside the EU)* (Brussels: Bruylant, 2010).
- J.-P. Schneider, 'Strukturen des Europäischen Verwaltungsverbunds—Einleitende Bemerkungen', in J.-P. Schneider/F. Velasco Caballero (eds), *Strukturen des Europäischen Verwaltungsverbunds* (Ergebnisse einer deutsch-spanischen Forschungsgruppe, 2009), pp 9–28.
- J.-P. Schneider, 'European Information Systems and Data Protection as Elements of the European Administrative Union', in D. Dörr/R. Weaver (eds), *The Right to Privacy in the Light of Media Convergence—Perspectives from Three Continents*, 2012, pp 374–85 (extended version in German: Informationssysteme als Bausteine des Europäischen Verwaltungsverbunds, Neue Zeitschrift für Verwaltungsrecht 2012, pp 65–70).
- U. Stelkens/H. Schröder, 'EU Public Contracts—Contracts passed by EU Institutions in Administrative Matters', FÖV Discussion Papers N° 70, 2012 (an updated version of this paper has been published in M. Trybus/R. Caranta/G. Edelstam, (eds), *EU Public Contract Law—Public Procurement and Beyond* (Brussels: Brylant, 2014), pp. 395–416 and pp 443–59).
- J. Ziller, Die Entwicklung des Verwaltungsverfahrensrechts in Frankreich, in H. Hill/K.-P. Sommermann/U. Stelkens/J. Ziekow (a cura di), 35 Jahre Verwaltungsverfahrensgesetz—Bilanz und Perspektiven (Duncker & Humblot, Berlin, 2011), pp 141–54.
- J. Ziller, 'Aspects Relating to Added Value for Citizens and Economic Operators, Research paper', Annex II, in European Parliament, *Law of Administrative Procedure of the European Union European Added Value Assessment*, PE_494.457, October (European Parliament, 2012).
- J. Ziller, 'Article 29 on European Administration', in Smit & Herzog on *The Law of the European Union* (Newark: LexisNexus, rev. ed., 2013), pp 298–1/298–6.

The final draft of the rules has been the result of continuing **deliberation and consultation** within ReNEUAL and with outside experts: a content check, in order to ensure the clarity and coherence of the proposed wording; a language compatibility check, in order to avoid the use of concepts that would lose their meaning in translation;[9] and an English-language check, as the rules have been drafted first in a single language. Other language versions, which have the same authoritative value as the present English version, already exist or are being prepared in the French, German, Italian, Polish, and Spanish languages. **65**

ReNEUAL highly appreciates the **input** its drafting teams have received **from the ReNEUAL membership as a whole, as well as from outside experts.** Details are provided in the editorial note of the ReNEUAL coordinators. **66**

B. Model Rules

Preamble

Public authorities are bound in administrative procedures by the rule of law, the right to good administration and other related principles of EU Administrative law.

In the interpretation and development of these model rules, regard should be had especially to equal treatment and non-discrimination, legal certainty, fairness, objectivity and impartiality, participation, proportionality, protection of legitimate expectations, transparency, and due access to effective remedies.

Public authorities shall have regard to efficiency, effectiveness and service orientation.

Within European administrative procedures due respect must be given to the principles of subsidiarity, sincere cooperation, and clear allocation of responsibilities.

I-1 Scope of application

(1) These model rules are applicable to all EU authorities when they are implementing Union law through administrative action.
(2) These model rules do not apply to Member State authorities unless sector-specific EU law renders them applicable.
(3) The model rules of Books V and VI are applicable to Member State authorities as defined in Articles V-1 and VI-1.

I-2 Relation to specific procedural rules of the European Union

(1) These model rules shall apply where no specific procedural rules exist in EU law.
(2) Specific procedural rules in EU law shall be interpreted in coherence with and may be complemented by these model rules.

[9] The composition of ReNEUAL's Steering Committee allows for a first level linguistic/conceptual check in the Danish, Dutch, English, French, German, Italian, Polish, Portuguese, and Spanish languages.

I-3 Relation to Member State law

Member State authorities may use these model rules as guidance when they are implementing EU law in accordance with their national procedural law.

I-4 Definitions

For the purpose of these model rules the following definitions apply to all Books:

(1) 'Administrative action' means activity of a public authority as defined in paragraph (7) that results in:
  (a) a legally binding non-legislative act of general application as defined in Book II,
  (b) a decision as defined in Book III,
  (c) a contract as defined in Book IV,
  (d) mutual assistance as defined in Book V,
  (e) information management activities as defined in Book VI.

(2) 'Administrative procedure' means the process by which a public authority prepares and formulates administrative action as defined in paragraph (1) lit. a. to c.

(3) 'Competent authority' means the public authority in the sense of paragraph (7) which is responsible for performing administrative action according to the applicable law.

(4) 'Composite procedure' means an administrative procedure where EU authorities and the authorities of a Member State or of different Member States have distinct functions which are inter-dependent. A composite procedure may also mean the combination of two administrative procedures that are directly linked.

(5) 'EU authority' means an institution, body, office or agency of the Union. Other bodies are also to be considered as EU authorities when they are entrusted with administrative action on behalf of the EU.

(6) 'Person' means any natural or legal person. Other associations, organizations or groups may be considered as a person on the basis of sector-specific EU law or the case law of the Court of Justice of the European Union.

(7) 'Public authorities' means EU authorities according to paragraph (5) and Member State authorities, insofar as these model rules apply to them.

C. Explanations

Preamble

1 As highlighted in the introduction,[10] as well as by the EP's resolution of 15 January 2013,[11] rules on EU administrative procedures must be based on **constitutional principles.** These principles **are already laid down in various provisions of the EU treaties** and the ReNEUAL Model Rules do not intend to duplicate those provisions. Instead, the preamble briefly refers to them in order to remind all addressees

[10] See paras 11–14, 62 of the introduction.

[11] European Parliament Resolution of 15 January 2013 with recommendations to the Commission on a Law of Administrative Procedure of the European Union (2012/2024(INI)); see also the Council of Europe Recommendation CM/Rec(2007)7 of the Committee of Ministers to member states on good administration.

and other readers of the constitutional background of the detailed rules which must be interpreted 'in the light' of these principles. Paragraph 1 refers to the rule of law and the principle of good administration as these are fundamental standards of administrative procedural law.

The **list in paragraph 2 pinpoints more specific principles**, some of which are more concrete manifestations of the two fundamental principles mentioned earlier. The list follows, in principle, the approach of the EP's resolution of 15 January 2013. Paragraph 3 lists principles which are additional important guidelines for administrative action. Paragraph 4 highlights principles which are especially important for the design of composite procedures, but are also applicable to other types of European administrative procedures. The principle of clear allocation of responsibilities is very important with regard to composite procedures in order to provide due access to effective judicial review and other remedies. Further, responsibilities have to be allocated clearly, not only between different public authorities, but also within institutions, bodies, offices, and agencies, especially if they are powerful authorities such as the European Commission. 2

The Preamble refers to rules and principles which guide any administrative activity in the scope of EU law. The bases for such activity are restated in the first sentence and, as with other parts of the preamble, are applicable throughout the following Books. The first sentence of the preamble recalls that administrations are bound by the rule of law, the right to good administration and other related principles of EU Administrative law. The preamble then restates that all administrative activity will take place in the context of certain specific obligations, which may, as the case may be, also contain rights for individuals, such as the obligation to ensure equal treatment and non-discrimination, legal certainty, fairness, objectivity and impartiality. Furthermore, rights of participation shall be respected and participation fostered. The principles of proportionality, the protection of legitimate expectations, transparency, and access to effective legal remedies need to be complied with. The organization of this list or the order of restatements does not indicate any possible legal consequences of compliance or non-compliance with these principles. The same holds true for the requirement that administrations exercise their duties efficiently, effectively, and with service orientation. In the same sense, the preamble closes with the restatement of the obligation for administrations in the exercise of their duties, to give due respect to principles of subsidiarity, sincere cooperation, and clear allocation of responsibilities. 3

I-1 Scope of application

As explained in detail in the introduction,[12] the ReNEUAL Model Rules have an **asymmetric scope of application.** The Model Rules of Books II, III and IV are 4

[12] See paras 16, 55–9 of the introduction.

generally applicable to EU authorities only. However, if the EU legislator so decides, Model Rules of Books II, III and IV may become applicable through a sector-specific act to Member State authorities implementing EU law, as specified in paragraph 2. Under conditions specified in Books V (see Article V-I) and VI (see Article VI-1), the relevant Model Rules are also applicable to Member State authorities involved in mutual assistance and inter-administrative information management activities.

5 **Paragraph 1** stipulates the **general applicability of the ReNEUAL Model Rules to EU authorities**, which, according to the definition in Article I-4(5), include institutions, bodies, offices, and agencies of the Union. An important limitation in this regard is that the rules apply only to specific administrative actions of those authorities that are defined in Article I-4(1) and in more specific definitions in the various books. Legislative procedures and judicial court proceedings are not covered by the ReNEUAL Model Rules. As courts or legislative bodies might also act as administrative authorities, paragraph 1 and Article I-4(1) avoid a purely organizational definition of the scope of these model rules. Such an approach could jeopardize their uniform application.

6 According to **paragraph 2**, the Model Rules do **not generally apply to Member States' authorities**. This limited scope has its disadvantages, but after intense discussions within the drafting teams as well as with outside experts, ReNEUAL takes the view that at this stage of the integration process and of the scholarly debate those disadvantages are more than counterbalanced by advantages; ReNEUAL opts for this subsidiarity-friendly solution. This approach is mainly applicable to Books II, III and IV regulating rule-making, single-case decision-making and contracts and reflects the fundamental choice made by ReNEUAL to focus on the establishment of procedural standards for EU authorities. Nevertheless, the Model Rules may also inspire national legislators and provide them with best practice solutions for a wide range of issues of administrative procedural law. In addition, national authorities may be influenced by these Model Rules if they choose to do so.

7 In contrast, as discussed in paras 59 to 61 of the introduction, **such an approach is not feasible with regard to Books V and VI**. These Books regulate mutual assistance and inter-administrative information management activities which unavoidably also concern Member States' authorities. It would be extremely dysfunctional to regulate only the input or actions of EU authorities in such inter-administrative arrangements of intensive collaboration.

I-2 Relation to specific procedural rules of the European Union

8 Article I-2 stipulates the **lex specialis principle**. This means that the ReNEUAL Model Rules are not intended to substitute for existing specific legal provisions on

administrative procedures, or to prohibit the legislator from enacting new specific rules on administrative procedures. ReNEUAL is aware of the fact that in certain circumstances such specific rules are needed to cope with the peculiarities of a special field of law. Such sector-specific law, or subject-matter-specific transversal law, can deviate in both directions from the standard set by the ReNEUAL Model Rules by providing higher standards or—in duly justified cases—also lower standards. In accordance with Article 296(2) TFEU, such deviations from the general ReNEUAL Model Rules must be duly and explicitly reasoned and acknowledged by the legislator.

The **possibilities for deviation by specific EU acts** provide flexibility in a codified framework.[13] The possibility of deviation is justified because the Model Rules are not drafted with the intention of setting only a minimum standard.[14] The ReNEUAL Model Rules are intended to present and stipulate best practice solutions. In addition, the possibility of new rules is a protection against ossification, a widely discussed danger of any codification. New specific rules may present innovative solutions, which may be tested in a limited field of application and later integrated into the ReNEUAL Model Rules after they have proven to be successful. 9

This being said, as stated in paragraph 1, these Model Rules are, in principle, **generally applicable if no sector-specific law exists**. Moreover, as stated in paragraph 2, these Model Rules may have a **twofold function even if sector-specific rules exist**. They may serve as a point of reference for the interpretation of such specific procedural rules and they may constitute a valuable default solution if an unintended gap is identified in such a specific framework. The Model Rules thereby have the potential to simplify the overall framework for EU administrative procedural law as well as to prevent 'black holes' in the protection of citizens and in the efficient administrative implementation of EU law. 10

I-3 Relation to Member State law

Article I-3 on the relation between the Model Rules and Member States' law is a consequence of Article I-1(2), but does not prevent the applicability of Books V and VI to national authorities according to Article I-1(3). The ReNEUAL Model Rules are **in general not applicable to Member States' authorities**, but they can influence the actions of those authorities indirectly. As far as Member States' law 11

[13] See also para 24 of the introduction.

[14] In this regard the Draft Model Rules deviate from the approach of the European Parliament Resolution of 15 January 2013 with recommendations to the Commission on a Law of Administrative Procedure of the European Union (2012/2024(INI)), Recommendation 2 of the Annex: 'The regulation should include a universal set of principles and should lay down a procedure applicable as a *de minimis* rule where no *lex specialis* exists. The guarantees afforded to persons in sectoral instruments must never provide less protection than those provided for in the regulation.'

provides for discretion concerning the concrete design of administrative procedures by the competent authorities or leaves even normative gaps, Article I-3 **reminds Member States' officials that they can find guidance** in the ReNEUAL Model Rules. Consequently, officials can set up and apply their procedures under their Member State's law in accordance with European best practices. Such European best practices might help those officials to fulfil their duties under the principle of sincere cooperation and to implement EU law effectively and in a non-discriminatory manner. Furthermore, the ReNEUAL Model Rules can also support law reform at Member State level that promotes EU-friendly amendments.

I-4 Definitions

12 Article I-4 contains definitions of **terms** that are **used throughout the ReNEUAL Model Rules.** In addition, each Book provides definitions of terms with specific relevance for that Book only. There is no attempt to give an exhaustive list of definitions: only those corresponding to possible issues of interpretation are included.

Paragraph 1

13 **Paragraph 1** defines '**administrative action**', a term which is used in Article I-1(1) to define the applicability of the ReNEUAL Model Rules. The definition is **technical and restricted**, and not one that would apply in a broader context than the Model Rules. A general definition would probably be highly contestable, since it would need to take into account divergent ideas about the concept of administration as a whole and consequently also of administrative action in the various legal orders of the EU and its Member States.

14 **Paragraph 1** therefore lists **only** those administrative **actions** that are **regulated in the Books** and refers to the respective definitions of those specific activities in Books II to VI. In combination with Article I-1(1), such an approach limits the applicability of the Model Rules to such specified activities. ReNEUAL takes the view that this approach, i.e. a focused codification of rules for pivotal administrative activities, is not only a consequence of the resources of an academic network, but also adequately reflects the state of play in the scholarly and practical debate on EU Administrative law.[15]

15 It has to be emphasized that such a **limited approach does not preclude further evolution** of EU Administrative law concerning administrative activities that are not included in the scope of the present Model Rules. On the contrary, the ReNEUAL Model Rules may serve as guidance, or point of reference, for further development of legal requirements for such additional activities, if appropriate.[16]

[15] See also paras 22, 25 of the introduction.

[16] See also paras 17, 24 of the introduction.

Paragraph 2

The definition of '**administrative procedure**' in **paragraph 2** is also based—similar to the definition of 'administrative action'—on a rather **technical and restrictive approach** in order to set, as far as possible, clear boundaries for the application of the procedural requirements spelt out in the Books. **16**

A **first limitation** follows from the fact that **only processes which might result in clearly defined acts** (acts of general application, decisions, or contracts) **are taken into account. By contrast**, requests for **mutual assistance** or the response to such requests, as well as information management activities as defined in Articles V-1(1) and VI-1(1)–(3), do not constitute independent administrative procedures according to this technical and restrictive approach: they are (only) important elements of administrative procedures for the purposes of these Model Rules. As such, requests for mutual assistance or the response to such requests as well as information management are also regulated by the fundamental principles which are the basis of these Model Rules. Where appropriate such requests and responses are also submitted to the legal requirements spelt out in Books II, III or IV. It must be emphasized that this (technical) limitation does not preclude activities linked with mutual assistance or information management from being regarded by the courts as reviewable acts. In line with this, Books V and VI provide the necessary legal safeguards with regard to the relevant activities, irrespective of the fact that they are indeed performed as part of an administrative procedure in the strict meaning of Article I-4(2).[17] **17**

A **second limitation** follows from the **exclusion of activities which take place after the final act is adopted**, such as enforcement of a decision, administrative reviews, and supervisory monitoring. According to the definition adopted in this article, the procedure ends with the adoption of the respective act. A procedure preparing a potential withdrawal of a decision constitutes a separate administrative procedure,[18] and the same is true for administrative appeal or review procedures. **18**

It has to be emphasized, in order to avoid misconceptions, that the **adoption and notification of the final act itself** is captured by the term 'formulates' and is consequently **part of the procedure.** It should also be highlighted that **procedures which do not end** in a formal final act, but are initiated with the potential intent of adopting such an act, **constitute administrative procedures,** at least because they 'prepare' such an act. **19**

Paragraph 3

Paragraph 3 defines the term '**competent authority**' which is especially **important** for the clear allocation of responsibilities in **composite procedures** and **shared information management**. The ReNEUAL Model Rules do not determine the **20**

[17] See also paras 59–61 of the introduction.

[18] See also Arts III-35 and III-36.

competent authorities. Instead the definition refers this organizational matter to the respective legislator or heads of administrative authorities at EU or national level.

Paragraph 4

21 Paragraph 4 defines '**composite procedures**', which are a distinctive and important element of EU Administrative law.[19] The wording is based on a definition formulated in 1999 by the Committee of Independent Experts who reported on the need to reform the Commission.[20] The second sentence of this paragraph reflects the situation in which procedures at EU level are relevant for the preparation of decisions by EU authorities that are directly addressed to a Member State, whilst having also direct effects on third parties; the latter happens because the EU decision obliges the Member State to take a precisely determined action against that third party in a national procedure, such as, for instance, a beneficiary of a national state aid.

Paragraph 5

22 Paragraph 5 Sentence 1 defines '**EU authorities**' in line with the wording of a number of Treaty provisions.[21] Sentence 2 is inspired by Article 58(1)(c)(vii) of Regulation 966/2012.[22] The definition prevents avoidance of the application of these Model Rules by means of a delegation of administrative tasks to bodies not covered by sentence 1, for instance, persons who act on behalf of the EU. However, sentence 2 only renders the ReNEUAL Model Rules applicable to such bodies, it does not regulate the lawfulness of such a delegation; this is an issue for the relevant policy-specific or organizational law.

23 **Sentence 2 may also cover Member States' authorities** if they explicitly act not on their own account but 'as formal agents' on behalf of the EU. Nevertheless, it must be emphasized that Member States usually act on their own behalf, even if they implement EU law indirectly or in shared implementation and composite procedures. Therefore, sentence 2 does not compromise the general approach taken in

[19] See also paras 26–7 of the introduction.

[20] Compare Committee of Independent Experts, Second Report on Reform of the Commission, Analysis of Current Practice and Proposals for Tackling Mismanagement, Irregularities and Fraud (10 Sept 1999), Vol I, para 3.2.2.

[21] See *inter alia* Arts 15(1), (3) Subparagraph 3, 16(2), 24(4), 123(1), 228(1) Subparagraph 2 Sentences 2 and 3, (3) Sentence 2, 265(2) and (3), 267(1), 277, 282(3), 287(3) Sentence 2, 298(1), 325(1), (4) TFEU; see also Arts 71, 263(1), (5), 265(1), 287(1) Subparagraph 1, (3) Subparagraph 1 TFEU.

[22] Regulation (EU, Euratom) 966/2012 of the European Parliament and of the Council of 25 October 2012 on the financial rules applicable to the general budget of the Union and repealing Council Regulation (EC, Euratom) No 1605/2002 [2012] OJ L 298/1 last amended by Regulation (EU, Euratom) No 547/2014 of the European Parliament and of the Council of 15 May 2014 amending Regulation (EU, Euratom) No 966/2012 on the financial rules applicable to the general budget of the Union [2014] OJ L 163/18.

Article I-1(2), which provides that these Model Rules do not apply to Member State authorities.

Paragraph 6

Paragraph 6 defines '**persons**', a generic term used throughout the ReNEUAL Model Rules. The notion of natural person needs no further explanation, as it is common to the legal orders of the Union and of all Member States. By contrast, the definition of legal persons varies not only from one legal order to another, but also according to the issues at hand, e.g. the capacity to be an addressee of a decision, to be a party to a contract, or to have standing in courts, etc. The CJEU has established that the meaning of 'legal person' under Article 263 TFEU on the action for annulment 'is not necessarily the same as in the various legal systems of the member states'. In its ruling ***Groupement des Agences de voyages*** of 1982,[23] **for instance, the Court considered that an ad hoc association of ten travel agencies, grouped together in order to respond jointly to an invitation to tender, fulfilled 'the conditions required by community law for the purpose of recognition as having the character of a 'legal person' within the meaning of Article [263]', since it had been allowed by the Commission itself to take part in the invitation to tender, had been considered in the tender, and its tender had been rejected, although the Groupement as such was not constituted as a legal person in any Member State's system. Another example is evident in Regulation 1367/2006**[24] **on the application of the provisions of the Aarhus Convention, where Article 2 defines 'the public' as meaning 'one or more natural or legal persons, and associations, organisations or groups of such persons' whereas the same article defines 'applicant' as meaning 'any natural or legal person requesting environmental information'. A quite different definition is to be found in Regulation 1049/2001**[25] **on access to documents, where, according to Article 3, 'third party' is defined as meaning 'any natural or legal person, or any entity outside the institution concerned, including the Member States, other Community or non-Community institutions and bodies and third countries'. It has to be stressed that, whereas States and International Organizations have legal personality under International Law and under domestic law, albeit often with very specific features derived from their immunities, EU institutions and bodies do not have a legal personality of their own, and neither** 24

[23] Case 135/81 *Groupement des Agences de voyages, Asbl v Commission of the European Communities* [1982] ECR 3799, paras 10,11; see also Case 18/74 *Syndicat general du personnel des organismes européens v Commission* [1974] ECR 933, and Case 175/73 *Union syndicale, Massa & Kortner v Council* [1974] ECR 917.

[24] Regulation (EC) No 1367/2006 of the European Parliament and of the Council of 6 September 2006 on the application of the provisions of the Aarhus Convention on Access to Information, Public Participation in Decision-making and Access to Justice in Environmental Matters to Community institutions [2006] OJ L 264/13.

[25] Regulation (EC) No 1049/2001 of the European Parliament and of the Council of 30 May 2001 regarding public access to European Parliament, Council and Commission documents [2001] OJ L 145/43.

do many offices, whereas agencies often have such legal personality. The different Books of the ReNEUAL Model Rules give further indication about the capacities that legal and natural persons enjoy in the relevant field. It may thus well occur that a grouping will be considered as a person for the purpose of one Book and not for the purpose of another Book.

Paragraph 7

25 Paragraph 7 defines '**public authorities**', a generic term used throughout the ReNEUAL Model Rules in order to use a short and abstract term. It must be emphasized that using this term does not impede the restrictive approach concerning the applicability of the ReNEUAL Model Rules with regard to Member State authorities as indicated in Article I-1(2) and (3) and in the relevant articles of Books II to VI.

BOOK II—ADMINISTRATIVE RULEMAKING

A. Introduction to Book II

This Book addresses rule-making procedures by the EU authorities acting in an executive capacity, i.e. those that remain outside the formal legislative procedures provided for in EU law. The EU executive has increasingly diversified. The **scope of the proposed rules is not limited to rule-making by the Commission.** Importantly, it also includes the making of other non-legislative acts of general application by other EU institutions, bodies, offices, and agencies (see Article II-1). The **objective of the procedural rules proposed** is to ensure that the constitutional principles of participatory democracy and transparency, as well as principles of EU Administrative law, in particular, the 'duty of care' (full and impartial assessment of all relevant facts), are observed in procedures leading to the adoption of non-legislative acts of general application. The purpose of the model rules proposed is to ensure a higher degree of legitimacy in rule-making activities, in accordance with Article 11(1) TEU. Greater transparency of input into the procedure as well as the opportunity for public debate and deliberation on alternatives will ensure that all the relevant facts and legally protected interests are more fully taken into account, which will contribute to the overall quality of rule-making. 1

Book II **aims to fill a gap in the existing legal system of the EU**. It links the provisions, general principles of law, and values arising from primary law with the procedure for adoption of non-legislative acts of general application. Progressively, 2 over the past decades, a set of constitutional values have emerged as general principles of law both in the case law of the CJEU and in (incremental) Treaty amendments. Such principles have until now mainly shaped the EU's institutional structures and decision-making procedures with regard to the EU's formalized legislative procedure. Rule-making outside of legislative procedures, the subject matter of this book, has arguably been much less influenced by these constitutional principles. The implementation of such principles is, in any event, scattered across single provisions in some but not all policy areas. The provisions of this book are designed to ensure their systematic infusion into non-legislative rule-making more generally.

B. Model Rules

II-1 Scope of Application

(1) Book II applies to the procedures leading to the establishment, amendment and repeal of legally binding non-legislative acts of general application, including:
acts adopted by the Commission or the Council under Articles 290 and 291 TFEU;
legally binding non-legislative acts of EU authorities adopted on the basis of Treaty provisions or legislative acts.

(2) Book II also applies to preparatory acts by EU authorities leading to the establishment, amendment and repeal of Acts in the sense of Paragraph 1 of this article.

(3) Book II does not apply to acts of the Court of Justice of the European Union when acting in its judicial capacity.

II-2 Initiative

An EU authority planning an act mentioned in Article II-1 shall make public
(a) the draft title of the planned act;
(b) a short description of its objective and its legal basis;
(c) the name of the EU authority in charge of drafting the act.

II-3 Preparation of the Draft Act

(1) The EU authority in charge of drafting the act shall:
  (a) carefully and impartially examine the relevant aspects;
  (b) undertake an assessment of the societal and economic impact of the act, as well as its impact on fundamental rights and on other values protected under EU law such as the environment. Impact assessment may include a cost-benefit analysis;
  (c) write an accompanying explanatory memorandum including the impact assessment, explanation of the reasons for the choices made and their alternatives.

(2) If experts or interest groups are heard in the preparatory phase of drafting the act, the explanatory memorandum shall name them and publish their supporting documents indicating the source of such materials.

II-4 Consultation and Participation

(1) The EU authority in charge of establishing, amending or repealing the act, shall give effect to the obligations in Article 11 TEU by consultation in accordance with the following paragraphs.
(2) The draft act and the explanatory memorandum shall be published on a central EU website for consultations and shall
   (a) be accompanied by an open invitation to any person to electronically submit comments in any of the official languages of the Union;
   (b) contain information about the adoption procedure including the deadline for submissions which cannot be shorter than twelve weeks after publication;
   (c) in an annex contain studies, data and other supporting material used for the drafting of the act including the impact assessment; and
   (d) be made available in at least those languages which the EU authority in charge of drafting the act has identified as its working languages.
(3) The EU authority in charge of drafting the act may also identify and address persons who are likely to be affected by the draft act and invite them to comment.
(4) Comments are made public in a way that allows public exchange of views. Natural persons have the right to request their identity to be concealed in duly justified cases.
(5) Where the comments lead to the necessity of substantial revision of the initial draft act, the EU authority in charge of drafting the act must consider whether a new phase of consultation under paragraphs 1–4 of this article is necessary.

II-5 Reasoned Report

(1) After consultation, the EU authority in charge of drafting the act shall create a reasoned report which
   (a) shall be published in the languages referred to in Article II-4(2)(d), shall consist of the explanatory memorandum as well as the material listed in Article II-4(2)(c) and shall explain whether and how comments which were made during the consultation were taken into account or, as the case may be, why they were disregarded;
   (b) shall be sufficiently reasoned to enable effective administrative and judicial review.
(2) The reasoned report shall add specific mention of changes made to the initial draft act
   (a) following consultations with the Council and the European Parliament under Article 290 TFEU or
   (b) following consultations with the committee defined in the legal act establishing the power to adopt an implementing act under Regulation No 182/2011 and Article 291 TFEU.

II-6 Expedited Procedures

(1) Under the expedited procedure, the EU authority in charge of drafting the non-legislative act of general application may proceed to adopt and temporarily put into place an act without prior notification and consultation of the public. In that case, the EU authority in charge of drafting the act
   (a) shall make public that the act has been adopted by the expedited procedure and give reasons;

(b) shall start the consultation and participation procedure under Article II-4 within a period of four weeks after the adoption of the act. After consultation the EU authority in charge of drafting the act will undertake the necessary amendments.

(2) An act adopted by means of the expedited procedure is valid for a maximum duration of eighteen months after its adoption.

C. Explanations

II-1 Scope of Application

1 Regarding the scope of applicability of Book II, the drafting group considered **three main issues**: First, should these model rules be applicable to Union institutions, bodies, offices and agencies only, or should they also be applicable to Member State rule-making activities? Second, should a generic term for rule-making (as opposed to single-case decision-making addressed in Book III) be developed? Third, should informal rulemaking be covered by these rules?

2 The first question concerns the **institutional scope of the rules** arising from this Book. The definition of the institutional scope of applicability is decisive for answering the question whether the rationales of Book II—participation, transparency and the duty of care—would apply not only to rule-making activity of EU institutions, bodies, offices, and agencies, but also to Member States when giving effect to EU law via rule-making procedures. Within the drafting group, the necessity of applying these rules to rule-making by the EU was without question. But the drafters were not able, at this stage, to fully consider the possible conflicts that such an application could have with national rules of procedure. For this reason, in this initial stage of our work, the rules proposed in this book concern the action of EU authorities and not of Member State authorities.

3 Regarding the second question concerning the **term 'rule-making'**, the drafters of this Book discussed **alternative formulations**. One was the term 'Union regulatory act', which would coincide with the 'regulatory act' in Article 263 paragraph 4 TFEU. It has been interpreted by the GC by Order of 6 Sept 2011 in Case T-18/10 *Inuit v EP and Council* [2011] ECR II-nyr, paras 49–56, confirmed on appeal in C-583/11 P, as 'all acts of general application apart from legislative acts'. The second was the term 'non-legislative act of general application', which conveys a formal criterion, insofar as it is the 'negative mirror' of legislative acts as defined in the TFEU. We considered the term 'regulatory act' inadequate, because it is a term that is connected with judicial review, which does not express adequately our focus on the effects of the act. It is defined with a view to establishing which acts are challengeable. For this reason, the term opens up the issue of 'direct interest' (as inherent in Article 263(4) TFEU), which is not relevant to our definition of a rule.

Third, when considering **whether or not to include informal rules such as administrative guidelines and other informal publications** in the scope of applicability of Book II, two important considerations point in opposite directions. On the one hand, informal rules—including guidelines, notices, vade mecums, and many other forms of act sometimes collectively referred to as 'soft law'—play an important role in the institutional reality of the EU and its Member States. They, for example, fill gaps in formal regulation, structure the interaction between administrations on the European and national levels and inform individuals about the potential future decision-making of the institutions. In these functions, the dividing line between formally binding and formally non-binding acts can be significantly blurred, especially in cases where informal rules are used, for all practical purposes, to replace formal rule-making. 4

On the other hand, if the essence of informal rules is the absence of formal rules for their adoption, their informality may in some cases count as an added value for citizens in so far as they can be more flexibly adopted and amended. Although this might need to be confirmed by further studies of those jurisdictions that have applied the procedural rules designed for formal rule-making procedures also to informal rule-making, the latter consideration prevailed within the drafting group of Book II. As much as the drafters would hope for the ReNEUAL Model Rules to be applied as far as possible, **as a matter of good administrative practice**, to informal acts of general application, the drafters of the book decided **not to suggest any binding obligation** to do so at this stage of the procedure. 5

Paragraph 1

In view of these general considerations, Article II-1(1) applies to all procedures leading to acts that affect or are intended to affect in a legally binding manner an undetermined group of third parties. Applying the rules only to the adoption of such acts would be too limited because amendment and even repeal of such acts might have a significant impact on the rights of individuals or other protected values of EU law. Acts of general application, in any case, should be understood as acts that affect or are intended to affect in a legally binding manner an undetermined group of third parties. Paragraph 1, therefore, highlights **two categories of acts which are specifically covered:** 6

The first are **delegated acts** under Article 290 TFEU **and implementing acts** under Article 291 TFEU. Both under Article 290 TFEU and under Article 291 TFEU, the Commission (or the Council in the exceptional cases envisaged by Article 291) prepares a draft act which is then submitted to specific supervisory procedures. The model rules of Book II are mainly focused on the phase prior to the presentation of the draft act by the Commission; hence, they apply to the elaboration of the draft act prior to the institutional channels envisaged in the Comitology Regulation (Regulation No 182/2011). Since both delegated and 7 implementing acts can be used for executive rule-making, the set of rules we propose apply equally to delegated acts and to implementing acts. If there is need for a simplified set of procedural rules, the expedited procedure envisaged in Article II-6 can be applied.

8 The second group concerns **non-legislative acts adopted under the Treaty and EU legislation where specific provision is made for adoption of such acts.** See, for instance, Article 43(3) TFEU, on the basis of which the Council adopted Council Regulation 297/2013[1] and Council Regulation 44/2012;[2] and Article 108(4) TFEU, on the basis of which the Commission adopted Commission Regulation 360/2012.[3]

9 Acts of general application are also acts of EU institutions, bodies, offices, and agencies which have externally binding effect in that they bind Member State administrative bodies in implementation of EU law. **Internal acts** of the administration, by contrast, **are in principle excluded** unless they implicitly or explicitly produce externally binding legal effects.

Paragraph 2

10 **Some rule-making procedures are 'composite'** in the sense that several different institutions, bodies, offices, or agencies are involved in their creation. Paragraph 2 mainly addresses the case where an EU agency prepares a draft of an act to be adopted by the Commission under Article 290 or 291 TFEU (for example, the European Banking Authority is obliged to draft delegated or implementing acts later to be adopted by the Commission). But it also applies to other instances where EU institutions, offices, bodies, and agencies adopt preparatory acts which are then subject to formal adoption by another EU authority.

11 The establishment of a number of **agencies at EU level** adds to the diversity of composite rule-making procedures. Since in an increasing number of policy areas the drafting of such non-legislative acts of general application is undertaken in multiple steps, the rules on procedures have to be applicable to all actors involved in the process. For example, the European Banking Authority is obliged to draft delegated or implementing acts later to be adopted by the Commission. The agency, as drafter of the act, should, therefore, follow the procedure provided for in this

[1] Council Regulation (EU) 297/2013 of 27 March 2013 amending Regulations (EU) No 44/2012, (EU) No 39/2013 and (EU) No 40/2013 as regards certain fishing opportunities [2013] OJ L90/10.

[2] Council Regulation (EU) 44/2012 of 17 January 2012 fixing for 2012 the fishing opportunities available in EU waters and, to EU vessels, in certain non-EU waters for certain fish stocks and groups of fish stocks which are subject to international negotiations or agreement [2012] OJ L25/55 last amended by Council Regulation (EU) 297/2013 of 27 March 2013 amending Regulations (EU) No 44/2012, (EU) No 39/2013 and (EU) No 40/2013 as regards certain fishing opportunities [2013] OJ L90/10.

[3] Commission Regulation (EU) 360/2012 of 25 April 2012 on the application of Articles 107 and 108 of the Treaty on the Functioning of the European Union to *de minimis* aid granted to undertakings providing services of general economic interest [2012] OJ L114/8.

Book since the drafting is undertaken by the agency even though the formal adoption is implemented by the Commission.

In any case, the drafters of Book II contend that **the administrative organisation should have no effect** on procedural rights and compliance with requirements of participation and transparency. In the cases in which the formal author of the act (e.g. the Commission) merely endorses the preparatory act of another EU authority, there is no reason to double the procedure at the formal adoption phase. Where, instead, there is substantial revision of the act subject to consultation—e.g. cases in which the Commission changes the draft prior to its submission to the EP and Council in case of acts under Article 290 TFEU or to the competent comitology committee for acts adopted under Article 291 TFEU—paragraph 5 of Article II-4 applies *mutatis mutandis*. **12**

In that sense, the provision of paragraph 2 establishes **the basic obligation of compliance** with the rules of this book **by any body in charge of drafting** the actual content of the acts of general application in the sense of Paragraph 1. It must ensure that the procedural rules set out in this book are complied with during the actual drafting of the act even if this will become legally binding only at a later stage, for example, through formal adoption by the Commission. **13**

The rule established in paragraph 2 becomes all the more relevant since recent **legislative practice has attempted to limit the capacity of the Commission to amend or reject agency inputs.** A first set of limits springs from the imposition upon the Commission of a procedural obligation to state reasons for their amendment or rejection. For example, the European Aviation Safety Agency (EASA) and the European Securities and Market Authority (ESMA)[4] have been empowered, respectively, to adopt opinions and to draft implementing or delegated acts, obliging the Commission to observe certain procedural requirements before either rejecting or amending them. Regulations establishing the EASA show an attempt to impose certain substantive requirements upon the Commission. Thus, the Commission is not free to change any 'technical' rules proposed as part of a draft implementing act without prior coordination with the agency.[5] A second set of limits, established **14**

[4] Regulation (EU) 1095/2010 of the European Parliament and the Council of 24 November 2010 establishing a European Supervisory Authority (European Securities and Markets Authority), amending Decision 716/2009/EC and repealing Commission Decision 2009/77/EC [2010] OJ L331/84 last amended by Directive 2014/51/EU of the European Parliament and of the Council of 16 April 2014 amending Directives 2003/71/EC and 2009/138/EC and Regulations (EC) 1060/2009, (EU) 1094/2010 and (EU) 1095/2010 in respect of the powers of the European Supervisory Authority (European Insurance and Occupational Pensions Authority) and the European Supervisory Authority (European Securities and Markets Authority) [2014] OJ L153/1.

[5] Regulation (EC) 216/2008 of the European Parliament and of the Council of 20 February 2008 on common rules in the field of civil aviation and establishing a European Aviation Safety Agency (EASA) and repealing Council Directive 91/670/EEC [2008] OJ L79/1 last amended by Commission Regulation (EU) 6/2013 of 8 January 2013 amending Regulation (EC) 216/2008 of

more recently, subjects the Commission's capacity to make amendments to the goal of making a draft better in respect of certain principles such as proportionality. See, for example, Recital 23 of the ESMA Regulation.[6]

Paragraph 3

15 The exclusion of acts of the CJEU from the scope of applicability of Book II follows from the specific procedural rules set out for Court proceedings in the articles of the TFEU and the Statutes of the Court. This is ***lex specialis***, and the exception formulated in paragraph 3 **serves only as restatement** of this legal situation. Acts of other actors or policy areas can be also excluded by *lex specialis* under EU law resulting from Treaty provisions or legislation.

Further considerations

16 Book II's procedural rules specifically apply to non-legislative acts adopted by EU institutions, bodies, offices, and agencies that produce effects external to the EU administration. But many discussions concerning these Model Rules turned on the necessity of a wider and deeper rule-making agenda. **Several categories of further types of act were discussed.**

17 **Private regulatory acts**, are an important category of rule-making and should, in principle, be included in the scope of application of Book II, especially when a private entity's acts are given the authority of public law e.g. by reference in legislation to a standard set by the industry, science or a standardization organization. Some procedural rules currently bind private standardization bodies. They are often established ad hoc in agreements with the Commission. This inclusion raises issues that need to be further discussed. The extension of the ReNEUAL Model Rules to

the European Parliament and of the Council on common rules in the field of civil aviation and establishing a European Aviation Safety Agency, and repealing Council Directive 91/670/EEC, Regulation (EC) 1592/2002 and Directive 2004/36/EC [2013] OJ L4/34, Art 17(2)(b); Regulation (EU) 1095/2010 of the European Parliament and the Council of 24 November 2010 establishing a European Supervisory Authority (European Securities and Markets Authority), amending Decision 716/2009/EC and repealing Commission Decision 2009/77/EC [2010] OJ L331/84 last amended by Directive 2014/51/EU of the European Parliament and of the Council of 16 April 2014 amending Directives 2003/71/EC and 2009/138/EC and Regulations (EC) 1060/2009, (EU) 1094/2010 and (EU) 1095/2010 in respect of the powers of the European Supervisory Authority (European Insurance and Occupational Pensions Authority) and the European Supervisory Authority (European Securities and Markets Authority) [2014] OJ L153/1, Art 10(1).

[6] Regulation (EU) 1095/2010 of the European Parliament and the Council of 24 November 2010 establishing a European Supervisory Authority (European Securities and Markets Authority), amending Decision 716/2009/EC and repealing Commission Decision 2009/77/EC [2010] OJ L331/84 last amended by Directive 2014/51/EU of the European Parliament and of the Council of 16 April 2014 amending Directives 2003/71/EC and 2009/138/EC and Regulations (EC) 1060/2009, (EU) 1094/2010 and (EU) 1095/2010 in respect of the powers of the European Supervisory Authority (European Insurance and Occupational Pensions Authority) and the European Supervisory Authority (European Securities and Markets Authority) [2014] OJ L153/1.

these acts may require adjustments that could not be fully considered at this stage. Private rule-making is, therefore, an important issue to consider at a future stage of developing model rules for EU administrative procedure.

In the same vein, **'interinstitutional' acts** (such as MoU between, for instance, the Commission and agencies) raise relevant issues that should be considered in setting out comprehensive rules of rule-making procedures. These are, in principle, internal acts, which therefore fall outside of the scope of 'acts of general application'. They might nonetheless affect third parties in that they establish substantive law or procedural rules. In a next stage of our work a more complete consideration of these kinds of inter-institutional acts should be included. **18**

Various **types of non-legislative acts of general application present specific problems** which prevent them from being included in the scope of Book II without further consideration. This is the case for some acts that do not seem to have external effects, such as internal rules of procedure[7] and, to a more limited extent, guidelines and plans. Also, acts of general application may, in reality, have an individual rather than a general scope. Plans and guidelines may fall within this category as well. **19**

'Plans' are a category of acts that **require further consideration** for an additional reason. In certain cases, plans have an 'open' nature, being available to an unspecified variety of addressees, for example, in a consultation document,[8] while in others they take the shape of a 'closed' communication to other institutions.[9] In both cases, however, the substance of the act—the definition of the steps to implement a given policy and the definition of the time to realize it—does not seem to change. There are, however, also plans of a more binding nature.[10] **20**

[7] Rules of Procedure adopted by institutions, agencies, bodies, and offices establish internal rules to be followed as to convening and attendance of meetings, voting, minute taking, access to documents, etc. See, for instance Council Decision 2009/937/EU of 1 December 2009 adopting the Council's Rules of Procedure [2009] OJ L325/35 last amended by European Council Decision 2010/594/EU of 16 September 2010 amending the list of Council configurations [2010] OJ L263/12; Rules of Procedure of the Commission C(2000)3614 [2000] OJ L308/26 last amended by Commission Decision of 9 November 2011 amending its Rules of Procedure (2011/737/EU, Euratom) [2011] OJ L296/58. On the other hand, certain acts such as the Council security rules which are based on the Council's rules of procedure do have external effects for other institutions and third parties.

[8] See for example State Aid Action Plan—Less and Better Targeted State Aid: A Roadmap for State Aid Reform 2005–2009, COM(2005) 107 final adopted by the European Commission on June 7, 2005.

[9] See, for instance, Commission Communication EU State Aid Modernisation to the European Parliament, the Council and the European and Social Committee and the Committee of Regions, COM(2012) 209 final adopted on 8 May 2012.

[10] Regulation (EC) 178/2002 of the European Parliament and of the Council of 28 January 2002 laying down the general principles and requirements of food law, establishing the European Safety Authority and laying down procedures in matters of food safety [2002] OJ L31/1 last amended by Regulation (EC) 596/2009 of the European Parliament and of the Council of 18 June 2009 adapting a number of instruments subject to the procedure referred to in Article 251 of the Treaty to Council Decision 1999/468/EC with regard to the regulatory procedure with scrutiny—Adaptation to the

21 With respect to **guidelines**, it is necessary to distinguish whether they are addressed to actors on the Union level (e.g. one Commission service to another Commission service) or towards Member State agencies (e.g. the Commission or EU agencies adopting guidelines and recommendations aimed at guiding the implementing phase at national level). Whether these types of guidelines should be subject to the model rules depends on whether one assumes that Member State agencies should have the same procedural rights as those of individuals protected in this Book.[11]

22 During discussions about the model rules presented here, the **issue** was raised whether a **uniform way of regulating rule-making procedures** was a good approach. Would it not be better to establish, for example, a three-tier procedure since a one-size-fits-all procedure might be too inflexible and not be adapted to the importance or controversial character of the rule to be adopted. It was suggested that a three-tier procedure could contain one set of procedural rules for the vast majority of rules (normal procedure). A second, simplified or fast track procedure could be sufficient for routine rules and minor amendments of limited importance as well as for a limited group of rules requiring expedited procedure. A third set of rules could apply to particularly important or controversial rules which could be adopted in a special manner including a formal hearing procedure and possibly based on preparatory work by a working group or a committee. Such an approach would be predicated on a relationship between the complexity of the procedure and the importance of the subject matter. The drafting group opted against this for the following reasons: First, these model rules already contain two different procedures which are the ordinary procedure and an expedited procedure proposed in Article II-6. There would inevitably be difficulties in distinguishing between the scope of applicability of the various procedures, and it was therefore decided not to

regulatory procedure with scrutiny—Part Four [2009] OJ L188/14, Art 55 according to which the Commission draws up emergency plans, which it seeks to make more binding.

[11] A procedure for the adoption of guidelines is included in Regulation (EU) 1095/2010 of the European Parliament and the Council of 24 November 2010 establishing a European Supervisory Authority (European Securities and Markets Authority), amending Decision 716/2009/EC and repealing Commission Decision 2009/77/EC [2010] OJ L331/84 last amended by Directive 2014/51/EU of the European Parliament and of the Council of 16 April 2014 amending Directives 2003/71/EC and 2009/138/EC and Regulations (EC) 1060/2009, (EU) 1094/2010 and (EU) 1095/2010 in respect of the powers of the European Supervisory Authority (European Insurance and Occupational Pensions Authority) and the European Supervisory Authority (European Securities and Markets Authority) [2014] OJ L153/1, Art 16. Examples of guidelines of general scope can be found in the Guidance on centrally authorised products requiring a notification of a change for update of annexes adopted by the European Medicines Evaluation Agency (EMEA) (EMA/95003/2013) and in EASA's Acceptable Means of Compliance. Conversely, 'individual' guidelines are the 'non-binding framework guidelines' adopted according to Regulation (EC) 713/2009 of the European Parliament and of the Council of 13 July 2009 establishing an Agency for the Cooperation of Energy Regulators [2009] OJ L211/1 last amended by Regulation (EU) 347/2013 of the European Parliament and of the Council of 17 April 2013 on guidelines for trans-European energy infrastructure and repealing Decision 1364/2006/EC and amending Regulations (EC) 713/2009, (EC) 714/2009 and (EC) 715/2009 [2013] OJ L115/39, Art 6(4).

follow this approach at present. Should, however, at a later stage, the scope of applicability of these model rules be enlarged to also take into account types of legal act with a more soft-law effect, this position might need to be reviewed.

Further, the discussions of the ReNEUAL Model Rules on administrative procedure concerning rule-making also focused on **experiences in various jurisdictions**, including a debate on US rules on executive rule-making. With regard to US rules on rule-making, they—not unlike the provisions in Article II-4—require a 'notice and comment' procedure for draft rule-making. Moreover, they have led to a certain degree of jurisprudence which by some authors has been referred to as 'ossification' of rule-making. After in-depth analysis by US scholars about this matter, the drafting group of Book II came to the conclusion that the phenomenon of 'ossification', i.e. lengthy rule-making procedures due to frequent involvement of Courts to review compliance of agencies involved in rule-making with participation rights and subsequent obligations of justification of regulatory choices, was less due to the rule-making procedures per se but owed more to specific rules on standing in Court and the intensity of substantive review. Given the considerable differences between the judicial procedural rules of the US and the EU, the drawbacks of establishing formal procedural rules for rule-making appeared less relevant. Meanwhile, the benefits are considerable in terms of both the quality of rule-making and the compliance with constitutional provisions strengthened under the Treaty of Lisbon. **23**

II-2 Initiative

Article II-2 is informed by a **concern for transparency**. Publicity of a planned act is a first important step to ensure the possibility of effective consultation and participation, as envisaged in Article II-4. Various policy areas of the EU offer examples of how to achieve these objectives. For example, the European Aviation Safety Agency's (EASA) rule-making procedure lays down very precise provisions on the preparation of consultation through the early publication of rule-making intentions. EASA's executive rule-making is preceded in EASA's 4-Year rule-making programme by an indication of the terms of reference of the actual rule-making activity.[12] The terms of reference are then individually published on the agency's website.[13] The terms of reference, code-named differently according to the specific regulated field, generally include an indication of the subject matter, the problem (statement of issue and justification and reasons for regulatory evolution), the object- **24**

[12] See, for instance, the work programme for the year 2013, available at: http://easa.europa.eu/agency-measures/docs/agency-decisions/2012/2012-013-R/4-Year%20RMP%202013-2016.pdf.

[13] See http://easa.europa.eu/rulemaking/terms-of-reference-and-group-composition.php. See for instance EASA Terms of Reference (ToR) AMC 20/001 of 22 July 2004, on certification of aircraft propulsion systems equipped with electronic engine control systems, available at http://easa.europa.eu/rulemaking/docs/tor/20/EASA-ToR-20.001-00-17072004.pdf.

ive, specific tasks and interface issues, the working methods, and, finally, the timescale for the adoption of the intermediary acts as well as of the final measure.

25 Inspired by this particularly clear example of the preparation of future rule-making, Article II-2 provides that the **EU authority** planning an act **must make public the draft title** of the planned act,[14] as well as, for purposes of consultation under Article II-4, give a **short description of its objective.**

26 Further, it is established case law that **Union acts must mention the legal basis** upon which they are adopted.[15] Delegated and implementing acts routinely mention their basic act in their title as well as in the text of the act. Agency acts likewise mention their legal basis in the adopted acts. Under this provision, this requirement would simply be extended to the announcement. For purposes of legal certainty and transparency, the legal basis chosen should be indicated at an early stage, without prejudice to future changes or additions that may be required following changes to the content of the planned act during the administrative procedure.

27 Adding the **name of the EU authority in charge** of drafting the act is another requirement of clarity and transparency, especially because, in an increasing number of policy areas, although a final delegated or implementing act under Articles 290 and 291 TFEU is adopted by the Commission, an EU agency will be in charge of preparing the text of such a legal act. With respect to agency rule-making, it has become standard good practice for EU agencies to provide the information required in Article II-2(c) as 'terms of reference' of their future rule-making activities.

II-3 Preparation of the Draft Act

28 Article II-3 is designed, on the one hand, to provide procedures to **ensure good quality rule-making.** Rules in this respect are predominantly inspired by the case law of the CJEU on the basis of the enforcement of general principles of EU law such as principles of good administration and compliance with the principle of proportionality. On the other hand, provisions of Article II-3 are intended to **prepare for meaningful possibilities of consultation and participation** under Article II-4. They are thus predominantly informed by the practical necessities of consultation.

[14] See, for example, Commission Implementing Regulation (EU) 354/2013 of 18 April 2013 on changes of biocidal products authorised in accordance with Regulation (EU) 528/2012 of the European Parliament and of the Council [2013] OJ L109/4; Commission Delegated Regulation (EU) 114/2013 of 6 November 2012 supplementing Regulation (EU) 510/2011 of the European Parliament and of the Council with regard to rules for the application for a derogation from the specific CO2 emissions target for new light commercial vehicles [2013] OJ L38/1 last amended by Commission Delegated Regulation (EU) 482/2014 of 4 March 2014 amending Delegated Regulation (EU) 114/2013 as regards the 2010 average specific CO 2 emissions specified for the manufacturer Great Wall Motor Company Limited [2014] OJ L138/51.

[15] See Case C-203/86 *Spain v Council* [1988] ECR 4563.

Amongst the first category of requirements inspired by the case law of the CJEU on general principles of EU law is the duty under Article II-3(1)(a) to comply with **the 'duty to care' as a general principle of law** established by the CJ. Although the Court has often mostly stressed its protective dimension towards persons affected by single-case decision-making, this principle also has an objective dimension and is now often understood to be part of the rights and principles of good administration. The relevant aspects covered by it could include existing Union law (in particular, but not limited to the basic regulation), technical standards, the objective of cooperation with other EU and international institutions, practical (including time) considerations, a risk assessment,[16] and a cost-benefit analysis.[17] **29**

Although the CJEU has occasionally made reference to **the impact assessment report** as a tool for reviewing compliance with the principle of proportionality, the requirement for undertaking an impact assessment of executive rule-making (next to legislative acts) has been a self-imposed procedural requirement for the Commission. However, the Commission's practice is not uniform. In the different policy fields analysed, there are cases where the proposal for a non-legislative act (typically a delegated act) was accompanied by a fully-fledged impact assessment,[18] but there are also cases, where this does not happen.[19] **30**

---

[16] See e.g. Decision of the EASA Management Board 01/2012, amending and replacing Decision 8/2007 concerning the procedure to be applied by the Agency for the issuing of options, certification specifications and guidance material ('Rulemaking Procedure'), of 13 March 2012 (based on Regulation (EC) 216/2008 on common rules in the field of civil aviation and establishing a European Aviation Safety Agency, OJ 2008 L 79/1 last amended by Commission Regulation (EU) 6/2013 of 8 January 2013 amending Regulation (EC) 216/2008 of the European Parliament and of the Council on common rules in the field of civil aviation and establishing a European Aviation Safety Agency, and repealing Council Directive 91/670/EEC, Regulation (EC) 1592/2002 and Directive 2004/36/EC [2013] OJ L4/34, Arts 18 and 20), Arts 1–7.

[17] This can be found in Regulation (EU) 1095/2010 of the European Parliament and the Council of 24 November 2010 establishing a European Supervisory Authority (European Securities and Markets Authority), amending Decision 716/2009/EC and repealing Commission Decision 2009/77/EC [2010] OJ L331/84 last amended by Directive 2014/51/EU of the European Parliament and of the Council of 16 April 2014 amending Directives 2003/71/EC and 2009/138/EC and Regulations (EC) 1060/2009, (EU) 1094/2010 and (EU) 1095/2010 in respect of the powers of the European Supervisory Authority (European Insurance and Occupational Pensions Authority) and the European Supervisory Authority (European Securities and Markets Authority) [2014] OJ L153/1, Arts 10 and 15.

[18] See, for example, Commission impact assessment accompanying the document Proposal for a Commission Delegated Regulation supplementing Regulation (EU) 236/2012 of the European Parliament and the Council on short selling and certain aspects of Credit Default Swaps with regard to definitions, the calculation of net short positions, covered sovereign credit default swaps, notification thresholds, liquidity thresholds for suspending restrictions, significant falls in the value of financial instruments and adverse events, C(2012) 4529 Final, of 5 July 2012, p 22–47.

[19] See for example Commission Delegated Regulation (EU) 946/2012 of July 12, 2012, supplementing Regulation (EC) No 1060/2009 of the European Parliament and of the Council with regard to rules of procedure for fines imposed on credit rating agencies by the European Securities and Markets Authority, including rules on the right of defence and temporal provisions [2012] OJ L282/23.

31 The drafters of Book II believe that it is important to require an impact assessment for non-legislative acts covered by Book II. Although, so far, the main emphasis in the EU has been on requiring impact assessment for legislative acts, such legislative acts, however, benefit from public scrutiny within a parliamentary process and by the Council and its working groups. When it comes to **non-legislative acts**, the added value of **impact assessment procedures** which are made public is to introduce a procedural tool for including and making publicly visible the inclusion of facts, interests, values, and scientific opinions into decision-making.

32 During the discussions of the ReNEUAL Model Rules on administrative procedure, the question was raised whether a per-se requirement for impact assessment of rule-making would be appropriate. The drafters of Book II have decided, after much discussion with academic experts and practitioners alike, to require impact assessment as standard procedure. The reason is that **impact assessment is a flexible procedural tool.** The analysis of impact does not require the same intensity for all acts. In fact, the impact assessment will by nature be the more extensive, the more potential impact an act will have. The inverse is also true. The less potential impact an act will have, the more limited the assessment of its impact will be. Hence, Article II-3 incorporates impact assessment procedures into the rules followed for the establishment, amendment and repeal of legally binding non-legislative acts of general application.

33 Impact assessment **may**—but does not have to in all cases—**include a cost-benefit analysis.** The weighing of interests or values is not easily quantifiable in all cases. It may, therefore, not be opportune in all cases to submit a regulatory matter to a cost-benefit analysis. Cost-benefit analysis should be undertaken when the nature of the content of the planned regulation so permits—i.e. when there is sufficient possibility of quantifying the parameters which need to be evaluated through impact assessment.

34 On the other hand, Article II-3 is **strict about the types of values and principles to be taken into account in impact assessment** procedures. It thereby takes inspiration from the standards set in the EU for impact assessment by the Commission, which explicitly include the analysis of fundamental rights, environment, budget, and many other factors including the social and societal impact of a planned measure.[20] Not taking these important values into account in the assessment of the impacts of non-legislative acts of general application would risk de-legitimization of EU policies.

---

[20] See European Commission, Communication on Compliance with the Charter of Fundamental Rights in Commission legislative proposals, COM(2005) 172; European Commission, Impact Assessment Guidelines of 15 January 2009, SEC(2009) 92.

The rules in Book II make it obligatory to **publish** the results of the impact assessment **by means of an explanatory memorandum** according to Article II-3(1)(c) in order to allow for a subsequent informed and therefore meaningful public consultation. Making public the reasons underlying the act not only allows for scrutiny, but it is also crucial to support the consultation phase that follows. **35**

Additionally, Article II-3(1)(c) requires that the **regulatory choice retained** for the draft non-legislative act of general application **as well as possible alternative solutions** to the problem be explained in the explanatory memorandum. This is currently not established practice but would, in the eyes of the drafters of Book II, be a welcome innovation for the current practice in which agencies are not always required to make their choices and alternative considerations public,[21] and short explanatory memorandums exist also in the case of delegated acts,[22] but not (at least not generally) in the case of implementing acts. **36**

The requirement of Article II-3(2) to make public the identity and the **material submitted by experts** who were consulted during the preparation of an act is linked to the principle of transparency. It is normal practice, and also desirable, in view of the need to act on the basis of sufficient knowledge and information, that a body drafting an act works with or meets with experts or other third parties. However, these parties need to be identified as an important part of the background information for a rule. It would also appear necessary to make public the nature of the interchange or any data that the outsider has supplied. The considerations that are likely to govern the final act should be made public, and information is best assessed when the author is clear. This also gives incentives for parties to present accurate data because such data can be independently scrutinized upon publication. **37**

II-4 Consultation and Participation

Article II-4(1) specifies what the general principles listed in Article 11(1) TEU mean with respect to executive rule-making in the EU and restates that the principles of Article 11(1) TEU apply in the process of drafting a legally binding non-legislative act of general application. However, the **Commission and other** **38**

[21] ESMA's consultation papers on draft regulatory technical standards contain explanations of the reasons for the adoption of the act (attached to the different questions submitted for the attention of persons participating in the consultation), but do not always analyse the different available alternatives possible. See, for instance, ESMA's Consultation Paper on Draft Technical Standards on the Regulation (EU) xxxx/2012 of the European Parliament and the Council on Short Selling and certain aspects of credit default swap, ESMA/2012/30, of 24 January 2012, available at http://www.esma.europa.eu/system/files/2012-30_0.pdf.

[22] See for example General Secretariat of the Council (to Coreper/Council), 'I/A' Item Note regarding Commission Delegated Regulation (EU) No . . ./. . . of 6.11.2012 supplementing Regulation (EU) 510/2011 of the European Parliament and of the Council with regard to rules for the application for a derogation from the specific CO2 emissions targets for new light commercial vehicles [2012] Council Document, 17168/12.

institutions and bodies of the Union **can obviously develop additional means** of exchanging ideas and including the public in their activities.

39 The rules of Article II-4 are intended to allow **input** from the interested public at a stage **when the content of the draft act is sufficiently determined**, and, therefore, capable of grounding concrete comments and suggestions on specific solutions (rather than on broad policy options). Envisaging consultation and participation at this stage means that the solutions enshrined in the draft act need to be adjusted in view of the comments received, following the rules on paragraph 5 of this article.

40 Article II-4(2) requires that a **central EU website for consultation and participation** is designed. This would allow for a simplified access for citizens who would, by using a single site, be able to comment on draft rules without being obliged to monitor an indefinite number of websites of agencies and bodies of the Union. Such a requirement of publication would standardize the currently diverse practice of consultation on a 'draft act of general application' and its reasoned report,[23] established in the various policy areas of the EU. A uniform practice does not seem to exist.

41 The details of such publication need to be designed with a view to ensuring input into rule-making which reflects the various opinions and interests held within pluralistic societies. **No specific group in society should be able to influence rule-making unilaterally**, due to privileged access to the regulator. One way to guarantee that this does not occur is to harmonize the place of publication, the necessary contents of publication, and the standard deadlines to be applied, and to establish rules on the language regime to be followed.

42 Regarding the **deadlines**, for example, the deadline indicated in paragraph 2(b) is the one currently defined in the Commission's standards of consultation in the context of impact assessment analyses.[24] Yet, agency practice is not always clear.[25]

---

[23] See, for example Regulation (EC) 216/2008 of the European Parliament and of the Council of 20 February 2008 on common rules in the field of civil aviation and establishing a European Aviation Safety Agency (EASA) and repealing Council Directive 91/670/EEC [2008] OJ L79/1 last amended by Commission Regulation (EU) 6/2013 of 8 January 2013 amending Regulation (EC) 216/2008 of the European Parliament and of the Council on common rules in the field of civil aviation and establishing a European Aviation Safety Agency, and repealing Council Directive 91/670/EEC, Regulation (EC) 1592/2002 and Directive 2004/36/EC [2013] OJ L4/34, Art 52(1)(c); Decision of the EASA Management Board 01/2012 concerning the procedure to be applied by the Agency for the issuing of options, certification specifications and guidance material ('Rulemaking Procedure'), Art 6.

[24] See e.g. the formulation in European Commission, Impact Assessment Guidelines of 15 January 2009, SEC(2009) 92, p 19, introducing the possibility of longer consultation periods for justified cases. See also Commission Staff Working Document, 'Review of the Commission Consultation Policy', SWD(2012) 422 final, Strasbourg, 12.12.2012.

[25] For one rather clearly defined approach, see e.g. Decision of the EASA Management Board 01/2012, amending and replacing Decision 8/2007 concerning the procedure to be applied by the Agency for the issuing of options, certification specifications and guidance material ('Rulemaking Procedure'), of 13 March 2012 (based on Regulation (EC) 216/2008 on common rules in the field

The **language requirement** in paragraph 2(d) is an attempt to balance, on the one hand, the necessity of information being accessible to all Union citizens and, on the other hand, practical requirements of administrative work, which cannot cope with the continuous translation of so many documents in all official languages. It is a compromise solution. Practice seems to favour a restriction in the number of languages, but this practice is not without its critics. For example, the practice of ESMA highlights that the publication in all official languages concerns final rather than draft acts.[26] At the same time, the practice of EASA in publishing many documents only in a few languages was condemned by the EO as an instance of maladministration.[27] The solution we propose refers only to the draft act and to the reasoned report. It is a compromise solution, which follows the judgment, according to which both the Treaty references to the use of languages in the EU and the rules contained in secondary legislation, 'cannot be regarded as evidencing a general principle of Community law that confers a right on every citizen to have a version of anything that might affect his interests drawn up in his language in all circumstances'.[28] It may have the undesirable effect of limiting the access to consultation procedures for those who do not master the working languages of the EU authority in charge of drafting the act. Nevertheless, it ought to be stressed that this solution cannot restrict the scope of the language rights enshrined in the Treaty. As such, EU citizens may still 'address the institutions and advisory bodies of the Union in any of the Treaty languages and…obtain a reply in the same language' (Article 20(2)(d) TFEU) and 'write to any of the institutions, bodies, offices or agencies…and have an answer in the same language' (Article 24(4) TFEU). 43

In parallel to an open call for comments addressed to the public at large under Article II-4(2), the Commission or the agency in charge may also directly, under Article II-4(3), **target certain parties** who have an interest in the matter in order to encourage greater feedback on rule-making proposals. This approach is well established in the concept of consultation contained in the European Commission 44

of civil aviation and establishing a European Aviation Safety Agency, OJ 2008 L 79/1 last amended by Commission Regulation (EU) 6/2013 of 8 January 2013 amending Regulation (EC) 216/2008 of the European Parliament and of the Council on common rules in the field of civil aviation and establishing a European Aviation Safety Agency, and repealing Council Directive 91/670/EEC, Regulation (EC) 1592/2002 and Directive 2004/36/EC [2013] OJ L4/34, Arts 18 and 20), Art 6(4), (5), setting the duration for consultation at between 1 and 3 months.

[26] See for example ESMA, Final Report—Guidelines on Sound Remuneration Policies under the AIFMD [2013] 2013/201, p 4, available at: http://www.esma.europa.eu/system/files/2013-201.pdf.

[27] Decision of the European Ombudsman closing his inquiry into complaint 3419/2008/(AF)(BEH)KM against the European Aviation Safety Agency (20.12.2012), available at http://www.ombudsman.europa.eu/cases/decision.faces/en/48732/html.bookmark.

[28] Case C-361/01 P *Christina Kik v Office for Harmonisation in the Internal Market* [2003] ECR I-8283), para 82. See also, Case T-120/99 *Christina Kik v Office for Harmonisation in the Internal Market (Trade Marks and Designs) (OHIM)* [2001] ECR II-2235, para 58.

Impact Assessment Guidelines of 2009. It is also used in legal systems which have an explicit notice and comment procedure, e.g. US Administrative law. The idea is to allow for making the consultation period effective by having an open call for comments, while at the same time actively seeking comments by known stakeholders in a specific matter. This also appears to be the practice in EASA consultation procedures. The persons affected may also be identified during the phase of public consultation, as the comments received may alert the EU authority in charge of drafting the act to impacts it may initially not be aware of.

45 Article II-4(4) seeks to **ensure that all comments received** during the consultation period—whether submitted by the public at large or by persons affected **are published.** However, in specifically justified cases, there may be legitimate concern at making public the identity of the natural person making comments. The protection of natural persons' identity may be necessary in certain cases where the requirement to publish the identity of the person submitting a comment might compromise the willingness to comment. That might especially be necessary in matters where the public debate is highly emotional and the individual right to freely state an opinion requires protection. Protecting individuals in this sense will also allow for comments to be made by individuals who might otherwise not be willing to come forward. Thereby this rule might implicitly also serve the interest of the public at large by raising the overall quality of rule-making.

46 Article II-4(4) also requires, in the interest of ensuring that under Article 11(1) TEU, citizens and representative associations have the 'opportunity to make known and publicly exchange their views', that **subsequent commentators be able to comment on comments made earlier.** This exchange of views will allow for alternative approaches to be developed in a comment section and ensure a more complete exchange on a Commission proposal than would have been possible if earlier comments were not accessible to later commentators.

47 A second consultation may be needed to **avoid the substitution of the act that was subject to consultation.** However, the decision-maker should be given the discretion not to start a new consultation procedure if this becomes too cumbersome. EASA rule-making procedures provide an example of such practice.[29] This rule was the inspiration for Article II-4(5).

[29] Decision of the EASA Management Board 01/2012, amending and replacing Decision 8/2007 concerning the procedure to be applied by the Agency for the issuing of options, certification specifications and guidance material ('Rulemaking Procedure'), of 13 March 2012 (based on Regulation (EC) 216/2008 on common rules in the field of civil aviation and establishing a European Aviation Safety Agency, OJ 2008 L 79/1 last amended by Commission Regulation (EU) 6/2013 of 8 January 2013 amending Regulation (EC) 216/2008 of the European Parliament and of the Council on common rules in the field of civil aviation and establishing a European Aviation Safety Agency, and repealing Council Directive 91/670/EEC, Regulation (EC) 1592/2002 and Directive 2004/36/EC [2013] OJ L4/34, Arts 18 and 20), Art 7(5).

II-5 Reasoned Report

Article II-5(1) describes a subsequent step in the procedure of rule-making. It obliges the body to actively **review the comments** received **and** to **report the results** of that activity. This provision balances the need to ensure that comments received are duly taken into account against the flexibility that ought to be given to the deciding authority in assessing those comments in the light of the legal mandate it needs to pursue. The public should be able to see which points have been taken into account in the final rule-making proposal. Not all comments will be pertinent and justify a reaction. This provision does not prevent aggregation of answers to the comments received according to the criteria chosen by the deciding authority (e.g. subject matter). **48**

The **form of publication** is a reasoned report accompanying the final act. This shall be sufficiently detailed to allow for effective administrative and judicial review. This requirement is in accordance with the consistent interpretation of Article 296 TFEU by the CJEU, which applies to the degree of justification of final acts.[30] Although the parallels with the case law of the CJEU are evident, the wording of Article II-5(1)(b) is not designed to require or regulate judicial review. Instead, it requires that the act be reasoned to a degree which makes it possible for effective administrative or judicial forms of review to take place. For this purpose, the main points and the legal issues of the act need to be sufficiently reasoned. **49**

The **reasoned report** under Article II-5 **does not have to be made part of the preamble** of the final act. This is justified by the need to leave untouched the technique of drafting EU legal acts as drafting approaches may differ. For example, delegated acts under Article 290 TFEU are usually accompanied by a brief explanatory note when they are submitted to the EP and Council. By contrast, the objectives or goals of implementing acts under Article 291 TFEU can mainly be found in the preamble to the act itself. However, the accompanied reasoned report needs to be publicly available and ought to be considered part of the final act.[31] **50**

Article II-5(2) establishes the **link between the set of rules** proposed above **and the procedural mechanisms in place for the adoption of acts under Articles 290 and** **51**

---

[30] See for example Case C-89/08 P *Commission v Ireland* [2009] ECR I-11245, para 77; Case C-367/95 P *Commission v Sytraval and Brink's France* [1998] ECR I-1719, para 63.

[31] See e.g. Decision of the EASA Management Board 01/2012, amending and replacing Decision 8/2007 concerning the procedure to be applied by the Agency for the issuing of options, certification specifications and guidance material ('Rulemaking Procedure'), of 13 March 2012 (based on Regulation (EC) 216/2008 on common rules in the field of civil aviation and establishing a European Aviation Safety Agency, OJ 2008 L 79/1 last amended by Commission Regulation (EU) 6/2013 of 8 January 2013 amending Regulation (EC) 216/2008 of the European Parliament and of the Council on common rules in the field of civil aviation and establishing a European Aviation Safety Agency, and repealing Council Directive 91/670/EEC, Regulation (EC) 1592/2002 and Directive 2004/36/EC [2013] OJ L4/34, Arts 18 and 20), Art 8(2).

291 TFEU.[32] Making it compulsory to mention the changes made to delegated acts following consultations with the EP and Council may be controversial, given the current inter-institutional disagreements on the role of each of these institutions (and of the Commission) in the adoption of delegated acts. This duty is, however, justified by the requirements of transparency. Consultations with the Council, the EP, or a committee under Regulation 182/2011, as the case may be, may trump some of the solutions that could have been favoured on the basis of the comments received via public consultation. In current practice, where it exists, public consultations over delegated acts precede the institutional consultations (see the 2014 Invitation by the Council to revise the Common Understanding). The rules we propose do not require a change to this practice. But actual compliance with the previous paragraphs of this article could be compromised in the absence of the duty we now propose.

II-6 Expedited Procedures

52 Expedited procedures are the **exception**, which provide **a certain degree of flexibility** to administrative entities in charge of rule-making, without creating loopholes for circumvention of the standard rule-making process. At the same time, conducting a consultation after the adoption of the act might still indicate areas where the act could be improved a posteriori and could be justified by the need to ensure the procedural protection of the legally protected interests affected.

53 There are basically **two possible approaches** for delimiting the use of expedited procedures and thereby protecting the ordinary procedure from being circumvented. The first approach is to establish a list of instances in which an expedited procedure could be used. The second approach is to design the procedure in a way which does not lend itself to misuse. The drafting team of Book II discussed this issue with many commentators. The problem with the first approach is that any list will either be too vague to give legal certainty, or contain a list of cases in which expedited procedures might be used which is not complete enough for application in all instances. After much discussion, the drafting team decided to opt for a procedural approach. This envisages the exceptional use of expedited procedures but seeks to protect the ordinary procedure in the following ways. First, a requirement to undertake the ordinary rule-making procedure directly after the adoption of the act under the expedited procedure is included. Second, any amendments to the act

[32] Such mechanisms are described by the Communication from the Commission to the European Parliament and the Council on the Implementation of Article 290 of the Treaty on the Functioning of the European Union (COM (2009) 673 final) and the Common Understanding between Parliament and Council on Delegated Acts, which can, for example, be found in Council Document 8753/11 of 10 April 2011 or Regulation (EU) 182/2011 of the European Parliament and of the Council of 16 February 2011 laying down the rules and general principles concerning mechanisms for control by Member States of the Commission's exercise of implementing powers [2011] OJ L55/13.

in force, which result from the procedure provided under Article II-4, are required. Third, a sunset clause, which limits an act adopted under the expedited procedure to a period of eighteen months, is included. The text of Article II-5 does not, however, exclude the possibility of the act adopted under the expedited procedure being again adopted under an expedited procedure after eighteen months. But this option will most likely be rarely used given that it could be replaced by an act adopted in the ordinary procedure after the mandatory use of the procedure provided in Article II-4. The sunset clause proposed in paragraph 2 is designed to ensure that the expedited procedure is not misused by becoming the default procedure since all matters of rule-making may, by definition, be declared urgent.

BOOK III—SINGLE-CASE DECISION-MAKING

A. Introduction to Book III

Book III is concerned with single-case decision-making, which is central to any regime of administrative procedure. While only some national administrative procedure acts regulate administrative rule-making, as distinct from primary and secondary legislation, there **is no legislative regulation of administrative procedures that neglects single-case decision-making.** The legal reality is that much administrative action gives rise to the issuing of individual acts and measures (décision individuelle, provvedimento amministrativo, Verwaltungsakt), with either favourable or unfavourable effects. It is therefore not surprising that the remedies available against such administrative acts and measures are in general tailored to the model of adjudication. Thus this type of administrative action is at the heart of national systems of public law, in Europe and elsewhere. 1

2 **Single-case decision-making has also been central to the development of EU law** for at least three reasons. First, since the constitution of the ECSC, the distinction between individual and general decisions has been established by the Treaty of Paris and clarified by the case law of the ECJ. Second, the system of remedies, as interpreted by EU courts, traditionally makes it much easier to bring an action against an individual measure, as distinct from a measure of general application. Last but not least, it is especially in the vast field of single-case decision-making that shared implementation between EU and national administrations has developed, particularly during the last twenty to thirty years. Since a large part of the EU budget is spent in this manner—in areas such as agriculture and regional policy—the Financial Regulation contains provisions dealing with shared management.

3 The **rules of Book III are applicable to EU authorities** whenever they make administrative decisions, whether in the context of direct or composite or shared administration. They are only applicable to Member State authorities where EU sector-specific legislation so provides, or where a Member State chooses to adopt the rules. There **would be advantages in rendering the rules applicable to Member States** when they act in the scope of EU law. It would provide those affected by Member State administrative decisions made in the context of EU law with a clear set of procedural rights and also render it easier for the administration to understand and apply the procedural obligations incumbent on them. They would not have to determine afresh on each occasion whether national procedural rules in court decisions, national codes of procedure or an admixture of the two, suffice to meet the requirements of EU law.

4 It has nonetheless been decided for two reasons that the **rules should only be applicable to Member States when EU sector-specific legislation so provides, or where a Member State chooses to adopt the rules.** First, there are doubts as to whether the EU has legal competence to enact a general law on administrative procedure that is applicable to Member States as well as the EU. Second, while the application of such a law to Member States would have the advantages set out above it might at this stage of European integration be perceived as an undue intrusion into national legal traditions. It is for this reason that the drafting team adopted at this stage of the project a more cautious approach, which may however serve as a starting point for extension of the scope of application in specific sectors of EU law. Thus, for the present, national rules on administrative procedure remain applicable, subject to the duty that these procedures comply with the general principles of EU law laid down by the CJEU. If a Member State so chooses, the model rules can however serve as a template for the reform of existing procedural rules, or for the adoption of new procedural rules.

5 The model rules do not seek to eliminate the particularities of sector-specific legislation. EU legislation contains procedural and substantive conditions for eligibility to, for example, EU funds. Such conditions are mainly determined on a case-by-

case approach. The *lex specialis* applies, but it must be interpreted in the light of the model rules, as established by Book I.

The principle that informs this Book is that there should be a **clear set of rules applicable to all stages of the administrative procedure**, from its inception, through investigation and hearings to the making of the final decision and the obligations flowing therefrom, including a duty to give reasons. The legal status quo is that the precepts of administrative procedure apply to administrative decisions that affect an individual or a small number of individuals, through, for example, withdrawal of a benefit or imposition of a penalty. There are also administrative decisions addressed to a particular person, natural or legal, which may affect a large number of individuals. The **EU courts** have done a good job in this area. Their activist jurisprudence has provided the requisites of due process, and they have supplied the omission of the legislature when the latter has failed to provide for such hearings, or where the standards of procedural rectitude have been insufficiently demanding. **Sector-specific rules** have drawn on the case law and advanced beyond it through provision of more detailed regulatory precepts for different sectoral areas. **6**

There is nonetheless **much room for further improvement in this area.** Most EU lawyers, even specialists in this area, would be hard pressed to articulate the applicable rules on a range of issues that are central to single-case decision-making. These include: the procedural norms that regulate the way in which applications should be made; the duties of the administration when in receipt of an application; the duties of the administration when managing an administrative procedure; the administration's powers of investigation and inspection; the rules that govern who can be a party to a hearing; the legal or technical assistance that can be requested; the nature of the hearing that must be afforded; the due process rules that pertain respectively to the EU and national administration when both play a central role in the final decision as dealt with in Article III-24; and the procedural rules applicable when a single decision affects a large number of people. **7**

These issues lie at the heart of single-case decision-making. The well-trained EU lawyer will, given sufficient time, be able to work out the answers to at least some of these issues. But that does not suffice to show that the current system is adequate. **We should not rest content with a system in which the rules on such basic issues are difficult to discern** for the individual claimant. Nor should we rest content with a system in which hard-pressed administrators and draft legislators have to put together a package of procedural rules afresh on each occasion. There is little doubt that the existing regime could be significantly improved for claimants, for those devising legislation and those applying it if there were some boilerplate general law of the kind set out below. It provides a clear set of rules dealing with all the issues set out in the preceding paragraph. It addresses the issues in a straightforward manner, following the sequence of an administrative decision from the time of the initial application or ex officio initiation, **8** through the rules that pertain to management of the procedure, inspection and investigation, rules of evidence, and onward to the nature of the hearing, and procedural consequences that flow thereafter, such as the duty to give reasons and the provision of information about appeals. Book III does not cover all the issues that are dealt with in every national administrative procedure act, and it is in any event the case that national APAs vary in terms of the range of issues for which provision is made.

9 Chapter 1 contains Articles III-1 and III-2, which define the **scope of application** of Book III and set out certain **key definitions** used throughout the remainder of the Book.

10 Chapter 2 deals with the **initiation and management of procedures.** It begins with Article III-3, which sets out the general duty of fair decision-making and rules on impartiality, including in this respect rules relating to conflict of interest. Article III-4 deals with provision of online information concerning existing procedures. Article III-5 specifies the requirements that pertain when an administrative procedure is initiated, either ex-officio or through an application. Article III-6 contains more specific provisions dealing with applications, and this is followed in Article III-7 by provisions concerning the official responsible for managing the procedure. Article III-8 then deals with the management of the administrative procedure, and Article III-9 with the time-limits within which the procedure should be concluded.

11 Chapter 3 is concerned with the **investigation as a major preparatory step in each administrative procedure** and selected issues concerning the law of evidence. Article III-10 sets out the basic principle underlying administrative investigation, Article III-11 the procedural norms that apply when investigations are conducted by request, Article III-12 the procedural rules that pertain when an investigation is mandated by the relevant EU rules and Article III-13 sets out duties of the parties to cooperate. Article III-14 deals with the privilege against self-incrimination and legal professional privilege. Article III-15 regulates witnesses and experts. Articles III-16-21 set out the rules relating to **inspections** which are conceived as a specific instrument of administrative investigations.

12 Chapter 4 specifies the **rights relating to the hearing.** Article III-22 is concerned with access to the file, Article III-23 with the basic principles governing the right to be heard by those adversely affected, this being complemented in Article III-24 by the application of such precepts in circumstances where there is a composite administrative procedure. Article III-25 lays down the procedural rules applicable where consultation is used in relation to a single decision that affects a large number of people, and Articles III-26 and III-27 are concerned respectively with consultation with the Member States and EU authorities.

13 Chapter 5 establishes in Articles III-28 to III-34 the procedural precepts that apply at the **conclusion of the administrative decision-making**, which include the duty to

specify the decision, the duty to give reasons, the duty to indicate available remedies, obligations relating to the notification of decisions, and language requirements.

Chapter 6 deals with the distinct and complex problems concerning the **withdrawal and rectification of decisions**, with Article III-35 addressing issues concerning withdrawal or rectification of decisions that have an adverse effect, while Article III-36 is directed towards such withdrawal or rectification where the decisions have a beneficial effect. 14

B. Model Rules

Chapter 1: General Provisions

III-1 Scope of application

(1) Book III applies to administrative procedures by which an EU authority prepares and adopts a decision as defined in Article III-2.
(2) Book III applies to administrative procedures by which a Member State authority prepares and adopts a decision as defined in Article III-2 insofar as sector-specific EU law or the respective Member State law renders it applicable.

III-2 Definitions

(1) 'Decision' means administrative action addressed to one or more individualized public or private persons which is adopted unilaterally by an EU authority, or by a Member State authority when Article III-1(2) is applicable, to determine one or more concrete cases with legally binding effect.
(2) 'Public authority' for the purposes of Book III means an EU authority, and a Member State authority under the conditions specified in Article III-1(2).
(3) 'Party' means the addressee of the intended decision and other persons who are adversely affected by it and who request to be involved in the procedure. Sector-specific EU law may assign the status of party to persons not adversely affected.
(4) 'Interested public' for the purposes of Article III-25 means every natural or legal person and other associations, organizations or groups expressing an interest in the administrative procedure.
(5) 'Inspection' means an on-the-spot check for the purposes of information gathering.
(6) 'Responsible official' means the official charged by the public authority with managing the administrative procedure.

Chapter 2: Initiation and Management of Procedure

III-3 General duty of fair decision-making and impartiality

(1) Every person has the right to have his or her affairs handled impartially, fairly and within a reasonable time by public authorities as specified in these model rules.
(2) The responsible official as set out in Article III-7 has a duty to communicate any financial or familial interest in a decision to his or her superior and shall not take part in that decision.

(3) The responsible official has a duty to communicate any other possible conflict of interest to his or her superior, who should exclude the official from participating in the decision where the impartial and objective exercise of the official's function is compromised.
(4) A party may request that a responsible official affected by a conflict of interest should not take part in the making of the decision. This request must be filed as soon as possible and should be reasoned and made in writing. The decision whether to exclude the official shall be made by his or her superior after hearing the official.
(5) Any other person involved in a decision on behalf of a public authority shall *mutatis mutandis* be bound by the obligations in paragraphs 2 to 4 above.

III-4 Online information on existing procedures

(1) Public authorities shall promote the provision of general updated online information on the existing administrative procedures, wherever possible and reasonable. Priority shall be given to application procedures.
(2) Such information may include, among other things:
 (a) a link to the applicable legislation in its consolidated version,
 (b) a brief explanation of the main legal requirements and its administrative interpretation,
 (c) a description of the main procedural steps,
 (d) the indication of the authority competent to adopt the final decision,
 (e) the indication of the time-limit for the adoption of the decision,
 (f) the indication of remedies available,
 (g) a link to standard forms that may be used by parties in their communications with the public authority within the procedure.
(3) The information shall be presented in a clear and simple way. Access shall be free of charge.
(4) The European Commission shall foster the adoption of best practices in the provision of online information and may issue recommendations to that end.

III-5 Initiation

(1) Administrative procedures can be initiated ex-officio or by an application.
(2) The initiation of an administrative procedure ex-officio shall be notified to the parties. The notification may take place at a later stage if it might jeopardise the investigation of the case. The notification may be omitted when an immediate decision is strictly necessary in the public interest, or because of the serious risk involved in delay.
(3) The notification shall indicate:
 (a) registration number,
 (b) notice of the rationale for the initiation of the procedure,
 (c) the name and contact details of the responsible official for the procedure,
 (d) information referred to in letters (c), (d), (e) and (f) of Article III-4(2),
 (e) the address of the website mentioned in Article III-4 if such website exists.
(4) Once an administrative procedure is initiated, the competent authority shall adopt a final decision within the time-limit laid down in Article III-9.

III-6 Special rules on application procedures

(1) Applications shall not be subject to unnecessary formal and documentary requirements and may be submitted in writing to the competent authority in-person, by mail or by electronic means.

(2) Applications addressed or transmitted to a non-competent service shall be transferred without delay to the competent one if both of them belong to the same public authority. The service that originally received the application shall notify the applicant of this transfer and shall indicate the contact details of the service to which the file has been passed. In other cases, applications shall be returned and advice on the competent authority shall be given, wherever possible and reasonable.

(3) Applications shall be acknowledged in writing as quickly as possible. The acknowledgement of receipt shall indicate the information contained in letters (a), (c), (d) and (e) of Article III-5(3). In the event of a defective application, the acknowledgment shall specify the defects or missing documents and give an appropriate period for remedying or producing the missing documents. Pointless or manifestly unfounded applications may be rejected as inadmissible by means of a briefly reasoned acknowledgement of receipt. No acknowledgement of receipt needs to be sent in cases where successive applications submitted by the same applicant are abusive because such applications have a repetitive character.

(4) Where the number of applications to be granted is limited and a competitive award procedure is used the rules laid down in Book IV Chapter 2 Section 3 shall apply *mutatis mutandis*.

III-7 Responsible official

When an administrative procedure is initiated the public authority shall appoint a responsible official, who shall manage it subject to Article III-3(2)–(3), shall respect the rights in Article III-8(1) and shall keep an adequate file containing records of all information and documents produced.

III-8 Management of procedures and procedural rights

(1) The parties shall have the following rights related to the management of the procedure:
   (a) to be given information on all questions related to the procedure in a fast, clear and understandable manner;
   (b) to communicate and to complete, where possible and appropriate, all procedural formalities at a distance and by electronic means, including videoconferencing;
   (c) to use any of the official languages of the EU in accordance with Article III-31;
   (d) to be notified of all procedural steps and decisions that may affect them in accordance with Article III-33;
   (e) to be represented by a lawyer or some other person of their choice having legal capacity;
   (f) to pay only charges that are reasonable and proportionate to the cost of the procedure in question.

(2) Without prejudice to the existing legal remedies, the parties shall have the right to file a complaint against the responsible official, the deciding authority, or any other official who takes part in the procedure where they fail to comply with their obligations under these model rules, whether intentionally or through negligence.

(3) Where the number of persons adversely affected is large, and the adverse effect is the same or very similar, they may choose a representative or representatives from the affected group to be parties. If the affected group does not do so, the public authority may require them within a reasonable period to appoint a joint representative where otherwise the regular execution of administrative procedure

would be impaired. If these persons do not comply within the period set, the authority may ex-officio appoint a joint representative.

(4) Sector-specific EU law may stipulate a particular number of persons adversely affected for the purposes of paragraph 3.

III-9 Time-limits for concluding procedures

(1) The public authority shall adopt its decision within a reasonable time and without delay. The time-limits shall be fixed in the relevant sector-specific EU law. If no time-limit is established in the rules governing the specific procedure for the case at hand the time-limit for adopting the decision shall be three months.

(2) The period shall begin on the date of the receipt of a complete application, or on the date of initiation ex-officio.

(3) When complexity or other obstacles prevent examination of the case within the time-limit the parties shall be informed and the decision shall be adopted in the shortest possible time. The public authority shall inform the parties in writing, stating the reasons for the extension, and if possible the predicted time for adoption of the decision. This is without prejudice to any restrictions on the extension of duration of the procedures provided by sector-specific EU law.

(4) Sector-specific EU law shall stipulate the consequences for violation of the time-limit.

Chapter 3: Gathering of Information

Section 1: General Rules

III-10 Principle of investigation

(1) When taking decisions, the public authority shall investigate the case carefully and impartially. It shall take into consideration the relevant factors, including those favourable to the parties, and give each of them its proper weight in the decision, whilst excluding any irrelevant element from consideration. The public authority shall use such evidence as, after due consideration, it deems necessary in order to ascertain the facts of the case.

(2) The public authority may under the conditions laid down in Article III-11 and Article III-12 or in other provisions of EU law:
  (a) gather information of all kinds,
  (b) hear the evidence of the parties, witnesses and experts or gather statements in writing or electronically from parties, experts and witnesses,
  (c) obtain documents and records, and
  (d) under the conditions of Article III-16 visit and inspect the premises involved.

(3) Article VI-21 to VI-22 apply to information provided by a public authority to another public authority.

III-11 Investigation by request

(1) In order to fulfil investigatory duties under sector-specific EU law the public authority may request a party to be interviewed or to provide all necessary information.

(2) Notwithstanding the consequences laid down in sentence 3 and 4 in Article III-13(1), the party may refuse to comply with the request. If the party consents to be interviewed or to provide information, he or she may not supply incorrect or misleading information. Lawyers duly authorised to act may supply the

information on behalf of their clients. The latter shall remain fully responsible if the information supplied is incorrect or misleading.

(3) When sending a request for information to a party, the public authority shall state the legal basis and the purpose of the request, specify what information is required and fix the time-limit within which the information is to be provided, and indicate the penalties provided for in the relevant EU law for supplying incorrect or misleading information.

(4) An EU authority shall without delay forward a copy of the request to the competent authority of the Member State in whose territory the seat of the party is situated or the party resides and to the competent authorities of other Member States whose territory is affected by that request. In case of an interview the Member State in which the interview takes place may request that its officials assist the officials and other accompanying persons authorised by the EU authority to conduct the interview.

(5) The rules of paragraph 4 apply also in case of a request by a Member State authority if the addressee is situated in another Member State. The affected Member State may refuse the interview by authorities from another Member State, in which case the rules on mutual assistance of Book V become applicable.

(6) When sector-specific EU law grants to the public authority the power to interview a person who is not party, who consents to be interviewed for the purpose of collecting information relating to the subject-matter of an investigation, the procedural rules in this article apply *mutatis mutandis.*

III-12 Investigation by mandatory decision

(1) When sector-specific EU law grants to the public authority the power to investigate by a mandatory decision, the procedural rules in this article are applicable. The parties or their representatives shall supply the information requested. They may not supply incorrect or misleading information.

(2) The procedural rules laid down in Article III-11(2) sentence 3 to Article III-11(5) apply *mutatis mutandis.* In addition to the obligations laid down in Article III-11(3) the competent authority shall indicate the legal consequences for not responding to a mandatory decision.

III-13 Duties to cooperate of parties

(1) The parties shall assist in ascertaining the facts of the case. In particular they shall state such facts and evidence as are known to them and which can reasonably expected to be presented by them. If a participant fails to state such facts, the final decision shall be taken on the basis of the information available. The public authority is obliged to conduct additional investigations ex officio only if additional evidence or issues to be investigated are evident. A more extensive duty to assist in ascertaining the facts, and in particular the duty to appear personally or make a statement, shall exist only where the law specifically requires this.

(2) In application procedures according to Article III-6(3) the applicant supplies in an appropriate form the information specified in EU law. If the applicant so requests before submitting an application, the public authority shall give an opinion on the information to be supplied by the applicant. The public authority shall consult appropriate authorities in accordance with Articles III-26 and III-27 before it gives its opinion. The fact that the public authority has given an opinion under this paragraph shall not preclude it from subsequently requiring the applicant to submit further information. Any public authorities

holding relevant information must make this information available to the applicant on his or her specific request and on the condition that the applicant cannot reasonably be expected to obtain this information on his or her own.

III-14 Privilege against self-incrimination and legal professional privilege

(1) Where it is within the responsibility of public authorities to establish a violation of EU law and this violation may lead to an administrative sanction, they are under the obligation to respect a private party's privilege against self-incrimination as well as his or her legal professional privilege.
(2) Where the privilege against self-incrimination or the legal professional privilege referred to in paragraph 1 have been violated in the course of gathering information, the information must not be used as evidence in procedures by public authorities if this violation of defense rights could have an impact on the content of the decision.

III-15 Witnesses and experts

(1) Witnesses and experts shall be obliged to make a statement or prepare opinions, when the law specifically requires this.
(2) The parties may propose witnesses and experts.

Section 2: Inspections

III-16 Inspection powers of public authorities

(1) Without prejudice to on-the-spot-checks carried out by the Member States in accordance with their national law, EU authorities shall have the power to inspect premises
    (a) where they have been provided with the necessary powers of inspection in the relevant legislative act, and
    (b) where this is necessary, to fulfil their duties under EU law.
(2) Where EU law establishes a power or a duty to inspect for a public authority, it should specify the ways in which the power or duty is exercised. A power or duty to inspect may *inter alia* entail the following powers:
    (a) to enter any premises, land or means of transport, which can be inspected according to the basic act providing for inspection powers,
    (b) to search for, examine and take or obtain copies or extracts of documents,
    (c) to ask for explanations,
    (d) to take samples,
    (e) to exchange information gathered by an inspection under the conditions laid down in Book VI, and
    (f) to seal premises or documents.
(3) In order to allow the public authority to carry out inspections, it shall be granted access to relevant premises, land or means of transport. Those affected shall cooperate with the EU officials in their investigation.

III-17 Duties of inspecting officials

(1) Public authorities shall ensure that their inspectors act in accordance with EU law, and in particular respect the European Union Charter of Fundamental Rights and comply with EU and national provisions on the protection of personal data.

(2) Inspectors and other authorized persons shall exercise their power only on production of a written authorization showing their identity and position, together with a notification according to Article III-5(3) or a copy thereof. Unless otherwise indicated in EU law, the inspectors must comply with relevant national procedural rules, provided that these are consistent with EU law.
(3) Public authorities shall take all necessary steps to ensure the confidentiality of the information communicated or obtained in the course of an inspection.
(4) Where public authorities decide to carry out inspections under EU law, they shall ensure that similar inspections are not being carried out at the same time in respect of the same facts by other EU or Member State officials.
(5) Inspectors shall draw up a report with the results of the inspection, which shall be included in the file.

III-18 Duties of sincere cooperation during inspections by EU authorities

(1) Where an inspection by an EU authority is mandated or authorized by EU law the inspection shall be prepared and conducted in close cooperation with the authorities of the Member State concerned. To that end, the officials of the Member State concerned may participate in the inspection, unless the Member State itself is being inspected and participation of its officials would endanger the purpose of the inspection.
(2) Before carrying out such an inspection in a Member State EU authorities shall inform the Member State authorities in good time of an inspection, unless the Member State itself is being inspected and notification would endanger the purpose of the investigation.
(3) Where EU authorities conduct such an inspection they shall be required to inform the Member State authorities of the result of such inspections. Inspectors shall ensure that in drawing up their reports account is taken of the procedural requirements laid down in the national law of the Member State concerned. The reports thus prepared shall constitute admissible evidence in administrative or judicial proceedings of the Member State in which they are used, in the same way and under the same conditions as reports drawn up by national administrative inspectors. Where an inspection is carried out jointly, pursuant to paragraph 1, the national inspectors who took part in the operation shall be asked to countersign the report drawn up by the EU inspectors.
(4) Subject to the agreement of the Member State concerned, EU authorities may seek the assistance of officials from other Member States and call on outside bodies acting under their responsibility to provide technical assistance. The EU authorities shall ensure that these officials and bodies guarantee the necessary technical competence, independence, observance of professional secrecy and are subject to the same professional duties of impartiality as EU officials. Where they seek such outside assistance, EU authorities remain responsible for any misconduct or damage caused by these officials and bodies in the course of an inspection. The EU authorities shall inform the Member State concerned, in good time and in writing, of the identities of these officials and bodies.
(5) In accordance with the duty of sincere cooperation, the Member State on whose territory an inspection mandated or authorized by EU law takes place shall provide any assistance necessary, requesting where appropriate the assistance of the police or of an equivalent enforcement authority, so as to enable the EU

authorities to conduct their inspection. If such assistance requires authorisation from a judicial authority according to the law of the Member State concerned, such authorisation shall be applied for. Such authorisation may also be applied for as a precautionary measure.

(6) Where authorization as referred to in paragraph 5 is applied for, the national judicial authority shall ensure that the authorization of the inspection is authentic and that the coercive measures envisaged are neither arbitrary nor excessive having regard to the subject matter of the inspection. In subjecting the coercive measures to proportionality control, the national judicial authority may ask the EU authorities, directly or through the Member State authority, for detailed explanations of: the grounds for suspecting a violation of EU law; the seriousness of the suspected infringement; and the nature of the involvement of the subject being inspected. However, the national judicial authority may not call into question the necessity for the inspection, nor demand that it be provided with the information in the assembled file.

III-19 Participation of EU authorities in Member State inspections

EU officials may participate in an inspection conducted by and under the responsibility of officials of a Member State on the basis of an agreement with the respective Member State, or if so provided by sector-specific EU law. In this case they shall have access to the same premises and to the same documents as national officials. EU officials may only participate in Member State inspections where they are able to produce written authorization stating their identities and their functions. They may not, on their own initiative, use the powers of inspection conferred on national officials or be present at inspections based on national criminal law.

III-20 Joint inspections of Member State authorities

(1) In cases where an inspection is necessary to fulfil the tasks of authorities from several Member States under EU law, inspectors of each Member State concerned may conduct a joint inspection on the basis of an agreement, or if so provided by sector-specific EU law. The authority in whose territory the inspections are conducted (the host authority) shall invite inspectors of each Member State (invited inspectors) to take part in the respective joint inspection. The host authority shall respond to the request of an authority from another Member State to participate in the operations without delay.

(2) A host authority may, in compliance with its own national law, and with the agreement of the invited inspector's authority, confer executive powers, including investigative powers on the invited inspector. The invited inspector may exercise executive powers only under the guidance and, as a rule, in the presence of inspectors from the host authority. The invited inspector shall be subject to the host authority's national law. The host authority shall assume responsibility for the actions of the invited inspector.

III-21 Relation to Book V

At the request of an EU authority or an authority of another Member State, a Member State authority may conduct inspections in accordance with its national law and subject to the rules formulated in Book V. In such cases, the Member State authority undertakes the inspection on behalf of the requesting authority and not in its own interest.

Chapter 4: Right to a Hearing and Inter-Administrative Consultations

Section 1: Access to the File

III-22 Access to the file

(1) Every party has a right of access to his or her file, while respecting the legitimate interests of confidentiality and of professional and business secrecy.
(2) If documents contain confidential information or professional or business secrets, the public authority must, where possible, provide a non-confidential version or summary of the documents.
(3) Every party shall have the opportunity to examine all documents in his or her file, which may be relevant for its defence, including incriminating and exculpatory evidence, before the decision is taken.
(4) The way in which access to the file is provided is for the public authority to determine, and may be regulated through sector-specific EU law, provided that it does not undermine the substance of the right. Subject to this caveat, access to the file may be provided either through copies of documentation, or the opportunity to study the file in the office of the public authority, or a combination of both.
(5) The right of access to the file does not cover access to documentation that is irrelevant and bears no relation to the allegations of fact or law in the particular case.

Section 2: Hearing, Participation and Consultation

III-23 Right to be heard by persons adversely affected

(1) Every party has the right to be heard by a public authority before a decision, which would affect him or her adversely, is taken.
(2) The hearing prior to the taking of the individual decision may be omitted when an immediate decision is strictly necessary in the public interest or because of the serious risk involved in delay, but a hearing shall be provided after the decision was taken, unless there are very compelling reasons to the contrary. The public authority shall provide reasons as to why these conditions are applicable and has the burden of proof in relation to showing that the evidence supports the reasons given.
(3) Every party has the right to notice of the central issues that are to be decided by the public authority and the core arguments that inform its reasoning, in order that the party can effectively make known its views on the matter and can exercise its rights of defence.
(4) Every party must have adequate time in which to respond after notice in accord with paragraph 3 has been provided. The public authority should set clear time-limits within which the response is to occur.
(5) The public authority has discretion as to the form and content of the hearing. This includes the choice as to whether the hearing should be written or oral, and whether to allow cross-examination. In choosing how to exercise this discretion the public authority should take into account the objectives of the legislation, the legislative provisions, the importance of the person's interests, the importance of the additional procedural safeguards for protection of the person's interest, and the costs of granting such specific procedural safeguards.

III-24 Right to be heard in composite procedures

(1) The right to be heard must be respected at all stages of a composite procedure between the EU and the Member States leading to a decision in the manner set out in this article. The application of the right to be heard will depend on the division of responsibility in the decision-making process.

(2) In a case of composite procedure, where an EU authority makes the decision it must comply with the procedural requirements in Article III-23. Where the decision is made by a Member State authority it must comply with the requirements of Article III-23 where sector-specific EU law renders the procedural rules in Book III applicable. In the absence of such sector-specific EU law, or any other EU law specifying applicable procedural requirements, the Member State authority will apply national rules of administrative procedure, which must comply with general principles of EU law concerning fair hearings.

(3) In a case of composite procedure, the form and content of the hearing provided pursuant to Article III-23(5) by the public authority that makes the decision will be affected by the extent to which the rights of the defence were adequately protected at a prior stage in the administrative proceedings by another public authority.

(4) In a case of composite procedure, where the public authority making the decision is legally bound by a recommendation made by an EU authority, then the right to be heard must be adequately protected before the EU authority that makes the recommendation, including through application of the principles in Article III-23(3)-(5). Where sector-specific EU law renders Book III applicable to Member States, the preceding obligation applies *mutatis mutandis* where a Member State authority makes the recommendation. In the absence of such an EU provision, or any other EU law specifying applicable procedural requirements, the Member State authority will apply national rules of administrative procedure, which must comply with general principles of EU law concerning fair hearings.

(5) In a case of composite procedure, where the EU authority's decision is predicated on a recommendation made by another public authority and where there was no opportunity for a hearing before such a public authority, the right to be heard before the decision is taken shall include knowledge of the recommendation and the ability to contest its findings. Where sector-specific EU law renders Book III applicable to Member States, the preceding obligation applies *mutatis mutandis* where a Member State authority makes the decision pursuant to a recommendation made by another public authority. In the absence of such an EU provision, or any other EU law specifying applicable procedural requirements, the Member State authority will apply national rules of administrative procedure, which must comply with general principles of EU law concerning fair hearings.

(6) For the avoidance of doubt, this article is also applicable to cases of composite procedure where EU law imposes legal obligations on Member State authorities to coordinate or co-operate action that leads to individual decisions.

III-25 Consultation of the interested public

(1) An EU authority making the decision may give effect to the obligations in Article 11 TEU by consultation of the interested public in accordance with the following paragraphs. Where sector-specific EU law renders Book III applicable

to a Member State authority making the decision it may give the interested public the opportunity to make known and publicly exchange their views by consultation. This is without prejudice to the obligation in Article III-23(1).

(2) The public authority may choose to consult through provision of a public hearing. This hearing must be notified through public announcement, which must be posted on an official website. The relevant documentation, including expert opinions, shall be available for inspection online prior to the hearing, unless excluded for legally defensible reasons. The notification must be given in sufficient time, which should not be less than two weeks, to enable those who wish to participate to be able to do so and to study the relevant documentation. The notification must be given and a public hearing must be held in sufficient time before the decision is made.

(3) If a public hearing pursuant to paragraph 2 is held it should be organized such that there is opportunity for those attending to express their views orally, subject to practical and organizational limits. Provision should be made for those who wish to express their views in writing, either prior to or instead of attendance at the public hearing. The written views should be available online in a clearly accessible part of the relevant website. The minutes of the public hearing should be available for public inspection online within a reasonable time after the end of the oral hearing, and there should be an opportunity for the persons involved to raise objections during two weeks thereafter about the alleged incompleteness or incorrectness of the minutes.

(4) The public authority may choose to conduct an online consultation exercise. This must be posted on an official website. The relevant documentation, including expert opinions, shall be available for inspection online, unless excluded for legally defensible reasons. The notification and documentation must be given in sufficient time to enable those who wish to participate to be able to do so. The notification must be given in sufficient time before the decision is made.

(5) The website referred to in the previous paragraphs of this article must be clear, simple and easy to use. The website should be so designed as to enable users to see the views of those who have already offered written comments.

(6) If consultation is mandated by Union law which provides no indication as to the form of the consultation, then it will be for the public authority to decide whether to fulfill this obligation by provision of a public hearing or an online consultation exercise. The relevant provisions of this article will then apply accordingly.

III-26 Consultation with Member States

When consultation with the Member States is required or permitted by EU law the EU authority shall inform without delay the Member States about initiation of any such consultation. It shall make available to the Member States all information that is required for the Member States to submit properly informed views on the subject-matter of the consultation exercise. The Member States must have adequate time in which to respond to the consultation.

III-27 Consultation with EU authorities

(1) Consultation with EU authorities shall take place when it is required by the constituent treaties, general principles of EU law or sector-specific EU law, and the consultation shall be in accord with the source of the obligation where that is specified.

(2) Where the format for the consultation is not specified then the following principles should apply. The bodies taking part in the consultation shall be given all information that is required to enable them to express a properly informed view on the subject matter of the consultation exercise. The bodies must have adequate time in which to respond to the consultation.

Chapter 5: Conclusion of the Procedure

III-28 Duty to specify the decision

A decision made by the public authority shall be clearly specified in order to enable the parties to understand their rights or duties.

III-29 Duty to give reasons

(1) The public authority shall state the reasons for its decisions in a clear, simple and understandable manner. The statement of reasons must be appropriate to the decision and must disclose in a clear and unequivocal fashion the reasoning followed by the public authority which adopted the decision in such a way as to enable the parties to ascertain the reasons for the decision and to enable the competent court to exercise its powers of review.

(2) The duty to provide reasons in cases of composite procedures will be shaped by the respective roles of the EU and the Member State in making the decision, as set out in Article III-24.

III-30 Duty to indicate available remedies

(1) Decisions shall provide information to the addressee concerning:
   (a) the possibility of administrative appeal, where this exists, including cases where an appeal can be made to a public authority other than that which adopted the decision, and
   (b) the time-limit for making an appeal.

(2) Decisions shall also inform the addressee of the possibilities of judicial challenge, including the time-limits within which this can be brought, and of possible recourse to an Ombudsman.

III-31 Formal and language requirements

(1) Decisions shall be in writing, shall be signed and identify the deciding authority.

(2) Where the decision is made by an EU authority it shall be written in the language chosen by the addressee, provided it is one of the official languages of the EU.

III-32 Decisions in electronic form

(1) A decision in written form may be replaced by electronic form unless otherwise stipulated by a legal provision. In this event, it must be provided with a qualified signature.

(2) If the addressee claims to be unable to process the electronic document communicated by the public authority, the latter shall send it again in a suitable electronic format or as a written document.

III-33 Notification of a decision

(1) Decisions shall be notified to the parties as soon as they are adopted. They shall take effect for a party upon notification.

(2) A decision may be publicly promulgated where this is permitted by EU law.

III-34 Correction of obvious inaccuracies in a decision

(1) The public authority that adopted a decision may at any time correct typographical mistakes, errors in calculation and similar obvious inaccuracies in a decision.
(2) Such corrections may be requested by the addressees of that decision. If the corrections are carried out ex-officio, the addressees shall be informed before any correction is implemented.

Chapter 6: Rectification and Withdrawal of Decisions

III-35 Rectification and withdrawal of decisions that have an adverse effect

(1) The public authority may rectify or withdraw an unlawful decision which adversely affects a party. Rectification or withdrawal shall have retroactive effect.
(2) The public authority may rectify or withdraw a lawful decision which adversely affects a party. Rectification or withdrawal shall have prospective effect.
(3) The public authority may exercise the power in paragraphs 1 and 2 ex-officio, or following a request by that party. The power may be exercised outside the time-limits for legal challenge.
(4) The public authority when exercising the power in this article shall take into account the effect of the rectification or withdrawal on other parties and on third parties.
(5) Rectification or withdrawal pursuant to this article constitutes an administrative procedure as defined in Article I-4(2).

III-36 Rectification and withdrawal of decisions that are beneficial

(1) The public authority may rectify or withdraw an unlawful decision that is beneficial to a party. It may exercise this power ex-officio, or following a request by another party. This power may be exercised outside the time-limits for legal challenge.
(2) The public authority shall take into account the extent to which a party has a legitimate expectation that the decision was lawful and the extent to which a party has relied on it when deciding,
    (a) whether to exercise the power in paragraph 1,
    (b) whether, if the power to rectify or withdraw is exercised, it should have retroactive or prospective effect.
(3) The public authority may rectify or withdraw a lawful decision that is beneficial to a party. It may exercise this power ex-officio, or following a request by another party. This power may be exercised outside the time-limits for legal challenge in the following circumstances:
    (a) where it is permitted by sector-specific EU law,
    (b) where the party has not complied with an obligation specified in the decision, or has not done so within the time-limit set for compliance,
    (c) in order to prevent or eliminate serious harm. The public authority shall upon application make good the disadvantage to the party affected deriving from reliance on the continued existence of the decision to the extent that this merits protection.
(4) The public authority when exercising the power in this article shall take into account the effect of the rectification or withdrawal on other parties and on third parties.

(5) Rectification or withdrawal shall have retroactive effect only if it occurs within a reasonable time.
(6) Rectification or withdrawal pursuant to this article constitutes an administrative procedure as defined in Article I-4(2).

C. Explanations

Chapter 1: General Provisions

III-1 Scope of application

1 Chapter 1 of Book III contains two general provisions. While Article III-1 concerns the scope of application of Book III, Article III-2 defines some key concepts of Book III and provides definitions of the following terms: decision, public authority, party, interested public, inspection, and responsible official.

2 **Article III-1 specifies the boundaries of Book III.** The first paragraph stipulates that the scope of application of Book III is limited to the 'administrative procedures by which an EU authority prepares and adopts a decision', while the second paragraph adds that the model rules only apply to the public authorities of the Member States when EU sector specific legislation so provides.

III-2 Definitions

3 Article III-2(1) is concerned with decisions, which may be addressed either to a State or a group of States, or to an individual or group of individuals, insofar as the latter is determined or can be determined ex ante. This is exemplified by: (i) the decision taken by the Commission as to whether or not a State aid is to be regarded as compatible with the common market (Article 107 TFEU); (ii) the decision by which the Commission finds that an agreement between undertakings is incompatible with the prohibition laid down by Article 101 TFEU; (iii) the decision to grant or to refuse subsidies or loans in the framework of the Common agricultural policy or of the EU structural funds; and (iv) the decision concerning the funding of a project in the framework of EU policy aiming at promoting research and development.

4 **Article III-2(1) excludes several kinds of acts and measures.** It excludes (i) legislative acts, which lie outside the scope of application of the model rules considered as a whole; (ii) non-legislative acts of general application which are subject to the rules established in Book II; (iii) judicial decisions; (iv) contracts, which are mainly regulated by Book IV which refers for their preparation to some specific articles of Book III.

5 Under Article III-2(1) **'decision'** therefore has four main features. It is adopted in the context of administrative action, and therefore excludes legislative and judicial acts. It is addressed to one or more individualized public or private persons, and therefore includes acts of a collective nature such as those addressed to a group of people, but

excludes administrative rule-making. It is adopted unilaterally, unlike a contract, although this does not necessarily preclude some form of agreement on the content of the decision that is made formally or informally between the public authority and private parties. Finally, it is important to note that decisions for the purpose of this Book 'determine' one or more concrete cases with legally binding effects. This Book regulates certain aspects that are preparatory to the final decision, such as a decision that a responsible official should be excluded from the administrative procedure, but these do not themselves constitute decisions for the purposes of this Book, because they do not determine the concrete case with legally binding effect. The definition of decision also means that decisions made by the Commission pursuant to an infringement procedure against a Member State are not covered by Book III.

A '**public authority**' means both an EU authority and a Member State authority, under the conditions set by Article III-1(2). This may include also a private body fulfilling a public function, if it is entrusted with the power to take a decision, in the sense of Article III-2(1). Reference should also be made to the definition of public authority in Book I, Article I-4(7) and the Explanations attached to this article. **6**

The following definition, that of '**party**', refers to (i) the addressee of the intended decision and (ii) other persons, as defined in Book I Article I-4(6), who are adversely affected by it and who request to be involved in the procedure. The definition of 'party' does not cover persons who are merely interested. A person who is merely interested does not qualify as being adversely affected merely because he or she subjectively thinks that this is so. It is an objective test, determined by the body providing the procedure, albeit subject to judicial review. **7**

It is **only those 'adversely' affected** by the intended decision who enjoy procedural rights. This is in accord with the criterion enshrined in Article 41(2)(a) CFR. This formulation does not require that the contested measure should be initiated against the claimant, although some requirement of this kind is included in some language versions of the CFR. The case law in different areas varies, with some judgments framed in terms of the need to show that the case was initiated against the claimant. The general trend of the case law is however towards an emphasis on adverse impact, either by expanding the notion of initiated against, or by not requiring it in certain types of cases. It should moreover be noted that the person adversely affected must request to take part in the procedure, which thereby serves to limit the number taking part. In addition, Article III-8(3) makes provision for the choice of a representative or representatives to take part in the procedure where there are many who are adversely affected in the same manner. **8**

A related, but distinct, concept is that of '**interested public**'. Article III-2(4) specifies that this concept is relevant for the purposes of Article III-25 and that it means 'every natural or legal person and other associations, organizations or groups expressing an interest in an administrative procedure'. This definition is justified by **9** the fact that the effects of the intended decision can sometimes be very far-reaching and affect the collective interests of a community. If a large number of people are affected by such a decision, the procedure should allow the public to be consulted, albeit with discretion as to how this should be done, and this is the rationale for the broad definition of 'interested public'.

10 **'Inspection'** means an on-the-spot check for the purposes of information gathering.

11 The definition of **'responsible official'** serves to identify the person who has the primary responsibility for managing the administrative procedure from the stage when it is initiated.

Chapter 2 : Initiation and Management of Procedures

12 According to the procedural approach adopted, the present Book is structured on the sequence of a standard procedure leading to an administrative decision: initiation, gathering of all information needed to take a sound and lawful decision—including the hearing and consultation of the public and of other public authorities—and conclusion of the procedure.

13 Chapter 2 focuses on the initiation stage and contains also some general rules related to the management of the procedure, such as the duty to appoint a responsible official, the rights of the parties that shall be respected when managing the procedure, and the mandatory time-limit within which the final decision is to be adopted.

14 The Chapter also deals with two other issues: the general duty of fair decision-making, with a particular emphasis on the duty of impartiality of all persons who are involved in making a decision on behalf of a public authority, and the provision of online information on the administrative procedures envisaged by the legislation.

III-3 General duty of fair decision-making and impartiality

15 The first substantive article of Book III begins by reproducing paragraph 1 of Article 41 CFR. This is considered to be the **umbrella principle of good administration** at the EU level, from which the courts and the legislator may derive more specific procedural rights, which go beyond the concrete rights listed in Article 41(2) CFR. The whole Book is thus intended to develop the fundamental right to good administration with regard to single-case decision-making. The title of Article III-3 aims to highlight this approach.

16 A particular right of Article 41(1) CFR, the **right to be treated impartially** by EU authorities, is regulated in more detail in paragraphs 2–5 of Article III-3. Currently, the duty of impartiality is regulated at EU level in the Financial Regulation and in the Staff Regulations.[1] However, it is also necessary to address this central issue, which is also connected to the principles of equality and non-discrimination,[2] from a procedural perspective, in order to ensure adequate protection of the (other) parties. Similar rules on impartiality are indeed contained in many national APAs.[3]

According to paragraph 2, the official responsible for managing the procedure[4] and any other person involved in a decision on behalf of a public authority shall abstain from participating in the procedure where they have any financial or familial interest in that decision. Such conflicts of interest are considered particularly relevant and are therefore not left to the superior's interpretation. The affected official must abstain in any case after communicating the conflict of interest to his or her superior. **17**

All other possible conflicts of interest shall be examined by the superior, who shall decide whether to exclude the official or not. The exclusion is mandatory where the impartial and objective exercise of the official's function is compromised.[5] **18**

Consistently with the procedural perspective mentioned earlier and with the right to be treated impartially of Article 41(1) CFR, paragraph 4 expressly grants the right of **19**

[1] Regulation (EU, Euratom) 966/2012 of the European Parliament and of the Council of 25 October 2012 on the financial rules applicable to the general budget of the Union and repealing Council Regulation (EC, Euratom) 1605/2002 [2012] OJ L298/1 last amended by Regulation (EU, Euratom) 547/2014 of the European Parliament and of the Council of 15 May 2014 amending Regulation (EU, Euratom) 966/2012 on the financial rules applicable to the general budget of the Union [2014] OJ L163/18, Art 57; Regulation 31 (EEC), 11 (EAEC), laying down the Staff Regulations of Officials and the Conditions of Employment of Other Servants of the European Economic Community and the European Atomic Energy Community ('Staff Regulations') [1962] OJ 45 last amended by Regulation (EU, Euratom) 1023/2013 of the European Parliament and of the Council of 22 October 2013 amending the Staff Regulations of Officials of the European Union and the Conditions of Employment of Other Servants of the European Union [2013] OJ L287/15, Art 11(a).

[2] Charter of Fundamental Rights of the European Union [2007] OJ C 303/1, Arts 20, 21.

[3] See for example Allgemeines Verwaltungsverfahrensgesetz 1991 (BGBl. Nr. 51/1991) das zuletzt durch Artikel 1 des Bundesgesetzes vom 31. Juli 2013 (BGBl. I Nr. 161/2013) geändert worden ist (§§ 7 and 36a); Wet van 4 juni 1992 houdende algemene regels van bestuursrecht (Stb. 1992, 315) in werking getreden op 1 juli 1994, laatstelijk gewijzigd bij Wet van 25 juni 2014, in werking getreden op 1 augustus 2014, Art 2:4; Verwaltungsverfahrensgesetz in der Fassung der Bekanntmachung vom 23. Januar 2003 (BGBl. I S. 102), das zuletzt durch Artikel 3 des Gesetzes vom 25. Juli 2013 (BGBl. I S. 2749) geändert worden ist, §§ 20, 21; Ley 30/1992, de 26 de noviembre, de Régimen Jurídico de las Administraciones Públicas y del Procedimiento Administrativo Común (BOE núm. 285, de 27.11.1992), modificada por última vez por la Ley 27/2013, de 27 de diciembre, de racionalización y sostenibilidad de la Administración Local (BOE núm. 312, de 30.12.2013), Arts 28, 29.

[4] On the responsible official, see paras 33 and 34 of the explanations.

[5] This criterion is taken from Regulation (EU, Euratom) 966/2012 of the European Parliament and of the Council of 25 October 2012 on the financial rules applicable to the general budget of the Union and repealing Council Regulation (EC, Euratom) 1605/2002 [2012] OJ L298/1 last amended by Regulation (EU, Euratom) 547/2014 of the European Parliament and of the Council of 15 May 2014 amending Regulation (EU, Euratom) 966/2012 on the financial rules applicable to the general budget of the Union [2014] OJ L163/18, Art 57(2).

the parties to request the exclusion of an official affected by a conflict of interest.[6] This request should be made as soon as possible, as soon as the requesting party knows the potential conflict of interest, in order to avoid undue delay of the procedure.[7]

20 Paragraph 5 extends the impartiality obligations laid down in the previous paragraphs to any other person involved in a decision on behalf of a public authority. This includes *inter alia* any other official—different from the responsible official—who participates in the management of the procedure or the person or persons in charge of adopting the final decision. The obligations are extended *mutatis mutandis* because it may happen, for example, that the affected person does not have a superior strictly speaking. If this is the case, the decision whether to exclude this person shall be taken by the appointing authority or by the collegiate body to which he or she belongs.[8]

III-4 Online information on existing procedures

21 The provisions laid down in Article III-4 are not yet very common from a comparative law perspective,[9] but seem necessary in order to adapt the regulation of administrative procedures to the information society and to fulfil the expectations of citizens with regard to e-government. The idea behind this article is that public authorities should use the internet extensively in order to inform the citizens in a clear and simple way on the different administrative procedures envisaged by the legislation. Such general online information is important to make a reality of the **principle of citizen access to the regulations** emphasized by the Mandelkern Report on Better Regulation,[10] and goes beyond the official websites with consolidated legislation that have proliferated recently at EU and at national level.[11]

[6] Paragraph 4 is inspired by European Parliament resolution of 15 January 2013 with recommendations to the Commission on a Law of Administrative Procedure of the European Union (2012/2024(INI)), Recommendation 4.3.

[7] See, for example, Council Regulation (EC) 207/2009 of 26 February 2009 on the Community trade mark (codified version) ('Community trade mark Regulation') [2009] OJ L78/1 last amended by the Act concerning the conditions of accession of the Republic of Croatia and the adjustments to the Treaty on European Union, the Treaty on the Functioning of the European Union, and the Treaty establishing the European Atomic Energy Community [2012] OJ L112/6, Art 137(3).

[8] See, for example, Council Regulation (EC) 207/2009 of 26 February 2009 on the Community trade mark (codified version) ('Community trade mark Regulation') [2009] OJ L78/1 last amended by the Act concerning the conditions of accession of the Republic of Croatia and the adjustments to the Treaty on European Union, the Treaty on the Functioning of the European Union and the Treaty establishing the European Atomic Energy Community [2012] OJ L112/6, Art 137(4).

[9] Wide online information duties on administrative procedures are laid down at the very beginning of the Administrative Procedure Act of 1946, Pub.L 79–404, §§ 500–96, 60 Stat. 237 (1946), § 552(a)).

[10] Mandelkern Group on Better Regulation, Final Report (13 November 2001), available at: http://ec.europa.eu/smart-regulation/better_regulation/documents/mandelkern_report.pdf, p 10, pp. 40–6.

[11] The EUR-Lex website of the EU being one of the more advanced examples.

The creation and updating of well-designed informative websites requires many resources. For this reason, it is left to the public authorities' discretion to decide when and how to implement them. However, it seems that **priority should be given to application procedures**, in order to relieve the many potential applicants from the burden of finding out which is the applicable legislation and the legal requirements that have to be fulfilled, and in order to avoid the public authority incurring the costs of informing the applicants individually.[12] Ex-officio procedures (such as penalty procedures or sanctions) are of course also very important and may adversely affect citizens, but the information rights of the addressees may be satisfied by imposing on public authorities the duty to inform them individually about the procedure when it is initiated.[13] The demand on online procedural information is higher with regard to application procedures. In fact, the official websites that already exist inform mainly about application procedures, and often allow citizens to submit their application online. 22

Paragraph 2 contains a **non-exhaustive and non-compulsory list of information items** that are considered particularly relevant. The websites should not only describe the main procedural steps and indicate the authority competent to adopt the final decision, the time-limit, and the remedies available, but also provide a link to the applicable legislation in its consolidated version,[14] a brief explanation of the main legal requirements and its administrative interpretation[15] and a link to standard forms that may be used by parties in their communications with the public authority within the procedure.[16] 23

Considering the importance that general online information on administrative procedures may have to promote the effective exercise of the EU internal market freedoms and to achieve a real European administrative space, the **European Commission is best placed to foster best practices** and to issue recommendations that might be followed by other EU and Member State authorities. 24

[12] See the information duties imposed on the public authority according to Art III-6(3) and Art III-8(1)(a).

[13] See Art III-5(2), (3).

[14] Source of inspiration are the Recommendations on the access to regulation contained in the Mandelkern Group on Better Regulation, Final Report (13 November 2001), available at: http://ec.europa.eu/smart-regulation/better_regulation/documents/mandelkern_report.pdf, (pp 40–6).

[15] Source of inspiration: Directive 2006/123/EC of the European Parliament and of the Council of 12 December 2006 on services in the internal market [2006] OJ L376/36, Art 7. Para 3 is also inspired by Directive 2006/123/EC of the European Parliament and of the Council of 12 December 2006 on services in the internal market [2006] OJ L376/36, Art 7(3), (5).

[16] See for example Ley 30/1992, de 26 de noviembre, de Régimen Jurídico de las Administraciones Públicas y del Procedimiento Administrativo Común (BOE núm. 285, de 27.11.1992), modificada por última vez por la Ley 27/2013, de 27 de diciembre, de racionalización y sostenibilidad de la Administración Local (BOE núm. 312, de 30.12.2013), Art 70(4); Spanish Act 11/2007 on electronic access of the citizens to public services (Ley 11/2007, de 22 de junio, de acceso electrónico de los ciudadanos a los Servicios Públicos, BOE núm. 150, de 23.6.2007, modificada por última vez por la Ley 2/2011, de 4 de marzo, de Economía Sostenible, BOE núm. 55, de 5.3.2011), Art 35.

III-5 Initiation

25 Paragraph 1 of Article III-5 lists the two ways administrative procedures may be initiated according to sector-specific legislation: ex-officio or by an application.[17] And paragraphs 2-4—and Article III-6(3)—regulate two relevant legal consequences that derive from both forms of initiation.

26 The first consequence is the **duty of the public authority to inform the parties** about the procedure that will be carried out. In ex-officio procedures this information takes place through the notification envisaged in paragraphs 2 and 3, while in application procedures it is provided through the acknowledgement of receipt regulated in Article III-6(3). The information that has to be given is the same in both cases, with only one difference: in ex officio procedures the parties must be informed about the rationale for the initiation of the procedure, while in application procedures this is not necessary. If an ex-officio procedure aims, for example, at the detection of possible violations of EU law, it is important that the concerned individual can discern this at the very beginning of the procedure.[18] This notice of the rationale for the initiation should be distinguished from the stronger duty to give reasons in Article III-29 with regard to the final decision of the procedure. It is important that parties are informed about the available remedies already at this early stage of the procedure, since the authority may not adopt the final decision and thus the remedies will not be indicated pursuant to Article III-30.[19]

27 Paragraph 2 contains **two exceptions** to the duty to notify immediately the initiation of ex-officio procedures. First, the notification may take place at a later stage if an immediate notification might jeopardize the investigation of the case. This can occur, for example, when an unannounced inspection is needed to obtain evidence. In this case, the previous notification of the initiation might jeopardize the effectiveness of the inspection and of the whole investigation. To avoid this risk, the notification can therefore take place at the very moment the inspection is carried out (Article III-17(2)). The second exception addresses situations of urgency where an immediate decision may be adopted under certain strict conditions.[20] An example

[17] This twofold distinction is envisaged by European Parliament resolution of 15 January 2013 with recommendations to the Commission on a Law of Administrative Procedure of the European Union (2012/2024(INI)), Recommendation 4.1; Council of Europe Recommendation CM/Rec(2007)7 of the Committee of Ministers to member states on good administration, Art 12; and by many national APAs.

[18] With regard to inspections e.g. Joined Cases C-97/87 to C-99/87 *Dow Chemical Ibérica and Others v Commission* [1989] ECR 3165, paras 12, 26, 45–7; Case C-94/00 *Roquette Frères v Directeur général de la concurrence, de la consommation et de la répression des fraudes, and Commission* [2002] ECR I-9039, paras 47–8.

[19] Source of inspiration: Council of Europe Recommendation CM/Rec(2007)7 of the Committee of Ministers to member states on good administration, Art 13(4).

[20] Source of inspiration Verwaltungsverfahrensgesetz in der Fassung der Bekanntmachung vom 23. Januar 2003 (BGBl. I S. 102), das zuletzt durch Artikel 3 des Gesetzes vom 25. Juli 2013 (BGBl. I S. 2749) geändert worden ist, § 28(2).

would be emergency measures adopted by the Commission in the field of food safety.[21] This immediate decision shall be notified in accordance with Article III-33(1). In such cases also the hearing may be omitted (Article III-23(2)).

The second legal consequence of both forms of initiation is the **duty of the public authority to manage the corresponding procedure and to adopt a final decision within the mandatory time-limit** laid down in Article III-9.[22] According to Article III-9(2), the time-limit fixed in sector-specific law, or the default time-limit of three months established in Article III-9(1), shall begin on the date of the receipt of a complete application in application procedures, or on the date of initiation ex-officio. This duty to decide is excluded in case of pointless, manifestly unfounded, or abusive applications (Article III-6(3)). 28

III-6 Special rules on application procedures

Article III-6 contains some special rules on the initiation of application procedures and is therefore closely related to Article III-5. In line with the **non-formalistic approach** of the whole Book, paragraph 1 establishes that applications shall not be subject to unnecessary formal and documentary requirements. This paragraph also allows applicants to submit their applications by electronic means, in accordance with the general right to communicate and to complete all procedural formalities by electronic means laid down in Article III-8(1)(b). 29

Paragraph 2 deals with the problem of **applications submitted to non-competent services.** Such applications shall be transferred ex-officio without delay to the competent one, but only if both services belong to the same public authority.[23] A more ambitious option would be to extend the transfer duty to services belonging to *other* authorities of the EU or of the Member States, but considering the large 30

[21] Regulation (EC) 178/2002 of the European Parliament and of the Council of 28 January 2002 laying down the general principles and requirements of food law, establishing the European Food Safety Authority and laying down procedures in matters of food safety [2002] OJ L31/1 last amended by Regulation (EC) 596/2009 of the European Parliament and of the Council of 18 June 2009 adapting a number of instruments subject to the procedure referred to in Article 251 of the Treaty to Council Decision 1999/468/EC with regard to the regulatory procedure with scrutiny—Part Four [2009] OJ L188/14, Art 53.

[22] The duty of EU authorities to adopt a definitive decision within a reasonable time derives implicitly from Art 265 TFEU (giving a remedy for undue delays in decision-making) and has been affirmed by the ECJ on many occasions (even with regard to complaints, see for example Case C-282/95 P *Guérin automobiles v Commission* [1997] ECR I-1503, para 37). At national level, see for example Ley 30/1992, de 26 de noviembre, de Régimen Jurídico de las Administraciones Públicas y del Procedimiento Administrativo Común (BOE núm. 285, de 27.11.1992), modificada por última vez por la Ley 27/2013, de 27 de diciembre, de racionalización y sostenibilidad de la Administración Local (BOE núm. 312, de 30.12.2013), Art 42(1).

[23] The expression 'public authority' is used in this context instead of the more precise of 'legal person', because at EU level—and in many Member States—the different administrations are not granted legal personality.

number, complexity and diversity of the authorities that exist in Europe such a solution could jeopardize administrative efficiency.[24]

31 Paragraph 3 imposes the **duty to provide the applicant with an acknowledgement of receipt** containing relevant information about the procedure.[25] Sentences 3, 4 and 5 of this paragraph regulate **how authorities should react when receiving a defective application.** Their duties depend on the importance of the defect. As a general rule, they shall specify in the acknowledgment of receipt the existing defects or missing documents and give an appropriate period for remedying or producing them. Pointless or manifestly unfounded applications may however be rejected as inadmissible by means of a briefly reasoned acknowledgement of receipt. No acknowledgement of receipt needs to be sent at all in cases where successive applications submitted by the same applicant are to be considered abusive because of their repetitive character. This paragraph is complemented by Article III-13(2), which allows applicants, before submitting an application, to request an opinion of the public authority on the information to be supplied by them.[26]

32 Paragraph 4 refers *mutatis mutandis* to the **competitive award procedure** regulated in Book IV Chapter 2 Section 3 with regard to the conclusion of EU contracts, where the number of applications to be granted is limited and such a competitive procedure is to be used, in order to grant a fair competition between all possible candidates.[27]

III-7 Responsible official

33 Article III-7 includes an **innovative provision** imported from the Italian APA:[28] the duty of the public authority to appoint an official responsible for managing the

[24] Paragraph 2 is inspired by the European Ombudsman—The European Code of Good Administrative Behaviour, Art 15; European Parliament resolution of 15 January 2013 with recommendations to the Commission on a Law of Administrative Procedure of the European Union (2012/2024(INI)), Recommendation 3 ('Principle of efficiency and service'); Council of Europe Recommendation CM/Rec(2007)7 of the Committee of Ministers to member states on good administration, Art 13(3).

[25] See paras 25–6 of the explanations.

[26] Art III-6(3) is inspired by European Ombudsman—The European Code of Good Administrative Behaviour, Art 14; European Parliament resolution of 15 January 2013 with recommendations to the Commission on a Law of Administrative Procedure of the European Union (2012/2024(INI)), Recommendation 4.2; Directive 2006/123/EC of the European Parliament and of the Council of 12 December 2006 on services in the internal market [2006] OJ L376/36, Art 13(5); Council of Europe Recommendation CM/Rec(2007)7 of the Committee of Ministers to member states on good administration, Art 13(4).

[27] Paragraph 4 is inspired by Directive 2006/123/EC of the European Parliament and of the Council of 12 December 2006 on services in the internal market [2006] OJ L376/36, Art 12(1).

[28] Legge 7 agosto 1990 n. 241, Nuove norme in materia di procedimento amministrativo e di diritto di accesso ai documenti amministrativi (pubblicata nella Gazzetta Ufficiale del 18 agosto 1990 n. 192), Arts 4–6. See also European Ombudsman—The European Code of Good Administrative Behaviour, Art 14(2).

procedure, whose name and contact details are communicated to the parties at the very moment of its initiation.[29] This official may be the person who adopts the final decision or a different one. The rationale of this provision is therefore not to separate the managing of the procedure and the adoption of the final decision and hence to reinforce the impartiality of the deciding authority.[30] It aims rather to strengthen procedural transparency, to avoid the dilution of responsibilities that may occur when no particular person is formally denoted as responsible for management of the procedure[31] and hence to **promote a better management of the procedure** and a stronger protection of the parties' procedural rights. The responsible official is the visible face of the procedure and the contact person of the parties throughout.

When managing the procedure, the responsible official shall **respect and actively promote the rights** listed in Article III-8(1) as well as the other procedural rights of the parties granted in other parts of Book III. Article III-7 also obliges him or her to **keep an adequate file** containing records of all information and documents produced during the procedure,[32] which is crucial to ensuring transparency and administrative efficiency, to allow the parties to exercise their rights of defence and to enable judicial review. **34**

III-8 Management of procedures and procedural rights

Paragraph 1 of Article III-8 lists some **general rights of the parties** that shall be respected in all stages of the procedure.[33] They **complement other rights** of the parties related to specific stages of the procedure such as the right to be notified of the initiation ex-officio (Article III-5(2)), the right to receive an acknowledgement of receipt in application procedures (Article III-6(3)), the right to request the exclusion of non-impartial officials (Article III-3(4)), the right to propose witnesses and experts (Article III-15(2)), the right to access one's own file (Article III-22), the right **35**

[29] See Art III-5(3)(c) and Art III-6(3), second sentence.

[30] The ECJ has rejected a general duty of separation between both functions, even in administrative penalty procedures, see for example Case 100/80 *Musique Diffusion Française v Commission* [1983] ECR 1825, paras 6–7.

[31] This is what happens for example in Spain according to Ley 30/1992, de 26 de noviembre, de Régimen Jurídico de las Administraciones Públicas y del Procedimiento Administrativo Común (BOE núm. 285, de 27.11.1992), modificada por última vez por la Ley 27/2013, de 27 de diciembre, de racionalización y sostenibilidad de la Administración Local (BOE núm. 312, de 30.12.2013), Art 41.

[32] See European Parliament resolution of 15 January 2013 with recommendations to the Commission on a Law of Administrative Procedure of the European Union (2012/2024(INI)), Recommendation 3 ('Principle of transparency') and European Ombudsman—The European Code of Good Administrative Behaviour, Art 24.

[33] A similar general list is contained in the Ley 30/1992, de 26 de noviembre, de Régimen Jurídico de las Administraciones Públicas y del Procedimiento Administrativo Común (BOE núm. 285, de 27.11.1992), modificada por última vez por la Ley 27/2013, de 27 de diciembre, de racionalización y sostenibilidad de la Administración Local (BOE núm. 312, de 30.12.2013), Art 35.

to confidentiality and to professional and business secrecy (Article III-22 paragraphs 1 and 2), the right to be heard (Articles III-23 and III-24), the right to be given reasons for the final decision (Article III-29), the right to be informed of the available remedies (Article III-30) or the right to be notified of the final decision (Article III-33).

36 The Services Directive contains interesting provisions on administrative procedures that should also be applicable to the procedures managed by EU authorities.[34] It inspires some of the rights listed in paragraph 1. This is the case for the right to be given information on all questions related to the procedure in a fast, clear, and understandable manner. This right does not include legal advice in individual cases, but only general information on the way in which requirements are usually interpreted or applied.[35] It is also the case for the right to communicate and to complete, where possible and appropriate, all procedural formalities at a distance and by electronic means,[36] including videoconferencing,[37] and for the right to pay only charges that are reasonable and proportionate to the cost of the procedures in question.[38]

37 Paragraph 1(e) allows lay representation when it grants the **right to be represented** not only by a lawyer, but also by some other person of his or her choice having legal capacity according to national law.[39] Paragraph 3 addresses the problem of procedures where the number of persons adversely affected is large by allowing the public

---

[34] Regulation (EC) 764/2008 of the European Parliament and of the Council of 9 July 2008 laying down procedures relating to the application of certain national technical rules to products lawfully marketed in another Member State and repealing Decision 3052/95/EC [2008] OJ L218/21, Art 6 also establishes some interesting general procedural standards for the Member States which have been taken into consideration when drafting the present Book.

[35] Directive 2006/123/EC of the European Parliament and of the Council of 12 December 2006 on services in the internal market [2006] OJ L376/36, Art 7. See also European Parliament resolution of 15 January 2013 with recommendations to the Commission on a Law of Administrative Procedure of the European Union (2012/2024(INI)), Recommendation 3 ('Principle of efficiency and service') and European Ombudsman—The European Code of Good Administrative Behaviour, Arts 10(3), 15(3) and 22.

[36] Directive 2006/123/EC of the European Parliament and of the Council of 12 December 2006 on services in the internal market [2006] OJ L376/36, Art 8(1). This right shall not apply for example to the inspection of premises or of equipment used or to physical examination of the capability or of the personal integrity of the interested party (Directive 2006/123/EC of the European Parliament and of the Council of 12 December 2006 on services in the internal market [2006] OJ L376/36, Art 8(2)).

[37] Council Directive 2004/80/EC of 29 April 2004 relating to compensation to crime victims [2004] OJ L261/15, Art 9.

[38] Directive 2006/123/EC of the European Parliament and of the Council of 12 December 2006 on services in the internal market [2006] OJ L376/36, Art 13(2); see also Council of Europe Recommendation CM/Rec(2007)7 of the Committee of Ministers to member states on good administration, Art 16.

[39] See for example Ley 30/1992, de 26 de noviembre, de Régimen Jurídico de las Administraciones Públicas y del Procedimiento Administrativo Común (BOE núm. 285, de 27.11.1992), modificada por última vez por la Ley 27/2013, de 27 de diciembre, de racionalización y sostenibilidad de la Administración Local (BOE núm. 312, de 30.12.2013), Art 32(2).

authority to appoint ex-officio a joint representative for all those parties affected in a similar way.[40]

In order to reinforce the rights listed in paragraph 1 and in the rest of the Book, paragraph 2 explicitly grants **the right of the parties to file a complaint** against the responsible official, the deciding authority, or any other official who takes part in the procedure where they fail to comply with their obligations under the model rules, whether intentionally or through negligence.[41] Purely private disputes are not covered. **38**

III-9 Time-limits for concluding procedures

If there are no time limits for making decisions it can lead to legal uncertainty for the individuals concerned, and can also foster administrative inefficiency. It is for this reason that time limits are common in sector-specific legislation and national legislation. **39**

Paragraph 1 establishes a **default time-limit** where no specific time-limit has been set elsewhere.[42] This is a time-limit regulating the duration of administrative procedures—irrespective of whether they are concluded by the intended administrative decision—or the decision on closing the proceedings, as is the case for many investigations. **40**

Paragraph 3 establishes an **exception to the general rule** set out in paragraph 1, if 'complexity or other obstacles' prevent the authority from completing its examination **41**

[40] This provision is inspired by the Verwaltungsverfahrensgesetz in der Fassung der Bekanntmachung vom 23. Januar 2003 (BGBl. I S. 102), das zuletzt durch Artikel 3 des Gesetzes vom 25. Juli 2013 (BGBl. I S. 2749) geändert worden ist, §18.

[41] See for example Ley 30/1992, de 26 de noviembre, de Régimen Jurídico de las Administraciones Públicas y del Procedimiento Administrativo Común (BOE núm. 285, de 27.11.1992), modificada por última vez por la Ley 27/2013, de 27 de diciembre, de racionalización y sostenibilidad de la Administración Local (BOE núm. 312, de 30.12.2013), Arts 35(j), 41(2); Council of Europe Recommendation CM/Rec(2007)7 of the Committee of Ministers to member states on good administration, Art 23(4). The material liability standard is taken from Regulation 31 (EEC), 11 (EAEC), laying down the Staff Regulations of Officials and the Conditions of Employment of Other Servants of the European Economic Community and the European Atomic Energy Community ('Staff Regulations') [1962] OJ 45 last amended by Regulation (EU, Euratom) 1023/2013 of the European Parliament and of the Council of 22 October 2013 amending the Staff Regulations of Officials of the European Union and the Conditions of Employment of Other Servants of the European Union [2013] OJ L287/15, Art 86(1) on disciplinary liability of EU officials.

[42] See European Parliament resolution of 15 January 2013 with recommendations to the Commission on a Law of Administrative Procedure of the European Union (2012/2024(INI)), Recommendation 4.6; Ley 30/1992, de 26 de noviembre, de Régimen Jurídico de las Administraciones Públicas y del Procedimiento Administrativo Común (BOE núm. 285, de 27.11.1992), modificada por última vez por la Ley 27/2013, de 27 de diciembre, de racionalización y sostenibilidad de la Administración Local (BOE núm. 312, de 30.12.2013), Art 42(3); Verwaltungsverfahrensgesetz in der Fassung der Bekanntmachung vom 23. Januar 2003 (BGBl. I S. 102), das zuletzt durch Artikel 3 des Gesetzes vom 25. Juli 2013 (BGBl. I S. 2749) geändert worden ist, §42a(2); Legge 7 agosto 1990 n. 241, Nuove norme in materia di procedimento amministrativo e di diritto di accesso ai documenti amministrativi (pubblicata nella Gazzetta Ufficiale del 18 agosto 1990 n. 192), Art 2.

in the required time period. The spectrum of situations may be wide and range from *vis maior* to the unavoidable length of proceedings. Other examples are a) justified suspension of the proceedings, b) delays caused by the party, c) time spent on waiting for delivery of the documents requested from the party or other relevant entities or authorities, which are necessary to decide the case.[43]

42 As a way of securing the concept of fair proceedings (Article 41 CFR), the **legislature may consider** including **a maximum number of possible extensions** of proceedings into sector-specific law. However, it should be noted that the setting of such a maximum time-limit for expansion, or a maximum number of extensions, may in practice not always be realistic.

43 It is important to highlight that **paragraph** 4 does not exclude liability for damages of the EU stipulated in the Treaties (Article 263 read with Articles 268 and 340 of the TFEU). National legislation and EU sector-specific law provide a variety of consequences for the violation of a particular time-limit, including, for instance, a penalty for the responsible officer, the payment of damages or even an *implied decision* in favour of the applicant (also called *tacit authorization*).[44] There are however conflicting imperatives here. On the one hand, setting up certain time-limits without specifying the consequences of violating them would strongly diminish the significance of such limits. On the other hand, for any consequences to be realistic they must be different depending on the facts of the specific case. For example, an *implied decision* is the most far reaching solution for protecting the interests of the applicant, but it may not work in cases where there is more than one party, and they have conflicting interests. The lack of a written decision might also lead to serious doubts as to the content of the implied decision and it might be difficult for a party to prove its existence.

Chapter 3: Gathering of Information

44 The gathering of information and evidence is a **centre piece of any administrative procedure** leading to the adoption of a single case decision. 'Administrative procedure' can thus be understood as a structured process of choice between different alternatives through acquiring, processing, and evaluating information. The ReNEUAL Model Rules set out in Chapter 3 of this book an investigatory concept of procedure as the generally applicable standard.

[43] Inspired by Ustawa z 14 czerwca 1960 r. Kodeks postępowania administracyjnego (Dziennik Ustaw Nr 30, poz. 168), tekst jednolity z dnia 30 stycznia 2013 r. (Dziennik Ustaw z 2013 r. poz. 267), zmiana z dnia 10 stycznia 2014 r. (Dziennik Ustaw z 2014 r. poz. 183), Art 35.

[44] See for instance Regulation of the European Parliament and the Council (EC) 1829/2003 on genetically modified food and feed [2003] OJ L268/1 last amended by Regulation (EC) 298/2008 of the European Parliament and of the Council of 11 March 2008 amending Regulation (EC) 1829/2003 on genetically modified food and feed as regards the implementing powers conferred on the Commission [2008] OJ L97/64, Art 11(4).

The **Chapter is split into two sections.** The first section establishes a set of general rules, the second section deals with specific issues relating to an especially important instrument of investigation, i.e. inspections. Therefore, inspections are not conceived as an alternative to investigations, but as an important subcategory of the instruments needed for performing effective investigations. This supplementary relationship between the two sections is also highlighted in Article III-10(2)(d). It should be emphasized that, as already highlighted in the explanations to Book I, procedures which do not end in a formal, final, act but are initiated with an intent to potentially formulate such an act serve the preparation of the act and are consequently also covered by the rules of Book III.[45] **45**

Section 1: General Rules

III-10 Principle of investigation

In accordance with the general approach explained above, Article III-10 (1) establishes the **principle of investigation as the general standard for administrative information gathering.** Its wording is based on several sources of inspiration from EU as well as national law.[46] It reflects the jurisprudence of the CJEU on the duty of careful consideration,[47] which is a counterpart to the principle of investigation. As the CJEU has established in its jurisprudence, this procedural right to a careful investigation has to be distinguished from substantive questions of law. It should not be used in such a way as to minimize substantive, administrative discretion. **46**

The duty of careful investigation is an **important element of the principle of good administration**, and as such implied in Article 41(1) CFR. In other words, the duty of careful investigation is a centre-piece of procedural impartiality and fairness. Nevertheless, the authority does not bear the responsibility for accurate fact finding alone. According to Article III-13 the parties are obliged to assist the authority in this regard. **47**

---

[45] See Book I, paragraph 19 of the explanations and para 62 of the explanations of this Book.

[46] Wording taken from European Ombudsman—The European Code of Good Administration (2013), Art 9 with one addition from Verwaltungsverfahrensgesetz in der Fassung der Bekanntmachung vom 23. Januar 2003 (BGBl. I S. 102), das zuletzt durch Artikel 3 des Gesetzes vom 25. Juli 2013 (BGBl. I S. 2749) geändert worden ist, §24(2). See also Wet van 4 juni 1992 houdende algemene regels van bestuursrecht (Stb. 1992, 315), in werking getreden op 1 juli 1994, laatstelijk gewijzigd bij Wet van 25 juni 2014, in werking getreden op 1 augustus 2014, Art 3:2; Legge 7 agosto 1990 n. 241, Nuove norme in materia di procedimento amministrativo e di diritto di accesso ai documenti amministrativi (pubblicata nella Gazzetta Ufficiale del 18 agosto 1990 n. 192), Sec. 6(1)(b); see also Ustawa z 14 czerwca 1960 r. Kodeks postępowania administracyjnego (Dziennik Ustaw Nr 30, poz. 168), tekst jednolity z dnia 30 stycznia 2013 r. (Dziennik Ustaw z 2013 r. poz. 267), zmiana z dnia 10 stycznia 2014 r. (Dziennik Ustaw z 2014 r. poz. 183), Arts 77–79.

[47] Case C-269/90 *TU München v Hauptzollamt München-Mitte* [1991] ECR I-5469, para 14. See Case T-13/99 *Pfizer Animal Health v Council of the EU* [2002] ECR II-3305 on the integration and consideration of scientific know-how.

48 It is **important to differentiate the duty of careful investigation from the administrative instruments created to fulfil this duty.** Information gathering can interfere with the fundamental rights of private parties. According to the principle of legality as laid down in Article 52(1)1 CFR, such interference needs a specific legislative justification. By contrast, the duty of careful investigation itself does not provide such a legal basis. For this reason, Article III-10(2) refers to the conditions under which such instruments may be used, which are laid down in other (specific) model rules within Book III or in other provisions of EU law.

III-11 Investigation by request

III-12 Investigation by mandatory decision

49 Article III-11 and Article III-12 codify **two typical investigatory powers** widely used in many sectors of administrative investigations. Their wording is inspired mainly by provisions in competition law.[48] It must be highlighted that the model rules follow a differentiated approach with regard to these two provisions and instruments. While Article III-11 empowers public authorities directly to investigations on the basis of a simple request, Article III-12 only establishes a 'standby-power' to conduct investigations by a mandatory decision. Sector-specific law must explicitly grant a public authority this 'standby-power'. This differentiation is justified as individuals cannot legally be forced to provide information by a simple request (Article III-11(2) sentence 1), while a mandatory decision to provide information is a legally enforceable act (compare Article III-12(1) sentence 2 and (2) sentence 2). In accordance with these significantly different legal consequences, investigations by simple request are even accepted as an inherent power of investigating authorities in some fields of EU law. The first sentence of Article III-12(2) refers to the procedural rules stipulated in Article III-11 as far as they are adequate in the context of a mandatory decision concerning investigations. It does not refer to all other procedural rules of Book III. As existing sector-specific law like Article 27(1) Regulation 1/2003[49] shows, the applicability of all these procedural rules would not be an adequate general rule for this sort of decision. Consequently, it is for the sector-specific provisions to render applicable additional model rules.

---

[48] Compare Council Regulation (EC) 1/2003 of 16 December 2002 on the implementation of the rules on competition laid down in Articles 81 and 82 of the Treaty [2003] OJ L1/1 last amended by Council Regulation (EC) 487/2009 of 25 May 2009 on the application of Article 81(3) of the Treaty to certain categories of agreements and concerted practices in the air transport sector [2009] OJ L148/1, Arts 18, 19.

[49] Council Regulation (EC) 1/2003 of 16 December 2002 on the implementation of the rules on competition laid down in Articles 81 and 82 of the Treaty [2003] OJ L1/1 last amended by Council Regulation (EC) No 487/2009 of 25 May 2009 on the application of Article 81(3) of the Treaty to certain categories of agreements and concerted practices in the air transport sector [2009] OJ L148/1.

An important aspect of both instruments concerns the **interaction of the investigating EU authority with the authorities of the Member State** in whose territory the seat of the relevant party is situated and with the competent authorities of other Member States whose territory may be affected by a specific investigation. These aspects are regulated for investigations by request in Article III-11(4). Article III-12(2) sentence 1 refers to this provision in case of investigations by mandatory decisions. The objective of these rules is the protection of national sovereignty and the building of mutual trust between the respective authorities. In times of e-government such an obligation should not be very burdensome. If it proves to be too burdensome in a specific field of law, specific procedural rules can provide an exemption (Article I-2). **50**

Article III-11(5) provides a similar rule in case of **an investigatory request by a Member State authority.** This rule shall not compromise the limited applicability of Book III to national authorities in accordance with Articles I-2(2) and III-1(2). Therefore, it is only applicable under the conditions set in Article III-1(2). **51**

III-13 Duties to cooperate of parties

Article III-13 establishes duties for the parties to cooperate with regard to information gathering. Such rules **supplement but must not compromise the principle of investigation.** Public authorities continue to bear the final responsibility. This relationship between the two principles is highlighted in the wording of Article III-13(1) sentence 1 ('assist'). Consequently, the authority shall consider statements made according to Article III-13, but not without carefully evaluating them. For instance, this means that the authority cannot blindly trust information provided by an applicant but has to scrutinize the statements. Useful instruments in this regard are specifications for the private fact-finding to be agreed upon beforehand, or the contrasting of the applicant's statement with information from experts, witnesses or from third, potentially adversely affected, parties as well as the conduct of investigations by the authority itself. **52**

The **duty to cooperate varies in different types of administrative procedures.** The duty is intensified in application procedures (paragraph 2), but it also exists in all other procedures (paragraph 1) although to a more limited extent. **53**

Paragraph 1 stipulates the generally applicable standards for the duty to cooperate in order to balance administrative efficiency and procedural fairness. These standards are based on the assumption that each party shall inform the authority about facts which are known to this party, or which can reasonably expected to be presented by it. The latter is the case with regard to facts within the 'sphere' of this party. Examples are its state of health, its income, its personal qualifications, experiences, or other personal affairs. Such a duty is not very burdensome, whereas it may be very cumbersome for the authority to investigate such facts. Sentences 2 and 3 **54**

stipulate that the authority does not neglect its duty of careful investigation if it takes its decision on the basis of the information available[50] and refrains from further investigations concerning such facts as long as they are not evidently required. Nevertheless, the authority has a duty to investigate non-evident but noticeable facts itself in accordance with Article III-10(1), if those facts cannot reasonably be expected to be presented by a party. This is, for instance, the case for information on public affairs, or on the affairs of persons who are not a party to the proceeding. It should be highlighted that these rules are purely procedural.

55 Paragraph 2 regulates important issues with regard to **intensified duties to cooperate of applicants** in application procedures. It supplements the basic rule in Article III-6(3) sentence 3. In this context, intensified duties to cooperate relate primarily to information duties. Sentence 1 refers to EU law for the concrete standards of cooperation. This is justified as the concrete information to be supplied by the applicants depends on the subject matter of an application and can therefore only be regulated in sector-specific law.[51] The other sentences specify certain standards for information and advice which must be provided to the applicant by public authorities. They thereby concretize the general right to be given information on all questions related to the relevant procedure under Article III-8(1)(a). These rules balance the objectives of service orientation with the objectives of independent and impartial performing of administrative investigations.

[50] The wording of sentence 3 is inspired by Council Regulation (EC) 659/1999 of 22 March 1999 laying down detailed rules for the application of Article 108 of the treaty on the functioning of the European Union [1999] OJ L83/1 last amended by Council Regulation (EU) 734/2013 of 22 July 2013 amending Regulation (EC) 659/1999 laying down detailed rules for the application of Article 93 of the EC Treaty [2013] OJ L204/15, Art 13(1).

[51] For example Directive 2001/18/EC of the European Parliament and of the Council of 12 March 2001 on the deliberate release into the environment of genetically modified organisms and repealing Council Directive 90/220/EEC [2001] OJ L106/1 last amended by Directive 2008/27/EC of the European Parliament and of the Council of 11 March 2008 amending Directive 2001/18/EC on the deliberate release into the environment of genetically modified organisms, as regards the implementing powers conferred on the Commission [2008] OJ L81/45, Arts 4(2),13(2)(b) read in conjunction with Annex II; Directive 2001/83/EC of the European Parliament and of the Council of 6 November 2001 on the Community code relating to medicinal products for human use [2001] OJ L311/67 last amended by Directive 2012/26/EU of the European Parliament and of the Council of 25 October 2012 amending Directive 2001/83/EC as regards pharmacovigilance [2012] OJ L299/1, Art 8(3), Annex 1; Council Directive 85/337/EEC of 27 June 1985 on the assessment of the effects of certain public and private projects on the environment [1985] OJ L175/40 last amended by Directive 2009/31/EC of the European Parliament and of the Council of 23 April 2009 on the geological storage of carbon dioxide and amending Council Directive 85/337/EEC, European Parliament and Council Directives 2000/60/EC, 2001/80/EC, 2004/35/EC, 2006/12/EC, 2008/1/EC and Regulation (EC) 1013/2006 [2009] OJ L140/114, Art 3; now Directive 2011/92/EU of the European Parliament and of the Council of 13 December 2011 on the assessment of the effects of certain public and private projects on the environment [2012] OJ L26/1 last amended by Directive 2014/52/EU of the European Parliament and of the Council of 16 April 2014 amending Directive 2011/92/EU on the assessment of the effects of certain public and private projects on the environment [2014] OJ L124/1, Art 3.

III-14 Privilege against self-incrimination and legal professional privilege

The privilege against self-incrimination and legal professional privilege are **two important facets to the rights of defence.** Other notions which are usually subsumed under the heading 'defence rights' include the right to be heard (Articles III-23, III-24), the right of access to file (Article III-22), the right to have proceedings concluded within an adequate period of time (Article III-9), as well as the protection of (private) premises. The EU courts have highlighted the need for the Commission to comply with the rights of defence in administrative procedures in which administrative sanctions of a punitive nature may be imposed.[52] This includes the obligation to ensure that such rights are not being 'irremediably impaired during preliminary inquiry procedures which may be decisive in providing evidence'.[53] By limiting the scope of this article to administrative sanctions which are imposed in administrative procedures, but are at least partially punitive measures, the article is both in line with Article 6 ECHR[54] and respects the need for EU authorities (or their agents) to investigate possible violations of EU law. The two privileges featured in Article III-14 also apply to legal persons, for instance in the area of competition law.[55] **56**

The drafting team decided against including detailed provisions on the privilege against self-incrimination and legal professional privilege for two reasons. First, while the case law of the CJEU (in the area of competition law) and the ECtHR in this area has been extensive, it is not completely homogeneous. Second, both privileges are closely related to administrative sanctions, and should therefore be addressed in detail in a comprehensive set of rules on administrative sanctions which could be provided at a later stage as a separate Book of these model rules. However, the drafting team decided to include at least a basic provision on these issues in order to highlight their importance even where a sanction procedure has not yet been formally initiated. The privileges in this article should therefore be understood as providing a minimum procedural standard. Nothing stated within these model rules prevents legislatures or courts from extending the scope of protection. **57**

Paragraph 2 applies where defence rights have been violated and the information in question could otherwise not have been gathered and have affected the content of the decision. To **prohibit the use as evidence** of information under such circumstances is a logical consequence of the protection of said rights. Moreover, it is the **58**

[52] Case C-511/06 P *Archer Daniels Midland Co. v Commission* [2009] ECR I-5843, para 84; Case C-328/05 P *SGL Carbon v Commission* [2007] ECR I-3921, para 70.

[53] Joined Cases 46/87 and 227/88 *Hoechst AG v Commission* [1989] ECR 2859, para 15, 16.

[54] *Engel and Others v The Netherlands*, Applications 5100/71; 5101/71; 5102/71; 5354/72; 5370/72 (1976) Series A No 22, para 82–83.

[55] Compare Case 347/87 *Orkem v Commission* [1989] ECR 3283; Case 155/79 *AM&S Limited v Commission* [1982] ECR 1575.

only way to adequately ensure a private party's defence rights under such circumstances. Currently, jurisprudence protects defence rights at a later stage in the proceedings, namely through annulment of the contested act if it can be established that 'had it not been for such an irregularity, the outcome of the procedure might have been different'.[56]

III-15 Witnesses and experts

59 According to Article III-10 (1) sentence 3 it is the public authority that takes the final decision as to which experts and witnesses shall be asked for a statement. Therefore, the parties may propose such experts and witnesses without thereby legally binding the investigating authority. However, the authority is obliged under Article III-10 to consider whether a proposed expert or witness should be interviewed in order to investigate the case carefully.

Section 2: Inspections

60 Section 2 of Chapter 3 focuses on **one of the main instruments of information gathering**, inspections. Inspections mainly serve **two functions**: an inspection may serve as a control mechanism with regard to citizens, and especially undertakings, and their obligations according to EU Law. Or it may constitute a supervisory power of EU bodies in controlling the compliance of national bodies with EU obligations. In both cases, these inspections are one expression of the many ways in which Member States and the Union frequently cooperate in the implementation of Union law. Indeed, EU inspections occur in Member State territory and are therefore inherently cooperative. Where such cooperation occurs, rules are needed to provide authorities with sufficient guidance on how to operate.

61 This being said, it is the **degree of cooperation between Member State and EU authorities** which **varies**, depending on the sector in which it occurs and the respective division of competences under EU law. To create a comprehensive set of rules applicable to all aspects of inspections cannot therefore be the objective of this section. Instead, Section 2 provides a set of basic rules which primarily focus on the duties of Member State and EU officials in their cooperation with each other.

62 **Inspections are part of the decision-making process** and rules of administrative procedure should exist that regulate how they are carried out. Where inspections provided for by Union law fall within the scope of Book III they are covered by the proposed rules, regardless of whether they are referred to as inspections, on-the-spot checks, or on-site monitoring visits. The scope of Section 2 is limited to inspections which take place within an administrative procedure intended to end in a decision 'with legally binding effect' (Article III-2(1)). Book III therefore does

[56] Case C-301/87 *French Republic v Commission* [1990] ECR I-307, para 31.

not cover OLAF inspections,[57] as long as reports following from these inspections are not considered as legally binding by the CJEU[58] and conclude the OLAF procedure. This differentiates the OLAF procedures from administrative procedures as defined in Article I-4(2). This definition, and consequently Book III, also covers **procedures which do not end** in a formal final decision, but only if they are initiated with the potential intent of adopting such an act.[59]

As far as the **structure of** Chapter 3 **Section 2** is concerned, a line can be drawn between Articles III-16 and III-17 and Articles III-18-21. Articles III-16 and III-17 establish both the powers of inspecting officials and their obligations, thereby taking the need to protect subjective rights into account. Articles III-18 to III-21 coordinate inspections, which must take place on Member State territory by necessity and thereby automatically occur in a multilevel system. To coordinate the ensuing interaction implies rules regulating certain aspects of Member State actions. In line with the limited scope of Book III under Article III-1(2) this is however conditional on the agreement of the respective Member State, or must be provided for in sector-specific law. **63**

III-16 Inspection powers of public authorities

III-17 Duties of inspecting officials

Article III-16 limits an EU authority's power to undertake an inspection through **two conditions:** first, EU law must provide an EU authority with the powers of inspection in the respective area and, second, the inspection must be necessary to fulfil its duties under EU law. The underlying notion behind this provision is the fact that while EU authorities may have been granted the power to conduct an investigation, an inspection may not be necessary in a specific case in order to achieve the relevant objective. As such, it is an innovative addition. As far as the inspection powers themselves are concerned, paragraph 2 provides a non-exhaustive list of powers which may be subsumed under the power to inspect.[60] The specific inspection powers **64**

[57] OLAF inspections instead are subject to a number of legal instruments, such as Regulation 883/2013 of the European Parliament and of the Council of 11 September 2013 concerning investigations conducted by the European Anti-Fraud Office (OLAF) and repealing Regulation (EC) 1073/1999 of the European Parliament and of the Council and Council Regulation (Euratom) 1074/1999 [2013] OJ L248/1.

[58] In line with the Court of First Instance in Case T-193/04 *Hans-Martin Tillack v Commission of the European Communities* [2006] ECR II-3995, para 69.

[59] See para 19 of the explanations to Book I.

[60] Compare Council Regulation (EC) 1/2003 of 16 December 2002 on the implementation of the rules on competition laid down in Articles 81 and 82 of the Treaty [2003] OJ L1/1 last amended by Council Regulation (EC) 487/2009 of 25 May 2009 on the application of Article 81(3) of the Treaty to certain categories of agreements and concerted practices in the air transport sector [2009] OJ L148/1, Art 20(2); Council Regulation (Euratom, EC) 2185/96 of 11 November 1996 concerning on-the-spot checks and inspections carried out by the Commission in order to protect the European Communities' financial interests against fraud and other irregularities [1996] OJ L292/2,

of an authority can differ, depending on the EU law provision on which they are based. In relation to the premises to be inspected, these can be both the premises of Member State authorities and those of private parties, depending on the purpose of the inspection. In light of the fact that the home enjoys a stronger protection than business premises, the relevant legal basis needed under Article III-16(1)(a) must regulate whether they are covered by the respective power to inspect.

65 **Article III-17** includes a number of important **duties for inspecting officials.** In line with the principle of legal certainty, the word 'production' in Article III-17(2) obliges the authorities to show their authorization to the affected persons prior to inspecting the premises. The second obligation to present a notification guarantees the coherence with Article III-5(2) and (3). Article III-17(4) is directed at the inter-administrative level. Its purpose is to ensure that the different authorities cooperate and coordinate in order to avoid unnecessary burdens for inspected persons as well as duplications of inspections jeopardizing administrative efficiency.[61] It is not meant to prevent a parallel inspection if the same facts lead to different infringements of EU law or where EU law foresees parallel inspections.[62] Article III-17(5) in turn obliges the inspecting officials to **draft a report.**[63] These reports summarize the results of an inspection as a step before the authority adopts a formal, legally

Art 7(1); Council Regulation (EC) 659/1999 of 22 March 1999 laying down detailed rules for the application of Article 93 of the EC Treaty [1999] OJ L83/1 last amended by Council Regulation (EU) 734/2013 of 22 July 2013 amending Regulation (EC) 659/1999 laying down detailed rules for the application of Article 93 of the EC Treaty [2013] OJ L204/15, Art 22(2).

[61] Compare Council Regulation (Euratom, EC) 2185/96 of 11 November 1996 concerning on-the-spot checks and inspections carried out by the Commission in order to protect the European Communities' financial interests against fraud and other irregularities [1996] OJ L292/2, Recital (13), Art 3.

[62] For example Regulation (EU) 1306/2013 of the European Parliament and of the Council of 17 December 2013 on the financing, management and monitoring of the common agricultural policy and repealing Council Regulations (EEC) 352/78, (EC) 165/94, (EC) 2799/98, (EC) 814/2000, (EC) 1290/2005 and (EC) 485/2008 [2013] OJ L347/549 last amended by Regulation (EU) 1310/2013 of the European Parliament and of the Council of 17 December 2013 laying down certain transitional provisions on support for rural development by the European Agricultural Fund for Rural Development (EAFRD), amending Regulation (EU) 1305/2013 of the European Parliament and of the Council as regards resources and their distribution in respect of the year 2014 and amending Council Regulation (EC) 73/2009 and Regulations (EU) 1307/2013, (EU) 1306/2013 and (EU) 1308/2013 of the European Parliament and of the Council as regards their application in the year 2014 [2013] OJ L347/865, Art 59(4).

[63] Sources of inspiration: Council Regulation (Euratom, EC) 2185/96 of 11 November 1996 concerning on-the-spot checks and inspections carried out by the Commission in order to protect the European Communities' financial interests against fraud and other irregularities [1996] OJ L292/2, Art 8(2); Regulation 883/2013 of the European Parliament and of the Council of 11 September 2013 concerning investigations conducted by the European Anti-Fraud Office (OLAF) and repealing Regulation (EC) 1073/1999 of the European Parliament and of the Council and Council Regulation (Euratom) 1074/1999 [2013] OJ L248/1, Art 11(1); see also para 69 of the explanations.

binding decision or refrains from doing so, for instance because an inspection reveals that there is no infringement of EU law. Relevant material and supporting documents can be annexed to these reports. The reports may also be used to inform other authorities (also Article III-18(3)) or—if legally justified—the wider public.

With regard to EU inspections four forms of cooperation exist which structure Section 2: (i) EU authorities need to conduct an inspection on Member State territory to fulfil their tasks and require the cooperation of one or more Member States (Article III-18);[64] (ii) a Member State conducts an inspection on its own territory to fulfil a task which has a Union dimension (Article III-19);[65] (iii) several Member States need to conduct a joint inspection to fulfil their tasks (Article III-20),[66] or (iv) an EU or Member State authority may request an authority from another Member State to conduct an inspection to be able to fulfil its task (Article III-21 and Book V).[67] **66**

III-18 Duties of sincere cooperation during inspections by EU authorities

Where an **inspection is undertaken by an EU authority in the territory of a Member State**, Article III-18 establishes duties of basic cooperation both for Member State as well as for EU authorities: EU and Member State authorities are obliged to prepare and conduct inspections in close cooperation with each other under **paragraph 1**. This paragraph also gives Member State officials the option to participate in EU inspections.[68] This **presence of Member State officials during EU inspections** will not only facilitate the inspection itself, but it may also have the added benefit of fostering mutual trust which in turn can strengthen the effective implementation of Union law. **67**

According to **Article III-18(2)**, EU authorities are under an **obligation to inform the respective Member State authorities of the planned inspection.**[69] This is sub- **68**

[64] See paras 67–71 of the explanations.

[65] See para 72 of the explanations.

[66] See para 73 of the explanations.

[67] See para 74 of the explanations.

[68] Compare Council Regulation (EC) 139/2004 of 20 January 2004 on the control of concentrations between undertakings (the EC Merger Regulation) [2004] OJ L24/1, Art 13(5).

[69] Compare Council Regulation (EC) 1/2003 of 16 December 2002 on the implementation of the rules on competition laid down in Articles 81 and 82 of the Treaty [2003] OJ L1/1 last amended by Council Regulation (EC) 487/2009 of 25 May 2009 on the application of Article 81(3) of the Treaty to certain categories of agreements and concerted practices in the air transport sector [2009] OJ L148/1, Art 20(3); Council Regulation (EC) 139/2004 of 20 January 2004 on the control of concentrations between undertakings (the EC Merger Regulation) [2004] OJ L24/1, Art 13(3); Council Regulation (EC, Euratom) 2988/95 of 18 December 1995 on the protection of the European Communities financial interests [1995] OJ L312/1 last amended by Corrigendum to Council Regulation (EC, Euratom) 2988/95 of 18 December 1995 on the protection of the

ject to a narrow exception, namely where the notification would endanger the purpose of the investigation.

69 **Article III-18(3)** obliges EU authorities to **inform the respective Member State about the results** of the inspection. For this purpose, the EU authority may use the report according to Article III-17(5). In drafting these reports the inspector should also be aware of his duty under Article III-18(3) to take the national law of the Member State in whose territory the inspection takes place into account.[70] This is connected to the idea that these reports should also be allowed as admissible evidence in national administrative or judicial proceedings in accordance with the relevant law. The underlying intent here is to ensure that individuals are treated in a manner which is equal to how they would have been treated had the situation occurred in a purely national context.

70 **Article III-18(4)** regulates cases where EU authorities intend to seek outside assistance for a specific inspection.[71] **Outside assistance** is made conditional on agreement by the Member State in whose territory the inspection occurs. However, according to Article I-2, there might be cases in which specific legislative acts could mandate the participation of outside assistance; in such cases these more specific rules take precedence over the model rules. Such outside assistance may be provided either by the authorities of another Member State, or outside bodies such as private parties and third country officials. The participation of such outside experts

European Communities financial interests (Official Journal of the European Communities L 312 of 23 December 1995) [1998] OJ L36/16, Art 9(2); Council Regulation (EC) 659/1999 of 22 March 1999 laying down detailed rules for the application of Article 108 of the treaty on the functioning of the European Union [1999] OJ L83/1 last amended by Council Regulation (EU) 734/2013 of 22 July 2013 amending Regulation (EC) 659/1999 laying down detailed rules for the application of Article 93 of the EC Treaty [2013] OJ L204/15, Art 22(3).

[70] Sources of inspiration Regulation 883/2013 of the European Parliament and of the Council of 11 September 2013 concerning investigations conducted by the European Anti-Fraud Office (OLAF) and repealing Regulation (EC) 1073/1999 of the European Parliament and of the Council and Council Regulation (Euratom) 1074/1999 [2013] OJ L248/1, Art 11(2); Council Regulation (Euratom, EC) 2185/96 of 11 November 1996 concerning on-the-spot checks and inspections carried out by the Commission in order to protect the European Communities' financial interests against fraud and other irregularities [1996] OJ L292/2, Art 8(3).

[71] For example, Council Regulation (Euratom, EC) 2185/96 of 11 November 1996 concerning on-the-spot checks and inspections carried out by the Commission in order to protect the European Communities' financial interests against fraud and other irregularities [1996] OJ L292/2, Art 6(2). The wording 'other accompanying persons' in Council Regulation (EC) 1/2003 of 16 December 2002 on the implementation of the rules on competition laid down in Articles 81 and 82 of the Treaty [2003] OJ L1/1 last amended by Council Regulation (EC) 487/2009 of 25 May 2009 on the application of Article 81(3) of the Treaty to certain categories of agreements and concerted practices in the air transport sector [2009] OJ L148/1, Art 20(3) and Council Regulation (EC) 139/2004 of 20 January 2004 on the control of concentrations between undertakings (the EC Merger Regulation) [2004] OJ L24/1, Art 12(2) is less clear but suggests that these two instruments also leave the Commission with the option to contract assistance from persons who are not Commission officials.

could be warranted if, *inter alia*, they possess special expertise or knowledge linked to the case. However, it is important that the participation of these experts does not lower procedural standards. Thus, these officials have to observe the same standards of professional secrecy[72] as EU officials and as with EU officials carefully investigate with objectivity. To further safeguard the procedural standards established in Book III, paragraph 4 provides that EU authorities remain responsible for any misconduct or damage caused by the external officials.[73]

Article III-18(5) sets out the obligation of Member States to provide **enforcement assistance** to EU authorities, where such assistance is needed to guarantee that an inspection can be undertaken. This is complemented by **paragraph 6** which focuses on setting guidelines for national judicial control where such control is necessary under national law before the Member State concerned can provide enforcement assistance. Of course, this does not create judicial control for Member State courts independent of the parameters set in paragraph 6.[74] As is emphasized in Article V-1(4) and in the introduction to Book V,[75] enforcement assistance is not covered by the rules on mutual assistance. As a consequence, paragraphs 5 and 6 complement Book V in this respect, at least with regard to inspections in single-case decision-making. **71**

III-19 Participation of EU authorities in Member State inspections

Inspections may be conducted by Member State authorities in their own name in order to fulfil their tasks under national or EU law. These may have a Union dimension in the sense that they have either been prepared together with Union authorities, or are of special interest to a Union authority. In these cases, EU officials may participate so long as they adhere to the rules set out in III-19. Its applicability is dependent on either a sector-specific legislative provision or Member State agreement.[76] They must carry written authorization with them and respect the relevant **72**

[72] Compare Council Regulation (Euratom, EC) 2185/96 of 11 November 1996 concerning on-the-spot checks and inspections carried out by the Commission in order to protect the European Communities' financial interests against fraud and other irregularities [1996] OJ L292/2, Art 6(2).

[73] This is an innovative proposal.

[74] Sources of inspiration for paragraphs 5 and 6: Council Regulation (EC) 1/2003 of 16 December 2002 on the implementation of the rules on competition laid down in Articles 81 and 82 of the Treaty [2003] OJ L1/1 last amended by Council Regulation (EC) 487/2009 of 25 May 2009 on the application of Article 81(3) of the Treaty to certain categories of agreements and concerted practices in the air transport sector [2009] OJ L148/1, Art 20(6), (7), (8); Council Regulation (EC) 139/2004 of 20 January 2004 on the control of concentrations between undertakings (the EC Merger Regulation) [2004] OJ L24/1, Art 13(6), (7), (8). Compare Council Regulation (EC, Euratom) 2988/95 of 18 December 1995 on the protection of the European Communities financial interests [1995] OJ L312/1 last amended by Corrigendum to Council Regulation (EC, Euratom) 2988/95 of 18 December 1995 on the protection of the European Communities financial interests (Official Journal of the European Communities L 312 of 23 December 1995) [1998] OJ L36/16, Art 9(2).

[75] See Book V, para 8 of the introduction.

[76] This is consistent with the limited scope of this Book (see paras 3–5 of this explanation).

national law, considering that the inquiry is conducted under the responsibility of the respective Member State authorities.[77]

III-20 Joint inspections of Member State authorities

73 Different Member State authorities may also decide to undertake an inspection jointly. This form of horizontal cooperation, where both act in their own name to fulfil their tasks, is regulated by **Article III-20**. This article constitutes an innovative proposal. It is dependent on either a sector-specific legislative provision or Member State agreement.[78] Article III-20 provides authorities with basic rules which will structure such an inspection. Its source of inspiration is Article 56 of the Commission Proposal for a General Data Protection Regulation.[79] The national law of the Member State in whose territory the inspection takes place is the applicable law. Moreover, the host authority remains responsible for actions of the visiting authority vis-à-vis third parties in its territory. A division of judicial control depending on the nationality of the inspector would inevitably threaten the rights of the affected individual and should be avoided. The more detailed arrangements to ensure a smooth exercise of any joint inspection should be laid down by the host authority in the respective agreement where it is not laid down already in the national law.

III-21 Relation to Book V

74 Finally, there are inspections which a Member State authority conducts at the request of another authority in accordance with the rules of Book V on mutual assistance. Under these rules, the Member State authority is obliged to assist another authority by conducting an inspection. **Article III-21** clarifies the relationship between Book III and Book V.

Chapter 4: Right to a Hearing and Inter-Administrative Consultations

Section 1: Access to the File

III-22 Access to the file

75 Article III-22(1) establishes that a party has a right of access to his or her file, subject to the legitimate interests of confidentiality and of professional and business secrecy.

76 The right of access to the file is **embodied in Article 41(2)(b) CFR**. It is dealt with by a separate article in Book III, because the right of access to the file may be relevant independently of whether there is a right to be heard.

---

[77] This is consistent with the limited scope of this Book (see paras 3–4 of this explanation).

[78] This is consistent with the limited scope of this Book (see paras 3–5 of this explanation).

[79] Commission Proposal for a Regulation of the European Parliament and of the Council on the protection of individuals with regard to the processing of personal data and on the free movement of such data (General Data Protection Regulation) COM(2012) 11 final, Art 56.

Article III-22(2)–(5) sets out more specific rules concerning the application of the right of access to the file. These **rules are derived from the case law of the CJEU.**[80] 77

Section 2: Hearing, Participation and Consultation

III-23 Right to be heard by persons adversely affected

Article III-23 deals with the procedural rights associated with the hearing. **The core right** is provided in Article III-23(1), which accords a right to be heard by a public authority to every party before a decision is made that would adversely affect that person. As mentioned earlier (see para 8 above), this formulation is in accord with that in Article 41(2)(a) of some language versions of the CFR, which do not require that the contested measure should be initiated against the claimant, although some requirement of this kind is included in some other language versions of the CFR. The legal reality is that **the CJEU case law is mixed in this respect**, with some cases containing the requirement that the contested measure should be initiated against the claimant, while other cases either do not contain this requirement, or interpret it in different ways. The general trend in the case law was towards an emphasis on adverse impact, either by expanding the notion of initiated against, or by not requiring it in certain types of case. 78

Article III-23(2) provides an **exception** for the need to hold a hearing when an immediate decision is strictly necessary in the public interest or because of the serious risk involved in delay.[81] It is incumbent on the public authority to provide reasons and evidence as to why these conditions are applicable. This exception is then qualified by the obligation to hold a hearing thereafter, unless there are very compelling reasons to the contrary. 79

Article III-23(3) is concerned with **notice of the core issues that will be dealt with at the hearing.** The case law of the CJEU is authority for such an obligation.[82] The formulation in Article III-23(3) is designed to ensure that the person adversely affected has sufficient notice of the nature of the case that is to be brought against him or her, which is an essential condition precedent to being able to exercise the right of defence, while at the same time not being unduly burdensome on the public authority. This is the rationale for the formulation that is cast in terms of the 80

[80] The leading decision is Case C-204-205/00 *Aalborg Portland A/S and Others v Commission* [2004] ECR I-123.

[81] Compare Verwaltungsverfahrensgesetz in der Fassung der Bekanntmachung vom 23. Januar 2003 (BGBl. I S. 102), das zuletzt durch Artikel 3 des Gesetzes vom 25. Juli 2013 (BGBl. I S. 2749) geändert worden ist, § 28(2). This exception coheres with the exception to notify the initiation of ex-officio procedures established in Art III-5(2), third sentence.

[82] See for example Cases C-48 and 66/90 *Netherlands and Koninklijke PTT Nederland NV and PTT Post v Commission* [1992] ECR 565; Case C-135/92 *Fiskano AB v Commission* [1994] ECR I-2885; Cases C-402 and C-415/05 P *Kadi and Al Barakaat International Foundation v Council and Commission* [2008] ECR I- 6351.

addressee being informed of the 'central issues' that are to be decided by the public authority and the 'core arguments' that underlie its reasoning. This obligation may, depending on the nature of the case, be met through discharge of the duty imposed by Article III-5(3)(b).

81 Article III-23(4) is designed to ensure that the person adversely affected has **adequate time** in which **to respond** to the draft decision. This is a fundamental aspect of administrative procedure. It is not possible to specify precise time limits, because of the great variety of draft decisions that fall within the ambit of EU law. However, each public authority should insofar as possible set clear time-limits.

82 Article III-23(5) deals with the **nature of the hearing.** The first two sentences reflect the existing case law of the CJEU. They stipulate that the public authority has discretion as to the form and content of the hearing, including the choice as to whether the hearing should be written or oral, and whether to allow cross-examination and the nature of the evidence. The last sentence specifies factors that should influence a public authority when deciding how to exercise its discretion. There is no direct articulation of this test in the case law of the CJEU, but it is nonetheless consistent with that case law and captures the approach of the CJEU. There is moreover a virtue in providing legal guidance to the public authority as to the factors that it should take into account when exercising its discretion.

III-24 Right to be heard in composite procedures

83 Article III-24 deals with the right to be heard in composite procedures between the EU and Member States, and **Article III-24(1) states the general principle** that application of the right to be heard in such procedures will depend on the division of responsibility in the decision-making process.

84 Administration in many areas is shared between the EU and the Member States. The rules of Book III do not apply to Member States, unless they are rendered applicable in whole or in part by sector-specific legislation. It is nonetheless **necessary within the framework of Book III** to deal with this type of administrative interaction. The strategy throughout this article has therefore been to **address three issues.** First, to specify the procedural obligations incumbent on the EU authorities when they engage in such procedures. Second, to set out the obligations of Member State authorities where sector-specific legislation renders Book III applicable to them. Third, to clarify the procedural obligations of Member States where no such sector-specific legislation exists.

85 Article III-24(2) exemplifies the way in which these three issues are dealt with in relation to one form of **composite procedure**, which is that **in which the final operative decision is made by the EU authority or the Member State authority.** First, it provides that where the EU authority makes the relevant decision, it must comply with the requirements in Article III-23. Second, where the relevant decision is made by a Member State authority, it must comply with Article III-23 where sector-specific legislation renders Book III applicable. Third, where there is no such legislation, Member State authorities apply national rules of procedure, although these must comply with EU general principles of law concerning fair hearings, since these principles have been deemed applicable to Member States by the CJEU when they act in the scope of EU law.

Article III-24(3) contains a **guiding principle** that informs the remainder of Article **86** III-24, which covers **more complex forms of composite procedure**. The guiding principle is that in deciding on the form and content of the hearing to be provided by the public authority that makes the decision pursuant to Article III-23(5) regard should be given to the extent to which the rights of the defence were adequately protected at a prior stage in the administrative proceedings.

Article III-24(4) deals with the situation where the public authority that makes **the** **87** **decision is legally bound by a recommendation from another EU authority**. The logic here is that the principles of due process guaranteed in Article III-23 must be observed by the body that makes the recommendation, since it is in effect making the operative determination. The same principle applies, *mutatis mutandis*, in circumstances where a Member State authority makes the recommendation, if there is sector-specific legislation rendering the rules of Book III applicable. Where no such legislation exists the administrative procedure requirements are determined by national law, subject to compliance with the general principle of fairness that is part of EU law.

Article III-24(5) deals with a variant of the situation covered in the preceding para- **88** graph. This is the situation where there is a **recommendation** from another public authority, but it is **not formally binding** on the public authority that makes the final decision. If there was no hearing by the public authority that made the recommendation, the right to be heard before the decision is taken includes knowledge of the recommendation and the ability to contest its findings by the public authority that makes the decision. Where sector-specific legislation renders Book III applicable to Member States, the preceding obligation applies *mutatis mutandis* where a Member State authority makes the decision pursuant to a recommendation made by another public authority. If there is no such legislation, the Member State authority applies national rules of administrative procedure, which must, as in the previous instances, comply with EU general principles of law concerning fair hearings.

III-25 Consultation of the interested public

The subject matter dealt with by Article III-25 is close to that covered by Book II, **89** insofar as it establishes rules concerning consultation by interested members of the public. The distinguishing feature is however that Book II is concerned with rules that may affect a large number of people, whereas Article III-25 is concerned with decisions on a particular issue in relation to which the public may be interested, the classic example being a decision that may have wide-reaching environmental impact on which sector-specific legislation exists.[83] Such sector-specific legislation on public consultations may be framed in mandatory or non-mandatory terms. Article III-25 is however framed in discretionary terms, for the following reason. While Article 11 TEU is framed in obligatory terms, discretion is also accorded to the EU institutions, as manifest in language such as 'by appropriate means', within Article 11(1) TEU. It is as yet unclear how the CJEU will interpret Article 11 TEU. It was therefore felt to be advisable at this stage of the development of EU law to frame Article III-25 in discretionary terms, in the sense that public hearings or online consultation could be ways in which the duties established in Article 11 TEU could be fulfilled, albeit without prejudice to the possibility that these duties might be met in other ways.

90 Article 11 TEU imposes an obligation on EU institutions to give by appropriate means citizens and representative institutions the opportunity to make known and publicly exchange their views in all areas of Union action. It also imposes an obligation on the European Commission to carry out broad consultations with parties concerned to ensure that the Union's actions are coherent and transparent. Article III-25 provides an authority with **two different solutions** to the logistical problems which are inherent in a consultation exercise that involves the interested public and thereby a higher number of individuals. The first is a form of consultation through a public hearing mechanism. The second is essentially an online consultation mechanism. Where Book III is made applicable to Member States, they may decide to allow the interested public to participate in a procedure by means of one of the modes of consultation provided for in the model rules.

91 Article III-25(2)–(3) specifies the administrative procedure requirements that must be satisfied where the public authority opts for a **public hearing.** There is an obligation for the hearing to be notified through public announcement posted on an official website, with documentation available for inspection prior to the hearing.[84]

[83] Directive 2011/92/EU of the European Parliament and of the Council of 13 December 2011 on the assessment of the effects of certain public and private projects on the environment [2012] OJ L26/1 last amended by Directive 2014/52/EU of the European Parliament and of the Council of 16 April 2014 amending Directive 2011/92/EU on the assessment of the effects of certain public and private projects on the environment [2014] OJ L124/1, Art 6; Directive 2003/35/EC of 26 May 2003 providing for public participation in respect of the drawing up of certain plans and programmes relating to environment and amending with regard to public participation and access to justice council directives 85/339/EEC and 96/61/EC [2011] OJ L 156/2003.

[84] Verwaltungsverfahrensgesetz in der Fassung der Bekanntmachung vom 23. Januar 2003 (BGBl. I S. 102), das zuletzt durch Artikel 3 des Gesetzes vom 25. Juli 2013 (BGBl. I S. 2749) geändert worden ist, § 67 is the inspiration for the second sentence of Article III-25(2); Allgemeines Verwaltungsverfahrensgesetz 1991 (BGBl. Nr. 51/1991) das zuletzt durch Artikel 1 des Bundesgesetzes

This notification must be given in sufficient time, which should not be less than two weeks, to enable those who wish to participate to do so and to study the relevant documentation. The notification must be given and a public hearing must be held in sufficient time before the decision. The article is also designed to ensure that there is an opportunity for those attending the public hearing to express their views orally, subject to practical and organizational limits, and for the minutes of the public hearing to be available for public inspection online within a reasonable time after the end of the oral hearing.[85]

Article III-25(4)–(5) specifies the administrative procedure requirements that must be complied with where the public authority opts for **an online consultation exercise.**[86] Notification of such an exercise must be posted on an official website, and there is once again an obligation to make the documentation available for inspection online, this being done in sufficient time to enable those who wish to participate to be able to do so. **92**

III-26 Consultation with Member States

Article III-26, in contrast to Article III-25, considers inter-administrative consultations which occur in a vertical relationship, more specifically between EU and Member State authorities. In this case, Member States should be informed of the views of other Member States and given the opportunity to consider them. The analogy here would be with the way in which consultation exercises are generally conducted at present, meaning that parties can access the views of others. If this is so for individuals, then it should apply a fortiori for Member States. **93**

III-27 Consultation with EU authorities

This article complements Article III-26 and approaches the vertical relationship in inter-administrative consultations from the opposite angle: while Article III-26 establishes rules for when an EU authority is obliged to consult Member State authorities, Article III-27 establishes a number of basic principles which should apply where the method of consultation is not specified further. **94**

---

vom 31. Juli 2013 (BGBl. I Nr. 161/2013) geändert worden ist, § 44a.(1) and 44b.(2) have also been considered.

[85] See for example Polish Telecommunications Law of 2004 (Prawo telekomunikacyjne), Arts 15–17a.

[86] Directive 2002/21/EC on a common regulatory framework for electronic communications [2009] OJ L108/33 last amended by Corrigendum to Directive 2009/140/EC of the European Parliament and of the Council of 25 November 2009 amending Directives 2002/21/EC on a common regulatory framework for electronic communications networks and services, 2002/19/EC on access to, and interconnection of, electronic communications networks and associated facilities, and 2002/20/EC on the authorisation of electronic communications networks and services [2013] OJ L241/8, Art 6.

Chapter 5: Conclusion of the Procedure

95 As observed earlier,[87] a general feature of Book III is the focus on procedures, as distinct from 'acts'. However, three lines of reasoning suggested that **provisions should concern the 'acts'** or measures that are adopted at the end of an administrative procedure. They are the legal constraints on power, a trend that is common to most codes of administrative procedure and, more specifically, the tradition of EC/EU law.

96 The view that public authorities enjoy wide decision-making powers, which permit them to make discretionary choices with respect to a variety of interests, public and private, is premised—in liberal democracies—ultimately on the assumption that all such powers are exercised subject to the existing criteria of legal validity. Viewed from this perspective, a variety of constraints on power are introduced by modern legal orders. Some such constraints, such as the duty to give reasons, are concerned with the connection between the decision-making process and the final act or measure. Other constraints relate to the final act or measure in itself. There can be formal irregularities, which do not affect the validity of the choices made by the public authority, but that must be corrected. There can also be formal or substantive errors that lead to the invalidity of the act. From this perspective, as the ECJ held in *Algera* (1957) unlawful acts can be withdrawn,[88] the background principle being the rule of law.

97 It is therefore necessary to ensure that formal and substantive legal requirements are duly respected. For example, an obligation to state the reasons that justify a certain decision can help to ensure that the rationale for the action has been duly considered and that administrators are diligently implementing political will. From the perspective of affected parties, an obligation to give reasons can enable them to know why a measure was adopted. From the perspective of the courts, the existence of reasons facilitates judicial review of administrative action.[89]

98 There is a **tradition of procedural constraints on power** within the EC/EU. The Treaty of Rome encapsulated an important process right, the duty to provide reasons, in Article 190, for all kinds of acts having binding force. Another requirement was that 'decisions shall be notified to those to whom they are addressed and shall take effect upon such notification' (Article 191). These procedural requirements have been interpreted and applied by EU courts. More recently, other requirements have emerged through EU case law and the EO Code.[90]

---

[87] See para 13 of the introduction.

[88] Joined Cases 7/56, 3/57, 7/57, *Algera and others v Common Assembly of the ECSC* [1957–1958] ECR 39 (English special edition), Section III (p 61) affirming that 'only unlawful administrative measures are revocable, lawful measures remaining irrevocable'.

[89] Case 222/86, *UNECTEF v Heylens* [1987] ECR 4097, establishing that national authorities must state the reasons for any limitation of the rights stemming from the legal order of the EC.

[90] European Ombudsman—The European Code of Good Administrative Behaviour.

III-28 Duty to specify the decision

III-29 Duty to give reasons

Articles III-28 and 29 have common and distinctive aspects. They **have a common rationale**, that is to say, the need that public authorities comply with the duties of care and transparency, so as to avoid any misuse or abuse of power. Another important aspect is the emphasis placed on clarity. The decision taken by a public authority under Article III-28 must be 'clearly specified in order to enable the parties' to understand their rights and duties. Any public authority must likewise state the reasons for its decision in a 'clear, simple and understandable manner'. However, while Article III-28 concerns the decision as such, Article III-29 deals specifically with the requirement to give reasons. **99**

Article III-28 is designed to ensure that it is possible for the parties to understand their rights or duties, which are influenced by the favourable or unfavourable effects ensuing from that decision. In this respect, Article III-28 is very similar to some national norms.[91] This does not imply that the parties may express a subjective judgment as to whether the decision is adequately or sufficiently clearly specified. It is, rather, an objective test, determined by the public authority and subject to review by either the courts or other public authorities. **100**

Whether we regard the **duty to give reasons** as a requirement of a legal-rational bureaucracy or as a rights-based constraint on the exercise of power, that is to say as a right to a reasoned decision, or as a manifestation of democracy, Article III-29 has some innovative features. A helpful way to shed some light on them is to begin by illustrating briefly the traditional norm governing reasons. **101**

Article 296(2) TFEU provides that 'Legal acts shall state the reasons on which they are based and shall refer to any proposals, initiatives, recommendations, requests or opinions required by the Treaties'.[92] This generates two obligations. The first is a procedural requirement, in the sense that what is required is to give reasons, as distinct from a more substantive requirement, consisting in giving adequate or good reasons. The second requirement is procedural in another sense, because it implies that all the documents which were legally necessary and which influenced **102**

[91] See Verwaltungsverfahrensgesetz in der Fassung der Bekanntmachung vom 23. Januar 2003 (BGBl. I S. 102), das zuletzt durch Artikel 3 des Gesetzes vom 25. Juli 2013 (BGBl. I S. 2749) geändert worden ist, § 37(1); and the Ley 30/1992, de 26 de noviembre, de Régimen Jurídico de las Administraciones Públicas y del Procedimiento Administrativo Común (BOE núm. 285, de 27.11.1992), modificada por última vez por la Ley 27/2013, de 27 de diciembre, de racionalización y sostenibilidad de la Administración Local (BOE núm. 312, de 30.12.2013), Art 53(2).

[92] This is not the only provision of the Treaty that considers reasons. For example, under Art 225 TFEU, if the European Parliament requests the Commission to submit any appropriate proposal, if the Commission does not submit any proposal, 'it shall inform the European Parliament of the reasons'. An identical requirement is established by Art 241 TFEU with regard to the Council's requests.

the final act are referred to, in order to ensure the transparency of administrative action. The settled case law of EU courts has specified that the statement of reasons must be appropriate to the act at issue. The intensity of this fundamental requirement thus varies as a function of both the interests that are affected by the measure adopted by the public authority and its content.[93]

103 An obvious **difference between the provision of the Treaty and Article III-29(1)** is that the former's scope of application is much broader, it applies to regulations, directives and other 'legal acts', while the latter only applies to decisions, as defined by Article III-2(1). There are three other distinctive elements as regards the content of Article III-29(1). First, following the jurisprudence of EU courts, it goes beyond the procedural obligation to state reasons, by specifying that such reasons must be stated 'in a clear, simple and understandable manner'. Since there is no specification of the contents of the statement of reasons, this requirement refers to both elements of fact and law.[94] Second, Article III-29(1) codifies the jurisprudential view that the statement of reasons 'must be appropriate to the decision'. In this regard, attention must be focused not only as to how the legal order of the EU regulates a certain type of decision, but also as to how that specific decision was taken, particularly in view of the interest that the addressees and other parties may have in obtaining explanations. Third, the requirement of clarity is reinforced by the obligation that the reasoning used by the public authority should be disclosed in an 'unequivocal fashion', because it enables the affected parties to ascertain the reasons that lie behind the decision and facilitates judicial review. While this reveals the lasting influence of an instrumentalist approach to the requirement to give reasons, the importance of an obligation to provide not only reasons, but adequate and clear reasons should not be underestimated.[95]

104 **Article III-29(1) also has distinctive features by way of comparison to national APAs.** First, unlike some APAs, its scope of application has no limitation concerning a specific kind of act or matter.[96] Nor is there any exception to the requirement

---

[93] This is settled case law: see Case C-367/95 P, *Commission of the European Communities v Chambre syndicale nationale des entreprises de transport de fonds et valeurs (Sytraval) and Brink's France SARL* [1998] ECR I-1719; Case C-301/96, *Commission v Germany* [2003] ECR I-9919.

[94] See Art 18(1) of the European Code of Good Administrative Behaviour, providing that 'Every decision of the institution which may adversely affect the rights or interests of a private person shall state the grounds on which it is based by indicating clearly the relevant facts and the legal basis of the decision'. See also the Verwaltungsverfahrensgesetz in der Fassung der Bekanntmachung vom 23. Januar 2003 (BGBl. I S. 102), das zuletzt durch Artikel 3 des Gesetzes vom 25. Juli 2013 (BGBl. I S. 2749) geändert worden ist, § 39, establishing that the 'statement of grounds must contain the chief material and legal grounds that led the authority to take its decision'.

[95] The fifth principle of public service, according to the EU Ombudsman's Public service principles for the EU civil service is transparency (implying that 'Civil servants should be willing to explain their activities and to give reasons for their actions').

[96] See for example Verwaltungsverfahrensgesetz in der Fassung der Bekanntmachung vom 23. Januar 2003 (BGBl. I S. 102), das zuletzt durch Artikel 3 des Gesetzes vom 25. Juli 2013 (BGBl. I S. 2749) geändert worden ist, § 39(2) and the Ley 30/1992, de 26 de noviembre, de Régimen

if, for example, the decision-maker deems that it is unnecessary.[97] Second, Article III-29(1) does not require any dissenting opinion to be reported.[98] Third, there is no explicit reference to the results of the preliminary phases of the procedure.[99] However, the duty of diligence can be interpreted as obliging the public authority to refer to them.

Article III-29(2) deals with the duty to provide reasons in cases of composite administrative procedures. Since such procedures are characterized, in a variety of ways, by the involvement of both EU and national authorities, Article III-29(2), following the approach in Article III-24, provides that the duty to state reasons will be 'shaped' by their respective roles in making the decision. The underlying assumption is, therefore, that reasons must always be given, coherently with the general principle of law recognized by the CJEU. **105**

III-30 Duty to indicate available remedies

While the previous model rule reiterates an obligation that derives directly from the Treaties, **Article III-30 introduces a new obligation**, by analogy with several national APAs of EU Member States. **106**

The **precise nature of this obligation varies depending on the national statute.** Sometimes, it simply requires that the decision-maker indicate the judicial remedies that are available against its decision. In other cases, a more elaborate requirement is established, including indication of the way in which to seek judicial protection.[100] A more extensive formulation may require consideration of judicial and non-judicial remedies, such as filing of a complaint to an Ombudsman or to another public agency. **107**

Jurídico de las Administraciones Públicas y del Procedimiento Administrativo Común (BOE núm. 285, de 27.11.1992), modificada por última vez por la Ley 27/2013, de 27 de diciembre, de racionalización y sostenibilidad de la Administración Local (BOE núm. 312, de 30.12.2013), Art 54.

[97] A power of this kind is provided by Förvaltningslag (1986:223) Utfärdad: 1986-05-07, last amended by Lag (2014:630) om ändring i förvaltningslagen (1986:223), Section 20 (1)); and the Legge 7 agosto 1990 n. 241, Nuove norme in materia di procedimento amministrativo e di diritto di accesso ai documenti amministrativi (pubblicata nella Gazzetta Ufficiale del 18 agosto 1990 n. 192), Art 21-*octies* (2), in the latter case due to the controversial interpretation of 'form' followed by some lower administrative courts.

[98] See for example Förvaltningslag (1986:223) Utfärdad: 1986-05-07, last amended by Lag (2014:630) om ändring i förvaltningslagen (1986:223), Section 19.

[99] See Allgemeines Verwaltungsverfahrensgesetz 1991 (BGBl. Nr. 51/1991) das zuletzt durch Artikel 1 des Bundesgesetzes vom 31. Juli 2013 (BGBl. I Nr. 161/2013) geändert worden ist, § 60.

[100] See Legge 7 agosto 1990 n. 241, Nuove norme in materia di procedimento amministrativo e di diritto di accesso ai documenti amministrativi (pubblicata nella Gazzetta Ufficiale del 18 agosto 1990 n. 192), Art 3(4); Allgemeines Verwaltungsverfahrensgesetz 1991 (BGBl. Nr. 51/1991) das zuletzt durch Artikel 1 des Bundesgesetzes vom 31. Juli 2013 (BGBl. I Nr. 161/2013) geändert worden ist, § 61 also requires the 'prerequisites' for an application for judicial review to be indicated.

108 **Article III-30 is based on the last of these models.** It requires the public authority to enshrine in the decision information concerning the possibility of administrative appeal, both direct and indirect (that is to say to another public authority) and, if so, of the time-limits for making such an appeal. It also requires the addressees to be informed of the possibilities of judicial review, with the related time-limits, as well as of filing a complaint to an Ombudsman.

109 It is important, nonetheless, to note that **Article III-30 does not introduce any innovation with regard to existing judicial and non-judicial remedies at EU level.** Rather, it facilitates their use by parties, by introducing an obligation to provide information about them. It confirms, in this respect, Article 19 EO Code.[101]

III-31 Formal and language requirements

110 Article III-31 deals with **formal and language requirements**, which have different implications.

111 **National APAs** deal with formal requirements in a variety of ways. Some APAs do not prescribe any specific form, though establishing that where any such requirement is established by the law, its infringement renders the act void or voidable.[102] Other APAs are more directly prescriptive, to the extent to which they require either a specific form or stipulate matters[103] such as signature.[104]

112 **Article III-31(1) opts for the latter model.** Not only does it require that decision shall be in writing, but it also requires that the decision be signed and the authority that makes the decision be identified. The former can be regarded as a manifestation of the general rule enshrined into Article 297 TFEU,[105] while the latter is a consequence of the obligation to respect the competence of the various institutions and bodies,[106] which is confirmed by the inclusion of competence among the grounds for judicial review of the acts of the Union.[107]

---

[101] European Ombudsman—The European Code of Good Administrative Behaviour.

[102] See Legge 7 agosto 1990 n. 241, Nuove norme in materia di procedimento amministrativo e di diritto di accesso ai documenti amministrativi (pubblicata nella Gazzetta Ufficiale del 18 agosto 1990 n. 192), Art 21-*octies* (2).

[103] See the Ley 30/1992, de 26 de noviembre, de Régimen Jurídico de las Administraciones Públicas y del Procedimiento Administrativo Común (BOE núm. 285, de 27.11.1992), modificada por última vez por la Ley 27/2013, de 27 de diciembre, de racionalización y sostenibilidad de la Administración Local (BOE núm. 312, de 30.12.2013), Art 55.

[104] Verwaltungsverfahrensgesetz in der Fassung der Bekanntmachung vom 23. Januar 2003 (BGBl. I S. 102), das zuletzt durch Artikel 3 des Gesetzes vom 25. Juli 2013 (BGBl. I S. 2749) geändert worden ist, § 34.

[105] Art 297(2) TFEU provides that non-legislative acts adopted in the form of regulations, directives or decisions, when the latter do not specify to whom they are addressed, shall be signed by the President of the institution which adopted them.

[106] Art 5 TEU.

[107] Art 263(2) TFEU.

There are a variety of rules concerning linguistic requirements in national APAs. 113
Some give the issue little attention,[108] while others regulate the translation of acts and documents, both during and at the end of an administrative procedure.[109]

The **need to accommodate linguistic diversity is obviously stronger in the EU,** 114
due to its multi-national and multi-lingual social base. This is acknowledged by Article 22 CFR, according to which 'the Union shall respect cultural, religious and linguistic diversity'. The centrality of language was apparent from the very outset of the EEC, as evidenced in Regulation 1 of 1958, which determined the languages to be used by the EEC. It finds expression once again in Article 41(4) CFR, which provides that 'Every person may write to the institutions of the Union in one of the languages of the Treaties and must have an answer in the same language', and this obligation is echoed by Article 13 EO Code.[110]

In line with the CFR's emphasis on linguistic diversity, Article III-31(2) requires 115
that a decision taken by an EU authority shall be written in the language chosen by the addressee. No distinction is made in this respect between procedures initiated by private parties and *ex officio*. This rule is, however, subject to **two limitations.** The first derives from the circumstance that the model rule only refers to decisions issued by EU authorities. A second limitation derives from the circumstance that Article III-31(2) refers to the 'official languages of the EU'.

III-32 Decisions in electronic form

Article III-32 concerns the instruments by which public authorities can communi- 116
cate acts and measures. The basic rule is that decisions must be notified in a **written form,** and, in accord with modern technology, public authorities are encouraged or obliged to promote the use of electronic communications.[111] The consequence is that there are legal frameworks to regulate the adoption, signature, and transmis-

[108] Verwaltungsverfahrensgesetz in der Fassung der Bekanntmachung vom 23. Januar 2003 (BGBl. I S. 102), das zuletzt durch Artikel 3 des Gesetzes vom 25. Juli 2013 (BGBl. I S. 2749) geändert worden ist, § 23.

[109] Förvaltningslag (1986:223) Utfärdad: 1986-05-07, last amended by Lag (2014:630) om ändring i förvaltningslagen (1986:223), Section 8; Ley 30/1992, de 26 de noviembre, de Régimen Jurídico de las Administraciones Públicas y del Procedimiento Administrativo Común (BOE núm. 285, de 27.11.1992), modificada por última vez por la Ley 27/2013, de 27 de diciembre, de racionalización y sostenibilidad de la Administración Local (BOE núm. 312, de 30.12.2013), Art 36 (dealing with the issue of diversity of official languages that may be chosen by the parties in certain parts of Spain).

[110] European Ombudsman—The European Code of Good Administrative Behaviour

[111] See for example Legge 7 agosto 1990 n. 241, Nuove norme in materia di procedimento amministrativo e di diritto di accesso ai documenti amministrativi (pubblicata nella Gazzetta Ufficiale del 18 agosto 1990 n. 192), Art 3-*bis*.

sion of electronic documents.[112] In line with this trend, the EU has laid down a common framework for **electronic signatures.**[113]

117 **Drawing on this common background**, the model rules set out a general rule and an exception. The general rule set by Article III-32(1) is that a decision in written form may be replaced by electronic form, in which case a qualified signature is required. A legal provision may, however, establish otherwise. Second, under Article III-32(2), if the addressee of the decision makes a reasonable claim to be unable to process the electronic document sent by the public authority, the latter must send it again either in a suitable electronic format or as a written document.[114]

III-33 Notification of a decision

118 **National APAs** regulate the notification of individual acts and measures. There are **common** and distinctive **elements.** The former include rules according to which (i) an administrative act must be made known, or capable of being known, by the person to whom it is addressed or who is affected by it,[115] (ii) as a matter of principle, the effect of the act can take place only after the notification,[116] which is relevant also for judicial protection, and (iii) only in the circumstances specified by legal provisions may other forms of communication, including publication,[117] be used.

[112] See for example Verwaltungsverfahrensgesetz in der Fassung der Bekanntmachung vom 23. Januar 2003 (BGBl. I S. 102), das zuletzt durch Artikel 3 des Gesetzes vom 25. Juli 2013 (BGBl. I S. 2749) geändert worden ist, § 3a and Spanish Act 11/2007 on electronic access of the citizens to public services (Ley 11/2007, de 22 de junio, de acceso electrónico de los ciudadanos a los Servicios Públicos, BOE núm. 150, de 23.6.2007, modificada por última vez por la Ley 2/2011, de 4 de marzo, de Economía Sostenible, BOE núm. 55, de 5.3.2011).

[113] See Directive 1999/93/EC of the European Parliament and of the Council of 13 December 1999 on a Community framework for electronic signatures [2000] OJ L13/12 last amended by Regulation (EC) No 1137/2008 of the European Parliament and of the Council of 22 October 2008 adapting a number of instruments subject to the procedure laid down in Article 251 of the Treaty to Council Decision 1999/468/EC, with regard to the regulatory procedure with scrutiny—Adaptation to the regulatory procedure with scrutiny—Part One [2008] OJ L311/1.

[114] Art III-32 was inspired by Verwaltungsverfahrensgesetz in der Fassung der Bekanntmachung vom 23. Januar 2003 (BGBl. I S. 102), das zuletzt durch Artikel 3 des Gesetzes vom 25. Juli 2013 (BGBl. I S. 2749) geändert worden ist, § 3a.

[115] Legge 7 agosto 1990 n. 241, Nuove norme in materia di procedimento amministrativo e di diritto di accesso ai documenti amministrativi (pubblicata nella Gazzetta Ufficiale del 18 agosto 1990 n. 192), Art 7 includes notification within the duties of the responsible official.

[116] Verwaltungsverfahrensgesetz in der Fassung der Bekanntmachung vom 23. Januar 2003 (BGBl. I S. 102), das zuletzt durch Artikel 3 des Gesetzes vom 25. Juli 2013 (BGBl. I S. 2749) geändert worden ist, § 41(1).

[117] Verwaltungsverfahrensgesetz in der Fassung der Bekanntmachung vom 23. Januar 2003 (BGBl. I S. 102), das zuletzt durch Artikel 3 des Gesetzes vom 25. Juli 2013 (BGBl. I S. 2749) geändert worden ist, § 41(3) (distinguishing between an individual and a general order, which can be published); Wet van 4 juni 1992 houdende algemene regels van bestuursrecht (Stb. 1992, 315), in werking getreden op 1 juli 1994, laatstelijk gewijzigd bij Wet van 25 juni 2014, in werking getreden op 1 augustus 2014, Art 3:40; Ley 30/1992, de 26 de noviembre, de Régimen Jurídico de las Administraciones Públicas y del Procedimiento Administrativo Común (BOE núm. 285, de

The latter distinctive aspects include the way in which the notification is carried out, the period within which it must be done,[118] and the deadlines or time-limits at the expiry of which a presumption of knowledge may arise.[119]

Article 297(2) TFEU is coherent with rules (i) and (ii). It provides that decisions which specify to whom they are addressed shall be notified to them and take effect upon such notification. This does not prevent a decision from being published in the Official Journal, but this does not dispense with the need for notification, which is the only way to render the act enforceable against those to whom it is addressed. Further rules are established by the last section of Article 263 TFEU concerning judicial review.[120] The EO Code confirms the first rule and adds another, according to which the responsible officer must abstain from communicating the decision to others, until the person or persons concerned has received it.[121] **119**

The **model rules are coherent with the three common elements mentioned earlier.** Article III-33(1) establishes that (i) decisions shall be notified to all the parties (and specifies that this must be done 'as soon as they are adopted') and (ii) clarifies that it is only after the notification that the decision 'shall take effect'. The third rule is implemented by Article III-33(2), which provides for promulgation where this is permitted by EU law. **120**

III-34 Correction of obvious inaccuracies in a decision

Article III-34 allows for the **correction of obvious inaccuracies** in a decision. This rule is inspired by many national APAs.[122] The correction of such obvious inaccuracies **121**

27.11.1992), modificada por última vez por la Ley 27/2013, de 27 de diciembre, de racionalización y sostenibilidad de la Administración Local (BOE núm. 312, de 30.12.2013), Arts 59(6) and 60.

[118] The Ley 30/1992, de 26 de noviembre, de Régimen Jurídico de las Administraciones Públicas y del Procedimiento Administrativo Común (BOE núm. 285, de 27.11.1992), modificada por última vez por la Ley 27/2013, de 27 de diciembre, de racionalización y sostenibilidad de la Administración Local (BOE núm. 312, de 30.12.2013), Art 58(2) indicates a time-limit of ten days.

[119] For example, the Verwaltungsverfahrensgesetz in der Fassung der Bekanntmachung vom 23. Januar 2003 (BGBl. I S. 102), das zuletzt durch Artikel 3 des Gesetzes vom 25. Juli 2013 (BGBl. I S. 2749) geändert worden ist, § 41(2) requires three days after posting.

[120] It provides that 'The proceedings provided for in this Article shall be instituted within two months of the publication of the measure, or of its notification to the plaintiff, or, in the absence thereof, of the day on which it came to the knowledge of the latter, as the case may be'. See Case T-296/97 *Alitalia—Linee aeree italiane SpA v Commission* [2000] ECR II-3871.

[121] European Ombudsman—The European Code of Good Administrative Behaviour, Art 20.

[122] See for instance Verwaltungsverfahrensgesetz in der Fassung der Bekanntmachung vom 23. Januar 2003 (BGBl. I S. 102), das zuletzt durch Artikel 3 des Gesetzes vom 25. Juli 2013 (BGBl. I S. 2749) geändert worden ist, § 42; Förvaltningslag (1986:223) Utfärdad: 1986-05-07, last amended by Lag (2014:630) om ändring i förvaltningslagen (1986:223), Section 26; Ley 30/1992, de 26 de noviembre, de Régimen Jurídico de las Administraciones Públicas y del Procedimiento Administrativo Común (BOE núm. 285, de 27.11.1992), modificada por última vez por la Ley 27/2013, de 27 de diciembre, de racionalización y sostenibilidad de la Administración Local (BOE núm. 312, de 30.12.2013), Art 105(2).

does not conflict with the legitimate expectations of any party. Therefore, this matter is regulated in a distinct chapter.

Chapter 6: Rectification and Withdrawal of Decisions

III-35 Rectification and withdrawal of decisions that have an adverse effect

III-36 Rectification and withdrawal of decisions that are beneficial

122 **Articles III-35 and III-36 regulate the power of a public authority to withdraw a formally adopted and notified decision.** The power includes the option to withdraw a decision completely, or to rectify only certain aspects of a decision which cannot be qualified as obvious inaccuracies as regulated in Article III-34.

123 Any withdrawal of a decision may **conflict with the protection of legitimate expectations and the principle of legal certainty.** The protection of legitimate expectations is an accepted general principle of EU law according to the jurisprudence of the CJEU. This is especially the case with regard to the withdrawal of formal Commission decisions. The CJEU differentiates in this regard between lawful and unlawful decisions and between favourable decisions or decisions which confer rights or similar benefits on one side and non-favourable decisions.

124 The ReNEUAL Model Rules follow this structure and **differentiate between the withdrawal of decisions that have an adverse effect (Article III-35) and decisions that are beneficial (Article III-36).** If a decision has adverse effects on one party and is beneficial to another party the authority must balance the conflicting interests of both parties (Articles III-35(4) and III-36(4)). Within these two basic categories the model rules differentiate further between lawful decisions (Articles III-35(2), III-36(3)) and unlawful decisions (Articles III-35(1), III-36(1), (2)). The model rules provide a set of different legal requirements for a lawful withdrawal of a decision for the four categories following from this structure. These requirements reflect the jurisprudence of the CJEU and translate the complex case law into a transparent legal structure.

125 Even **in the case of an unlawful decision** that has an adverse effect, the authority is not strictly obliged to withdraw that decision but has been **left with discretion.** Otherwise, time-limits for legal challenges of unlawful decisions would become meaningless. On the other hand, the expiry of a time-limit does not prohibit an authority from withdrawing an unlawful decision (Articles III-35(3) and III-36(3)). In the case of an unlawful decision that is beneficial, the authority may choose to withdraw that decision either with retrospective effect, only with prospective effect, or not at all (Article III-36(2)). This set of different actions provides for an adequate balancing of the interests of the public with those of the beneficiary. Important criteria for this balancing test are the extent to which the illegality that taints the decisions is obvious, whether the beneficiary had provoked the earlier decision through false or incomplete information and the extent to which the beneficiary undertook irreversible investments because he or she relied on the decision.

The **withdrawal of lawful decisions** that are beneficial is an especially important and delicate category, because the respective beneficiaries generally have increased legitimate expectations. Therefore, Article III-36(3) sentence 3 empowers public authorities only under very restrictive conditions to withdraw such a decision. Alternative (b) reflects settled case law of the CJEU.[123] Alternative (c) is inspired by national law.[124] The provision allows a withdrawal of a lawful decision in case of serious harm to public or private interests which outweigh the legitimate expectations of the beneficiary. In order to provide a fair balance the legitimate expectations of the beneficiary might demand (financial) compensation of his or her disadvantages deriving from reliance on the continued existence of the decision. **126**

The **time-limit** set in Article III-36(5) for a withdrawal with retroactive effect restates the existing case law.[125] In accordance with the jurisprudence, the time-limit starts with the notification of the decision to the relevant party. Under such circumstances, it is not suitable to set a definite time-limit.[126] Therefore, the ReNEUAL Model rule provides for a flexible time-limit, which is used by the courts and allows the circumstances in the individual case to be taken into account. Articles III-35(5) and III-36(6) clarify that the procedural rules provided by Book III apply to procedures to prepare a **decision** to withdraw or rectify an earlier decision. **127**

[123] Case 54/77 *Herpels v Commission* (1978) ECR 585, para 38; Case T-81/95, *Interhotel-sociedade Internacional de Hotéis SARL v Commission* (1997) ECR II-1265, paras 42, 46–47, 61–62.

[124] Compare Verwaltungsverfahrensgesetz in der Fassung der Bekanntmachung vom 23. Januar 2003 (BGBl. I S. 102), das zuletzt durch Artikel 3 des Gesetzes vom 25. Juli 2013 (BGBl. I S. 2749) geändert worden ist, § 49 (2) sentence 1 no. 5 with (6) sentence 1.

[125] Case 14/61 *Koninklijke Nederlandsche Hoogovens en Staalfabrieken N.V. v High Authority of the European Coal and Steel Community* [1962] ECR 253 (English special edition); Case 15/85 *Consorzio Cooperative d'Abruzzo v Commission* [1987] ECR 1005, para 12.

[126] Compare in contrast Verwaltungsverfahrensgesetz in der Fassung der Bekanntmachung vom 23. Januar 2003 (BGBl. I S. 102), das zuletzt durch Artikel 3 des Gesetzes vom 25. Juli 2013 (BGBl. I S. 2749) geändert worden ist, § 48(4) which set a time-limit of one year. On the other side the German courts hold that the time-limit does not start before the authority has investigated all factors which are important for the decision whether to withdraw the earlier decision or not.

BOOK IV—CONTRACTS

A. Introduction to Book IV

1 The 'model rules' on contracts that are presented in Book IV are to be understood as a contribution to the debate on **EU contracts**, the **administrative procedure leading to their conclusion, and their execution**. There is very little existing mandatory law on contracts with EU authorities that can be drawn upon for this purpose. Although the proposed rules often derive from existing practice, there is **usually no common approach** shared by all or even most of the EU institutions, bodies, offices, and agencies. Even within the European Commission, approaches vary from one policy sector and DG to another.

I. Problems of a Restatement of EU Law with Regard to Public Contracts

2 Work on public contracts at an EU level entails several problems. To begin with, one has to screen an **abundant amount of restatement material** (EU legislation, case law, ombudsprudence (the 'jurisprudence' of the EO), standard contracts, and contract templates developed by the Commission), which coincidentally is **very ambiguous and fragmentary** in nature. What is more, there is no consensus among lawyers on how to understand this material. The same rules and clauses are interpreted in different ways by different contracting authorities, courts, lawyers, advocates general, and scholars. Thus, a **very heterogeneous landscape presents itself on the European level**. This landscape becomes even more complex when the national levels are taken into account. Member States apply very different national concepts to public contracts (and public contract law), regardless of whether these contracts are governed by national public or national private law, or by a mixture comprising public and private law elements.

3 Furthermore, there is **no consensus on the substance of 'public contract law'** itself. Many questions arise in this context, *inter alia*: Does public contract law only concern public procurement or does it also involve the conclusion and execution of all contracts concluded by public authorities (including transactions, settlements, grant agreements, employment contracts)? Are contracts between public entities (regarding the division of competences) contracts which should be made subject to the same rules as public contracts between public administration and private persons?

II. The Starting Point

4 The working group leaders for this book began their research on public contract law long before the commencement of the ReNEUAL project. The preparatory scientific work, within and outwith ReNEUAL, which served as a basis for the rules of Book IV, can be seen in the resources of the **research network 'Public Contracts in Legal Globalization'** (https://www.public-contracts.org/), headed by Jean-Bernard

Auby. This network is composed of an international group of experts working on public contracts and involves regular meetings for workshops and seminars on this topic. Various publications on International, European, and Comparative Public Contract Law have resulted from the scientific exchange within this network. Another **forum for scholarly discussions** has been the research network ReNEUAL, in which the different concepts of EU contracts, represented by different scholars, have been the subject of lively debate within the working group on contracts and during various workshops with experts in EU Law and national Administrative law. The ideas developed within the working group have subsequently been amended and further developed to take account of new literature and case law.

III. The 'Life' of Public Contracts in a Nutshell

In general, the 'life' of a public contract can be divided roughly into **three phases**, 5
which are, *in nuce*, usually common to all legal systems:

1. Administrative procedure leading to the conclusion of a public contract

This phase is governed by administrative procedure and public procurement rules.

2. Conclusion of the contract

This phase is governed by the rules establishing the prerequisites for the validity of a contract and the right to invoke invalidity.

3. Execution and end (expiration) of the contract

This phase is above all governed by the law of obligations. However, one should also consider whether the decision-making process of the public authority, for instance with regard to the exercise of contractual rights, the termination of the contract or the decision to enact a unilateral act in order to enforce contractual rights, has to be subject to administrative procedure rules.

IV. Between Ambition and Self-Restraint: The Decision on the Scope of Book IV

Taking these three phases of the 'life' of public contracts into consideration, the 6
working group had to engage with several questions prior to the completion of Book IV. Should Book IV only include rules regarding the administrative procedure leading to the conclusion of a public contract (especially public procurement rules)? Or should rules concerning administrative procedures in execution of a contract (for example regarding the decisions to terminate a contract, to exercise contractual rights etc.) also be incorporated? Moreover, should the work only consider **administrative procedure rules in sensu stricto** or also **provisions concerning the consequences of non-observance of such rules in**

view of the validity of the contract and judicial review? Is it at all **possible to differentiate between procedural and substantive law in public contract law?** Should the Model Rules only provide a restatement with regard to public contracts with EU authorities, or also in relation to public contracts between Member State administrations and third parties? More challenging still: Should Book IV also deal with the problems of sub-contractors?

7 In order to answer the majority of these questions, **several aspects were discussed** in the working group:

8 First of all, extending the scope of Book IV to public contracts concluded by Member State authorities would only be possible if its focus were limited to the administrative procedures leading to the conclusion of a public contract (especially public procurement rules). **Member State laws on the validity and execution of public contracts are too heterogeneous for any harmonization on EU level.** Furthermore, the **issue of a legal basis for codification** of administrative procedure law which is discussed in the Introduction to Book I of these model rules **is even more complicated** in the case of contracts by Member State authorities.

9 Second, **public procurement rules are already exhaustively laid out** in the various public procurement directives, Title V of Regulation 966/2012 on the financial rules applicable to the general budget of the Union (Financial Regulation), and the Commission's Interpretative Communication on the Community law applicable to contract awards not or not fully subject to the provisions of the Public Procurement directives (2006/C 179/02).

10 Third, **ombudsprudence and the case law of the CJEU** demonstrate important **gaps of legislation** with regard to the principles of good administration in the execution phase of public contracts and in relation to the practice of subcontracting.

11 Fourth, **public contracts typically create continuing obligations.** This fact justifies placing the **focus on the execution of public contracts** (without neglecting the procedure leading up to the conclusion of the contract).

12 Fifth, national laws on public contracts have some clear shortcomings, particularly with regard to the consequences of the illegality of such public contracts, and may therefore not always serve as suitable models for the solution of these problems on an EU level. Book IV therefore also proposes some new solutions which should not be considered as a restatement, but as a proposal on how to improve public contract law.

13 Discussing all these questions and assessing the arguments presented during the drafting period finally led to the following compromise between ambition and necessary self-restraint.

Only contracts regarding administrative activity concluded between EU authorities and private entities or, with some reservations, with Member State administrations fall within the scope of Book IV. Hence, the scope of application of the Model Rules of Book IV is the same as for Books II and III. 14

Book IV covers all three phases of the 'life' of an EU contract, as well as the problems of subcontracting. 15

It is necessary to align the Model Rules of Book IV with primary law on judicial review, Articles 272 and 335 TFEU, and the case law concerning 'acts' within the meaning of Articles 263 and 299 TFEU. 16

Furthermore, with regard to questions of validity, execution, and judicial review, it is necessary to distinguish between, on the one hand, **EU contracts that are governed solely by EU law** and on the other hand **EU contracts that are governed solely by the law of a Member State**, or even a Third State. By contrast, there is generally no need to differentiate between these two kinds of EU contracts with regard to the administrative procedures that lead to their conclusion, or concern the execution or termination of such contracts. 17

V. EU Contracts Solely Governed by EU Law and EU Contracts Governed by the Law of a Member State

The necessary distinction between EU contracts solely governed by EU law and EU contracts governed by the law of a Member State, or a third State, brings about the need to outline the respective **characteristics of these two types of EU contracts.** It could be said that under the present state of EU law, **EU contracts solely governed by EU law** are usually contracts **serving as a tool to implement EU policies** (bearing only few similarities to contracts concluded between private parties), *inter alia* grant agreements, transactions, and settlement agreements (but also staff contracts in the sense of the EU Staff Regulations). They require a **'uniform contract law'** assuring a uniform implementation of EU law across the whole EU territory. 18

By contrast, under the present state of EU law, **EU contracts governed by the law of a Member State** are usually **contracts which could also be concluded between private parties,** *inter alia* contracts concerning the purchase and sale of goods or real estate, rental and lease contracts, or contracts for the supply of services. They do **not require separate EU contract law** as the application of national private law in relation to the validity and the execution of these contracts is sufficient. In this instance, special rules for EU contracts would be considered as unjustified 'privileges' for the contracting EU authority. 19

Yet, even with regard to EU contracts governed by the law of a Member State, the **EU authority does not enjoy the contractual freedom** (in the sense of the German concept of '*Privatautonomie*') **typical of private persons** in either the award 20 procedure or during the execution of the contract. The EU authority is bound by the right to good administration which finds its expression, *inter alia*, in Article 41 CFR. Therefore, Book IV contains rules on administrative procedures with regards to the conclusion, execution, and termination of such contracts.

VI. Background on the Application of Member State Law

21 It could be argued that for reasons of primacy EU law could establish a special legal regime for EU contracts subject in principle to national law. The implementation of this approach would result in a parallel application of national and EU law to contracts and, moreover, in special cases this approach would create a certain dominant position for the EU authority in the contractual relationship. This **book is however based on the opposite view**, which also corresponds to the *de lege lata* situation, namely **that there is not a special EU law regime for all EU contracts.**

22 Article 335 TFEU gives the EU the most extensive legal capacity accorded to legal persons under the respective national law, but it does not have the characteristics of a legal basis and certainly could not be used in order to provide EU authorities with additional powers in a contracting situation. Hence, for reasons of legal certainty it seems obvious and desirable that there be a clear distinction between EU law and national law on this topic. Therefore, it would also be logical that, if a relation is governed by national law, such law has to be applied exclusively without further interference or exemptions. Otherwise the contract would no longer be subject to a regime of national contract law, but to a special regime, a mixture of national law with some reservations drawn from EU law. This would necessitate the drafting of a new intermediate regime, but not the application of a national law of contracts.

23 Such an **intermediate regime**, which would be comparable to the German concept of '*Verwaltungsprivatrecht*' ('administrative private law'), **would furthermore contribute to legal uncertainty and a lack of transparency** as the contractors would neither be able to assess the rules applicable to the contract, nor their substantive content (as the German experiences with '*Verwaltungsprivatrecht*' show).

24 This being said, even if the contract is governed by national law, **standard terms or contractual clauses** should make it **possible to adapt the contract to EU law specifications**, especially those that serve to guarantee rights protected by the CFR and further consequences of the right to good administration. Standard clauses on the core issues of national contract law regimes, such as those about validity or performance of contracts for instance, would however be excluded, as the relevant national contract law should apply without reservations to its core regime.

25 Following a strict division of contract law regimes—as opposed to the creation of a new intermediate regime—seems to also be in line with the opinion of the European

Commission.[1] Article IV-35(3) and Article IV-36 are the clearest illustration of the option made in favour of such a strict division.

VII. Rules on Transactions, Settlements, and Mediation?

The working group considered including a chapter on **special rules on transactions, settlement, and mediation** in Book IV. They could have been based on Recommendation Rec(2001)9 of the Committee of Ministers of the Council of Europe to Member States on alternatives to litigation between administrative authorities and private parties. Article 147(1) of the Rules of Procedure of the Court of Justice[2] presumes for direct execution of EU law that the parties are able to settle a controversy on arguable questions of the case, which means that basically a (non-judicial) dispute settlement is licit in general. For reasons of the prevalence of the objective legal protection function, **this basic presumption does not hold true for proceedings based on Articles 263 and 265 TFEU** (Article 147(2) of the Rules of Procedure of the Court of Justice[3]), which are in practice very important. Nevertheless, some sort of **amicable dispute settlement** is possible in proceedings under Article 263 and 265 TFEU by withdrawal of the claim or, in cases which do not proceed to judgments (disposal of a case), application of Articles 148–151 Rules of Procedure of the Court of Justice.[4] **Settlements by compromise** through contracts on rights and obligations of EU law between EU authorities and private persons are not uncommon.[5] **Settlements in the field of EU anti-trust and merger control law** also appear comparable to compromise settlements. For the EU, anti-trust law settlement agreements are explicitly provided for in Article 10a of Commission Regulation 773/2004 amended by Commission Regulation 622/2008.[6] Nevertheless the working group on this book **refrained from drafting a 'law on settlements agreements'**. The question whether and under which circumstances settlement agreements and mechanisms for alternative settlement of disputes are licit is **assessed very differently in the Member States.** This heterogeneity is based on different views on the principle of legality of administration. In the end, 26

[1] Commission Regulation (EC, Euratom) 478/2007 of 23 April 2007 amending Regulation (EC, Euratom) 2342/2002 laying down detailed rules for the implementation of Council Regulation (EC, Euratom) 1605/2002 on the Financial Regulation applicable to the general budget of the European Communities [2007] OJ L111/13.

[2] Rules of Procedure of the Court of Justice of 25 September 2012 [2012] OJ L265/1, last amended by the Amendment of the Rules of Procedure of the Court of Justice [2013] OJ L173/65.

[3] Rules of Procedure of the Court of Justice of 25 September 2012 [2012] OJ L265/1, last amended by the Amendment of the Rules of Procedure of the Court of Justice [2013] OJ L173/65.

[4] Rules of Procedure of the Court of Justice of 25 September 2012 [2012] OJ L265/1, last amended by the Amendment of the Rules of Procedure of the Court of Justice [2013] OJ L173/65.

[5] On such cases where Member States concluded contracts in the name and for account of the European Community: Joined Cases C-80-82/99 *Flemmer/Christoffel v Council and Commission* [2001] ECR I-7211 paras 29 f.

[6] Commission Regulation (EC) 622/2008 of 30 June 2008 amending Regulation (EC) 773/2004, as regards the conduct of settlement procedures in cartel cases [2008] OJ L171/3.

this **question is a topic of substantive law, not of administrative procedure law.** Hence, **Book IV does not provide for rules on the question if a settlement agreement or alternative dispute resolution can be closed at all.** However, we would like to stress that if the EU authority seeks to conclude a transaction contract or a settlement contract, the standard procedure of Articles IV-7 and IV-8 will apply. Furthermore, for the execution of such contracts, Chapter 3 of this Book IV is directly applicable. As regards the applicable substantive law, the law of the Member States is only applicable, if the transaction serves to settle a conflict about contractual obligations arising from a contract which is governed by Member State law. In all other cases EU law applies.

B. Model Rules

Chapter 1: General Provisions

IV-1 Scope of application

(1) Book IV applies to all contracts and legally binding agreements concluded
    (a) between an EU authority and a private entity;
    (b) between an EU authority and a Member State authority, if the Member State authority acts as a service provider on the market and concludes the contract with an EU authority as a private person would.
    (c) Book IV applies also to contracts between an EU authority and a Member State authority other than those mentioned in (b) if these rules are appropriate in view of the nature of the contract constituting an arrangement relating to administrative organisation.
(2) Paragraph (1)(a) and (b) of this article applies *mutatis mutandis* to contracts between EU authorities.
(3) Where an EU contract involves subcontracting, only the special rules of Chapter 4 of Book IV shall apply to the latter.
(4) Book IV does not apply to agreements concluded by EU authorities under public international law.

IV-2 Definitions

(1) 'Contract' means an agreement between two or more parties which is intended to create a binding legal relationship or to have some other legal effect.
(2) 'Contractor' means the person that has entered into a contractual relationship with an EU authority.
(3) 'EU contract' means all contracts as defined in Article IV-1(1) and (2).
(4) 'General terms of contract' means contractual terms which have not been individually negotiated. A term shall be regarded as not individually negotiated where it has been drafted in advance by one of the parties and the other party has therefore not been able to influence the substance of the term.
(5) 'Participant' means any person that made an application or a tender in a competitive award procedure in the sense of Chapter 2 Section 3 of Book IV.
(6) 'Party' means the EU authority or the contractor as parties of an EU contract.
(7) 'Potential Contractor' means any person that expressed an interest in concluding an EU contract in cases where a competitive award procedure in the sense

of Chapter 2 Section 3 of Book IV did not take place or where he or she was excluded from the participation in such a procedure.

(8) 'Specific obligations of EU authorities as public authorities' mean the obligations of an EU authority to comply with fundamental rights in accordance with Article 6 TEU as well as with general principles of EU Law, with EU rules applicable to the conclusion of contracts, EU budgetary and financial rules, and with other general or specific obligations imposed under EU law on EU authorities as public authorities.

(9) 'Subcontractor' means any person who has entered into a contractual relationship with the contractor for the purpose of implementing an existing EU contract.

(10) 'Third party' means any person who is not a party to the EU contract.

IV-3 Determination of the law applicable to an EU contract

(1) An EU contract is governed by either EU law or by the law of a Member State or by the law of a Third State. Where an EU legal act determines the law applicable to contracts, the parties cannot choose to submit a contract to another law.

(2) An EU contract is governed solely by EU law in the following cases:
   (a) if explicitly provided for by an EU legal act;
   (b) if the contract is a contract within the meaning of Article IV-1(1)(c);
   (c) if the contract is modifying or abrogating pre-existing EU law relations between the parties;
   (d) if the obligations of the EU authority can only be fulfilled through an act within the meaning of Article 288 TFEU or through similar measures implying the exercise of public authority conferred on the EU authority by EU law;
   (e) if an EU legal act establishes homogeneous rules regarding the principal obligations under the respective contract which are directly binding upon the contracting parties. The present rule applies in particular when unilateral powers to modify the contract or to enforce the contractual obligations are not explicitly enshrined in contractual clauses.

(3) For the purpose of paragraph (2)(e) of this article, the following contracts in particular are to be considered as contracts governed solely by EU law:
   (a) staff contracts within the meaning of the EU Staff Regulations;
   (b) grant agreements within the meaning of the EU Financial Regulations;
   (c) grant agreements within the meaning of the EU Regulations implementing Framework Programmes on Research.

(4) If an EU contract is not governed by EU law, it is governed by the law of a Member State chosen by the parties pursuant to the criteria under Regulation (EC) No 593/2008 on the law applicable to contractual obligations (Rome I). To the extent that the applicable Member State law has not been chosen by the parties, or if the choice of law clause is invalid, the criteria of Regulation (EC) No 593/2008 shall be applied to determine which Member State law is applicable.

(5) All 'public contracts' within the meaning of Article 101(1) of Regulation (EU, EURATOM) No. 966/2012 on the financial rules applicable to the general budget of the Union are to be considered as contracts subject to paragraph (4) of the present article.

(6) The law of a Third State shall apply to a contract in the case of paragraph (4) of the present article, if the application of Regulation (EC) No 593/2008 on the law applicable to contractual obligations (Rome I) stipulates this result. All the rules of Book IV pertaining to EU contracts governed by Member State law shall apply accordingly to EU contracts governed by the law of third countries.

IV-4 Rules applicable to EU contracts solely governed by EU law

EU contracts in the sense of Article IV-3(2) are governed by the rules of Book IV, by their respective contractual provisions, by sector-specific EU law, by general principles of EU contract law as well as other general principles of EU law.

IV-5 Rules applicable to EU contracts governed by Member State law

(1) If an EU contract is governed by the law of a Member State, the EU authority shall enjoy the most extensive legal capacity accorded to legal persons under the law of the respective Member State pursuant to Article 335 TFEU. The EU authority cannot refer to the exercise of public authority conferred by the law of the respective Member State on its own public authorities. Article 343 TFEU on privileges and immunities shall remain unaffected.
(2) The applicability of Member State law to an EU contract cannot relieve the EU authority of its obligations to comply with fundamental rights in accordance with Article 6 TEU, general principles of EU Law, with EU rules applicable to the conclusion of contracts, EU budgetary and financial rules, and with other general or specific obligations imposed under EU law on EU authorities as public authorities.

Chapter 2: Procedures for the Conclusion of Contracts

Section 1: Preparation of General Terms of Contracts

IV-6 Procedure for drafting general terms of contract

(1) The rules of Book II shall apply *mutatis mutandis* to the procedure for drafting general terms of the contract by the EU authority. This does not apply
   (a) to general terms of contracts corresponding to model contracts which are part of a legislative act or an act of general application in the sense of Article II-1(1);
   (b) to non-substantial modifications of general terms of contracts especially if such modifications serve to adapt contracts to new legislation or jurisprudence, or if they are solely advantageous for the contractor.
(2) General terms of contract can be adopted through the expedited procedure of Article II-6. In such a case they may only be used for eighteen months after their first use. If new general terms of contract are adopted following the regular rule-making procedure, the EU authority is obliged to offer its contractor the opportunity to change the contract in order to incorporate the new general terms of contract. The second sentence of this paragraph is not applicable
   (a) if the contract has been fully performed by both parties;
   (b) if the new general terms of contract are disadvantageous for the contractor in comparison to the general terms of contract adopted in the expedited procedure.
(3) The second and third sentence of paragraph (2) shall apply *mutatis mutandis*
   (a) if the general terms of contract included in an EU contract have not been drafted according to paragraph (1) of the present Article, or if the general terms have been adopted before the entry into force of these Model Rules;

(b) if the act of general application referred to in paragraph (1)(a) of the present article can be adopted through the expedited procedure of Article II-6.

(4) General terms of contract submitted by the EU authority and not individually negotiated may be invoked against the contractor only if the contractor was aware of them, or if the EU authority took reasonable steps to draw the contractor's attention to these terms, before or during the conclusion of the contract. A mere reference to such terms within a contractual document will not suffice for these to be considered as brought to the contractor's attention in a sufficient manner, even if the contractor signs the document. Section 3 of Chapter 3 of Book IV remains unaffected.

Section 2: General Rules on Procedure

IV-7 Applicability of Book III

(1) The following articles of Book III shall apply *mutatis mutandis* to the decision of an EU authority on whether or not to conclude an EU contract unless stipulated otherwise in Book IV:
- Article III-3 – General duty of fair decision-making and impartiality;
- Article III-5 – Initiation;
- Article III-6 – Special rules on application procedures;
- Article III-7 – Responsible official;
- Article III-8 – Management of procedures and procedural rights;
- Article III-10 – Principle of investigation;
- Article III-11 – Investigation by request;
- Article III-13 – Duties to cooperate of parties;
- Article III-14 – Privilege against self-incrimination and legal professional privilege;
- Article III-15 – Witnesses and experts;
- Article III-22 – Access to the file;
- Article III-23 – Right to be heard by persons adversely affected;
- Article III-29 – Duty to give reasons;
- Article III-30 – Duty to indicate available remedies;
- Article III-31 – Formal and language requirements;
- Article III-32 – Decisions in electronic form.

(2) Paragraph (1) of this article applies *mutatis mutandis* to the decision of an EU authority to suggest or to accept a modification of an existing contract, or its cancellation. Article IV-9(3) remains unaffected.

IV-8 Effects on judicial procedure

(1) The refusal to conclude or to modify a contract is a decision in the sense of Article III-2 of the present Model Rules.

(2) Any person having participated in a competitive award procedure or having expressed an interest in concluding the contract may institute proceedings within the meaning of Article 263 TFEU against the contract award decision in the sense of Article IV-18, in cases where a correct procedure did not take place, even if the decision is not addressed to that person.

(3) The time limit established under Article 263 TFEU shall begin after the notification of the decision leading to the conclusion of the contract to the plaintiff, or in the absence thereof, on the day in which the decision came to the knowledge of the plaintiff.

(4) A contracting EU authority whose decision leading to the conclusion of an EU contract, has been declared void by the Court of Justice of the European Union is required to render the contract ineffective in compliance with the judgment, if the contractor has not fully met his part of the contractual obligations. This duty only allows the contracting EU authority to terminate or modify the contract, or to claim its invalidity under the conditions laid down in Chapter 3 of the present Book. This duty shall not affect any obligation which may result from the application of Article 340(2) TFEU.

Section 3: Competitive Award Procedure

IV-9 Scope

(1) The competitive award procedure is applicable to the conclusion of EU contracts
   (a) if the contracting EU authority is not legally obliged to conclude an EU contract with every person satisfying the criteria for the award;
   (b) if the contracting EU authority is not legally bound by a framework contract, decision or otherwise to conclude the contract with a specific person.

(2) The special rules regarding award procedures applicable to EU contracts in the sense of Article IV-3(3) and (5) as well as any other rules on competitive award procedures laid down in sector-specific EU law, take precedence over the rules of this section.

(3) A substantial modification of the provisions of an EU contract during its term shall be considered as a new award subject to the provisions of this section. A modification shall be considered substantial, where it renders the contract substantially different from the one initially concluded. Modifications arising from the rights provided under Article IV-6(2) and (3), Article IV-8(4), Article IV-23(3), Article IV-24(3), Article IV-28, Article IV-32 should in general not be deemed substantial.

IV-10 General principles

(1) The rules in Article IV-7(1) are applicable in a residual way to competitive award procedures.

(2) The rules of the present section will be considered as respected if the contracting EU authority applies the rules mentioned in Article IV-9(2) *mutatis mutandis* in appropriate cases. This includes provisions relating to exceptions from obligations resulting from the rules mentioned in Article IV-9(2).

IV-11 Prior advertising

(1) The contracting EU authority has to ensure the publication of a sufficiently accessible advertisement prior to the award of the contract in order to guarantee competitive tendering and impartiality of the award procedure. An advertisement is sufficiently accessible if, in light of the relevant market, every person who may have a reasonable interest in the contract has access to appropriate information prior to its award, which enables this person to express his or her interest in obtaining the contract.

(2) The contracting EU authorities are responsible for deciding the most appropriate medium for advertising the contracts. Their choice should be guided by an assessment of the relevance of the contract for the respective market, in particular in view of the subject matter and value of the contract as well as the customary practices in the relevant sector.

(3) Adequate means of publication include:
- Advertisements on the website of the EU authority,
- Publication in the Official Journal of the European Union/ TED (Tenders Electronic Daily),
- Publication in National journals specializing in public procurement announcements, newspapers with national or regional coverage, or specialist publications where there is only a local, regional or specialized market for the contract in question.

IV-12 Content of the advertisement and the contract documents

(1) The advertisement may be limited to a short description of the essential details of the contract and of the award method along with an invitation to contact the respective EU authority. If necessary, it might be complemented with additional information available on the Internet, or accessible upon request from the contracting EU authority. The advertisement and any additional documentation should provide as much information as is reasonably necessary for the persons interested to be able to make a decision on whether to express their interest in obtaining the contract.

(2) The subject matter of the contract shall be described in a non-discriminatory manner within the contract documents. The description of the characteristics required of a product or service should not refer to a specific make or source, a particular process, or to trade marks, patents, a specific origin or types of production, unless such a reference is justified by the subject matter of the contract and is accompanied by the words 'or equivalent'.

IV-13 Cases justifying use of the negotiated procedure without prior advertisement

Contracting EU authorities may award EU contracts by means of a negotiated procedure without prior advertisement in the following cases:

(a) when for technical or artistic reasons, or for reasons pertaining to the protection of exclusive rights, the contract may only be awarded to a particular person;

(b) insofar as is strictly necessary when, for reasons of extreme urgency brought about by events unforeseeable by the EU authority in question, the rules laid down in this section cannot be complied with. The circumstances invoked to justify extreme urgency must not in any event be attributable to the contracting EU authority;

(c) in similar cases, especially if the EU authority has developed and applies an award procedure pursuant to Article IV-10(2).

IV-14 Equal access for economic operators from all Member States

(1) The contracting EU authority shall only impose conditions which do not cause direct or indirect discrimination against persons who might be interested in the contract.

(2) If participants are required to submit certificates, diplomas or other forms of written evidence, documents from all Member States certifying an equivalent level of guarantee must be accepted.

(3) Time limits for expressing interest and for submitting offers should be long enough to allow persons from all Member States to make a meaningful assessment and prepare their tender.

(4) All participants must have prior access to the applicable rules along with the certainty that these rules shall apply without discrimination.

IV-15 Limit on the number of participants invited to submit a tender

(1) The contracting EU authority may take measures to appropriately limit the number of participants, provided this is done in a transparent and non-discriminatory manner. The respective EU authority must apply objective factors, such as the experience of the participants in the relevant sector, the size and infrastructure of their business, their technical and professional abilities, or other factors. Contracting EU authorities may opt for a drawing lots procedure, either exclusively or in combination with other selection criteria. In any event, the number of shortlisted participants shall take account of the need to ensure adequate competition.
(2) Alternatively, EU authorities may establish qualification systems where a list of qualified persons is compiled by means of a sufficiently advertised, transparent and open procedure. In the event of an award of individual contracts falling within the scope of this system, the EU authority may select the persons to be invited to submit a tender from the list of qualified persons on a non-discriminatory basis, in particular by drawing in rotation from the list.

IV-16 Equal treatment

(1) While the competitive award procedure is running, all contacts between the contracting EU authority and the participants shall satisfy conditions ensuring transparency and equal treatment. Such contacts shall not lead to an amendment of the terms and conditions of the contract or of the original tender.
(2) In procedures allowing for negotiation with shortlisted participants, negotiations should be organized in a way that gives all participants access to the same amount of information, excluding any unjustified advantages for a specific participant.

IV-17 Contracts of low value

(1) Contracts of low value may be awarded without prior advertisement on the basis of an appropriate market analysis and, if appropriate, through a negotiated procedure based on an adequate number of applications. The threshold for contracts of low value shall be established and published on a regular basis by each EU authority. In the absence of a published threshold, the threshold established by the Commission for the implementation of the EU Financial Regulations shall apply.
(2) For the purpose of this article the contracting EU authority should accept unsolicited applications and establish open lists with qualified persons. If it comes to the knowledge of the EU authority that a number of qualified persons are interested in concluding such low value contracts, the contracts should be awarded on the principle of rotation where the offered prizes and terms of contracts are similar, and where the negotiated procedure would be inappropriate with respect to the value of the contracts.

IV-18 Contract award decision

(1) The final decision awarding the contract has to comply with the procedural rules laid down at the outset as well as with the principles of non-discrimination and equal treatment.

(2) The contracting EU authority shall notify simultaneously all participants whose application or tender have been rejected of the grounds on which the decision was taken. The contracting EU authority shall notify all participants meeting the exclusion and selection criteria who make a request in writing, the characteristics and relative advantages of the successful tender along with the name of the participant to whom the contract is awarded. Article III-32 on decisions in electronic form applies *mutatis mutandis*. However, specific details need not be disclosed if their disclosure would hinder the application of the law, would be contrary to the public interest or would harm legitimate business interests or could distort fair competition.
(3) The contracting EU authority shall invite all participants and known potential contractors to present their concerns or make their comments within the standstill period provided under Article IV-19.

IV-19 Standstill period before signature of the contract

(1) The contracting EU authority shall not sign the contract with the successful participant until 14 calendar days have elapsed. This period shall begin to run after the simultaneous dispatch of the notifications to successful and unsuccessful participants.
(2) If necessary, the contracting EU authority may suspend the conclusion of the contract for the purpose of additional examination if this is justified on the grounds of requests or comments made by unsuccessful or aggrieved participants or potential contractors or on the grounds of any other relevant information received.
(3) The non-observance of the standstill period or its expiry has no effect on the time limit mentioned in Article IV-8(3), or on the obligation of the contracting EU authority to render the contract ineffective pursuant to Article IV-8(4) and Article IV-31.

Chapter 3: Execution and Validity of EU Contracts

Section 1: General Provisions

IV-20 Representation of EU authorities and formal requirements for EU contracts

(1) The representation of EU authorities and the question whether a person is able to legally bind an EU authority are solely governed by EU law.
(2) Any provision pertaining to the form of an EU contract which is laid down in an EU legal act is to be understood as a rule limiting the representative power of the person representing the EU authority.

IV-21 Claims of the EU authority in the context of contracts

Procedures which lead to the EU authority's exercise of contractual rights or its claim of invalidity shall be subject to the principles of good administration, in particular those enshrined in the following Articles of Book III:

- Article III-3 – General Duty of Fair Decision-making and impartiality;
- Article III-5 – Initiation;
- Article III-7 – Responsible official;
- Article III-8 – Management of procedures and procedural rights;
- Article III-10 – Principle of investigation;
- Article III-11 – Investigation by request;

- Article III-13 – Duties to cooperate of parties;
- Article III-14 – Privilege against self-incrimination and legal professional privilege;
- Article III-15 – Witnesses and experts;
- Article III-22 – Access to the file;
- Article III-23 – Right to be heard by persons adversely affected;
- Article III-29 – Duty to give reasons;
- Article III-30 – Duty to indicate available remedies;
- Article III-31 – Formal and language requirements;
- Article III-32 – Decisions in electronic form.

IV-22 Decisions of the EU authority on an extra-contractual basis

(1) Neither the terms of an EU contract nor Member State law applicable to such a contract can exclude the exercise of public authority powers on extra-contractual grounds by an EU authority. Such powers may not be misused by the EU authority in its intention to suspend or cease its own contractual obligations. The exercise of public authority powers by EU authorities, which are unrelated to contracts, shall leave unaffected:
- the rights of parties under Article 340(2) TFEU;
- any claim by the contractor on the basis of the contract.

(2) If the powers referred to in paragraph (1) are executed by means of a decision that is enforceable within the meaning of Article 299 TFEU, and if the pecuniary obligation imposed by this decision is also contractually due, the contractual obligation shall be deemed fulfilled if the contractor complies with the decision.

IV-23 Review by the European Ombudsman

(1) The scope of review by the European Ombudsman includes the fulfilment of EU authorities' obligations arising both from Article IV-21 and from EU contracts.

(2) The recommendation issued by the European Ombudsman does not affect the right of the parties to have their contractual dispute examined and authoritatively settled by a court of competent jurisdiction.

(3) A conclusion by the European Ombudsman that his inquiry has revealed an instance of maladministration on the part of the EU authority does not affect the validity of the contract or its terms and clauses, nor the validity of claims pursuant to Article IV-21. The EU authority has to remedy its maladministration by using its contractual powers or by accepting offers from the contracting party to re-negotiate or modify the respective contract, or by means of financial compensation.

IV-24 Arbitration clauses

(1) The validity of an arbitration clause within the meaning of Article 272 TFEU is solely determined by EU law even if the EU contract is governed by Member State law. The clause shall be incorporated into the written contract. If the arbitration clause is not incorporated into the contract, the parties can still conclude it by signing a separate document with reference to the contract. If there is no written arbitration clause whatsoever, it shall be presumed irrefutably that no arbitration clause has been concluded. The written form can be replaced by an electronic form. Article III-32 on decisions in electronic form applies *mutatis mutandis*.

(2) An arbitration clause within the meaning of Article 272 TFEU can be concluded until an application for court proceedings has been submitted.
(3) The EU authority shall agree to annul an arbitration clause within the meaning of Article 272 TFEU upon the request of the contractor:
  (a) if the arbitration clause has not been individually negotiated;
  (b) if the jurisdiction of courts or tribunals of the Member States or a Third State would be more appropriate in view of the law applicable to the contract and the principle of effective legal protection;
  (c) if the request has been made shortly after the contractor became aware of the intention of the EU authority to file an action based on the clause before the Court of Justice of the European Union.

A decision of the EU authority refusing the annulment of an arbitration clause shall give reasons as to why the conditions under b) of the present paragraph were not deemed to be fulfilled.

IV-25 Exclusion of compensation

Compensation as provided for in this chapter is excluded if the contractor

(a) has obtained the award of the contract or a beneficial contractual position through false pretences, threat or bribery;
(b) has obtained the award of the contract or a beneficial contractual position by providing substantially incorrect or incomplete information;
(c) was aware of the illegality of the contract or was unaware thereof due to gross negligence on his part.

Section 2: EU Contracts Governed by EU Law

Subsection 1: Execution and Performance

IV-26 Good faith and fair dealing

(1) The contracting parties have a duty to act in accordance with good faith and fair dealing when performing an obligation, exercising a right to performance, pursuing or disputing a remedy for non-performance, or when exercising a right to terminate an obligation or the contractual relationship.
(2) The duty under paragraph (1) may not be excluded or limited by contract.

IV-27 Contractual rules

(1) The EU authority should ensure that any EU contract solely governed by EU law contains a provision specifying a law of obligations, or specific model rules, applicable on a complementary basis to issues not covered by the rules mentioned in Article IV-4, such as the place and time of performance, remedies for non-performance, refusal of performance, termination, damages and interest, and limitation rules.
(2) In order to guarantee uniformity in the execution of EU contracts, the EU authority should ensure that the provision introduced in paragraph (1) refers to the same law of obligations or model rules in all contracts serving the same purposes.

Subsection 2: Change of Circumstances and Related Clauses

IV-28 Change of circumstances

If the circumstances which determined the content of an EU contract have changed so substantially since the conclusion of the contract that one of the parties cannot reasonably be expected to adhere to the original contractual provisions, this disadvantaged party may request the adaptation of the agreement or, where such an adaptation is not possible or cannot reasonably be expected of the other party, the disadvantaged party may terminate the contract.

IV-29 Termination to avoid grave harm to the common good

(1) The EU authority may also terminate an EU contract in order to avoid or eliminate a risk of grave harm to the common good. The termination shall have no retroactive effect.
(2) Following an application, the EU authority shall compensate any disadvantage suffered by the contractor which resulted from its reliance on the continued existence of the EU contract, provided such reliance deserves protection (legitimate expectation) and only to the extent that such reliance merits protection.

IV-30 Termination for non-performance

(1) Each party may terminate the contract if the other party's non-performance of a contractual obligation is fundamental. A non-performance of a contractual obligation is fundamental:
    (a) if it substantially deprives the creditor of what the creditor was entitled to expect under the contract, as applied to the whole or relevant part of the performance, unless at the time of conclusion of the contract the debtor did not foresee and could not reasonably be expected to have foreseen that result; or
    (b) if it is intentional or reckless and gives the creditor reason to believe that the other party's future performance cannot be relied upon.
(2) Each party may terminate the contract in a case of delay in performance of a contractual obligation which is not in itself fundamental if the party gives a notice fixing an additional period of time of reasonable length for performance and the debtor does not perform within that period. If the period fixed is unreasonably short, termination is possible only after a reasonable period from the time of the notice.
(3) Each party may terminate the contract before performance of a contractual obligation is due if the debtor has declared that there will be a non-performance of the obligation, or it is otherwise clear that there will be such a non-performance, and if the non-performance would have been fundamental.
(4) Each party which reasonably believes that there will be a fundamental non-performance of a contractual obligation by the other party may terminate if it has requested an adequate assurance of due performance and no such assurance has been provided within a reasonable time.
(5) The right to seek damages is not excluded by the termination.

Subsection 3: Consequences of Illegality and Unfair Terms

IV-31 Termination due to an infringement of the provisions of Chapter 2

(1) For the purpose of complying with Article IV-8(4), or if the EU authority becomes aware that the rules on the procedure regarding the conclusion of an EU contract have not been respected to the detriment of a third party, the EU authority may terminate the contract in order to re-open this procedure.
(2) This right of termination does not apply
    (a) if there is no possibility that the infringement has influenced the decision on the matter;

(b) if the contract award decision has become definitive due to the expiration of the time limit for the actions provided under Article IV-8(2);
(c) if the award decision has been confirmed by court;
(d) if the contractor has irreversibly executed his main obligations in whole or in substantial part.

(3) A termination in the sense of paragraph (1) has no retroactive effect.
(4) The EU authority shall compensate the other party for a disadvantage suffered due to its reliance on the existence of the EU contract provided such reliance deserves protection (legitimate expectation) and only to the extent that such reliance merits protection. The contractor cannot request to be treated as if the contract had been fulfilled.

IV-32 Renegotiation due to an infringement of the specific obligations of EU authorities as public authorities

(1) If the content of an EU contract is illegal due to the non-observance of the specific obligations of the EU authority as a public authority, the EU authority may request that the content of the agreement be adapted to restore lawful conditions.
(2) If the content of the contract is illegal because the unobserved rules intended to protect the rights and interests of the other party, then that party may request that the content of the agreement be adapted to restore lawful conditions.
(3) These adaptations may consist *inter alia* in a change of terms and clauses, price adjustments, modifications of the main obligations, or in the cancellation of the agreement with or without compensation.
(4) If the competitive award procedure was applicable to the contract, only a cancellation of the agreement with compensation may be negotiated. A change of terms and clauses is only possible if the modification is not substantial in the sense of Article IV-9(3).

IV-33 Invalidity

An EU contract is invalid

(a) if an equivalent contract between private persons would be considered invalid and thus not binding in accordance with the general principles common to the laws of the Member States;
(b) if a single case decision of the EU authority with equivalent content would be nonexistent.

Each party may request the other party to confirm the invalidity.

IV-34 Unfair terms

EU legislation on unfair terms in consumer contracts shall apply *mutatis mutandis* if the contractor is a consumer within the meaning of this legislation.

Section 3: EU Contracts Governed by Member State Law

IV-35 Applicable law

(1) The conditions for the validity and termination of EU contracts governed by the law of a Member State shall be determined by the respective Member State law.
(2) If an EU contract infringes EU law, this shall not be considered a ground for invalidity or termination of the contract if a similar contract concluded between private parties would be considered valid and binding in accordance with the applicable Member State law.

(3) If the exercise of contractual rights of the EU authority is effective according to the law of the Member State in spite of an infringement of the rules mentioned in Article IV-5(2), this shall not preclude the obligation of the EU authority, which follows from its duties mentioned in Article IV-5(2), to conclude or re-negotiate the contract with the contractor, or to compensate the contractor by other means for the damage he or she suffered because of the illegal decision.

IV-36 Contractual clauses for compliance with EU Law

(1) The exercise of public authority by an EU authority may not give rise to contractual obligations on the part of the contractor. The specific obligations of an EU authority as a public authority may only entail direct consequences for the validity or termination of the contract if they have been made constituent components of that contract. The EU authority shall ensure that an EU contract includes a clause enabling the EU authority to terminate the contract where it is subsequently established that the specific obligations of the EU authority as a public authority have not been complied with.
(2) The validity of the standard terms and clauses described in paragraph (1) is determined in accordance with the Member State law applicable to the contract. These standard terms and clauses should provide adequate protection for the legitimate expectations of the contractor to the extent that his reliance on the continued existence of the contract merits protection.

Chapter 4: Subcontracts

IV-37 Admissibility and scope of subcontracts

(1) The contractor may subcontract the performance of the EU contract in whole or in part without the EU authority's consent, unless personal performance is required under the EU contract. Any subcontractor so engaged must be of adequate competence. The contractor must ensure that any tools and materials used for the performance of the EU contract are in conformity with the EU contract and the applicable laws, and fit to achieve the particular purpose for which they are to be used. The EU Financial Regulations are applicable to the contractor's choice of subcontractors and to the financial accountability of the contractor.
(2) A contract concluded for the performance of an EU contract by the contractor with a subcontractor does not create any direct relationship between the subcontractor and the relevant EU authority in the absence of an explicit provision within the EU contract indicating the scope and consequence of such a relationship.
(3) The contractor remains responsible for performance of the EU contract. Nothing can limit the contractor's liability vis-à-vis the contracting EU authority for the breach of contractual duties caused by a subcontractor.
(4) The EU authority is not liable to third parties for the negligence of a subcontractor.

IV-38 Choice of the law applicable to subcontracts

(1) In the absence of a specific provision on the law applicable to subcontracts, such law shall be determined by the law applicable to the contractor's activities.
(2) Article IV-37(1) remains unaffected.

IV-39 Duties of the EU authorities towards subcontractors

(1) The absence of a direct relationship between an EU authority and a subcontractor, and the limitations that derive thereof for the standing of subcontractors in actions based upon Articles 263, 265 and 340 TFEU, shall not exempt that authority from its duties to apply the principles of good administration, especially those established in Book III under the following articles:
- Article III-3 – General duty of fair decision-making and impartiality;
- Article III-5 – Initiation;
- Article III-7 – Responsible official;
- Article III-8 – Management of procedures and procedural rights;
- Article III-9 – Time limits for concluding procedures;
- Article III-10 – Principle of investigation;
- Article III-11 – Investigation by request;
- Article III-13 – Duties to cooperate of parties;
- Article III-14 – Privilege against self-incrimination and legal professional privilege;
- Article III-15 – Witnesses and experts;
- Article III-22 – Access to the file;
- Article III-23 – Right to be heard by persons adversely affected;
- Article III-29 – Duty to give reasons;
- Article III-30 – Duty to indicate available remedies;
- Article III-31 – Formal and language requirements;
- Article III-32 – Decisions in electronic form.

(2) The EU authority shall ensure that the contractor informs the subcontractor of the applicability of principles of good administration.

(3) A subcontractor shall have the right to know of any criticism by the EU authority which is party to the EU contract regarding his or her performance. The subcontractor shall also have the right to be heard in relation to such criticism. If the EU authority intends to request the replacement of a subcontractor, it shall inform the latter of its intention and give reasons for doing so. The request shall only be made to the contractor after the subcontractor has had an opportunity to present his or her observations.

(4) In order to also protect subcontractors, the EU authority shall check a contractor's financial stability before awarding it an EU contract, and shall continue to do so throughout the term of the contract.

C. Explanations

Chapter 1: General Provisions

IV-1 Scope of application

Paragraph 1(a)

For the definition of EU authority see **Article I-4(5)**. 1

Paragraph 1(b)

This rule on special types of contracts between EU authorities and Member State 2
authorities takes in the criteria developed by the CJEU concerning the application

of EU public procurement law to public-public cooperation.[7] It could also be referred to Article 12(4) Directive 2014/24,[8] which is more detailed in regard to public procurement objectives.

Paragraph 1(c)

3 Contracts between public entities which do not fulfil the criteria of Article IV-1(1)(b) are almost always considered as contracts submitted to a special regime, or they are at least treated in a special way by jurisprudence in Member State law. However, the limited applicability of Book IV does not affect the capacity of the EU authorities to conclude such a contract. Such a contract may lead to modifications in the distribution of competences and areas of responsibility between the EU authority and the Member State's administration only if it is based upon an enabling provision of EU law.

Paragraph 2

4 **Interinstitutional agreements** generally do **not** fall within the scope of Book IV; that is also justified by their 'constitutional' character.[9] This being said, it may be possible that Book IV applies to contracts between the EU Commission and an EU Agency if the Agency acts as a service provider for the Commission.

Paragraph 3

5 As the topic of subcontracting has not been well elaborated in EU law so far, but gives rise to many problems in a very specific field of public contract law, only the rules of Chapter 4 of this book should be applied to subcontracting issues.

Paragraph 4

6 The conclusion and the execution of **international treaties** is a question of public international law and therefore cannot fall within the scope of an Administrative Procedure Act.

IV-2 Definitions

Paragraph 1

7 The definition of **contract** is taken from **Article II-1:101 of the DCFR**[10] which has, however, a slightly different wording: '*A contract is an agreement which is intended*

[7] See e.g. Commission Staff Working Paper, SEC(2011)1169 final concerning the application of EU public procurement law to relations between contracting authorities.

[8] Directive 2014/24/EU of the European Parliament and of the Council of 26 February 2014 on public procurement and repealing Directive 2004/18/EC [2014] OJ L94/65.

[9] See e.g. Art 17(1) Sentence 4 TEU and Art 295 TFEU.

[10] Draft Common Frame of Reference: Principles, Definitions and Model Rules of European Private Law—Draft Common Frame of Reference (DCFR)—Outline Edition, Prepared by the Study Group on a European Civil Code and the Research Group on EC Private Law (Acquis Group), Based in part on a revised version of the Principles of European Contract Law, available at http://ec.europa.eu/justice/policies/civil/docs/dcfr_outline_edition_en.pdf http://ec.europa.eu/justice/contract/files/european-private-law_en.pdf.

to give rise to a binding legal relationship or to have some other legal effect. It is a bilateral or multilateral juridical act.'

Paragraph 4

The definition of general terms of contract is taken from Article 3 Directive 93/13.[11] 8

Paragraph 8

The definition of **specific obligations of EU authorities as public authorities** seeks 9
to **address the specific obligations of administrative authorities** which arise from their status as a public authority subject to special rules that are not applicable to private persons, and which administrative authorities must comply with even when acting like private persons. For example, according to the **ombudsprudence**, EU authorities have to comply with Article 41 CFR even if executing an EU contract submitted under a Member State's private law.

IV-3 Determination of the law applicable to an EU contract

Paragraph 1

Primary law **does not provide for any specific provision on the determination of** 10
the law applicable to an EU contract. However primary law presupposes that there are EU contracts which are solely governed by EU Law and EU contracts which are governed by the law of a Member State (or a third country), see **Article 335** TFEU.

Paragraph 2(c)

A typical contract modifying or abrogating pre-existing EU law relations between 11
the parties would be a **settlement** or **transaction.**

Paragraph 3

(a) **staff contracts in the sense of EU Staff Regulation** refers to Regulation 31 12
(EEC), 11 (EAEC), laying down the Staff Regulations of Officials and the Conditions of Employment of Other Servants of the European Economic Community and the European Atomic Energy Community [1962] OJ 1385 in its up-to-date version. These cover also e.g. temporary staff and other forms of employment as laid down in the aforementioned Regulations.

(b) **grant agreements in the sense of EU Financial Regulations** refers to Article 13
121 Regulation 966/2012 in its up-to-date version.[12]

[11] Council Directive 93/13/EEC of 5 April 1993 on unfair terms in consumer contracts [1993] OJ L95/29 last amended by Directive 2011/83/EU of the European Parliament and of the Council of 25 October 2011 on consumer rights, amending Council Directive 93/13/EEC and Directive 1999/44/EC of the European Parliament and of the Council and repealing Council Directive 85/577/EEC and Directive 97/7/EC of the European Parliament and of the Council [2011] OJ L304/64.

[12] Regulation (EU, Euratom) No 966/2012 of the European Parliament and of the Council of 25 October 2012 on the financial rules applicable to the general budget of the Union and repealing Council Regulation (EC, Euratom) No 1605/2002 [2012] OJ L298/1 last amended by Regulation

14 (c) **grant agreements in the sense of EU Regulations implementing the Framework Programme for Research** refers to Regulation 1290/2013 in its up-to-date version.[13]

Paragraph 4

15 The reference to Regulation 593/2008 on the law applicable to contractual obligations (Rome I)[14] concerns **primarily Article 3 and 4 of this regulation.** Those rules are appropriate to be applied *mutatis mutandis* to EU contracts even when not directly applicable: not all EU contracts may be qualified as contracts in 'civil and commercial matters', but some may be qualified as contracts in 'revenue, customs or administrative matters' in the sense of Article 1(1) of the Rome I Regulation. However, there is **no reason why the criteria set out in the rules of the Rome I Regulation would not be appropriate** to determine the applicable law even in these cases.

Paragraph 5

16 Article 101 of Regulation 966/2012 on the financial rules applicable to the general budget of the Union uses the term **public contracts** in the sense of *marché public* and *öffentlicher Auftrag*. Public contracts are defined as 'contracts for pecuniary interest concluded in writing between one or more economic operators and one or more contracting authorities within the meaning of Articles 117 and 190, in order to obtain, against payment of a price paid in whole or in part from the budget, the supply of movable or immovable assets, the execution of works or the provision of services. Such contracts comprise: (a) building contracts, (b) supply contracts, (c) works contracts, (d) service contracts.'

17 It is general practice to apply the (private) law of a Member State to these EU contracts.

IV-4 Rules applicable to EU contracts solely governed by EU law

18 In practice the **general principles of EU contract law** will be derived (foremost) from **the French law on public contracts,** as it is the country whose system of public contract law is closest to the existing EU rules that apply to EU contracts.

(EU, Euratom) No 547/2014 of the European Parliament and of the Council of 15 May 2014 amending Regulation (EU, Euratom) No 966/2012 on the financial rules applicable to the general budget of the Union [2014] OJ L163/18.

[13] Regulation (EU) 1290/2013 of the European Parliament and of the Council of 11 December 2013 laying down the rules for participation and dissemination in 'Horizon 2020—the Framework Programme for Research and Innovation (2014-2020)' and repealing Regulation (EC) No 1906/2006 [2013] OJ L 347/81.

[14] Regulation (EC) 593/2008 of the European Parliament and of the Council of 17 June 2008 on the law applicable to contractual obligations (Rome I) [2008] OJ L177/6 last amended/corrected by Corrigendum to Regulation (EC) No 593/2008 of the European Parliament and of the Council of 17 June 2008 on the law applicable to contractual obligations (Rome I) (OJ L 177, 4.7.2008) [2009] OJ L309/87.

Chapter 2: Procedures for the Conclusion of Contracts

Section 1: Preparation of General Terms of Contract

IV-6 Procedure for drafting general terms of contract

Paragraph 1

The draft breaks new ground insofar as it renders the elaboration of general terms of contracts, and the necessary adaptations, to the rule-making procedure of Book II. The reason is that in public contract law the elaboration of general terms of contracts may serve as a substitute for administrative rule-making. Particular terms of contracts may be included systematically in all public contracts, because they standardize the content of these contracts, simplify matters for the contracting EU authority, and foster equal treatment of contractors. 19

As general terms of contracts may serve as a substitute for administrative rule-making, the elaboration of general terms of contracts should **be submitted to the rules of Book II** in the same way as proper administrative rule-making to ensure that in the drafting phase the constitutional principles of participatory democracy and transparency, and the principles of EU Administrative law, specifically participation and the obligation to conduct a full and impartial assessment of all relevant facts ('duty of care'), are complied with. 20

A positive secondary effect of the proposed rules may be a **reduction in the variety of models of general terms of contracts** used by different EU authorities and therefore a reduction in complexity thanks to the transparency and the publication of general terms of contract ensured by the application of Book II. The formalities foreseen by Book II may lead an EU authority to apply existing models of general terms of contract rather than inventing new ones. 21

Paragraphs 2 and 3

Paragraphs 2 and 3 take into account the **specific operation and effect of general terms of contracts**. In contrast to proper administrative rules, general terms of contracts do not apply directly but have **to be transposed into a contract in order to be effective**. It is therefore impossible to give retroactive effect to general terms of contract in order to make them also apply to contracts which have been concluded **before** their drafting. In order to ensure that general terms of contract drafted in the regular rule-making procedure are also applicable to contracts that have been previously concluded, it is necessary **to impose an obligation** on the EU authority to include new general terms of contract **by way of a modification of the contract** so as to guarantee equal treatment of the contractors. 22

Paragraph 4

See Article II-9:103 DCFR.[15] 23

[15] Draft Common Frame of Reference: Principles, Definitions and Model Rules of European Private Law—Draft Common Frame of Reference (DCFR)—Outline Edition, prepared by the

Section 2: General Rules on Procedure

IV-7 Applicability of Book III

24 The general rules on procedure are applicable to all EU contracts, including those which can **only be concluded with one specific person.** This is, for example, the case as regards transactions and settlements,[16] and also for all cases in which a contractual relationship exists already and will be changed by a new contract, as is provided under Article IV-6(2) and (3), Article IV-8(4), Article IV-23(3), Article IV-24(3), Article IV-28, Article IV-32.

IV-8 Effects on judicial procedure

Paragraph 3

25 For the time limit see **Article 263(6) TFEU.**

Paragraph 4

26 The provision deals with the **consequences of a successful annulment action on a contract that has already been signed.** According to **Article 266(1) TFEU**, '[t]he institution whose act has been declared void [according to Article 264(1) TFEU] ... shall be required to take the necessary measures to comply with the judgement of the Court of Justice of the European Union'. In the framework of an action for annulment, the CJEU refuses to determine the consequences of the annulment of an act. Thus, the organ that has issued the annulled act has to 'take the necessary measures to comply with the judgement'.[17] Hence, CJEU judgements declaring void acts that preceded the conclusion of contracts are **silent as to the consequences of the illegality of that act** for the contract.[18]

27 In our view, this uncertainty concerning the consequences of illegality means that an institution whose decision to enter into a contract has been declared void **is required to terminate the contract in question.** Inspiration may be found in the case law concerning the violation of European public procurement law by Member State administrations, as established in infringement procedures. The legal consequences of a judgement establishing an infringement under Articles 258–260 TFEU, and those of a judgement declaring void an act of an EU institution under Articles 263–266

Study Group on a European Civil Code and the Research Group on EC Private Law (Acquis Group), Based in part on a revised version of the Principles of European Contract Law, available at http://ec.europa.eu/justice/policies/civil/docs/dcfr_outline_edition_en.pdf.

[16] See Section VII of the introduction.

[17] See e.g. Case 1/54 *French Republic v High Authority* [1954] ECR 1, p 16; Joined Cases 42 and 49/59, *S.N.U.P.A.T.* [1961] ECR 53, p 88; Cases T-114/92, *BEMIM* [1995] ECR II-147, para 33; T-89/07, *VIP Car Solutions SARL v European Parliament* [2009] ECR II-1403, para 112.

[18] In most cases, the claims are admissible but the Court declares them unfounded and does not annul the challenged acts. In the rare cases where such acts are (partially) annulled, the Court does not address the question of the consequences of the annulment for the contract. See e.g. Case T-365/00, *AICS v European Parliament* [2002] ECR II-2719, para 73 f.

TFEU, are the same: the party who has committed a violation of EU law—in the first case, the concerned Member State; in the second case, the institution whose act has been declared void—'shall be required to take the necessary measures to comply with the judgement of the Court' (see Articles 260(1) and 266(1) TFEU).

In infringement procedures, it appears according to the CJEU that a **substantial illegality** committed by a contracting Member State administration in the pre-contractual phase **leads to the illegality of the subsequent contract itself**, because 'the adverse effect on the freedom to provide services arising from the infringement of Directive... must be found to subsist throughout the entire performance of the contracts concluded in breach thereof'.[19] Thus, an infringement consisting of a violation of EU law through the conclusion of a contract by a Member State administration **can be remedied only by providing for the ineffectiveness of the contract in question**, which thus appears to be the 'necessary measure to comply with the judgement' according to Article 260(1) TFEU.[20] Article 73(c) Directive 2014/24 presumes this. **28**

Consequently, the 'necessary measure', under Article 266(1) TFEU, to comply with a judgement declaring void an act of an EU administration that is constitutive of the conclusion of a contract must also consist in providing for the ineffectiveness of the contract in question. Otherwise the violation of EU law subsists as long as the contract remains in force, just as in the case of infringement by a Member State. **29**

Section 3: Competitive Award Procedure

Chapter 2 Section 3 is inspired by the Commission Interpretative Communication on the Community law applicable to contract awards that are not, or not fully, subject to the provisions of the Public Procurement directives (2006/C 179/02—hereafter Commission Communication on contract awards),[21] by Title V of Regulation 966/2012 on the financial rules applicable to the general budget of the Union and by Title V of Regulation 1268/2012.[22] **30**

---

[19] Joined Cases C-20 and C-28/01 *Bockhorn and Braunschweig I* [2003] ECR I-3609, para 36.

[20] Cases C-20 and C-28/01 *Bockhorn and Braunschweig I* [2003] ECR I-3609 paras 21, 31, 40f; Case C-125/03 *Commission v Germany* [2004] ECR I-4771 paras 15f; Case C-126/03 *Commission v Germany* [2004] ECR I-11197 paras 25f; Case C-414/03 *Commission v Germany* paras 10f [not yet reported]; Case C-503/04 *Bockhorn and Braunschweig II* [2007] ECR I-6153 paras 28ff.; Case C-199/07 *Commission v Greece* [2009] ECR I-10669 paras 22f; Case C-536/07 *Commission v Germany* [2009] ECR I-10355 paras 22f; Case C-275/08 *Commission v Germany* [2009] ECR I-168 paras 26 f.

[21] Commission Interpretative Communication on the Community law applicable to contract awards not or not fully subject to the provisions of the Public Procurement directives (2006/C 179/02).

[22] Commission Delegated Regulation (EU) 1268/2012 of 29 October 2012 on the rules of application of Regulation (EU, Euratom) No 966/2012 of the European Parliament and of the Council on the financial rules applicable to the general budget of the Union [2012] OJ L362/1.

IV-9 Scope

Paragraphs 1 and 2

31 Due to existing EU specific legislation the rules of this chapter **will only have a limited scope of application.**

32 **Public procurement** of EU authorities is in general subject to Title V of **Regulation 966/2012** on the financial rules applicable to the general budget of the Union.

33 **Granting of financial aids** in competitive award procedures is in general subject to Title VI of **Regulation 966/2012** on the financial rules applicable to the general budget of the Union.

34 The **selection of contractual agents** is in general subject to the **specific procedure of competition** foreseen in Annex III of Regulation 31 (EEC), 11 (EAEC), laying down the Staff Regulations of Officials and the Conditions of Employment of Other Servants of the European Economic Community and the European Atomic Energy Community [1962] OJ 1385 in its up-to-date version.

35 However, the **sale of assets** by EU authorities and contracts below the thresholds of these special rules may be governed by the competitive award procedure providing a minimum level of protection.

Paragraph 3

36 This paragraph transposes the main principles of **Article 72 Directive 2014/24** to EU Contract law. The more detailed Article 72 may be used as a source of inspiration to flesh out the notion of substantial modification.

37 A **specific difficulty** may arise when EU contracts are modified due to the obligation of the EU-authority to offer or accept modifications of contracts arising from Article IV-6(2) and (3), Article IV-8(4), Article IV-23(3), Article IV-24(3), Article IV-28, Article IV-32, or similar provisions arising from Member State Law. Whereas it is not possible to consider all **transactions** as non-substantial and exempt them from the scope of the competitive award procedure, it should in general be possible to consider **modifications** of a contract as non-substantial, if they are **the consequence of an enforceable right** of one of the parties to a contract modification and if the **modification does not exceed the 'frame' of this right**.

IV-10 General principles

Paragraph 1

38 For the compatibility of the award procedure with the rules and principles of the Treaties, especially the **principles of transparency, equal treatment and proportionality**, see also Article 102 **Regulation 966/2012.**

Paragraph 2

This paragraph contains an **experimental clause** for the development of new forms of competitive award procedures. **39**

IV-11 Prior advertising

On prior advertising see 2.1. of the Commission Communication on contract awards (2006/C 179/02). **40**

IV-12 Content of the advertisement and the contract documents

On the content of the advertisement, see 2.1.3. of the Commission Communication on contract awards (2006/C 179/02). **41**

IV-13 Cases justifying use of the negotiated procedure without prior advertisement

For cases without prior publication of the advertisement, see 2.1.4. of the Commission Communication on contract awards (2006/C 179/02). **42**

IV-14 Equal access for economic operators from all Member States

For equal access, see 2.2.1. of the Commission Communication on contract awards (2006/C 179/02). **43**

IV-15 Limit on the number of participants invited to submit a tender

For the limit on the number of applicants invited to submit an offer, see 2.2.2. of the Commission Communication on contract awards (2006/C 179/02). **44**

IV-17 Contracts of low value

Paragraph 1

The threshold established by the Commission for the implementation of the EU Financial Regulations is laid down in Commission Delegated Regulation (EU) 1268/2012 in its up-to-date version. **45**

IV-18 Contract award decision

For the award decision see Article 113 Regulation 966/2012. **46**

IV-19 Standstill period before signature of the contract

Paragraph 1

For the standstill period, see Article 118 Regulation 966/2012, for the starting of the period see Article 171 Regulation 1268/2012. **47**

Paragraph 3

48 Due to the mandatory character of Article 263(6) TFEU, it is impossible to modify the time limit for judicial action in order to coordinate it with the standstill period.

Chapter 3: Execution and Validity of EU Contracts

Section 1: General Provisions

IV-20 Representation of EU authorities and formal requirements of EU contracts

Paragraph 2

49 This **rule reflects the German way of dealing with formal requirements** provided for in the law of the *Länder* (federated states) concerning public contracts governed by private law concluded by the administration of the relevant *Land* (one of the federated states). These rules are regarded as rules limiting the representative power of the person representing the *Land* authority, because the *Land* has no legislative power to impose additional formal requirements for contracts governed by (federal) private law.

IV-21 Claims of the EU authority in the context of contracts

50 This article makes clear that all decisions of the EU authority taken in the course of executing the contract shall be subject to administrative procedure rules and the principle of good administration. If the judgement of the GC in T-116/11[23] paragraph 245 were to be understood as meaning that the principle of good administration is not applicable due to the contractual status between private parties and the EU authority—which means substantively excluded—we would not agree with this position.[24] Our view is also not in line with the so-called ombudsprudence.[25] We assume that the aforementioned judgement is limited to the restricted types of claims in the CJEU court proceedings and that despite this judicial statement Article 41 CFR is applicable.

51 However, the contractor **cannot institute proceedings in the sense of Article 263 TFEU** against the decision mentioned in Article IV-21. The rules concerning the definitive character of acts not challenged within the time limit foreseen in Article 263 TFEU **do not apply to those decisions.** Therefore this article shall not affect the right of the parties to have their contractual dispute arising from the decision examined and authoritatively settled by a court of competent jurisdiction.

---

[23] Case T-116/11 *EMA v European Commission* [not yet published].

[24] See also Case F-1/05 *Landgren v ETF* [2007] I-A-1–00123, II-A-1–00459 paras 70 ff; confirmed by Case T-404/06 P [2009] ECR II-2841 para 148.

[25] For ombudsprudence in the field of contracts see e.g.: European Ombudsman, *Annual Report 2012*, p. 46 ff.

IV-22 Decisions of the EU authority with extra-contractual basis

This article deals with problems arising from the **unclear jurisprudence of the CJEU** concerning the relationship between contractual litigation and the enforcement of decisions of an EU authority following Article 299 TFEU.[26] The article is **premised on the assumption that** the contractor may not challenge the legality of decisions in the sense of this article on the basis of the contract. That being said, the **definitive character of such decisions does not block a claim** by the contractor **on the basis of the contract**: the respective pecuniary obligations under the contract remain unaffected. **52**

IV-23 Review by the European Ombudsman

The **article** transposes **the practice of the EO** concerning the execution of EU contracts[27] and develops it further. **53**

IV-24 Arbitration clauses

Background of the article

Article IV-24 is meant to deal with **some particularities of EU contract litigation between the parties to the EU contract.** The rules on the competent **courts** for this kind of litigation are not coordinated with the law applicable to the contract. **54**

The **CJEU** is competent as a venue for litigation between the parties of an EU contract only if an **arbitration clause within the meaning of Article 272 TFEU** has been concluded.[28] If an arbitration clause in the sense of Article 272 TFEU has been included in an EU contract governed by the law of a Member State, the CJEU is **not limited to reviewing manifest errors of interpretation of the Member State's law** by the contracting parties, **but shall apply Member State's law as it is understood by the Member State's courts.** However, the CJEU should as far as possible **avoid applying national rules without taking cognisance of the jurisprudence of national courts on these rules.**[29] **55**

[26] See Case C-334/97 R-EX *Commission v Comune di Montorio al Vomano* [2001] ECR I-4229; Case T-220/10 *Commission v EU Research Projects Ltd.* [not yet published]; Case T-260/04 *Centro di educazione sanitaria e tecnologie appropriate sanitarie (Cestas) v Commission* [2008] ECR II-701; Case T-224/09 *Centre d'étude et de valorisation des algues SA (CEVA) v Commission* [2001] ECR II-277.

[27] See e.g. European Ombudsman, *Annual Report 2012*, p 46 ff.

[28] Article 272 TFEU: 'The Court of Justice of the European Union shall have jurisdiction to give judgment pursuant to any arbitration clause contained in a contract concluded by or on behalf of the Union, whether that contract be governed by public or private law.'

[29] See for examples the 'handling' of national law in **Belgium** *inter alia* Case 318/81 *Commission v Co. De. Mi.Spa* [1985] ECR 3693 paras 18f; Case 249/87 *Mulfinger et al. v Commission* [1989] ECR 4127 paras 2f; Case C-42/94 *Heidemij Advies BV v European Parliament* [1995] ECR I-1417 paras 16f; for **German law** *inter alia* Case C-209/90 *Commission v Feilhauer* [1992] ECR I-2613 paras 16f; Case C-156/97 *Commission v Van Balkom Non-Ferro Scheiding BV* [2000] ECR I-1095 paras 10f; Case C-77/99 *Commission v Oder-Plan-Architektur GmbH et al.* [2001] ECR I-7355 para 4; for **French law** *inter alia* Case C-172/97 *SIVU v Commission* [1999] ECR I-3363 para 5; for

56 If **no arbitration clause in the sense of Article 272 TFEU** has been concluded, the courts or tribunals of the Member States are competent in accordance with Article 274 TFEU. To determine the jurisdiction of the Member State's courts, the relevant **rules of the Member State's law and the relevant EU regulations** on jurisdiction in legal disputes of a civil or commercial nature between individuals resident in different Member States[30] **apply, as far as the EU contract falls into their scope.** Where Member State's courts have jurisdiction this will extend to the validity and interpretation of EU contracts. Article 267(1)(b) TFEU is **only applicable** in determining whether decisions leading to the conclusion of an EU contract were in conformity with the relevant EU law rules.

57 Article IV-24 has to be understood in this context. It deals with arbitration clauses within the meaning of Article 272 TFEU.

Paragraph 1

58 The **jurisdiction of the CJEU** based on Article 272 TFEU **is independent of national provisions conflicting with Article 272 TFEU.** Even if substantive national law is applicable and national law conflicts with the jurisdiction of the CJEU, the jurisdiction nevertheless is given to the CJEU, if such a clause has been agreed on in the contract. According to the CJEU:

> This objection of lack of jurisdiction cannot be upheld. While, under an arbitration clause entered into pursuant to Article 181 of the EEC Treaty [now: 272 TFEU], the Court may be called on to decide a dispute on the basis of the national law governing the contract, its jurisdiction to determine a dispute concerning that contract falls to be determined solely with regard to Article 181 of the EEC Treaty and the terms of the arbitration clause, and this cannot be affected by provisions of national law which allegedly exclude its jurisdiction.[31]

59 The **validity of an arbitration clause** is determined by Union law and by Union law only. According to the CJEU:

> Article 38(6) of the rules of procedures stipulates that any application submitted under Article 153 of the Euratom Treaty [now: 272 TFEU] shall be accompanied by

Italian law *inter alia* Case 23/76 *Pellegrini v Commission* [1976] ECR 1807 paras 17ff; Case 109/81 *Porta v Commission* [1982] ECR 2469 para 11; Case C-299/93 *Bauer v Commission* [1995] ECR I-839 paras 11ff; Case C-334/97 *Commission v Comune di Montiorio al Vomano* [1999] ECR I-3387 para 6.

[30] Council Regulation (EC) No 44/2001 of 22 December 2000 on jurisdiction and the recognition and enforcement of judgments in civil and commercial matters [2001] OJ L012/1 last amended by Commission Regulation (EU) No 566/2013 of 18 June 2013 amending Annex I to Council Regulation (EC) No 44/2001 on jurisdiction and the recognition and enforcement of judgments in civil and commercial matters [2013] OJ L167/29.

[31] Case C-209/90 *Commission v Feilhauer* [1992] ECR I-2613 para 13. For further jurisprudence, see Case C-299/93 *Bauer v Commission* [1995] ECR I-839 para 11; Case T-271/04 *Citymo SA v Commission* [2007] ECR I-01375 para 55.

a copy of the arbitration clause. Since these requirements have been fulfilled in this instance by the production of the contractual documents, consisting in the 'Draft Agreement' and the correspondence referring thereto, the bringing of the matter before the Court of Justice under Article 153 is valid.[32]

For **reasons of legal certainty**, the arbitration clause has to be concluded **in written form**. Although this might conflict with some case law of the CJEU—it has been acknowledged[33] that if both parties appeal to the CJEU, this could be sufficient even without a written clause—the policy of the proposed rule is to **protect the contractor**. It **should not be possible for the European Commission to sue a contractor before the CJEU without a written document** that establishes the jurisdiction of the CJEU. This is to avoid the implication that a mere response to the CJEU by the contractor as a consequence of a claim by the European Commission leads to an implied arbitration agreement, which was maybe not intended. The requirement of a **written** arbitration clause **is also fulfilled by another separate document** that contains a written arbitration clause **and which refers to the contract.**[34] 60

Paragraph 2

The arbitration clause can be concluded **later than the contract itself**, and before the initiation of court proceedings.[35] 61

Paragraph 3

Paragraph 3 is included to **harmonize jurisdiction with the applicable law**. EU authorities seem sometimes to include arbitration clauses in EU contracts even if giving jurisdiction to the CJEU seems inappropriate due to the nature of the contract, of the applicable law, and of the sometimes more effective Member State judicial system that would apply due to Article 274 TFEU if there were no arbitration clause. **In these cases it should be possible to avoid such problems by cancelling the arbitration clause.** 62

IV-25 Exclusion of compensation

This general clause is **designed to avoid repetitions** in Article IV-29(2), Article IV-31(4), Article IV-32(3) and Article IV-36(2). It is **inspired by § 48(2) of the German APA.**[36] 63

[32] Case 23/76 *Pellegrini v Commission* [1976] ECR 1807 para 10.

[33] With regard to Case T-180/95 *Nutria AE v Commission* [1997] ECR II-01317 para 38 and Case T-44/96 *Oleifici Italiani SpA v Commission* [1997] ECR II-01331 para 37.

[34] Compare Case 318/81 *Commission v Co. De. Mi. Spa* [1985] ECR 3693 paras 9 ff.

[35] Compare Case 109/81 *Teresita Pace, née Porta v Commission* [1982] ECR 2469 para 10.

[36] Verwaltungsverfahrensgesetz in der Fassung der Bekanntmachung vom 23. Januar 2003 (BGBl. I S. 102), das zuletzt durch Artikel 3 des Gesetzes vom 25. Juli 2013 (BGBl. I S. 2749) geändert worden ist.

Section 2: EU Contracts Governed by EU Law

Subsection 1: Execution and Performance

IV-27 Contractual rules

64 According to Article IV-27(2) clauses should make clear:

a) if the clause refers to the common contract law of the relevant Member State,

or

b) if the EU authority may avail itself of the specific privileges granted to public authorities in the contractual law of the relevant Member State,

or

c) if the contract should be treated like a contract governed by public law of the relevant Member State.

65 Instead of referring to the law of a Member State, the contract may refer to the DCFR,[37] to Unidroit rules[38] or to other qualified model codes.

Subsection 2: Change of Circumstances and Related Clauses

IV-28 Change of circumstances

66 For changes of circumstances see: **§ 60 of the German APA.**[39] **Article III-1:110** of the **DCFR**[40] provides for the following solution concerning private law contracts:

> III.—1:110: Variation or termination by court on a change of circumstances
>
> (1) An obligation must be performed even if performance has become more onerous, whether because the cost of performance has increased or because the value of what is to be received in return has diminished.

---

[37] Draft Common Frame of Reference: Principles, Definitions and Model Rules of European Private Law—Draft Common Frame of Reference (DCFR)—Outline Edition, Prepared by the Study Group on a European Civil Code and the Research Group on EC Private Law (Acquis Group), Based in part on a revised version of the Principles of European Contract Law, available at http://ec.europa.eu/justice/policies/civil/docs/dcfr_outline_edition_en.pdf.

[38] International Institute for the Unification of Private Law (UNIDROIT): UNIDROIT Principles of International Commercial Contracts, http://www.unidroit.org/instruments/commercial-contracts/unidroit-principles-2010.

[39] Verwaltungsverfahrensgesetz in der Fassung der Bekanntmachung vom 23. Januar 2003 (BGBl. I S. 102), das zuletzt durch Artikel 3 des Gesetzes vom 25. Juli 2013 (BGBl. I S. 2749) geändert worden ist

[40] Draft Common Frame of Reference: Principles, Definitions and Model Rules of European Private Law—Draft Common Frame of Reference (DCFR)—Outline Edition, Prepared by the Study Group on a European Civil Code and the Research Group on EC Private Law (Acquis Group), Based in part on a revised version of the Principles of European Contract Law, available at http://ec.europa.eu/justice/policies/civil/docs/dcfr_outline_edition_en.pdf.

(2) If, however, performance of a contractual obligation or of an obligation arising from a unilateral juridical act becomes so onerous because of an exceptional change of circumstances that it would be manifestly unjust to hold the debtor to the obligation a court may:
   (a) vary the obligation in order to make it reasonable and equitable in the new circumstances; or
   (b) terminate the obligation at a date and on terms to be determined by the court.

(3) Paragraph (2) applies only if:
   (a) the change of circumstances occurred after the time when the obligation was incurred;
   (b) the debtor did not at that time take into account, and could not reasonably be expected to have taken into account, the possibility or scale of that change of circumstances;
   (c) the debtor did not assume, and cannot reasonably be regarded as having assumed, the risk of that change of circumstances; and
   (d) the debtor has attempted, reasonably and in good faith, to achieve by negotiation a reasonable and equitable adjustment of the terms regulating the obligation.

In comparison with the solution of Article III-1:110 of the DCFR,[41] the solution proposed in this article seems better adapted to EU contracts, above all because it avoids the necessity of a court action. **67**

IV-29 Termination to avoid grave harm for the common good

This article is inspired by **§ 60 of the German APA.**[42] The reasons for termination must be **very limited** i.e. only in cases where adherence to the contract would be **absolutely intolerable.** In Germany, this clause is therefore considered to be a 'fear clause' (*Angstklausel*) or 'emergency valve' (*Notventil*) and there are to our knowledge no actual cases of application of this clause. **68**

IV-30 Termination for non-performance

The article **takes over Article III-3:502 to Article III-3:505** of the **DCFR**[43] and reveals the difficulties and problems of the divide of procedural rules and substantive provisions. It reveals, moreover, the difficulties of defining substantive provisions and therefore underlines **the decision of the working group on contracts not to** **69**

---

[41] Draft Common Frame of Reference: Principles, Definitions and Model Rules of European Private Law—Draft Common Frame of Reference (DCFR)—Outline Edition, Prepared by the Study Group on a European Civil Code and the Research Group on EC Private Law (Acquis Group), Based in part on a revised version of the Principles of European Contract Law, available at http://ec.europa.eu/justice/policies/civil/docs/dcfr_outline_edition_en.pdf.

[42] Verwaltungsverfahrensgesetz in der Fassung der Bekanntmachung vom 23. Januar 2003 (BGBl. I S. 102), das zuletzt durch Artikel 3 des Gesetzes vom 25. Juli 2013 (BGBl. I S. 2749) geändert worden ist.

[43] Draft Common Frame of Reference: Principles, Definitions and Model Rules of European Private Law—Draft Common Frame of Reference (DCFR)—Outline Edition, Prepared by the Study Group on a European Civil Code and the Research Group on EC Private Law (Acquis Group), Based in part on a revised version of the Principles of European Contract Law, available at http://ec.europa.eu/justice/policies/civil/docs/dcfr_outline_edition_en.pdf.

define a new substantive law on EU contracts, but to stick to the rules necessary for the administrative procedure for the conclusion and execution of EU contracts.

Subsection 3: Consequences of Illegality and Unfair Terms

IV-31 Termination due to an infringement of the provisions of Chapter 2

70 This provision reflects what can be considered as common sense among scholars and is oriented towards Article 2d Directive 89/665[44] and Article 73 Directive 2014/24.

IV-32 Renegotiation due to an infringement of the specific obligations of EU authorities as a public authority

IV-33 Invalidity

71 We are aware of the fact that this rule **is not common in the Member States' Administrative law systems.** However, the problem is that there is **actually no convincing common standard** for the solution of infringements of the specific obligations of EU authorities. There is moreover **little discussion about such a rule among scholars** and in many Administrative law systems the questions of illegality of a public contract is not decisive, as there are several quite simple ways to terminate a public contract. Often, as in **France**, a substantively illegal public contract is seen as coincidentally invalid, whereas illegality is only granted if the contract contradicts certain legal provisions on formalities of public contracts or certain strict legal prohibitions. These cases are therefore **very rare in actual contracting** with the consequence that a specific common national standard cannot be identified. Moreover, there is to our knowledge **no jurisprudence of the CJEU or of the ECHR** on this issue. The **principle of legality of administration does not provide a solution to the legal consequences of such infringements.**

72 For **direct execution by EU authorities,** the following appears to represent **current practice:** only if the contract is solely subject to EU law do the infringement rules of EU law apply to the contract. Our position is basically that if there is no secondary legislation the consequences of infringements should be borrowed from the French system (comments on Article IV-4). That would mean that a substantively illegal public contract is invalid, but invalidity can only be asserted if a court has declared invalidity. However, transposing this solution to EU contracts would require the existence of a type of remedy with the CJEU resembling the French *plein contentieux*—where both annulment and damages or other claims may be

[44] Council Directive 89/665/EEC of 21 December 1989 on the coordination of the laws, regulations and administrative provisions relating to the application of review procedures to the award of public supply and public works contracts [1989] OJ L395/33 last amended by Directive 2014/23/EU of the European Parliament and of the Council of 26 February 2014 on the award of concession contracts [2014] OJ L94/1.

presented in the same proceeding. But such a comparable concept does not exist in EU law so far. Thus another solution had to be found.

The rule has been drafted in this manner for the preceding reason. The rule **seeks to uphold the contract by giving the possibility of action back to the parties of the contract**, which is the basic idea of contracts. It is then for the parties to make an initial decision about the future of the contract. The idea behind the **suggestion of a renegotiation** is that **each party can only refer to its protected rights,** which have been violated when renegotiating, but **not to the rights of the other party.** For instance, the EU authority cannot call for invalidity because of the violation of rights of the contractor in the procedure, if the contractor has no problem with the violation and does not want any further changes. This idea is based upon the assumption that the contractor may anyway renounce its right. Therefore, the parties should have the opportunity to renegotiate the contract and **hence uphold the contract in substance with the renegotiated changes.** Thus, the solution given here **does not lead automatically to invalidity** because of infringements of obligations while contracting, but it provides the possibility of settlement by facilitating the conclusion of a new contract based on the earlier one. In addition, this provision **attempts to adapt the rules on infringement of single-case decisions, and the possible legal consequences, to the needs of contracts.** The all-or-nothing principle is not sufficient in such cases. 73

As a result, one can state clear rules of invalidity without a judgement of the court as a prerequisite (as mandatory in the French model). **Only in very distinctive and restricted cases** does an infringement lead automatically to the **invalidity** of a contract. In other instances the renegotiation procedure applies. 74

IV-34 Unfair terms

If the contractor acts as a consumer, see **Directive 93/13**[45] in its up to date version. 75

Section 3: EU Contracts Governed by Member State Law

IV-35 Applicable law

Paragraph 3

This paragraph safeguards the duty of EU authorities to observe special (fundamental) rights of the contractor deriving from legal sources mentioned in Article IV-5(2). Even if the EU authority can exercise its contractual rights towards the contractor, although rights of the contractor deriving from legal sources mentioned 76

[45] Council Directive (EEC) 93/13 of 5 April 1993 on unfair terms in consumer contracts [1993] OJ L95/29 last amended by Directive 2011/83/EU of the European Parliament and of the Council of 25 October 2011 on consumer rights, amending Council Directive 93/13/EEC and Directive 1999/44/EC of the European Parliament and of the Council and repealing Council Directive 85/577/EEC and Directive 97/7/EC of the European Parliament and of the Council [2011] OJ L304/64.

in Article IV-5(2) have been infringed, this national validity cannot spare the EU authority from the consequences of disregard of the laws mentioned in Article IV-5(2). As a consequence of this disregard, a new contract has to be concluded, or re-negotiation has to take place, or compensation for damages has to paid.

Chapter 4: Subcontracts

77 Subcontractors are **third parties who are in a particularly weak position** for two reasons. **First**, when a number of activities for the performance of a contract have to be performed by different persons, it is advisable, especially for sound financial management, for an EU authority to delegate the burden of managing those persons to a sole contractor, who in turn will establish the necessary subcontracts. Having delegated that burden, EU authorities usually consider that nothing in the relationship between a contractor and its subcontractors is their concern.

78 **Second, there are difficulties concerning judicial review.** Decisions taken by an EU authority in the implementation of a contract are not considered by the EU courts to be decisions in the sense of Article 263 TFEU. While contractors can have such decisions reviewed by the judge of the contract, which may be an EU court, or a Member State's court, or other court, **subcontractors have no standing to bring an action for annulment, or an action for failure to act under Article 265 against the EU authority.** In turn, the judge of the subcontract, (which is normally not an EU Court), cannot review the decisions made by the EU authority in the implementation of the EU contract, as these are not formally addressed to the subcontractor, as is clear from the limited case law of the GC on actions introduced by subcontractors.

79 A number of subcontractors have made complaints to the EO, who has developed an **ombudsprudence** on the applicability of the principles of good administration to the actions, or to the inaction, of EU authorities that have implications for subcontractors.

80 The proposed model rules **do not change the CJEU case law on standing of subcontractors**, since this would not be compatible with the wording of the relevant Treaty articles. The rules aim at clarifying and systematizing what has emerged from the relevant ombudsprudence, in order to apply it in the context of subcontracts.

IV-37 Admissibility and scope of subcontracts

Paragraph 1

81 The wording of paragraph 1 is **partly based on** the DCFR[46], Articles IV. C.—2:104: Subcontractors, tools and materials and IV. D.—3:302: Subcontracting. The word-

[46] Draft Common Frame of Reference: Principles, Definitions and Model Rules of European Private Law—Draft Common Frame of Reference (DCFR)—Outline Edition, Prepared by the

ing takes also into account the relevant provisions of the **EU Financial Regulations:** Article 161 Regulation 966/2012.

The rest of the article is mainly intended to clarify the consequences of paragraph 1. 82

IV-38 Choice of the law applicable to subcontracts

This article is mainly intended to clarify a situation in a way that is logical in terms 83
of contract law.

IV-39 Duties of the EU authorities towards subcontractors

Paragraph 1

This is the main provision of the model rules on subcontracts. The wording of para- 84
graph 1 fleshes out **the meaning of the principles of good administration as applied to subcontracts**. The references to Book III are—despite one exception—the same as those in Article IV-21 (Claims of the EU authority in the context of contracts).

Paragraphs 2 and 3

The wording of paragraphs 2 and 3 is trying to summarize a part of the relevant 85
recommendations of the EO. Paragraph 3 appears to be particularly relevant in view of the following EO cases: 53/2009/MF, paragraph 52, EO 2449/2007/VIK, paragraphs 73–75 and 2610/2009/(BU)MF, paragraph 35.

Paragraph 4

The wording of paragraph 4 is taken from a **recommendation of the EO in case** 86
1811/2009/(BB) FOR, paragraph 21, where it seemed that the Commission had neglected to verify the financial stability of a contractor and had refused to take over claims of subcontractors against the latter after the contractor went bankrupt.

Study Group on a European Civil Code and the Research Group on EC Private Law (Acquis Group), Based in part on a revised version of the Principles of European Contract Law, available at http://ec.europa.eu/justice/policies/civil/docs/dcfr_outline_edition_en.pdf.

BOOK V—MUTUAL ASSISTANCE

A. Introduction to Book V

I. The Concept of Mutual Assistance in the ReNEUAL Model Rules

1 This book understands mutual assistance as **a basic form of support between authorities in the exercise of administrative tasks** within the scope of EU law. Mutual assistance consists of an authority requesting administrative support from another authority that is located in a different EU jurisdiction. Such mutual assistance rests on a number of central elements which find their expression in Article V-2:

- the requesting authority cannot fulfil one of its tasks by itself;
- the requested authority from another Member State or the EU is in a position to give the requesting authority what is necessary for it to fulfil its task;
- the assistance requested can take various forms: the transmission of information, the conduct of an inspection, or the service of a document.

2 Thereby, as becomes apparent in Article V-1, mutual assistance **applies to requests for assistance between Member State authorities as well as between a Member State and an EU authority**, so long as these requests are within the scope of EU law.

II. Scope of Book V

The rules of Book V provide a minimum standard for mutual assistance **where EU law triggers a need for cooperation between two authorities.** Book V of the ReNEUAL Model Rules establishes mutual assistance between public authorities as a generally applicable default obligation. It is directly applicable to all fields of EU law as long as no more advanced forms of inter-administrative cooperation, such as those for information exchange established in Book VI, are applicable. While Book VI establishes a framework for information management activities which is supplemented by a basic act for the respective activity, the default rules of Book V are not dependent on such a combination. 3

The **need for such assistance** primarily arises out of the principle of the territorial reach of public authority, which hinders the requesting authority from completing the task itself. Therefore, assistance can either occur horizontally (between two administrative authorities from different Member States), or vertically (between the public authority of a Member State and another belonging to the EU). Against this background, Book V covers not only mutual assistance between EU authorities, but also between authorities from different Member States, or between authorities on the EU as well as on the national level. This comprehensive approach is justified by the fact that the variety of applicable legal rules transforms mutual assistance into an (unnecessarily) complex part of European Administrative law.[1] Although theoretically it would also have been possible to create two specific sets of minimum standards, one for horizontal and one for vertical assistance, this would have had the disadvantage of further complicating an already complex and little explored area of EU procedural law. 4

One of the main advantages of the concept proposed in Book V is its **ability to encompass not only simple forms of exchange of information, but also to be applicable to more complex forms of cooperation,** such as conducting inspections or the service of documents. Book V on mutual assistance is more far-reaching than Book VI which is confined to information cooperation. In so far as both Books V and VI cover exchange of information, they reflect different levels of administrative integration. The conventional forms of mutual assistance covered in Book V represent the lowest degree of informational integration. By contrast, the focus of Book VI is the resolution of some of the challenges created by more integrated structures of information exchange, *inter alia* structured information mechanisms.[2] This approach in Book V enables the creation of minimum standards across different sectors and for different types of administrative actions. 5

---

[1] See paras 11–13 of the introduction to Book V.

[2] See Book VI, Chapter 2.

6 The strict **distinction** between **mutual assistance addressed in Book V**, and **forms of information exchange in Book VI**, prevents the application of the rules of Book V to the more sophisticated forms of cooperation to which they are (at best) ill-suited. An example of this is the cooperative exchange of information under the Internal Market Information System (IMI), which functions through the use of pre-defined (and pre-translated) workflows. While the IMI seeks to facilitate what it refers to as 'mutual assistance',[3] it does so by means of a structured information system which poses distinct challenges. A one-size-fits-all rule cannot adequately cover both a system such as the IMI as well as the most basic form of assistance that one authority can provide another. By clearly distinguishing the two, this danger is avoided while all forms of information exchange are still covered by the model rules. As a result of this approach, the concept of mutual assistance adopted in Book V does not cover some of the instances EU law refers to as 'mutual assistance',[4] including the above-mentioned mechanism in the IMI. Instead such forms of cooperation fall within the scope of Book VI. This also means that the inherent challenges in such more advanced forms of information exchange that are evolving towards the creation of administrative networks, including, *inter alia*, rules on coordinated supervision or technical interoperability,[5] are also situated in Book VI.

7 The **focus** in Book V **on a more 'classical' concept** of mutual assistance **has a number of consequences.** Generally, the assistance rendered is supplementary. It is distinct from a 'delegation', by which an authority entrusts another authority with a task which would otherwise form part of its normal obligations, in its entirety. This supplementary function of mutual assistance affects the grounds on which an authority may refuse a request. Moreover, requests for mutual assistance operate without the safeguards necessary in information networks; hence they should not be used to create such ad-hoc information networks. Nor should requests be so excessive as to overburden the administrative authorities either of a Member State or of the EU. The principle of proportionality, which applies to requests for and acts of mutual assistance, serves as a safeguard against potentially excessive burdens.

[3] Regulation (EU) 1024/2012 of the European Parliament and of the Council of 25 October 2012 on administrative cooperation through the Internal Market Information System and repealing Commission Decision 2008/49/EC ('the IMI Regulation') [2012] OJ L316/1 last amended by Directive 2014/67/EU of the European Parliament and of the Council of 15 May 2014 on the enforcement of Directive 96/71/EC concerning the posting of workers in the framework of the provision of services and amending Regulation (EU) No 1024/2012 on administrative cooperation through the Internal Market Information System ('the IMI Regulation') [2014] OJ L 159/11, Recital (2).

[4] This is also the case for some forms of cooperation which are categorized as mutual assistance in European Parliament legislative resolution of 12 March 2014 on the proposal for a regulation of the European Parliament and of the Council on the protection of individuals with regard to the processing of personal data and on the free movement of such data (General Data Protection Regulation) P7_TA(2014)0212, Art 55(1), namely: requests to carry out 'prior authorization' and the duty of 'prompt information on the opening of cases and ensuing developments'.

[5] See Book VI, para 20, Explanations.

Book V has a **narrow scope of applicability** in that its rules apply to mutual assistance in the procedural phase leading up to and preparing administrative action and especially administrative decisions. Book V is not applicable to judicial and enforcement assistance. The latter is generally left to *lex specialis* and not covered in this Book. However, Article III-18(5) regulates enforcement assistance for inspections which are conducted within a single-case decision-making procedure. Judicial assistance between courts is likewise distinct from administrative mutual assistance and thus not included. 8

As a result, informational mutual assistance is the **main focus of this book for several reasons.** First, information is the basis underlying any administrative decision. Without information a public authority cannot take any necessary steps. Second, given that administrative authorities are under an obligation to collect all information and facts relevant to a decision in a careful and impartial manner, rules on informational mutual assistance become essential in the indirect implementation of EU law. Third, provisions on the exchange of information constitute a large part of European mutual assistance provisions. Therefore the creation of common minimum standards for mutual assistance is a good place to start. Fourth, in light of the frequent use of informational mutual assistance just mentioned, it is essential that concerns about protection of individual rights (both procedural and substantive) including data protection rights are not treated as secondary in a quest for increasing administrative efficiency. Despite its inter-administrative focus, Book V therefore creates a number of safeguards for the protection of information and personal data, most notably in Articles V-4(3) and V-5. 9

The **dividing line between Book III and Book V** is that Book III deals solely with Member State enforcement assistance in the case of EU inspections, the participation of EU authorities in Member State inspections which are of shared interest, and joint inspections of different Member State authorities. By contrast, Book V deals with horizontal as well as vertical requests to conduct an inspection for another authority. In these cases the requested Member State authority undertakes the inspection not in its own interest, but as a task in addition to its own obligations. 10

III. Justification for Covering Mutual Assistance in the ReNEUAL Model Rules

The **inclusion of rules on mutual assistance** within the project is not only useful, but in fact **necessary**. Today, no general piece of legislation exists which provides a clear procedure for cross-border or multi-level mutual assistance. Instead, EU and Member State Authorities rely either on sector-specific rules, which exist in a limited number of cases, or on conventions of the Council of Europe. The obligation to adhere to the principle of sincere cooperation pursuant to Article 4(3) TEU may positively influence the interpretation of sector-specific rules on mutual assistance, but it is not enough to deduce concrete obligations for mutual assistance. 11

12 Mutual assistance constitutes an important part of European Administrative law. At present, **diverse concepts of mutual assistance exist** in academic literature as well as in sector-specific EU law. The respective rules in sector-specific law are also quite diverse. Some sector-specific instruments simply establish an obligation to provide mutual assistance by means of a general reference, without further specifying the duties subsumed under this concept.[6] By contrast, the IMI seeks to facilitate the realization of 'mutual assistance' obligations (which are not defined further) by means of a structured information mechanism.[7] It operationalizes Directive 2006/123, which in turn does not clearly define mutual assistance but simply uses the term, apparently on the assumption that its meaning is obvious.[8] Directive 2006/123 is one of the legislative acts which provide a set of rules which are subsumed under the more general heading of 'mutual assistance'.[9] More generally speaking, the same legal phenomenon is sometimes referred to as mutual assistance and sometimes as administrative cooperation; sometimes the former is subsumed under the latter.[10]

[6] By means of a general reference without further specifying the duties subsumed under mutual assistance. See for example the Commission Regulation (EEC) 2454/93 of 2 July 1993 laying down provisions for the implementation of Council Regulation (EEC) 2913/92 establishing the Community Customs Code [1993] OJ L253/1 last amended by Commission Implementing Regulation (EU) 1099/2013 of 5 November 2013 amending Regulation (EEC) 2454/93 laying down provisions for the implementation of Council Regulation (EEC) 2913/92 establishing the Community Customs Code (enhancement of regular shipping services) [2013] OJ L294/40, Art 856a (6), Art 899(4).

[7] Regulation (EU) 1024/2012 of the European Parliament and of the Council of 25 October 2012 on administrative cooperation through the Internal Market Information System and repealing Commission Decision 2008/49/EC ('the IMI Regulation') [2012] OJ L316/1 last amended by Directive 2014/67/EU of the European Parliament and of the Council of 15 May 2014 on the enforcement of Directive 96/71/EC concerning the posting of workers in the framework of the provision of services and amending Regulation (EU) No 1024/2012 on administrative cooperation through the Internal Market Information System ('the IMI Regulation') [2014] OJ L 159/11, Art 3(1) read in conjunction with Art 5(b).

[8] Compare Directive 2006/123/EC of the European Parliament and of the Council of 12 December 2006 on services in the internal market [2006] OJ L376/36, Recital (107)-(109), Art 28.

[9] Directive 2006/123/EC of the European Parliament and of the Council of 12 December 2006 on services in the internal market [2006] OJ L376/36, Chapter VI.

[10] Compare for example Regulation (EC) 2006/2004 of the European Parliament and of the Council of 27 October 2004 on cooperation between national authorities responsible for the enforcement of consumer protection laws (the Regulation on consumer protection cooperation) [2004] OJ L364/1 last amended by Directive 2013/11/EU of the European Parliament and of the Council of 21 May 2013 on alternative dispute resolution for consumer disputes and amending Regulation (EC) 2006/2004 and Directive 2009/22/EC (Directive on consumer ADR) [2013] OJ L165/63, Arts 6–8; Council Regulation (EU) 389/2012 of 2 May 2012 on administrative cooperation in the field of excise duties and repealing Regulation (EC) 2073/2004 [2012] OJ L121/1 last amended by Council Regulation (EU) 517/2013 of 13 May 2013 adapting certain regulations and decisions in the fields of free movement of goods, freedom of movement for persons, company law, competition policy, agriculture, food safety, veterinary and phytosanitary policy, transport policy, energy, taxation, statistics, trans-European networks, judiciary and fundamental rights, justice, freedom and security, environment, customs union, external relations, foreign, security and defence policy and institutions, by reason of the accession of the Republic of Croatia [2013] OJ L158/1; Commission Regulation (EC) 1010/2009 of 22 October 2009 laying down detailed rules for the

This existing **diversity** of approaches **has** not only **created gaps** in protection, but **different solutions** have been created **for similar problems**. Nevertheless, some common features, or at least trends, can be observed. Uniform minimum standards would not only benefit administrations, but would also enhance the protection of European citizens.[11] **13**

B. Model Rules

V-1 Scope of Application of Book V

Book V applies to requests for mutual assistance which are sent from

(a) an EU authority to a Member State authority,
(b) a Member State authority to an EU authority, or
(c) a Member State authority to an authority of another Member State,

when the requesting authority is implementing EU Law through administrative action.

An act of mutual assistance may take one of the following forms:

(a) the transmission of information which is either already in the possession of the requested authority or which is gathered specifically in order to comply with the request for assistance.
(b) the conduct of an inspection
(c) the service of documents.

Book V does not apply when Member State authorities provide information as a party to a proceeding according to Articles III-11 to III-13.

Book V does not apply to judicial assistance or enforcement assistance. The model rules of Book V are without prejudice to provisions on mutual assistance in criminal matters and leave obligations arising out of the principle of sincere cooperation unaffected.

V-2 General Concept of Mutual Assistance

In order to receive the assistance necessary to fulfil its tasks under EU law, the requesting public authority may ask a Member State or EU public authority (the

implementation of Council Regulation (EC) 1005/2008 establishing a Community system to prevent, deter and eliminate illegal, unreported and unregulated fishing [2009] OJ L280/5 last amended by Commission Implementing Regulation (EU) 865/2013 of 9 September 2013 amending Regulation (EC) 1010/2009 as regards administrative arrangements with third countries on catch certificates for marine fisheries products [2013] OJ L241/1, Recital (9), Art 35.

[11] Examples for attempts to create such sector-specific minimum standards: Commission Proposal for a Regulation of the European Parliament and of the Council on the protection of individuals with regard to the processing of personal data and on the free movement of such data (General Data Protection Regulation), COM(2012) 11 final, Art 55; Directive 2006/123/EC of the European Parliament and of the Council of 12 December 2006 on services in the internal market [2006] OJ L376/36, Chapter VI; more detailed is Council Directive 2011/16/EU of 15 February 2011 on administrative cooperation in the field of taxation and repealing Directive 77/799/EEC [2011] OJ L64/1.

requested authority) for support, provided it cannot reasonably be expected to execute the necessary task itself.

Any communication shall be in written form and where possible by electronic means. Where provided for in EU law, a communication may be oral in urgent cases, especially by phone, on the condition that it will be confirmed in writing as soon as possible.

Except where otherwise agreed upon between the public authorities involved, requests and follow-up communication shall be conducted by the requesting authority in one of the official languages of the requested authority, or shall be accompanied by a translation in one of those languages. The requested authority shall formulate its response in one of its official languages. If necessary, the requesting authority shall provide a translation into another language. In the case of vertical mutual assistance, any communication must be undertaken in (one of) the official language(s) of the Member State unless otherwise agreed between the EU and Member State authorities involved.

Neither the requesting nor the requested authorities shall use mutual assistance to circumvent obligations or limitations existing under their applicable law.

In accordance with the principle of sincere cooperation, public authorities shall strive for an amicable solution to any dispute arising out of mutual assistance.

V-3 Duties of the Requesting Authority

A request for assistance shall

(a) state the provisions which provide the legal basis for the relevant administrative task of the requesting authority;
(b) state the provisions which provide the legal basis for the request itself;
(c) state the purpose of the requested assistance, its intended and desired use as well as reasons why the requesting authority could not conduct the necessary tasks itself. The request shall include relevant facts already known to the requesting authority and shall indicate if a similar request has been made to another public authority;
(d) contain sufficient information to enable a requested authority to fulfil the request. In case of a request for the service of documents, the relevant documents shall be the original or certified copies thereof, and the request shall indicate the name, address and any other relevant information for identifying the addressee, as well as a short summary of the attached document to be served, the purpose of the request and the period within which it should be served.

Where the request is not to be transmitted through information systems, or not to be sent to a designated contact or liaison point, the request should be sent through suitable ministerial channels. If the requested information is of a sensitive nature, the request may only be handled by specific authorities identified in the applicable law or it should be sent through suitable ministerial channels. Member States and EU authorities shall make suitable authorities as easily identifiable to outside authorities as possible.

The requesting authority may, at any time, withdraw the request for assistance which it has sent to the requested authority. The decision to withdraw shall be transmitted to the requested authority immediately. In the case of a request for the service of documents, the originals transmitted to the requested authority shall be returned forthwith. A request for the service of documents cannot be withdrawn once such documents have been served to the addressee. The requested authority shall inform the requesting authority immediately if this is the case.

The information transmitted in the course of mutual assistance may only be used for the purposes for which it was exchanged.

Any information, documents, findings, statements, certified true copies collected or information communicated in the course of mutual assistance may be invoked or used as evidence by all authorities of the Member State receiving it on the same basis as similar information or documents obtained within that State. An exception to such use exists where the requested authority has stated otherwise in accordance with EU law. Both the national laws of the requested and the requesting authority may prohibit the use of information as evidence if procedural or defence rights of the person concerned have been violated in the course of collecting the information.

The requested authority may ask the requesting authority to report back to it on the results of the assistance provided. In such cases the requesting authority is under an obligation to send a report.

V-4 Duties of the Requested Authority

(1) The requested authority shall
- (a) acknowledge the receipt of the request for assistance as soon as possible;
- (b) comply with the request within the shortest possible period of time. Where the requested authority cannot comply with the request, it shall inform the requesting authority thereof and of the reasons for its failure to do so. In case of difficulties in meeting a request, the requested authority shall promptly inform the requesting authority with a view to finding a solution. Where the addressed authority is not the authority competent to comply with the request, it shall forward the request to the competent public authority within its jurisdiction and inform the requesting authority thereof;
- (c) inform the requesting authority if it has evidence to suggest that information transmitted is inaccurate, or if it has been transmitted unlawfully.

(2) In order to comply
- (a) with a request for information, the requested authority shall provide any pertinent information in its possession or obtain the information sought. To obtain the information sought, the requested authority, or the public authority to which it has recourse, shall proceed as though acting on its own account or, if the requested authority is a Member State authority, at the request of another authority in its own Member State;
- (b) with a request for an inspection, the Member State authority shall conduct the inspection requested subject to existing constraints under national law and in accordance with EU law, or transfer the information required where it is already in its possession;
- (c) with a request for the service of documents, the requested authority shall in accordance with the rules governing the notification of similar instruments in its own Member State, provide the addressee with all of the documents which it has received for the purpose of service.

(3) The requested authority is obliged to comply with any lawful request for assistance. It shall refuse to provide personal data where the transfer would infringe applicable EU or national data protection law.

(4) It may refuse to comply in the following cases:
  (a) where the request does not comply with the requirements of Article V-3 (1);
  (b) to comply with the request would lead to the disclosure of a commercial, industrial or professional secret, or of information the disclosure of which would be contrary to public policy or national security;
  (c) the requesting authority could have reasonably been expected to fulfil the task itself;
  (d) to comply would pose a disproportionate administrative burden on the requested authority;
  (e) the law of the requested authority does not authorise the competent authority to carry out these enquiries or to collect or use that information for the requested authority's own purposes, and the refusal is in accordance with EU law.

V-5 Right of a Person Concerned to be Informed

Where the transfer of data has been requested the person concerned as defined in Article VI-2(7) has a right to be informed by the requested authority of the intended transmission. The requested authority is not obliged to inform the person concerned where this would threaten the purpose for which assistance is sought, and where the decision not to inform such person is proportionate.

(2) Information communicated in any form in the course of mutual assistance shall enjoy the protection extended to similar information under the national law of the receiving Member State and the corresponding provisions applicable to EU authorities.

V-6 Allocation of Costs

Member States and EU authorities shall renounce all claims against each other for the reimbursement of costs arising from any mutual assistance acts, except where mutual assistance involves particular problems leading to excessive costs. In such cases the requesting and requested authorities may agree on special reimbursement arrangements. A similar exception may be made, where appropriate, with respect to fees paid to outside actors, such as experts and translators.

C. Explanations

V-1 Scope and Application of Book V

Paragraph 1

1 Book V creates a **set of minimum rules for mutual assistance,** which is applicable between authorities—both horizontally, between authorities belonging to different Member States, as well as vertically, between a Member State and an EU authority. The rules equip administrative authorities with a set of **default rules.** They structure EU mutual assistance proceedings and provide authorities with a greater amount of clarity in their inter-administrative dealings. They apply to requests for mutual assistance which are sent when the requesting authority is implementing EU law through administrative action in the sense of Article I-4(1)(a)–(c). Book V does not regulate questions of judicial procedures.

Paragraph 2

Paragraph 2 contains a **non-exhaustive list of forms of mutual assistance.** This does not exclude other forms of mutual assistance. On the contrary, as observed in the introduction to Book V, mutual assistance owes much of its practical importance in the EU law sphere to its inherent flexibility. The obligation to transfer information upon request remains one of the forms of mutual assistance which is most used in the context of European administration. It can be found in a variety of sectors, for instance in the area of feed and food control or consumer protection.[12] The obligation to transfer such information also implies a duty to conduct enquiries as becomes apparent in the field of taxation.[13] Such considerations are also taken into account in the remainder of Book V, for instance in Article V-4(2)(a). The gathering of information can occur in a number of different ways, notably through investigations, interviews, inspections etc. 2

The inherent flexibility of mutual assistance allows for its use not only to request the transfer of information (the requested authority will also have to consider whether 3

[12] Regulation (EC) 882/2004 of the European Parliament and of the Council of 29 April 2004 on official controls performed to ensure the verification of compliance with feed and food law, animal health and animal welfare rules [2004] OJ L165/1 last amended by Commission Regulation (EU) 563/2012 of 27 June 2012 amending Annex VII to Regulation (EC) 882/2004 of the European Parliament and of the Council as regards the list of EU reference laboratories [2012] OJ L168/24, Art 36; Regulation (EC) 2006/2004 of the European Parliament and of the Council of 27 October 2004 on cooperation between national authorities responsible for the enforcement of consumer protection laws (the Regulation on consumer protection cooperation) [2004] OJ L364/1 last amended by Directive 2013/11/EU of the European Parliament and of the Council of 21 May 2013 on alternative dispute resolution for consumer disputes and amending Regulation (EC) 2006/2004 and Directive 2009/22/EC (Directive on consumer ADR) [2013] OJ L165/63, Art 6. Compare also European convention on the obtaining abroad of information and evidence in administrative matters [1978] ETS 100, Arts 13, 14.

[13] For example, Council Regulation (EU) 389/2012 of 2 May 2012 on administrative cooperation in the field of excise duties and repealing Regulation (EC) 2073/2004 [2012] OJ L121/1 last amended by Council Regulation (EU) 517/2013 of 13 May 2013 adapting certain regulations and decisions in the fields of free movement of goods, freedom of movement for persons, company law, competition policy, agriculture, food safety, veterinary and phytosanitary policy, transport policy, energy, taxation, statistics, trans-European networks, judiciary and fundamental rights, justice, freedom and security, environment, customs union, external relations, foreign, security and defence policy and institutions, by reason of the accession of the Republic of Croatia [2013] OJ L158/1, Art 8(2); Council Directive 2011/16/EU of 15 February 2011 on administrative cooperation in the field of taxation and repealing Directive 77/799/EEC [2011] OJ L64/1, Art 6(1); Council Directive 2010/24/EU of 16 March 2010 concerning mutual assistance for the recovery of claims relating to taxes, duties and other measures [2010] OJ L84/1, Art 5(1). Compare for feed and food control Regulation (EC) 882/2004 of the European Parliament and of the Council of 29 April 2004 on official controls performed to ensure the verification of compliance with feed and food law, animal health and animal welfare rules [2004] OJ L165/1 last amended by Commission Regulation (EU) 563/2012 of 27 June 2012 amending Annex VII to Regulation (EC) 882/2004 of the European Parliament and of the Council as regards the list of EU reference laboratories [2012] OJ L168/24, Art 36(1). For an example outside of the tax-law sector, see European convention on the obtaining abroad of information and evidence in administrative matters [1978] ETS 100, Art 15.

enquiries are needed), but **also to request the carrying out of specific inspections.**[14] The transfer of documents on behalf of another authority constitutes a third form of mutual assistance.[15] It is referred to as 'service of documents'.[16]

Paragraph 3

4 Paragraph 3 draws an **important distinction between Book III and Book V.** Where administrative authorities are themselves parties to a proceeding, for example when a Member State authority is the addressee of a decision by an EU authority within the meaning of Article III-2(1), they have corresponding duties as a party to the proceeding. Duties described under Articles III-11 to III-13 do not then fall within the scope of Book V. In addition, reporting duties of a Member State which exist under a duty to inform as defined in Article VI-2(2) do not fall within the scope of Book V either.

5 A point of discussion is the **relationship between the supervisory powers of EU authorities**, especially the Commission, with regard to Member States implementing EU law **and their obligations under mutual assistance.** Supervisory powers require a specific legal basis in EU law, which the rules on mutual assistance do not provide. Therefore, Book V does not establish a general supervisory power for EU authorities and the drafting team assumes that Book V does not create duties for supervised authorities in relation to the supervisory authority. Supervisory powers

[14] Council Regulation (EU) 389/2012 of 2 May 2012 on administrative cooperation in the field of excise duties and repealing Regulation (EC) 2073/2004 [2012] OJ L121/1 last amended by Council Regulation (EU) 517/2013 of 13 May 2013 adapting certain regulations and decisions in the fields of free movement of goods, freedom of movement for persons, company law, competition policy, agriculture, food safety, veterinary and phytosanitary policy, transport policy, energy, taxation, statistics, trans-European networks, judiciary and fundamental rights, justice, freedom and security, environment, customs union, external relations, foreign, security and defence policy and institutions, by reason of the accession of the Republic of Croatia [2013] OJ L158/1, Art 8(3); Council Directive 2011/16/EU of 15 February 2011 on administrative cooperation in the field of taxation and repealing Directive 77/799/EEC [2011] OJ L64/1, Art 6(2); Council Act of 18 December 1997 drawing up, on the basis of Article K.3 of the Treaty on European Union, the Convention on mutual assistance and cooperation between customs administrations [1998] OJ C24/1, Art 12 of the Annex.

[15] For example, The Schengen acquis—Convention implementing the Schengen Agreement of 14 June 1985 between the Governments of the States of the Benelux Economic Union, the Federal Republic of Germany and the French Republic on the gradual abolition of checks at their common borders [2000] OJ L239/19, Art 49(e) judicial documents.

[16] Compare Regulation (EC) 1393/2007 of the European Parliament and of the Council of 13 November 2007 on the service in the Member States of judicial and extrajudicial documents in civil or commercial matters (service of documents), and repealing Council Regulation (EC) 1348/2000 [2007] OJ L324/79 last amendment by Council Regulation (EU) 517/2013 of 13 May 2013 adapting certain regulations and decisions in the fields of free movement of goods, freedom of movement for persons, company law, competition policy, agriculture, food safety, veterinary and phytosanitary policy, transport policy, energy, taxation, statistics, trans-European networks, judiciary and fundamental rights, justice, freedom and security, environment, customs union, external relations, foreign, security and defence policy and institutions, by reason of the accession of the Republic of Croatia [2013] OJ L158/1.

will be regulated in sector-specific legislation, which will also address the specific duties of the supervised authority in providing information for the purpose of effective supervision.

Paragraph 4

As has already been explained in para 5 of the introduction, Book V focuses on mutual assistance and **does not cover judicial assistance and enforcement assistance.** 6

V-2 General Concept of Mutual Assistance

Paragraph 1

The concept of mutual assistance as proposed in these rules **shall not replace action by the administration in charge of a procedure,** but is only an auxiliary tool. This is inherent in the notion of mutual assistance, which is restricted to those instances when assistance is truly needed. The drafting team chose to use the term 'reasonably be expected' in order to limit the requesting authorities' right to seek assistance. It can be understood in a manner corresponding to a ground of refusal provided in Article 21(2)(g), Joint Council of Europe OECD Convention on Mutual Administrative Assistance in Tax Matters, which allows a requested State party to refuse a request for assistance 'if the applicant State has not pursued all reasonable measures available under its laws or administrative practice, except where recourse to such measures would give rise to disproportionate difficulty'.[17] In line with this reasoning, Article V-4(4)(c) allows for a request for assistance to be refused where the requesting authority could have reasonably been expected to carry out the task itself. 7

Reasons to request assistance may therefore fall into either **one of these categories:** legal obstacles render it difficult for the authority to fulfil the task on its own or factual circumstances exist which render the fulfilment of the task difficult. Mutual assistance may also be used for considerations of administrative efficiency. Lastly, any action linked to a request for mutual assistance, or its execution, has to be in compliance with the principles of EU Administrative law, especially legality, subsidiarity, proportionality, and effectiveness. 8

The **principle of proportionality** implies that an authority, when requesting assistance, should ensure that the assistance sought does not cause more work for the assisting authority than the assistance can reasonably be expected to be worth to the assisted authority. In other words, the request should not be more 9

[17] Convention on mutual administrative assistance in tax matters [1988] ETS 127 amended by the provisions of the Protocol amending the Convention on Mutual Administrative Assistance in Tax Matters [2010] ETS 208, Art 21(2)(g).

burdensome than the advantage that can be gained. Also, national administrative authorities have to take care that their national Administrative laws on how to proceed with mutual assistance requests do not render the implementation and application of EU law impossible or disproportionately difficult nor, inversely, undermine equivalence with national mutual assistance requirements and effectiveness with respect to being able to comply with assistance requests.

Paragraph 2

10 **Electronic forms of communication** are standard in present-day administration; their use should be encouraged wherever this is possible. Formal structures exist in a variety of fields such as taxation and customs, as well as in alert systems.[18] Nonetheless, other forms of communication continue to exist, such as written or oral communication.[19] Rules on standard and emergency situations should be designed to fit a variety of forms of communication.

Paragraph 3

11 Many existing legislative acts address the **question of the language** of either the request or its response or both.[20] It follows the general concept expressed in the first

[18] For example, Council Regulation (EU) 904/2010 of 7 October 2010 on administrative cooperation and combating fraud in the field of value added tax [2010] OJ L268/1 last amended by Council Regulation (EU) 517/2013 of 13 May 2013 adapting certain regulations and decisions in the fields of free movement of goods, freedom of movement for persons, company law, competition policy, agriculture, food safety, veterinary and phytosanitary policy, transport policy, energy, taxation, statistics, trans-European networks, judiciary and fundamental rights, justice, freedom and security, environment, customs union, external relations, foreign, security and defence policy and institutions, by reason of the accession of the Republic of Croatia [2013] OJ L158/1, Art 51; Directive 2006/123/EC of the European Parliament and of the Council of 12 December 2006 on services in the internal market [2006] OJ L376/36, Art 8; Council Regulation (EU) 389/2012 of 2 May 2012 on administrative cooperation in the field of excise duties and repealing Regulation (EC) 2073/2004 [2012] OJ L121/1 last amended by Council Regulation (EU) 517/2013 of 13 May 2013 adapting certain regulations and decisions in the fields of free movement of goods, freedom of movement for persons, company law, competition policy, agriculture, food safety, veterinary and phytosanitary policy, transport policy, energy, taxation, statistics, trans-European networks, judiciary and fundamental rights, justice, freedom and security, environment, customs union, external relations, foreign, security and defence policy and institutions, by reason of the accession of the Republic of Croatia [2013] OJ L158/1, Art 9; Council Directive 2010/24/EU of 16 March 2010 concerning mutual assistance for the recovery of claims relating to taxes, duties and other measures [2010] OJ L84/1, Art 21(1).

[19] For example, Council Act of 18 December 1997 drawing up, on the basis of Article K.3 of the Treaty on European Union, the Convention on mutual assistance and cooperation between customs administrations [1998] OJ C24/1, Art 9(4) of the Annex.

[20] For example, European Convention on the obtaining abroad of information and evidence in administrative matters [1978] ETS 100, Art 9; Council Directive 2010/24/EU of 16 March 2010 concerning mutual assistance for the recovery of claims relating to taxes, duties, and other measures [2010] OJ L84/1, Art 22(1); Council Framework Decision 2009/315/JHA of 26 February 2009 on the organisation and content of the exchange of information extracted from the criminal record between Member States [2009] OJ L93/23, Art 10; Regulation (EC) 2006/2004 of the European Parliament and of the Council of 27 October 2004 on cooperation between national authorities

paragraph of Article V-2, which confers upon the requesting authority the primary responsibility for the completion of its tasks. It can be expected that the necessary efforts of time and expense required for translation will be borne by the administration that will benefit from the acts of assistance of another authority. This proposed solution has two advantages: first, a requesting authority can better judge exactly which information is the most accurate for the purpose of its procedure than the requested authority; second, parties to the procedure will then be able to review the accuracy of the information by also having access to the original document and thereby being able to analyse the accuracy of the translation.

In relation to the service of a document, the **request and** the **document attached** (to be served to a third party) have to be distinguished from each other. In accordance with the inter-administrative focus of Book V, paragraph 3 mandates only the translation of the request, but not of the document itself. This inter-administrative focus is rooted in the concept of mutual assistance, while the language requirements concerning the document are an element of the legal relationship between the requesting authority and the addressee of the document. Where sector-specific law regulates the translation of the document itself (or parts thereof) for the protection of the rights of the individual, this is of course to be evaluated positively. Regulatory options can mandate the translation of the document before or after its transmission if the addressee complains of not being able to understand the document, potentially with a limited stay of proceedings where necessary.[21] **12**

Paragraph 4

As is apparent in Article V-2(4), as well as in Articles V-3(1)(a) and (b), Book V works on the basis of a divided standard of legality, the dividing line being the identity of the acting authority. The **law of the requesting Member State** governs the **permissibility of the request**, while the **law of the requested Member State** governs its **compliance** with a request and **any follow-up** assistance. Moreover, any action undertaken by the relevant authorities must adhere to the general principle of sincere cooperation and other specific conditions laid down by relevant EU law. Where a request is made or complied with by an EU authority, EU law governs the conduct of the respective authority. The decision to designate the national law of the acting authority as applicable law was motivated by the following considerations: first, it is a view which **13**

responsible for the enforcement of consumer protection laws (the Regulation on consumer protection cooperation) [2004] OJ L364/1 last amended by Directive 2013/11/EU of the European Parliament and of the Council of 21 May 2013 on alternative dispute resolution for consumer disputes and amending Regulation (EC) 2006/2004 and Directive 2009/22/EC (Directive on consumer ADR) [2013] OJ L165/63, Art 12(4).

[21] Compare Convention on mutual administrative assistance in tax matters [1988] ETS 127 amended by the provisions of the Protocol amending the Convention on Mutual Administrative Assistance in Tax Matters [2010] ETS 208, Art 17(5); European Convention on the service of documents abroad of documents relating to administrative matters [1977] ETS 94, Art 7.

corresponds to a number of EU law provisions on mutual assistance in sectors such as agriculture, customs, and tax law,[22] although the respective instruments do not necessarily reflect the wording chosen here; second, it minimizes the margin of error to a certain degree, as the public authority may be expected to be most familiar with its own national laws. The national laws are of course complemented by EU law. The latter comprises not only general principles, but also more specific, additional criteria, which in turn depend on the applicable sector-specific law. Such 'additional' criteria can, *inter alia*, be found in Article 27(3) of Directive 2004/38.[23]

Paragraph 5

14 The possibility of a Member State **initiating proceedings** against another Member State which has failed to fulfil its obligations under the treaties in accordance with Article 259 TFEU, or of the Commission to initiate proceedings against a Member State in accordance with Article 258 TFEU, of course remains unaffected by this paragraph.

---

[22] Council Directive 2010/24/EU of 16 March 2010 concerning mutual assistance for the recovery of claims relating to taxes, duties and other measures [2010] OJ L84/1, Recital (14); Council Regulation (EU) 389/2012 of 2 May 2012 on administrative cooperation in the field of excise duties and repealing Regulation (EC) 2073/2004 [2012] OJ L121/1 last amendment by Council Regulation (EU) 517/2013 of 13 May 2013 adapting certain regulations and decisions in the fields of free movement of goods, freedom of movement for persons, company law, competition policy, agriculture, food safety, veterinary and phytosanitary policy, transport policy, energy, taxation, statistics, trans-European networks, judiciary and fundamental rights, justice, freedom and security, environment, customs union, external relations, foreign, security and defence policy and institutions, by reason of the accession of the Republic of Croatia [2013] OJ L158/1, Art 8(4); Council Regulation (EU) 904/2010 of 7 October 2010 on administrative cooperation and combating fraud in the field of value added tax [2010] OJ L268/1 last amended by Council Regulation (EU) 517/2013 of 13 May 2013 adapting certain regulations and decisions in the fields of free movement of goods, freedom of movement for persons, company law, competition policy, agriculture, food safety, veterinary and phytosanitary policy, transport policy, energy, taxation, statistics, trans-European networks, judiciary and fundamental rights, justice, freedom and security, environment, customs union, external relations, foreign, security and defence policy and institutions, by reason of the accession of the Republic of Croatia [2013] OJ L158/1, Art 7(5); Council Regulation (EC) 515/97 of 13 March 1997 on mutual assistance between the administrative authorities of the Member States and cooperation between the latter and the Commission to ensure the correct application of the law on customs and agricultural matters [1997] OJ L82/1 last amended by Regulation (EC) 766/2008 of the European Parliament and of the Council of 9 July 2008 amending Council Regulation (EC) 515/97 on mutual assistance between the administrative authorities of the Member States and cooperation between the latter and the Commission to ensure the correct application of the law on customs and agricultural matters [2008] OJ L218/48, Art 4(2). Compare in the area of police and judicial cooperation Council Decision 2008/615/JHA of 23 June 2008 on the stepping up of cross-border cooperation, particularly in combating terrorism and cross-border crime [2008] OJ L210/1, Arts 13, 14, 26(1).

[23] Directive 2004/38/EC of the European Parliament and of the Council of 29 April 2004 on the right of citizens of the Union and their family members to move and reside freely within the territory of the Member States amending Regulation (EEC) 1612/68 and repealing Directives 64/221/EEC, 68/360/EEC, 72/194/EEC, 73/148/EEC, 75/34/EEC, 75/35/EEC, 90/364/EEC, 90/365/EEC and 93/96/EEC [2004] OJ L158/77 last amended by Regulation (EU) 492/2011 of the European Parliament and of the Council of 5 April 2011 on freedom of movement for workers within the Union [2011] OJ L141/1.

V-3 Duties of the Requesting Authority

Paragraph 1

Article V-3 contains the requesting authority's duties when seeking assistance from another authority. They **serve multiple purposes:** They enhance administrative efficiency, protect the individual and provide greater clarity by structuring mutual assistance across sectors. The formal requirements for a request which are established by this paragraph[24] serve a dual purpose. First, they seek to support the administration and to increase administrative efficiency. By providing the requested authority with all the relevant information, including the intended and desired use of the requested information, it is easier for the requested authority to comply with the request speedily and completely, minimizing risks of a second request for assistance. Moreover, if a request includes a statement of facts, this may limit the amount of data which the requesting authority deems relevant to satisfying the need for information and then transfers.[25] By contrast, a duty to justify a request protects the requested authority against an influx of requests for assistance, which may be useful for the requesting authority, but are not truly needed. Such a duty to justify the request already exists in some areas of EU law, for instance in Article 28(3) Directive 2006/123.[26] This need to indicate a specific purpose is also in line with data protection law.[27] The duty to justify the request is extended by the model rules to cover the reasons for the requesting authority's inability to conduct the task 15

[24] In less detail, see the European Convention on the obtaining abroad of information and evidence in administrative matters [1978] ETS 100, Art 5. Compare the Convention on mutual administrative assistance in tax matters [1988] ETS 127 amended by the provisions of the Protocol amending the Convention on Mutual Administrative Assistance in Tax Matters [2010] ETS 208, Art 18. Formal requirements can be (partly) laid down through the use of a standard form, i.e. European Convention on the service of documents abroad of documents relating to administrative matters [1977] ETS 94, Art 3.

[25] Opinion of the European Data Protection Supervisor on the Amended Proposal for a Regulation of the European Parliament and of the Council on mutual administrative assistance for the protection of the financial interests of the European Community against fraud and any other illegal activities [2007] OJ C94/1, Section II.2.

[26] Directive 2006/123/EC of the European Parliament and of the Council of 12 December 2006 on services in the internal market [2006] OJ L376/36.

[27] Regulation (EC) 45/2001 of the European Parliament and of the Council of 18 December 2000 on the protection of individuals with regard to the processing of personal data by the Community institutions and bodies and on the free movement of such data [2001] OJ L8/1 last amended by Corrigendum to Regulation (EC) 45/2001 of the European Parliament and of the Council of 18 December 2000 on the protection of individuals with regard to the processing of personal data by the Community institutions and bodies and on the free movement of such data [2007] OJ L164/35, Art 4(1)(b); Directive 95/46/EC of the European Parliament and of the Council of 24 October 1995 on the protection of individuals with regard to the processing of personal data and on the free movement of such data [1995] OJ L281/31 last amended by Regulation (EC) 1882/2003 of the European Parliament and of the Council of 29 September 2003 adapting to Council Decision 1999/468/EC the provisions relating to committees which assist the Commission in the exercise of its implementing powers laid down in instruments subject to the procedure referred to in Article 251 of the EC Treaty [2003] OJ L284/1, Art 6(1)(b).

itself. While this is not practiced currently, it seems warranted in light of the narrow notion of mutual assistance adopted in the model rules which is reflected in the grounds of refusal in Article V-4(4).

16 As a second aim, some of the obligations seek to **protect the individual**. For instance, the fact that the requesting authority should specify the legal basis for its request for assistance constitutes an innovative rule and is currently not standard practice in EU law in this form. Different EU legal acts often specify in detail which actions may be taken or which information may be transferred for the purposes of the instrument. The duty to specify the legal basis is intended to remind the authorities involved not to go beyond what is provided for in EU law. This notion of a *purpose limitation* can be found in Article 13 Regulation 1024/2012[28] and is also reflected in Article V-3(4). To oblige authorities to provide the relevant legal basis would thus provide a first tier of control by ensuring that all authorities are aware of the origin of their powers to ask for assistance and their limitations. Similarly, the obligation to specify if similar requests have been sent to other Member States is meant to render it more difficult for individual Member States to use mutual assistance to create an ad hoc information network. Such an ad hoc network would lack the safeguards necessary for such a system, which are provided for in Book VI.

Paragraph 2

17 Paragraph 2 follows **established practice.**[29]

Paragraph 3

18 Paragraph 3 ensures that where assistance is either not necessary within the meaning of Article V-2(1), but the requesting authority mistakenly assumed it was, or where it is no longer necessary due to changed circumstances, the requesting authority has the **ability to withdraw the request.**[30]

[28] Regulation (EU) 1024/2012 of the European Parliament and of the Council of 25 October 2012 on administrative cooperation through the Internal Market Information System and repealing Commission Decision 2008/49/EC ('the IMI Regulation') [2012] OJ L316/1 last amended by Directive 2014/67/EU of the European Parliament and of the Council of 15 May 2014 on the enforcement of Directive 96/71/EC concerning the posting of workers in the framework of the provision of services and amending Regulation (EU) No 1024/2012 on administrative cooperation through the Internal Market Information System ('the IMI Regulation') [2014] OJ L 159/11.

[29] For example European Convention on the obtaining abroad of information and evidence in administrative matters [1978] ETS 100, Arts 2, 11; European Convention on the service of documents abroad of documents relating to administrative matters [1977] ETS 94, Art 2.

[30] Compare Commission Implementing Regulation (EU) 1189/2011 of 18 November 2011 laying down detailed rules in relation to certain provisions of Council Directive 2010/24/EU concerning mutual assistance for the recovery of claims relating to taxes, duties and other measures, Art 9.

Paragraph 4

Where information is transmitted between authorities (especially where these are located in different jurisdictions) it is essential to **regulate the way in which this information may be used.**[31] This safeguards data protection standards which provide that authorities may not use personal data for purposes other than the one for which it was collected.[32] For the restriction on the usage of information in information systems, consult Article VI-24. Where the applicable law allows for the further use of the information exchanged, including access to information, these more specific norms take precedence over Article V-3(4). **19**

Paragraph 5

The **use of information** received in the course of mutual assistance **as evidence** by the authorities of the requesting Member State is regulated in a number of EU law provisions.[33] Article V-3(5) creates a **fall-back clause** which allows the use of such information. At the same time, it recognizes that the requested authority may prohibit the use of information as evidence in accordance with Union law. One example of such a prohibition is the refusal of the requested authority to consent where sector-specific law requires its consent before information can be used as evidence. An example of the latter is the cooperation of law enforcement authorities in Article 1(4) Council Decision 2006/960.[34] **20**

The drafting team did **not** include a **provision** in the model rules on the consequences of sharing information within a mutual **assistance procedure which** **21**

[31] For one example of how this is regulated see European Convention on the obtaining abroad of information and evidence in administrative matters [1978] ETS 100, Art 16.

[32] Commission Proposal for a Regulation of the European Parliament and of the Council on the protection of individuals with regard to the processing of personal data and on the free movement of such data (General Data Protection Regulation) COM(2012) 11 final, Art 55(3); compare Opinion of the European Data Protection Supervisor on the proposal for a Council Regulation on administrative cooperation and combating fraud in the field of value added tax (recast) (2010/C 66/01), para 37.

[33] For example, Council Directive 2010/24/EU of 16 March 2010 concerning mutual assistance for the recovery of claims relating to taxes, duties and other measures [2010] OJ L84/1, Art 23(6); Regulation (EC) 2006/2004 of the European Parliament and of the Council of 27 October 2004 on cooperation between national authorities responsible for the enforcement of consumer protection laws (the Regulation on consumer protection cooperation) [2004] OJ L364/1 last amended by Directive 2013/11/EU of the European Parliament and of the Council of 21 May 2013 on alternative dispute resolution for consumer disputes and amending Regulation (EC) 2006/2004 and Directive 2009/22/EC (Directive on consumer ADR) [2013] OJ L165/63, Art 13(2); Council Directive 2011/16/EU of 15 February 2011 on administrative cooperation in the field of taxation and repealing Directive 77/799/EEC [2011] OJ L64/1, Art 16(5).

[34] Council Framework Decision 2006/960/JHA of 18 December 2006 on simplifying the exchange of information and intelligence between law enforcement authorities of the Member States of the European Union [2006] OJ L386/89 last amended by Corrigendum to Council Framework Decision 2006/960/JHA of 18 December 2006 on simplifying the exchange of information and intelligence between law enforcement authorities of the Member States of the European Union [2007] OJ L75/26.

originated from procedures violating the rights of defence or other procedural rights of individuals. Not only does this book generally refrain from establishing remedies, but also the inclusion of such a provision might prove too controversial at this point in time since the consequences of violations of procedural rights and defence rights vary greatly between the various legal systems of the EU. As a consequence, the inclusion of such a prohibition in the model rules appeared to the drafting team too invasive of national Administrative law. Such violations may be remedied differently depending on the respective Administrative law framework. Therefore, Article V-3(5) states that Member State laws may prohibit the use of such information as evidence but this approach is not mandatory. This does not of course relieve courts of the obligation to consider whether such evidence must be excluded to avoid the violation of fundamental rights as formulated in Steffensen (2003).[35] Moreover, paragraph 5 does not allow authorities to circumvent the general restriction on the subsequent use of information established in paragraph 4.

Paragraph 6

22 The **obligation to report back** to the requested authority where this is desired is inspired by rules in the tax law sector.[36] It can build an authority's confidence and trust in the public authority of another Member State. Of course, this is only the case if the report is indeed useful and not too burdensome for the requesting authority.

V-4 Duties of the Requested Authority

Paragraph 1

23 Corresponding to Article V-3, Article V-4 creates duties for the requested authority, further structuring the mutual assistance procedure. Paragraph 1 sets out the **primary obligation** of the requested authority, which is to **comply with the request**.[37]

---

[35] Case C-276/01 *Steffensen* [2003] ECR I-3735, para 80 subparagraph (2).

[36] Council Regulation (EU) 904/2010 of 7 October 2010 on administrative cooperation and combating fraud in the field of value added tax [2010] OJ L268/1 last amended by Council Regulation (EU) 517/2013 of 13 May 2013 adapting certain regulations and decisions in the fields of free movement of goods, freedom of movement for persons, company law, competition policy, agriculture, food safety, veterinary and phytosanitary policy, transport policy, energy, taxation, statistics, trans-European networks, judiciary and fundamental rights, justice, freedom and security, environment, customs union, external relations, foreign, security and defence policy and institutions, by reason of the accession of the Republic of Croatia [2013] OJ L158/1, Art 16; Council Directive 2011/16/EU of 15 February 2011 on administrative cooperation in the field of taxation and repealing Directive 77/799/EEC [2011] OJ L64/1, Recital (16), Art 14. Compare, in the area of police and judicial cooperation, Council Decision 2008/615/JHA of 23 June 2008 on the stepping up of cross-border cooperation, particularly in combating terrorism and cross-border crime [2008] OJ L210/1, Art 32.

[37] Compare European Convention on the obtaining abroad of information and evidence in administrative matters [1978] ETS 100, Art 4.

The time-frame in which the requested authority has to confirm receipt of the request has to be interpreted in accordance with the different time-frames that exist in sector-specific instruments.[38] It should, in any event, occur as soon as possible in a given case.[39] The duty to communicate a refusal to comply under Article V-4(3) or V-4(4)[40] or any difficulties in complying with the request to the requesting authority, is a manifestation of the duty of sincere cooperation. The duty to provide the requesting authority with an update when the requested authority learns that the information it provided was either inaccurate or obtained unlawfully strengthens the protection of personal data and furthers mutual trust among the different administrative authorities.

Paragraph 2

In the drafting process of the duty to comply with a request for information, the question arose how to **limit** in the best possible way **the scope of information to be transmitted.** The drafting team ultimately opted for 'any pertinent information' which has to be read in light of restrictions which the different sector-specific laws impose. This means that limitations on the exchange which exist in sector-specific law are of course applicable and relevant legislation should specify as much as possible the type of information which may be transmitted. Where no or little specification is given, 'any pertinent information' has to be judged by the requested authority in light of the information it has been given under Article V-3(1). As far as the **24**

[38] To define a specific time-limit is not possible in light of the different periods opted for in sector-specific EU law, see for example Council Regulation (EU) 389/2012 of 2 May 2012 on administrative cooperation in the field of excise duties and repealing Regulation (EC) 2073/2004 [2012] OJ L121/1 last amended by Council Regulation (EU) 517/2013 of 13 May 2013 adapting certain regulations and decisions in the fields of free movement of goods, freedom of movement for persons, company law, competition policy, agriculture, food safety, veterinary and phytosanitary policy, transport policy, energy, taxation, statistics, trans-European networks, judiciary and fundamental rights, justice, freedom and security, environment, customs union, external relations, foreign, security and defence policy and institutions, by reason of the accession of the Republic of Croatia [2013] OJ L158/1, Art 11; Council Framework Decision 2006/960/JHA of 18 December 2006 on simplifying the exchange of information and intelligence between law enforcement authorities of the Member States of the European Union [2006] OJ L386/89 last amended by Corrigendum to Council Framework Decision 2006/960/JHA of 18 December 2006 on simplifying the exchange of information and intelligence between law enforcement authorities of the Member States of the European Union [2007] OJ L75/26, Art 4.

[39] European Convention on the obtaining abroad of information and evidence in administrative matters [1978] ETS 100, Art 10(1).

[40] Compare European Convention on the obtaining abroad of information and evidence in administrative matters [1978] ETS 100, Art 7(2); Convention on mutual administrative assistance in tax matters [1988] ETS 127 amended by the provisions of the Protocol amending the Convention on Mutual Administrative Assistance in Tax Matters [2010] ETS 208, Art 20(2); European Convention on the service of documents abroad of documents relating to administrative matters [1977] ETS 94, Art 14(2). Compare, in the area of judicial and police cooperation, Council Act of 29 May 2000 establishing in accordance with Article 34 of the Treaty on European Union the Convention on Mutual Assistance in Criminal Matters between the Member States of the European Union [2000] OJ C197/1, Art 4(3) of the Annex.

formulation 'as though acting on its own accord' is concerned, similar notions can be found in a variety of instruments, i.e. in Article 8(4) Regulation 389/2012 or Article 6(3) Directive 2011/16.[41]

25 In connection with the obligation to comply with a request for an inspection, it is important to recall the **dividing line between Book III and Book V**, which was explained in paragraph 10 of the introduction to this Book.

26 As far as the obligation to comply with a request for the service of documents is concerned, **similar wording can be found in different instruments.**[42] There are different ways in which this obligation can be given effect, such as notification by postal services or through consular agents. The specific manner of service depends on the requirement laid down in national and/or sector-specific law. The duty upon Member State authorities to serve documents when requested by EU authorities is based on Article 297(2) TFEU.

Paragraphs 3 and 4

27 Paragraphs 3 and 4 are an important element in the overall structure of Book V. They mandate that lawful requests for assistance have to be complied with unless a **ground for refusal** exempts the authority from this obligation. In order to protect personal data, the drafting team opted for a list of grounds of refusal divided

[41] Council Regulation (EU) 389/2012 of 2 May 2012 on administrative cooperation in the field of excise duties and repealing Regulation (EC) 2073/2004 [2012] OJ L121/1 last amended by Council Regulation (EU) 517/2013 of 13 May 2013 adapting certain regulations and decisions in the fields of free movement of goods, freedom of movement for persons, company law, competition policy, agriculture, food safety, veterinary and phytosanitary policy, transport policy, energy, taxation, statistics, trans-European networks, judiciary and fundamental rights, justice, freedom and security, environment, customs union, external relations, foreign, security and defence policy and institutions, by reason of the accession of the Republic of Croatia [2013] OJ L158/1; Council Directive 2011/16/EU of 15 February 2011 on administrative cooperation in the field of taxation and repealing Directive 77/799/EEC [2011] OJ L64/1; see also para 13 of the explanations.

[42] Council Regulation (EU) 389/2012 of 2 May 2012 on administrative cooperation in the field of excise duties and repealing Regulation (EC) 2073/2004 [2012] OJ L121/1 last amended by Council Regulation (EU) 517/2013 of 13 May 2013 adapting certain regulations and decisions in the fields of free movement of goods, freedom of movement for persons, company law, competition policy, agriculture, food safety, veterinary and phytosanitary policy, transport policy, energy, taxation, statistics, trans-European networks, judiciary and fundamental rights, justice, freedom and security, environment, customs union, external relations, foreign, security and defence policy and institutions, by reason of the accession of the Republic of Croatia [2013] OJ L158/1, Art 14(1); Council Regulation (EU) 904/2010 of 7 October 2010 on administrative cooperation and combating fraud in the field of value added tax [2010] OJ L268/1 last amended by Council Regulation (EU) 517/2013 of 13 May 2013 adapting certain regulations and decisions in the fields of free movement of goods, freedom of movement for persons, company law, competition policy, agriculture, food safety, veterinary and phytosanitary policy, transport policy, energy, taxation, statistics, trans-European networks, judiciary and fundamental rights, justice, freedom and security, environment, customs union, external relations, foreign, security and defence policy and institutions, by reason of the accession of the Republic of Croatia [2013] OJ L158/1, Art 25; Council Directive 2010/24/EU of 16 March 2010 concerning mutual assistance for the recovery of claims relating to taxes, duties and other measures [2010] OJ L84/1, Art 8(1).

between a mandatory ground of refusal in paragraph 3 and a number of voluntary grounds of refusal in paragraph 4.

In paragraph 3, the decision to include a **possible infringement of national data protection law** as a mandatory ground of refusal is necessary as long as large parts of data protection law are regulated on the national level. At present, national data protection laws remain the focal point of national data protection implementing Directive 95/46[43] (currently under review), also in the implementation of EU law. 28

Paragraph 4 lists **voluntary grounds of refusal.** Grounds of refusal in paragraph 4 are without prejudice to the obligations arising out of the principle of sincere cooperation and may of course be made mandatory in a specific EU legal act. 29

Paragraph 4's first ground of refusal is a **formal** one. It allows authorities to refuse requests where they do not comply with the standards set out in Article V-3(1). This in turn will encourage authorities to adhere to these standards and ensure that their purpose as set out in paragraphs 15 and 16 above is fulfilled.[44] 30

The second ground of refusal exempts the authority from the obligation to assist where this would **violate rules of professional or commercial secrecy, be contrary to public policy or violate national security.** Similar grounds of refusal can be found in a number of instruments in the tax law sector and Council of Europe Conventions.[45] The refusal to provide information due to national security concerns 31

[43] Directive 95/46/EC of the European Parliament and of the Council of 24 October 1995 on the protection of individuals with regard to the processing of personal data and on the free movement of such data [1995] OJ L281/31 last amended by Regulation (EC) 1882/2003 of the European Parliament and of the Council of 29 September 2003 adapting to Council Decision 1999/468/EC the provisions relating to committees which assist the Commission in the exercise of its implementing powers laid down in instruments subject to the procedure referred to in Article 251 of the EC Treaty [2003] OJ L284/1.

[44] Contrast European Convention on the obtaining abroad of information and evidence in administrative matters [1978] ETS 100, Art 6; European Convention on the service of documents abroad of documents relating to administrative matters [1977] ETS 94, Art 5, both of which oblige the requested authority to inform the requesting authority of perceived deficits, presumably with a view to remedying them to allow assistance action to be taken. Article V-4(4)(a) by contrast is stronger, yet it does not hinder a request to resubmit the request again in compliance with the formal requirements.

[45] For example Council Regulation (EU) 904/2010 of 7 October 2010 on administrative cooperation and combating fraud in the field of value added tax [2010] OJ L268/1 last amended by Council Regulation (EU) 517/2013 of 13 May 2013 adapting certain regulations and decisions in the fields of free movement of goods, freedom of movement for persons, company law, competition policy, agriculture, food safety, veterinary and phytosanitary policy, transport policy, energy, taxation, statistics, trans-European networks, judiciary and fundamental rights, justice, freedom and security, environment, customs union, external relations, foreign, security and defence policy and institutions, by reason of the accession of the Republic of Croatia [2013] OJ L158/1, Art 54(4); Council Regulation (EU) 389/2012 of 2 May 2012 on administrative cooperation in the field of excise duties and repealing Regulation (EC) 2073/2004 [2012] OJ L121/1 last amendment by Council Regulation (EU) 517/2013 of 13 May 2013 adapting certain regulations and decisions in the fields of free movement of goods, freedom of movement for persons, company law, competition policy, agriculture, food safety, veterinary and phytosanitary policy, transport policy, energy, taxation,

in the area of vertical mutual assistance is also in line with Article 346(1)(a) TFEU. Except for this exemption which is provided in the treaty, exemptions to the duty to provide vertical, informational mutual assistance have to be understood in a narrow manner. Already in early ECJ case law, namely two *Commission v Hellenic Republic of Greece* cases in 1988, the court has observed that Member States were under an obligation to provide the Commission with information to facilitate the tasks which were given to it under the treaty.[46]

32 The third ground of refusal mirrors the concept of mutual assistance explored in Article V-2(1), which is based on the understanding that the **primary responsibility for fulfilling the task rests with the requesting authority.**[47] Therefore, when the requesting authority can reasonably be expected to fulfil the task on its own, the requested authority may refuse the request.[48] However, this ground of refusal may not be used by Member States to attempt to escape their cooperative duties under EU law. To be able to claim this ground of refusal the requested authority must have good reasons to believe that the requesting authority could conduct the task

statistics, trans-European networks, judiciary and fundamental rights, justice, freedom and security, environment, customs union, external relations, foreign, security and defence policy and institutions, by reason of the accession of the Republic of Croatia [2013] OJ L158/1, Art 25(4); Council Directive 2011/16/EU of 15 February 2011 on administrative cooperation in the field of taxation and repealing Directive 77/799/EEC [2011] OJ L64/1, Art 17(4); Convention on mutual administrative assistance in tax matters [1988] ETS 127 amended by the provisions of the Protocol amending the Convention on Mutual Administrative Assistance in Tax Matters [2010] ETS 208, Art 21(2)(b),(d); European Convention on the service of documents abroad of documents relating to administrative matters [1977] ETS 94, Art 14(1)(b); European Convention on the obtaining abroad of information and evidence in administrative matters [1978] ETS 100, Art 7(1)(b).

[46] Case 240/86 *Commission v Hellenic Republic of Greece* [1988] ECR 1835; Case 272/86 *Commission v Hellenic Republic* [1988] ECR 4875, see especially para 30.

[47] Compare Council Directive 2011/16/EU of 15 February 2011 on administrative cooperation in the field of taxation and repealing Directive 77/799/EEC [2011] OJ L64/1, Art 17(1); Council Regulation (EU) 389/2012 of 2 May 2012 on administrative cooperation in the field of excise duties and repealing Regulation (EC) 2073/2004 [2012] OJ L121/1 last amendment by Council Regulation (EU) 517/2013 of 13 May 2013 adapting certain regulations and decisions in the fields of free movement of goods, freedom of movement for persons, company law, competition policy, agriculture, food safety, veterinary and phytosanitary policy, transport policy, energy, taxation, statistics, trans-European networks, judiciary and fundamental rights, justice, freedom and security, environment, customs union, external relations, foreign, security and defence policy and institutions, by reason of the accession of the Republic of Croatia [2013] OJ L158/1, Art 25(1)(a); Council Regulation (EU) 904/2010 of 7 October 2010 on administrative cooperation and combating fraud in the field of value added tax [2010] OJ L268/1 last amended by Council Regulation (EU) 517/2013 of 13 May 2013 adapting certain regulations and decisions in the fields of free movement of goods, freedom of movement for persons, company law, competition policy, agriculture, food safety, veterinary and phytosanitary policy, transport policy, energy, taxation, statistics, trans-European networks, judiciary and fundamental rights, justice, freedom and security, environment, customs union, external relations, foreign, security and defence policy and institutions, by reason of the accession of the Republic of Croatia [2013] OJ L158/1, Art 54(1)(b).

[48] Convention on mutual administrative assistance in tax matters [1988] ETS 127 amended by the provisions of the Protocol amending the Convention on Mutual Administrative Assistance in Tax Matters [2010] ETS 208, Art 21(2)(g).

itself without too much difficulty.[49] Where the Commission cannot fulfil the task itself because of practical hurdles, its administrative resources being significantly smaller than those of the Member States, it could not reasonably be expected to fulfil the task itself. In comparison, this ground will in all likelihood be much harder to use by a Member State authority to refuse a request by EU authorities than a request by other Member State authorities.

The fourth ground of refusal seeks to **prevent requests from becoming a disproportionate burden** on the requested authority and hindering it in fulfilling its own obligations.[50] In this scenario not only does the number of requests received by the requested authority have to be considered, but the relative importance of the respective tasks has to be taken into account as well, especially in view of Article 197(1) TFEU. 33

The fifth ground of refusal can be used both for horizontal[51] and vertical requests for assistance. Any refusal will be reviewed under the **principles of equivalence and effectiveness.** A simple refusal to cooperate due to a lack of national law permitting an authority to act, for instance, is contrary to the principle of effectiveness.[52] 34

The drafting group discussed but ultimately **excluded further possible grounds** for refusal other than those currently listed in paragraph 4. First, this applies to grounds which were considered not to be suitable for general rules on mutual 35

[49] Compare Revised Explanatory Report to Joint Council OECD Convention on Mutual Administrative Assistance in Tax Matters as amended by the protocol, para 201.

[50] Compare Council Regulation (EU) 904/2010 of 7 October 2010 on administrative cooperation and combating fraud in the field of value added tax [2010] OJ L268/1 last amended by Council Regulation (EU) 517/2013 of 13 May 2013 adapting certain regulations and decisions in the fields of free movement of goods, freedom of movement for persons, company law, competition policy, agriculture, food safety, veterinary and phytosanitary policy, transport policy, energy, taxation, statistics, trans-European networks, judiciary and fundamental rights, justice, freedom and security, environment, customs union, external relations, foreign, security and defence policy and institutions, by reason of the accession of the Republic of Croatia [2013] OJ L158/1, Art 54(1)(a); Council Regulation (EU) 389/2012 of 2 May 2012 on administrative cooperation in the field of excise duties and repealing Regulation (EC) 2073/2004 [2012] OJ L121/1 last amendment by Council Regulation (EU) 517/2013 of 13 May 2013 adapting certain regulations and decisions in the fields of free movement of goods, freedom of movement for persons, company law, competition policy, agriculture, food safety, veterinary and phytosanitary policy, transport policy, energy, taxation, statistics, trans-European networks, judiciary and fundamental rights, justice, freedom and security, environment, customs union, external relations, foreign, security and defence policy and institutions, by reason of the accession of the Republic of Croatia [2013] OJ L158/1, Art 25(1)(b).

[51] Compare Convention on mutual administrative assistance in tax matters [1988] ETS 127 amended by the provisions of the Protocol amending the Convention on Mutual Administrative Assistance in Tax Matters [2010] ETS 208, Art 21(2)(a),(c).

[52] Contrast European Convention on the obtaining abroad of information and evidence in administrative matters [1978] ETS 100, Art 7(1)(d) 'that its domestic law or customs prevent the assistance requested'. See also Explanatory Report to the European Convention on the obtaining abroad of information and evidence in administrative matters [1978] ETS 100, para 34.

assistance.[53] Second, the drafters propose not to include reciprocity as a ground for refusal. Currently, a number of instruments still provide for a ground of refusal which is linked, in a more or less direct way, to a notion of reciprocity.[54] In view of Article 197(1) TFEU, this might be regarded to be an outdated requirement which should be eliminated from EU law provisions on mutual assistance.

V-5 Right of a Person Concerned to be Informed

Paragraph 1

36 This article creates a **right to be informed where personal data is about to be transmitted** to another authority, both where the authority is from another Member State and where it is an EU authority. It is currently not standard practice in mutual assistance instruments, but it exists in Data Protection law and is an important innovation included in Book V. Existing standards of data protection provide for the data subject to be informed prior to transmission, or no later than before first disclosure of the data to a third party. The exact duties depend on whether the information was directly obtained from the data subject or stems from another source.[55] Article 18(1) Regulation 1024/2012 provides for a right to be informed

[53] For example Regulation (EU) 1227/2011 of the European Parliament and of the Council of 25 October 2011 on wholesale energy market integrity and transparency [2011] OJ L326/1, Art 16(5)(b),(c): '(b) judicial proceedings have already been initiated in respect of the same actions and against the same persons before the authorities of the Member State addressed; or (c) a final judgment has already been delivered in relation to such persons for the same actions in the Member State addressed.'

[54] For example Council Regulation (EU) 904/2010 of 7 October 2010 on administrative cooperation and combating fraud in the field of value added tax [2010] OJ L268/1 last amended by Council Regulation (EU) 517/2013 of 13 May 2013 adapting certain regulations and decisions in the fields of free movement of goods, freedom of movement for persons, company law, competition policy, agriculture, food safety, veterinary and phytosanitary policy, transport policy, energy, taxation, statistics, trans-European networks, judiciary and fundamental rights, justice, freedom and security, environment, customs union, external relations, foreign, security and defence policy and institutions, by reason of the accession of the Republic of Croatia [2013] OJ L158/1, Art 54(3); Council Regulation (EU) 389/2012 of 2 May 2012 on administrative cooperation in the field of excise duties and repealing Regulation (EC) 2073/2004 [2012] OJ L121/1 last amendment by Council Regulation (EU) 517/2013 of 13 May 2013 adapting certain regulations and decisions in the fields of free movement of goods, freedom of movement for persons, company law, competition policy, agriculture, food safety, veterinary and phytosanitary policy, transport policy, energy, taxation, statistics, trans-European networks, judiciary and fundamental rights, justice, freedom and security, environment, customs union, external relations, foreign, security and defence policy and institutions, by reason of the accession of the Republic of Croatia [2013] OJ L158/1, Art 25(3); Council Directive 2011/16/EU of 15 February 2011 on administrative cooperation in the field of taxation and repealing Directive 77/799/EEC [2011] OJ L64/1, Art 17(3).

[55] Compare Directive 95/46/EC of the European Parliament and of the Council of 24 October 1995 on the protection of individuals with regard to the processing of personal data and on the free movement of such data [1995] OJ L281/31 last amended by Regulation (EC) 1882/2003 of the European Parliament and of the Council of 29 September 2003 adapting to Council Decision 1999/468/EC the provisions relating to committees which assist the Commission in the exercise of its implementing powers laid down in instruments subject to the procedure referred to in Article 251 of the EC Treaty [2003] OJ L284/1, Arts 10, 11; Regulation (EC) 45/2001 of the European

without mentioning the point in time when this right is effective.[56] Article 37(2) Regulation 767/2008 provides for a right of information on the usage of the information at point of data collection, but this occurs within an information system.[57]

This being said, the ECJ observed in *Sabou* (2013), a case which concerned the implementation of Directive 77/799, that respect for the rights of the defence did not require that a taxpayer be notified of a decision to collect information, nor did it require him or her to be heard at the point of inquiry, or require him or her to be involved in the stage of information gathering, in particular the examination of witnesses.[58] The court held that these actions were still part of the investigatory phase of a procedure and the refusal to inform the person concerned did not negate his or her right to be heard before a decision adversely affecting him or her was taken. The drafting team, similar to the court in *Sabou,* does not view the **right to be informed prior to transmission** as a right which is mandated by the rights of defence. However, it **is the procedural right** of a natural or legal person. Several reasons speak in favour of establishing this procedural right which include, first, that not every transmission of data will lead to a decision adversely affecting the individual, in the process of which he or she will normally be informed of the transmission of information. Where no decision is reached this should not leave the individual unaware of information related to him or her being transmitted. Second, **37**

Parliament and of the Council of 18 December 2000 on the protection of individuals with regard to the processing of personal data by the Community institutions and bodies and on the free movement of such data [2001] OJ L8/1 last amended by Corrigendum to Regulation (EC) 45/2001 of the European Parliament and of the Council of 18 December 2000 on the protection of individuals with regard to the processing of personal data by the Community institutions and bodies and on the free movement of such data [2007] OJ L164/35, Arts 11, 12; Commission Proposal for a Regulation of the European Parliament and of the Council on the protection of individuals with regard to the processing of personal data and on the free movement of such data (General Data Protection Regulation) COM(2012) 11 final, Art 14.

[56] Regulation (EU) 1024/2012 of the European Parliament and of the Council of 25 October 2012 on administrative cooperation through the Internal Market Information System and repealing Commission Decision 2008/49/EC ('the IMI Regulation') [2012] OJ L316/1 last amended by Directive 2014/67/EU of the European Parliament and of the Council of 15 May 2014 on the enforcement of Directive 96/71/EC concerning the posting of workers in the framework of the provision of services and amending Regulation (EU) No 1024/2012 on administrative cooperation through the Internal Market Information System ('the IMI Regulation') [2014] OJ L 159/11.

[57] Regulation (EC) 767/2008 of the European Parliament and of the Council of 9 July 2008 concerning the Visa Information System (VIS) and the exchange of data between Member States on short-stay visas (VIS Regulation) [2008] OJ L218/60 last amended by Regulation (EC) 610/2013 of the European Parliament and of the Council of 26 June 2013 amending Regulation (EC) No 562/2006 of the European Parliament and of the Council establishing a Community Code on the rules governing the movement of persons across borders (Schengen Borders Code), the Convention implementing the Schengen Agreement, Council Regulations (EC) No 1683/95 and (EC) No 539/2001 and Regulations (EC) No 767/2008 and (EC) No 810/2009 of the European Parliament and of the Council [2013] OJ L182/1.

[58] Case C-276/12 *Jiří Sabou v Finanční ředitelství pro hlavní město Prahu* [2013] OJ C367/16, paras 44–46.

individuals may have the option to participate in the information gathering in the requested Member State. Such rights can only be effectively used if the individual is made aware of the data transmission in the first place.

38 Of course, there may be **instances where a refusal to inform the individual is justified** to protect the underlying purpose of the request for assistance. This need is also recognized in Directive 95/46.[59] Such cases were taken into account when drafting the second sentence of paragraph 1 allowing the requested authority to *defer* the individual's right to be informed when two conditions are fulfilled: the duty to inform would threaten the purpose of the request for assistance, and the refusal to inform the individual is in line with the principle of proportionality. By contrast, and in line with general data protection law, where these conditions are no longer fulfilled, the requested authority is under a duty to inform the individual ex post. Irrespective of these considerations, the right to be informed will not apply in the case of a service of documents. This is based on the assumption that in such cases persons concerned are informed by virtue of the documents served.

Paragraph 2

39 Paragraph 2 aims at ensuring that **all information which has been exchanged** under the procedure of mutual assistance **shall be protected,**[60] in compliance with

[59] Directive 95/46/EC of the European Parliament and of the Council of 24 October 1995 on the protection of individuals with regard to the processing of personal data and on the free movement of such data [1995] OJ L281/31 last amended by Regulation (EC) 1882/2003 of the European Parliament and of the Council of 29 September 2003 adapting to Council Decision 1999/468/EC the provisions relating to committees which assist the Commission in the exercise of its implementing powers laid down in instruments subject to the procedure referred to in Article 251 of the EC Treaty [2003] OJ L284/1, Art 13(1).

[60] Compare Art VI-28 on confidentiality and Council Regulation (EU) 904/2010 of 7 October 2010 on administrative cooperation and combating fraud in the field of value added tax [2010] OJ L268/1 last amended by Council Regulation (EU) 517/2013 of 13 May 2013 adapting certain regulations and decisions in the fields of free movement of goods, freedom of movement for persons, company law, competition policy, agriculture, food safety, veterinary and phytosanitary policy, transport policy, energy, taxation, statistics, trans-European networks, judiciary and fundamental rights, justice, freedom and security, environment, customs union, external relations, foreign, security and defence policy and institutions, by reason of the accession of the Republic of Croatia [2013] OJ L158/1, Art 55(1); Council Directive 2010/24/EU of 16 March 2010 concerning mutual assistance for the recovery of claims relating to taxes, duties and other measures [2010] OJ L84/1, Art 23(1); Council Regulation (EC) 1/2003 of 16 December 2002 on the implementation of the rules on competition laid down in Articles 81 and 82 of the Treaty [2003] OJ L1/1 last amended by Council Regulation (EC) 487/2009 of 25 May 2009 on the application of Article 81(3) of the Treaty to certain categories of agreements and concerted practices in the air transport sector [2009] OJ L148/1, Art 28; Regulation (EC) 2006/2004 of the European Parliament and of the Council of 27 October 2004 on cooperation between national authorities responsible for the enforcement of consumer protection laws (the Regulation on consumer protection cooperation) [2004] OJ L364/1 last amended by Directive 2013/11/EU of the European Parliament and of the Council of 21 May 2013 on alternative dispute resolution for consumer disputes and amending Regulation (EC) 2006/2004 and Directive 2009/22/EC (Directive on consumer ADR) [2013] OJ L165/63, Art 13(3); Council Framework Decision 2006/960/JHA of 18 December 2006 on simplifying the

the principles of equivalence and effectiveness (derived from the principle of sincere cooperation under Article 4(3) TEU), in the same way as any other information would be within the Member State. This is not only important for business secrets but also for personal data.

V-6 Allocation of Costs

Article V-6 regulates the financial aspects of mutual assistance. Its starting point is a **complete renunciation of claims** by the authorities involved subject to only **two exceptions.**[61] This is motivated by the need to ensure a smooth functioning of European administration, both between different Member State authorities and EU and MS authorities. It is inspired by three provisions: Article 20(2) Directive 2010/24, Article 26 Regulation 389/2012 and Article 21(2) Directive 2011/16.[62] The European Convention on Mutual Assistance in Criminal Matters started from a comparable premise already in 1959, the new Commission Proposal for a General Data Protection Regulation in turn prohibits any fee for 'any actions taken following **40**

exchange of information and intelligence between law enforcement authorities of the Member States of the European Union [2006] OJ L386/89 last amended by Corrigendum to Council Framework Decision 2006/960/JHA of 18 December 2006 on simplifying the exchange of information and intelligence between law enforcement authorities of the Member States of the European Union [2007] OJ L75/26, Art 9; Council Regulation (EU) 389/2012 of 2 May 2012 on administrative cooperation in the field of excise duties and repealing Regulation (EC) 2073/2004 [2012] OJ L121/1 last amended by Council Regulation (EU) 517/2013 of 13 May 2013 adapting certain regulations and decisions in the fields of free movement of goods, freedom of movement for persons, company law, competition policy, agriculture, food safety, veterinary and phytosanitary policy, transport policy, energy, taxation, statistics, trans-European networks, judiciary and fundamental rights, justice, freedom and security, environment, customs union, external relations, foreign, security and defence policy and institutions, by reason of the accession of the Republic of Croatia [2013] OJ L158/1, Art 28(1).

[61] Compare European Convention on the obtaining abroad of information and evidence in administrative matters [1978] ETS 100, Arts 8, 18, 21; European Convention on the service of documents abroad of documents relating to administrative matters [1977] ETS 94, Art 13; compare Convention on mutual administrative assistance in tax matters [1988] ETS 127 amended by the provisions of the Protocol amending the Convention on Mutual Administrative Assistance in Tax Matters [2010] ETS 208, Art 26.

[62] Council Directive 2010/24/EU of 16 March 2010 concerning mutual assistance for the recovery of claims relating to taxes, duties and other measures [2010] OJ L84/1; Council Regulation (EU) 389/2012 of 2 May 2012 on administrative cooperation in the field of excise duties and repealing Regulation (EC) 2073/2004 [2012] OJ L121/1 last amendment by Council Regulation (EU) 517/2013 of 13 May 2013 adapting certain regulations and decisions in the fields of free movement of goods, freedom of movement for persons, company law, competition policy, agriculture, food safety, veterinary and phytosanitary policy, transport policy, energy, taxation, statistics, trans-European networks, judiciary and fundamental rights, justice, freedom and security, environment, customs union, external relations, foreign, security and defence policy and institutions, by reason of the accession of the Republic of Croatia [2013] OJ L158/1; Council Directive 2011/16/EU of 15 February 2011 on administrative cooperation in the field of taxation and repealing Directive 77/799/EEC [2011] OJ L64/1.

a request for mutual assistance'.[63] However, since a request or a number of related requests may lead to excessive costs, it was deemed more feasible to provide for a narrow exception to the general prohibition. By contrast, no exception was provided for cases where requests for assistance have been withdrawn by the requesting authority. Such a rule could lead the requesting authority to refuse to withdraw a request even where a specific action is no longer necessary or a particular piece of information no longer needed. Where a requested authority is faced with excessive costs (be it due to the sheer number of 'withdrawn requests' or the scope of one request) or where it has to pay external experts, it can still reclaim the costs under Article V-6.

[63] European Convention on mutual assistance in criminal matters [1959] ETS 30, Art 20; Commission Proposal for a Regulation of the European Parliament and of the Council on the protection of individuals with regard to the processing of personal data and on the free movement of such data (General Data Protection Regulation) COM(2012) 11 final, Art 55(7).

BOOK VI—ADMINISTRATIVE INFORMATION MANAGEMENT

A. Introduction to Book VI

I. Scope of Application of Book VI and its Relation to Books II to V

Book VI deals with specific categories of inter-administrative information management activities consisting either in **certain forms of inter-administrative information exchange** or in **databases directly accessible to public authorities.** 1

Information management is a core feature of each administrative procedure. The sharing of information is **a key element of a decentralized yet effective implementation of EU law** within the internal market. Information-related activities are often the essence of composite decision-making procedures that have already been partially addressed in Books II–IV. This is especially true for Book III with extensive rules on information gathering, inspections, hearings, participation of third parties and consultation of other authorities. In addition, mutual assistance, as regulated in Book V, is a core element of EU Administrative law and consists to a large extent in informational mutual assistance. This means that Book VI, first, **only** regulates a **specific set of information activities**, and second, it **supplements** the **other books** by regulating certain horizontal aspects which give rise to distinct problems of information law. These various provisions on information management are essential pre-conditions for the realization of the right to good administration. In requiring fair and impartial decision-making good administration depends on procedures which allow administrations to take into account and reason about the relevant facts of a case including those which arise from other jurisdictions within the EU. 2

Existing information exchange schemes regularly involve EU as well as national authorities.[1] Similarly, the most important databases are those defined in Article VI-2(3) and thereby accessible to EU as well as to national authorities.[2] Consequently, Book VI follows a **comprehensive approach concerning its scope of application** 3

[1] For example Regulation (EU) 1024/2012 of the European Parliament and of the Council of 25 October 2012 on administrative cooperation through the Internal Market Information System and repealing Commission Decision 2008/49/EC ('the IMI Regulation') [2012] OJ L316/1 last amended by Directive 2014/67/EU of the European Parliament and of the Council of 15 May 2014 on the enforcement of Directive 96/71/EC concerning the posting of workers in the framework of the provision of services and amending Regulation (EU) No 1024/2012 on administrative cooperation through the Internal Market Information System ('the IMI Regulation') [2014] OJ L 159/11, Art 3; Commission Regulation (EU) 16/2011 of 10 January 2011 laying down implementing measures for the Rapid alert system for food and feed [2011] OJ L6/7, Art 1 No 2.

[2] For example Council Regulation (EC) 515/97 of 13 March 1997 on mutual assistance between the administrative authorities of the Member States and the cooperation between the latter and the Commission to ensure the correct application of the law on customs and agricultural matters [1997] OJ L82/1 last amended by Regulation (EC) 766/2008 of the European Parliament and of the Council of 9 July 2008 amending Council Regulation (EC) 515/97 on mutual assistance between the administrative authorities of the Member States and cooperation between the latter and the Commission to ensure the correct application of the law on customs and agricultural matters [2008] OJ L218/48, Art 24.

including not only the information management activities of EU authorities but also of national authorities. In other words, Book VI is applicable to all forms of composite information management activities. As these issues can only marginally be regulated by existing national Administrative law, such a comprehensive approach offers a solution compatible with the principle of subsidiarity.

4 At this stage of the ReNEUAL project, Book VI focuses only on inter-administrative information management activities as these are the basis of, or at least supportive of, administrative actions regulated in Books II to IV. This includes, importantly, provisions on tracing informational input into decision-making. This feature is an **important gap-filler** enabling judicial review of decision-making procedures with input from various jurisdictions and will thus contribute to ensuring effective judicial review within the EU under the principle restated by Article 47 CFR.

II. Relation to General Data Protection Law and Freedom of Information Rights

5 Book VI combines rules on structural issues (procedures, organization, inter-administrative obligations), as well as on data protection aspects of information law. The rationale behind this is that **data protection needs to be integrated into general information law** provisions in order to be effective. At the same time, it must be applied in the context of the general objectives of information law so as not to be excessively burdensome.

6 Therefore, Book VI attempts to find a **reasonable balance between** these **objectives of information law**, by not simply duplicating general data protection rules, but rather by adequately adapting them to the problems and needs of inter-administrative information exchange and databases.

7 For **example**, Article VI-9 establishes the **principle of transparent information management**, including, for instance, duties to record data-processing activities. This duty supports data protection, but it also fosters inter-administrative accountability and interaction with regard to collaborative information gathering. Article VI-19 establishes different obligations, to update, correct or delete data. While Article VI-19(3) explicitly provides an individual 'subjective' right for persons concerned (including data subjects) in line with general data-protection principles, other paragraphs are predominantly concerned with establishing obligations and rights applicable in the inter-administrative relationships not confined to data protection. Article VI-19(5) on data flagging combines the latter two approaches. Finally, Article VI-34 provides an obligation to establish internal supervision by data protection officers. This rule is declaratory with regard to EU authorities,[3] but

[3] See the general obligation in Regulation (EC) 45/2001 of the European Parliament and of the Council of 18 December 2000 on the protection of individuals with regard to the processing of personal data by the Community institutions and bodies and on the free movement of such data

innovative for national authorities at least at present.[4] Other examples will be highlighted in the respective explanations.

The process of reform of the EU's general legislative framework governing data protection law might result in the need to adjust these ReNEUAL Model Rules accordingly. However, **including data protection rules** in the general provisions on EU Administrative law can be a **contribution to the overall simplification of the legal system** in that sector-specific law,[5] which might in future refer to the general rules on administrative procedure. 8

At this stage of the project, Book VI does **not cover rules on access to documents or** the **proactive display of data** held by public authorities. Therefore, the rules in Regulation 1049/2001 on access to documents[6] as well as in the Directives 2003/4 (Access to environmental information)[7] and Directive 2007/2 (Infrastructure for Spatial Information in the European Community (INSPIRE))[8] remain unaffected (Article VI-1(3)). The same holds true with regard to specific standards for public announcements by public authorities, particularly product warnings. 9

III. Reasons for a Legal Framework for Composite Information Management Activities

A legal framework for composite information management activities is necessary to **steer the informational course** of composite administrative procedures **and** provide the various actors involved in such procedures with **legal certainty** as to their tasks and obligations. The objectives of such a legal framework are manifold. 10

[2001] OJ L8/1 last amended by Corrigendum to Regulation (EC) 45/2001 of the European Parliament and of the Council of 18 December 2000 on the protection of individuals with regard to the processing of personal data by the Community institutions and bodies and on the free movement of such data [2007] OJ L164/35, Art 24.

[4] It remains to be seen whether the similar Commission Proposal for a Regulation of the European Parliament and of the Council on the protection of individuals with regard to the processing of personal data and on the free movement of such data (General Data Protection Regulation) COM(2012) 11 final, Art 35 will be enacted.

[5] See Regulation (EU) 1024/2012 of the European Parliament and of the Council of 25 October 2012 on administrative cooperation through the Internal Market Information System and repealing Commission Decision 2008/49/EC ('the IMI Regulation') [2012] OJ L316/1 last amended by Directive 2014/67/EU of the European Parliament and of the Council of 15 May 2014 on the enforcement of Directive 96/71/EC concerning the posting of workers in the framework of the provision of services and amending Regulation (EU) No 1024/2012 on administrative cooperation through the Internal Market Information System ('the IMI Regulation') [2014] OJ L 159/11, Arts 13ff.

[6] Regulation (EC) 1049/2001 of the European Parliament and of the Council of 28 May 2001 regarding public access to European Parliament, Council and Commission documents [2001] OJ L145/43.

[7] Directive 2003/4/EC of the European Parliament and of the Council of 28 January 2003 on public access to environmental information and repealing Council Directive 90/313/EEC [2003] OJ L41/26.

[8] Directive 2007/2/EC of the European Parliament and the Council of 14 March 2007 establishing an Infrastructure for Spatial Information in the European Community (INSPIRE) [2007] OJ L108/1.

11 First, such rules must ensure the **transparency** of composite information management actions. When confronted with such composite administrative procedures, natural and legal persons should be in a position to identify the actors, their duties and to allocate responsibility accordingly.

12 Second, a framework should ensure that the various stages of the composite information management activities **comply with the procedural rights** afforded to concerned persons and third parties in EU administrative procedures. The complexity of composite procedures enhances the quality of administration in the common interest. At the same time, such complexity should not come at the cost of complying with procedural rights.

13 Third, a framework for composite information management activities should provide solutions to **overcome the challenges stemming from the inherent fragmentation of composite procedures.** In order to do so, it should address the resulting multi-jurisdictional aspect of composite information management activities and the conflicts of laws stemming therefrom. A legal framework for composite information management activities should also overcome the traditional horizontal and vertical split of supervisory competences. It should provide a solution adapted to the multi-level integrated nature of composite information management activities in addition to securing the effectiveness of judicial protection.

14 The supervisory and judicial procedures should ensure the efficiency of administrative action while at the same time guaranteeing that concerned persons are in a position to obtain enforcement of their rights.

15 With regard to **multi-jurisdictionalism**, it is also essential to reduce the potential for horizontal and vertical conflicts of laws to a minimum.

16 In light of the above considerations, Book VI complements procedural rules on composite information management activities with **suitable organizational structures.** These procedural and institutional structures must provide for satisfactory data quality. They must also regulate the conditions for lawful information gathering, exchange, and use within composite information procedures.

IV. Types of Information Management Activities and Adequate Regulatory Standards

17 In order to establish a legal infrastructure for information management activities that is not excessively burdensome on the one hand, but provides the legal standards necessary in an EU based on the rule of law, on the other hand, Book VI takes a differentiated approach. Book VI also provides for a very flexible legal infrastructure. We prefer such a **comprehensive**, while **at the same time differentiated and flexible**, legal arrangement to a very selective approach with only a few minimum standards.

First, the regulatory standards of Book VI **apply only to the specified information management activities** (Article VI-1 and Article VI-2). These standards vary for the different types of information management activities: 18

- databases,[9] which are necessarily supported by an information system as defined in Article VI-2(4);
- duties to inform[10] other authorities, if they are supported by an information system as defined in Article VI-2(4);
- structured information mechanisms,[11] if they are supported by an information system as defined in Article VI-2(4);
- (simple) duties to inform other authorities;
- (simple) structured information mechanisms.

As a consequence **only some rules apply to all information management activities** as defined in Article VI-1: Article VI-3 (need for a basic act);[12] Article VI-4(1), (2) (evaluation); Article VI-6 (competent authorities); Article VI-9 (principle of transparency, data tagging); Article VI-10 (principle of data quality); Article VI-40 (compensation); Article VI-41 (penalties for unlawful data processing). 19

Other rules apply only if an information management activity is supported by an information system (in the sense of the definition in Article VI-2): Article VI-5 (specific duties of sincere cooperation); Article VI-17 (access management rules); Article VI-21 (duty to independently assess information); Article VI-30 (Supervisory Authority); Article VI-31 (mediation procedure); Article VI-32 (binding inter-administrative decisions); Article VI-33 (powers of the Supervisory Authority to grant access to/to alter/delete data). In this context, some rules are applicable specifically to IT systems only such as Article VI-8 (management authorities for IT systems) and Article VI-29 (security standards). 20

Some rules apply only to databases (in the sense of the definition in Article VI-2): Article VI-4(3) (duty to report in the context of evaluations); Article VI-13 (general standards); Article VI-27 (storage, blocking, and deletion beyond administrative procedures); Article VI-34 (internal supervision by data protection officers); Article VI-35 (cooperative external data protection supervision); Article VI-36 (external supervision by EDPS); Article VI-37 (external data protection supervision by National Supervisory Authorities); Article VI-38 (cooperation of National Supervisory Authorities and the EDPS); Article VI-39 (data protection supervision by the European Data Protection Board). 21

[9] As defined in Art VI-2(3).
[10] As defined in Art VI-2(2).
[11] As defined in Art VI-2(1).
[12] But note the exemption in para 4 for pilot projects.

22 The following **rules apply only to duties to inform**: Article VI-12 (General standards); Article VI-26 (data storage, blocking, and deletion under a duty to inform)

23 Additionally, **some requirements** in this book are deliberately construed as a **legislative option**. In contrast to the *lex specialis* rule generally adopted in Article I-2 (opt-out solution), these requirements only apply if the legislator renders them expressly applicable in sector-specific law (opt-in solution): Article VI-7 (contact points); Article VI-8(4) (specification of the basic act for IT systems); Article VI-14 (verification); Article VI-18(2) (possibility of assigning the competence to alter/delete information to other bodies; Article VI-19(2) (possibility of establishing an obligation to update information regularly); Article VI-39(1) (external supervision of databases by the European Data Protection Board); Article VI-38(4) (representative supervision in the context of the cooperation between National Supervisory Authorities and the EDPS).

V. Rights, Obligations, and Organizational Structures

24 As Book VI regulates the inter-administrative information exchange and databases used by different authorities, many of its rules contain obligations on authorities (Articles VI-4; VI-5; VI-19(4); VI-22; VI-24(2); VI-31(2), (3); VI-40(2), (3)) or establish organizational structures (Articles VI-6 to VI-8; VI-14; VI-16; VI-18; VI-30 to VI-39). The creation of such innovative organizational structures contributes to the **objective of a clear allocation of responsibilities and transparent information management.** This would benefit legal certainty and create real possibilities of supervision and accountability either through control by a supervisory authority (Articles VI-31 and VI-32), or by the Commission when entering into an action for infringement under Articles 258, 259 TFEU before the CJEU. From this perspective, Book VI contributes to the legal infrastructure for implementing EU law in a decentralized structure, for which well-structured information management activities and new general supervisory powers are essential.

25 Nevertheless, an equally important element of the legal infrastructure provided by Book VI consists in rules which provide, explicitly or implicitly, **subjective rights for individuals** in order to effectively protect their legal interests. Some rights are explicitly provided. These include Article VI-15 (access for persons concerned); Article VI-19(3), (5) (obligations to correct or delete data); Article VI-26 (storage, blocking, and deletion of data exchanged under a duty to inform);[13] Article VI-27 (storage, blocking, and deletion of data beyond administrative procedures);[14] Article VI-32(3) (right to be heard by the supervisory authority); Article VI-33 (power to grant access to data and to alter or delete data); Article VI-37(2) (obligation of

[13] Read in conjunction with Art VI-19(3).

[14] Read in conjunction with Art VI-19(3).

national supervisory authorities to assist and advise a person concerned); third sentence of Article VI-38(1) (obligation of an incompetent authority to transfer a request of a person concerned to the competent authority); Article VI-40(1) (right to compensation in relation to composite information management activities). This does not, however, preclude the possibility that other provisions of this book containing obligations might not also be interpreted to contain rights, such as in: Article VI-13 (general standards for databases); Article VI-14 (verification); Article VI-16 (access for competent authorities); Article VI-19(1), (2), (4) (obligations to update, correct, or delete data); Article VI-21 (duty to independently assess information provided through information systems); Article VI-24 (restrictions on the use of data and information); Article VI-28 (confidentiality); Article VI-29 (security standards for IT systems).

B. Model Rules

Chapter 1: General Provisions

VI-1 Scope of application

(1) Book VI applies to the following information management activities of public authorities based on EU law
  (a) exchange of information according to a structured information mechanism,
  (b) exchange of information under a duty to inform without prior request,
  (c) establishment and use of a database.
  Book VI does not apply to information management activities legally confined to a single Member State with no information exchange with either another Member State or an EU authority.
(2) Rules in books I to V of these model rules on other information management activities remain unaffected.
(3) EU law and national laws on access to documents remain unaffected.

VI-2 Definitions

(1) 'Structured information mechanism' means a pre-defined workflow allowing authorities to communicate and interact with each other in a structured manner beyond the general obligations of mutual assistance according to Book V.
(2) 'Duty to inform' means an obligation for an authority which exists under EU law to provide data or information to another authority without prior request.
(3) 'Database' means a structured collection of data supported by an IT system and managed by a competent authority, which provides at least one other competent authority at EU or Member State level with access to stored data without prior request.
(4) 'Information system' means either a specific software or IT infrastructure (IT system) or an organizational infrastructure and supports inter-administrative information exchange or establishes a database.
(5) 'Participating authority' means any authority taking part in an information management activity within the scope of this book, be it as a competent authority,

a contact point, a management authority, a verification authority or a general supervisory authority.

(6) 'Data supplying authority' means a competent authority supplying data to other competent authorities according to a duty to inform or entering data into a database.

(7) 'Person concerned' means any natural or legal person identifiable, directly or indirectly, by reference to data exchanged or stored by an information management activity within the scope of this book.

VI-3 Need for a basic act

(1) A basic act shall be adopted before an information management activity within the scope of this book may be performed. No duty to perform such an activity shall exist without a basic act.

(2) A basic act may take the form of a regulation, directive, decision, or any other instrument which has binding legal effect.

(3) Notwithstanding additional requirements in other articles of this book, the basic act shall clearly establish

(a) either the power or the duty to perform the relevant information management activity,

(b) the purpose of the relevant information management activity,

(c) the competent authorities according to Article VI-6 and their responsibilities, or a power to designate such an authority,

(d) the Management Authority according to Article VI-8,

(e) the Supervisory Authority according to Article VI-30,

(f) limitations on the right to exchange and receive information or to store data in a database,

(g) the applicable law,

(h) any specific requirements concerning the mechanism for exchanging information including the structure and security requirements of information systems, and

(i) additional aspects specified in other articles of this book.

(4) By way of derogation from paragraphs 1 to 3 an information management activity may be performed without a basic act provided that the action falls within the competences of the Union and is performed in order to implement a pilot project of an experimental nature designed to test the feasibility of an action and its usefulness. The relevant information management action may be performed without a basic act for not more than two consecutive years.

VI-4 Evaluation of information management activities

(1) The Commission or another body adopting the relevant basic act shall produce an overall evaluation of each information management activity; the evaluation shall be transmitted to the European Parliament and the Council. The interval for evaluations shall be defined in the basic act.

(2) If applicable, the Management Authority under Article VI-8 shall submit to the Commission regular reports on the relevant IT system's technical functioning, communication infrastructure, technical and information security and the bilateral and multilateral exchange of information through the IT system. If a Supervisory Authority has been established pursuant to Article VI-30, it shall submit to the Commission regular reports on its findings resulting from its supervisory activities. These reports shall be annexed to the overall evaluation.

(3) With respect to the processing of personal data in databases, a joint report shall be established by the National Supervisory Authorities and the European Data Protection Supervisor and shall be sent to the European Parliament, the Council, the Commission and the concerned Management Authority or Supervisory Authority at regular intervals. If the legislator has assigned the external supervision to the European Data Protection Board according to Article VI-39(1) and (3) the board shall establish the report. The report shall take into account the results of data protection audits according to Articles VI-36(3) and VI-37(3).

VI-5 Duties of sincere cooperation with regard to information systems

(1) Public authorities using an information system shall ensure the efficient functioning of the system within their jurisdiction.
(2) Public authorities using an information system shall ensure effective communication between themselves and with the Management Authority.

VI-6 Competent authorities

(1) For every information management activity each relevant Member State shall establish or designate an authority, or authorities, which will be responsible for performing that activity. Each Member State shall communicate to the Commission or, if established, to the Management Authority a list of these competent authorities, as well as any amendments thereto, as soon as possible. If a Member State designates more than one competent authority the Member State shall clearly define the respective allocation of responsibilities in that list.
(2) The Commission shall maintain a list of all competent EU authorities. If the Union designates more than one competent authority the Commission shall clearly define their respective responsibilities in that list.
(3) The Commission shall maintain an aggregated list of all competent authorities for each information management activity, and shall distribute that list to all participating authorities. Where applicable the aggregated list shall also contain the allocation of responsibilities according to the preceding paragraphs. This aggregated list shall be reviewed and updated at regular intervals and at least once a year.

VI-7 Contact points

(1) If laid down in a basic act each Member State involved and the Union shall designate a contact point.
(2) Contact points shall support
    (a) competent authorities in performing their designated information management activities,
    (b) the resolution of conflicts,
    (c) and coordinate the use of information systems.
(3) Contact points shall ensure the availability of an on-duty officer reachable outside office hours for emergency communications on a 24-hour/7-day-a-week basis.

VI-8 Management authorities for IT systems

(1) If an information management activity is supported by an IT system a management authority is established or designated in the basic act. The management authority can be the European Agency for the operational management of large-scale IT systems.

(2) The management authority shall be responsible for the operational management of the respective IT system. The tasks of the management authority include:
   (a) ensuring the security, continuous and uninterrupted availability, high quality of service for users, high level of data protection, maintenance and development of the respective IT system,
   (b) registering the competent authorities according to Article VI-6 and, if applicable, the contact points, and granting them access to the respective IT system,
   (c) performing processing operations on personal data in the respective IT system, only where provided for in the respective basic act,
   (d) supporting the evaluation tasks of the Commission or the body adopting the relevant basic act in accordance with Article VI-4(1). For the purposes of performing this evaluation task, the management authority shall have access to the necessary information relating to the processing operations performed in the respective IT system.

(3) The management authority shall not participate in information management activities involving the processing of personal data except where required by EU law.

(4) Each basic act may provide for more detailed rules serving the specific needs of an IT system, and may confer additional operational tasks on the management authority.

VI-9 Principle of transparent information management

(1) Information management activities are undertaken in accordance with the principle of transparent and retraceable data processing.

(2) Data processed as a result of an information management activity performed through an IT system shall be tagged. In the absence of detailed regulation within the basic act or implementing acts, the tag shall contain:
   (a) a record of the data supplying authority, the source of data collection, the authority which collected the data if this is not the data supplying authority, and whether restrictions on the exchange or subsequent use apply to that data,
   (b) a record of each information exchange between competent authorities or access to data stored in a database, the subsequent use of that data, as well as the corresponding legal basis for each of these information management activities,
   (c) a flag as provided for in Article VI-19(5) or Article VI-14(3).

Where various data are linked, the tag shall identify such linkage, the authority having requested it, and the corresponding legal basis.

VI-10 Principle of data quality

The data supplying authority shall be responsible for ensuring that the data are accurate, up-to-date and lawfully recorded.

Chapter 2: Structured Information Mechanisms

VI-11 Standards for structured information mechanisms

(1) A basic act establishing a structured information mechanism should, when applicable, indicate the use of agreed workflows, the use of forms, dictionaries, tracking mechanisms and other standardising instruments for the members of the network to exchange the relevant information and to cooperate internally.

(2) With regard to information exchanged through a structured information mechanism the duties to update information laid down in Article VI-19 apply *mutatis mutandis*.

(3) Structured information mechanisms must be subject to a comprehensive data protection framework as provided for in the basic act in line with the principles underlying Articles VI-19, VI-25 to VI-29, VI-34 to VI-39. In any event the obligation to respect the applicable general data protection law remains unaffected.

Chapter 3: Duties to Inform Other Public Authorities Without Prior Request and Databases

Section 1: General Standards for Duties to Inform and Databases

VI-12 General standards for duties to inform

(1) The exchange of information under a duty to inform may either be regular, at certain time intervals, or triggered by an event as specified in the basic act. Personal data may only be exchanged if they are relevant and limited to the minimum necessary in relation to the purposes of the data exchange.

(2) Where a duty to inform exists, information may be exchanged using a variety of notification types. The data supplying authority selects the appropriate notification mechanism, taking into account the nature of the information, the circumstances and aim of its provision, and the specific rules laid down in the basic act and in national implementing rules which establish the duty to inform.

(3) Information may be exchanged by using notification types including:
   (a) emergency notifications,
   (b) standard alert notifications,
   (c) simple information notifications,
   (e) information notifications requiring action, and
   (f) follow-up notifications responding to an existing notification.

(4) In principle, the information will be exchanged in electronic form, including by entering data into an information system designed for the purpose of information exchange. In exceptional and duly justified cases, information may be exchanged in other forms.

VI-13 General standards for databases

(1) Data may only be entered into a database for legitimate purposes as specified in the basic act. Personal data may only be entered if they are relevant and limited to the minimum necessary in relation to the purposes of the database.

(2) Data entered into a database is subject to predefined storage times in accordance with Articles VI-26 and VI-27.

VI-14 Verification

(1) A basic act may provide that data and information exchanged between competent authorities under a duty to inform, or entered into a database, shall be verified ex ante by a separate verification authority. This verification authority may be the Supervisory Authority according to Article VI-30.

(2) The basic act shall specify a time limit for verification. If no limit is specified, the verification authority shall verify the data within the shortest time possible.

(3) Where, due to the nature of the exchange or to time constraints in urgent or emergency situations, it is not possible to verify data before its communication, it shall be flagged by either the verification or the data supplying authority as

unverified and efforts shall be made after dissemination to verify the information transmitted.

(4) The basic act shall specify the verification standards. If no standard is specified, the verification authority shall evaluate whether the information is complete, formally accurate, not evidentially false and legible.

Section 2: Management of Information

Subsection 1: Access to Data and Information

VI-15 Information and access for persons concerned

(1) The data supplying authority shall inform the person concerned in accordance with applicable data protection law about the storage and processing of data relating to him or her. The information shall at least include the categories of data relating to him or her being processed, the data supplying authority, the recipients of the data, and the purpose for which the data will be processed, including the legal basis for such processing in accordance with the relevant provisions of national law.

(2) The person concerned shall have the right to obtain from the data supplying authority or, subject to the conditions laid down in Articles VI-30 and VI-33, from the supervisory authority at any time, on request, confirmation as to whether or not data relating to the person concerned are being processed. Where personal data are being processed, the authority shall provide information in accordance with applicable data protection law. Paragraph (1) sentence 2 applies *mutatis mutandis*.

(3) The data supplying authority shall inform the person concerned of his or her rights to access data relating to him or her, including the right to request either that inaccurate data is corrected or that unlawfully processed data is deleted as soon as possible, and the right to receive information on the procedures for exercising these rights.

(4) The supervisory authority shall ensure that persons concerned can effectively exercise their right of access in accordance with applicable data protection law.

(5) Information may only be withheld in the context of paragraphs 1 and 2 for the purpose of:
   (a) prevention, investigation, detection and prosecution of criminal offences;
   (b) national security, public security or defence of the Member States;
   (c) protection of important economic or financial interests of a Member State or of the Union, including monetary, budgetary and taxation matters;
   (d) protection of the rights and freedoms of others.

The authority is obliged to inform the person concerned about the grounds of withholding of information and rights of recourse to the competent data protection supervisor. Article 20(3) to (5) Regulation (EC) No 45/2001 applies *mutatis mutandis*.

VI-16 Access for competent authorities

(1) Access to information supplied under a duty to inform or stored in a database shall be restricted to those authorities for which access is essential for the performance of their duties, and limited to the extent that the data is necessary for the fulfilment of their tasks in accordance with the purposes for which the information was shared.

(2) Clear and comprehensive rules regarding the authorities which may access and use such information, and the conditions under which access and use is

permissible, shall be laid down in the basic act and in relevant implementing provisions for each duty to inform or database.

VI-17 Access management rules in information systems

For each information system through which public authorities exchange data under a duty to inform or which establishes a database, clear and comprehensive access management rules shall be established in the basic act and in relevant implementing provisions.

Subsection 2: Alteration and Deletion of Data and Information

VI-18 Competences to alter and delete data

(1) Information contained within a database may be altered or deleted by:
  (a) the competent authority which has supplied data under a duty to inform or entered data into a database,
  (b) the Supervisory Authority under Article VI-33.
(2) Where explicitly authorised by the basic act, the right to alter or delete information within a database may also be conferred on one of the bodies listed pursuant to Article VI-6.

VI-19 Obligations to update, correct or delete data

(1) If the data supplying authority finds that information transmitted to other authorities, or that data entered into a database are inaccurate or were processed contrary to the relevant national or EU law, it shall check the information or data and, if necessary, correct or delete them immediately.
(2) The basic act may create an obligation for data supplying authorities to update information at specified regular intervals.
(3) Any person concerned may request that data relating to him or her which are inaccurate shall be corrected and that data recorded unlawfully or which may no longer be stored shall be blocked or deleted by the data supplying authority without delay.
(4) If a participating authority which did not supply the data has evidence to suggest that data are inaccurate or were processed contrary to the relevant national or EU law, this body must inform the data supplying authority immediately. The data supplying authority shall check the data and, if necessary, correct or delete them immediately.
(5) In cases where the person concerned or another participating authority contests the accuracy of the data but the accuracy cannot be established, the data shall, at the request of the person concerned, be marked by the data supplying authority with a flag denoting this dispute. If a flag exists, it may be removed only with the permission of the person concerned or of the other participating authority. Without prejudice to this limitation, a flag may be removed in accordance with a decision of the competent court or an independent data protection authority.
(6) The respective powers of the Supervisory Authority under Article VI-33 remain unaffected.

Subsection 3: Use of Data and Information

VI-20 Duty to use information in activities and to consult databases

Competent authorities are obliged to consider information supplied by other competent authorities under a duty to inform or entered into a database when carrying out their activities. They are particularly obliged to search for and to consult information available in databases.

VI-21 Duty to independently assess information provided through information systems

(1) Information provided through information systems must be subject to a separate assessment by the competent authority considering an administrative action based on such information. Where the acting competent authority doubts the validity of the information, it shall immediately consult the competent authority supplying that information through the information system.
(2) Competent authorities shall ensure that full use is made of the relevant features of an information system so as to obtain a clear and complete picture of the information and to avoid false statements of facts.

VI-22 Duty to take specific action as a result of information

Where an obligation to act as a result of a notification exists, the competent authorities shall ensure that measures as specified in the basic act are carried out and, where required, inform other relevant competent authorities of the actions taken by sending a follow-up notification.

VI-23 Exemption clause

In exceptional cases, competent authorities may be exempt from complying with the duties listed in Articles VI-21 and VI-22. Such non-compliance must be restricted to a limited number of justified situations which are clearly specified in the basic act or in relevant implementing rules.

VI-24 Restrictions on the use of data and information

(1) Competent authorities shall exchange and process data only for the purposes defined in the relevant provisions of EU law providing for the exchange of such information.
(2) Processing for other purposes shall be permitted solely with the prior authorisation of the data supplying authority data and subject to the applicable law of the receiving or retrieving competent authority. The authorisation may be granted insofar as the applicable law of the supplying authority permits.
(3) The dissemination of data and information shared between public authorities to third parties requires a specific legislative authorisation.

Subsection 4: Data Protection and Information Security

VI-25 General data protection duties

(1) All information management activities must comply with the requirements of specific data protection applicable to the matter.
(2) The basic act shall clearly define for each regulated information management activity the categories of data and information which may be gathered, exchanged and stored. Before supplying information, the competent authority shall ensure that the information falls within those categories of data and information.

VI-26 Storage, blocking and deletion of data exchanged under a duty to inform

(1) Data relating to a person concerned and stored in a database as a result of an information exchange under a duty to inform, shall be accessible only for so long as necessary to achieve the purposes for which they were supplied. If a duty

to inform is triggered by a specified event the data shall only be accessible until the administrative tasks connected with that event are accomplished and no longer than six months after the formal closure of the relevant procedure. After that period the data shall be blocked. The basic act shall set rules for the standard and maximum period within which data are accessible.

(2) Blocked data shall, with the exception of their storage, only be processed for purposes of proof of an information exchange with the consent of the person concerned, unless processing is necessary for a subsequent court proceeding or is requested for overriding reasons in the public interest.

(3) Blocked data shall not be searchable or accessible to competent authorities using the database. Searches which result in blocked data shall return a negative result to the requesting authority.

(4) Blocked data shall automatically be deleted three years after the start of the blocking period. Any decision to retain data for a longer period must be based on a comprehensive case-specific assessment, and shall regularly be reviewed.

(5) Nothing in this article shall prejudice the right of a Member State to keep national files of data relating to a particular notification issued by that Member State, or a notification in connection with which action has been taken on the Member State's territory. The duration of such data storage shall be governed by national law.

VI-27 Storage, blocking and deletion of data beyond procedures associated with a duty to inform

(1) Data may be accessible through databases irrespective of the limits set out in Article VI-26 in accordance with the rules of the basic act for the respective database.

(2) Without prejudice to the maximum data retention period provided for in the basic act, data stored in a database shall regularly be reviewed by the data supplying authority in order to assess whether they are still required for the purpose for which they were lawfully stored.

(3) Data relating to a person concerned and stored in a database shall be blocked by the supplying authority as soon as they are no longer necessary for the purpose for which they were lawfully stored or after the maximum total storage time provided for in the basic act.

(4) Sentence 4 of paragraph (1) and paragraphs (2) to (5) of Article VI-26 apply to databases *mutatis mutandis*.

(5) This article shall not exclude the possibility of deleting data earlier than the established storage time subject to an explicit request of the data supplying authority and the consent of the person concerned. Such a deletion must be notified to all participating authorities.

VI-28 Confidentiality

Public authorities, their officials and other servants, including independent experts or bodies appointed by a public authority, shall not disclose information which they have acquired through information management activities and which is covered by the obligation of professional secrecy or other equivalent duties of confidentiality. This obligation shall also apply after members of staff leave office or employment, or after the termination of their activities.

VI-29 Security standards for IT systems

For each IT system through which public authorities exchange data under a duty to inform or which establishes a database, clear and comprehensive standards for risk adequate security measures shall be established in the basic act and in relevant implementing provisions.

Chapter 4: Supervision and Dispute Resolution

Section 1: General Supervision and Dispute Resolution

VI-30 Establishment of a Supervisory Authority

(1) If an information management activity is supported by an information system, the relevant basic act shall establish or designate a Supervisory Authority and regulate its organisational structure.

(2) The Functions of the Supervisory Authority shall be:

(a) to supervise the information management activities of all participating authorities in order to ensure compliance with these model rules, the basic act and the relevant EU law,

(b) to resolve conflicts between participating authorities through mediation procedures according to Article VI-31, or through binding inter-administrative decisions according to Article VI-32,

(c) to assume the role of the appeal authority if EU law establishes an administrative appeal procedure,

(d) to assume the role of a verification authority pursuant to Article VI-14 if the relevant EU law requires the verification of data or information,

(e) notwithstanding the competences of external data protection supervisory authorities according to Section 2 of this chapter, to ensure compliance with the relevant data protection laws. The Supervisory Authority shall cooperate with the data protection authorities in order to establish an effective and efficient data protection supervision,

(f) to hear complaints about refusal of access to documents in a database as defined in Article VI-2(3), and to grant such access in accordance with the applicable EU law.

VI-31 Mediation procedure between participating authorities

(1) Where a participating authority is of the opinion that a measure taken by another participating authority is either incompatible with the basic act or is likely to affect the objectives of the information management activity, it shall refer the matter to the Supervisory Authority. The Supervisory Authority shall serve as mediator.

(2) The relevant participating authorities and the Supervisory Authority shall make every effort to solve the problem.

(3) Participating authorities concerned by the outcome of a mediation shall report on follow-up measures undertaken.

VI-32 Binding inter-administrative decisions

(1) The Supervisory Authority shall be vested with the power to review the legality of information management activities against the standards laid down in the basic act and other rules and principles arising from EU law. The Supervisory Authority may adopt a decision to order participating authorities to comply with the relevant provisions.

(2) The Supervisory Authority may act either on its own initiative or on the basis of a request lodged by a participating authority. The Supervisory Authority shall strive to resolve a conflict through a mediation process as per Article VI-31

before adopting a binding inter-administrative decision. The model rules of Book III apply *mutatis mutandis*.

(3) Save for the powers pursuant to Article VI-33, the Supervisory Authority shall hear and investigate complaints of concerned persons with respect to information management activities.

VI-33 Power to grant access to data and to alter or delete data

(1) On the request of a person concerned, the Supervisory Authority shall inform the respective person concerned in accordance with Article VI-15 about his or her data introduced into an information system.

(2) On the basis of a request by a person concerned pursuant to Article VI-19 (3), or following a decision by a Data Protection Authority, or a judicial authority, the Supervisory Authority shall be afforded the right to delete or alter inaccurate or unlawful data introduced into an information system.

Section 2: Data Protection Supervision of Databases

VI-34 Internal supervision by data protection officers

(1) All public authorities participating in a database shall appoint at least one person as data protection officer.

(2) For the appointment and tasks of the data protection officers, Article 24 of Regulation (EC) No 45/2001 applies insofar as no specific rules are applicable, in case of Member State authorities *mutatis mutandis*.

VI-35 Cooperative external data protection supervision of databases

If the legislator does not assign the external data protection supervision of databases to the European Data Protection Board under Article VI-39 the external data protection supervision of databases is organized in a cooperative structure according to Articles VI-36 to VI-38.

VI-36 External supervision by the European Data Protection Supervisor

(1) With respect to the processing of personal data in databases, the European Data Protection Supervisor shall be responsible for ensuring, in accordance with Regulation (EC) No 45/2001 and any other EU law relating to data protection, that the fundamental rights and freedoms of natural persons, and in particular their right to protection of personal data as established in Article 8 of the Charter of Fundamental Rights and Article 16 of the Treaty on the Functioning of the European Union, are respected by the EU authorities.

(2) With respect to the processing of personal data in databases, the European Data Protection Supervisor shall independently monitor the lawfulness of the processing of personal data by EU authorities, especially the data's transmission to and from the database. If a management authority is set up pursuant to Article VI-8, the European Data Protection Supervisor shall particularly monitor the exchange and further processing of supplementary information or actions undertaken by the management authority.

(3) The European Data Protection Supervisor shall ensure that an audit of the personal data processing activities of participating EU authorities is carried out in accordance with international auditing standards at least every four years. The participating authorities shall supply any information requested by the European Data Protection Supervisor, grant him access to all documents and records, and allow him access to all their premises, at any time.

(4) For the purpose of this article, the European Data Protection Supervisor shall fulfill the duties provided for in Article 46, and exercises the powers granted in Article 47 of Regulation (EC) No 45/2001.

VI-37 External data protection supervision by National Supervisory Authorities

(1) With respect to the processing of personal data in databases, the authority or authorities designated in each Member State and endowed with the powers referred to in Article 28 of Directive 95/46 or Article 25 of Council Framework Decision 2008/977/JHA (the "National Supervisory Authority") shall independently monitor the lawfulness of the processing of personal data by actors of their Member States, including the data transmission to and from the database and the exchange and further processing of supplementary information.
(2) The National Supervisory Authority of the Member State in which the data subject is located and, where necessary, the National Supervisory Authority of the Member State which transmitted the data, shall assist the data subject and, if requested, advise him or her on exercising his or her right to correct or erase data. Both national supervisory authorities shall cooperate to this end. Requests for such assistance may be made to the national supervisory authority of the Member State in which the data subject is located. This authority shall communicate the requests to the National Supervisory Authority of the Member State which transmitted the data.
(3) The National Supervisory Authority shall ensure that an audit of the personal data processing activities by participating Member State authorities is carried out in accordance with international auditing standards at least every four years. The participating authorities shall supply any information requested by the respective National Supervisory Authority, give it access to all documents and records, and allow it access to all their premises, at any time.

VI-38 Cooperation between National Supervisory Authorities and the European Data Protection Supervisor

(1) With regard to the processing of personal data in databases, the National Supervisory Authorities and the European Data Protection Supervisor, both acting within the scope of their respective competences, shall cooperate actively in the context of their responsibilities, and shall ensure coordinated supervision of the databases. To this end, they shall exchange relevant information, assist each other in carrying out audits and inspections, examine difficulties of interpretation or implementation of the applicable data protection rules, study problems related to the exercise of independent supervision or to the exercise of the rights of data subjects, draw up harmonised proposals for joint solutions to any problems and promote awareness of data protection rights, as necessary. If an incompetent authority is addressed by a data subject with a request, the incompetent authority shall transfer the request to the competent authority and shall inform the data subject of the transmission.
(2) Each supervisory authority shall take all appropriate measures necessary to attend to the request of another supervisory authority without delay and no later than one month after having received the request. Such measures may include, in particular, the transmission of relevant information on the course of an investigation, or enforcement measures to bring about the cessation or prohibition of processing operations contrary to the applicable law.

(3) Book V on mutual assistance shall apply without prejudice to the above paragraphs.
(4) The legislator can assign the supervision of the whole internal data processing in a database either to the European Data Protection Supervisor, a National Supervisory Authority or a group of Supervisory Authorities (representative supervision).

VI-39 Data protection supervision of databases by the European Data Protection Board

(1) With respect to the processing of personal data in databases, the legislator may assign the entire external supervision of such a database to a European Data Protection Board. The Board shall be composed of the head of one supervisory authority of each Member State and of the European Data Protection Supervisor and it shall take decisions by a simple majority of its members. If a European Data Protection Board is set up by general EU data protection law, the supervision of databases can only be assigned to this Board. In this case, the Board shall establish at least one subgroup for the supervision of databases. In no case, the Commission shall have the right to participate in the activities and meetings of the Board concerning the supervision of databases.
(2) The national supervisory authorities and the EDPS shall ensure that the European Data Protection Board or the subgroup is vested with adequate human, technical and financial resources, premises and infrastructure for the effective performance of its duties and tasks.
(3) The European Data Protection Board shall fulfill the tasks and duties provided for in Articles VI-36 and VI-37 and shall exercise the powers granted in these articles. For this purpose it shall adopt a supervision plan for each database every year. In this plan parts of the tasks and duties, namely the supervision of Member States activities, can be delegated to particular national supervisory authorities, groups of national supervisory authorities or the EDPS. In case of a delegation, the national supervisory authorities and the EDPS are bound by the delegation and other decisions of the Board. The delegation can be revoked at any time.
(4) For the purpose of fulfilling its tasks and contributing to foster consistency in the application of the rules and procedures for data processing, the European Data Protection Board shall cooperate as necessary with other supervisory authorities.

Chapter 5: Remedies and Liability

VI-40 Right to compensation in relation to composite information management activities

(1) Any person suffering damage from unlawful processing operation in the context of an information management activity, or any act incompatible with the provisions laid down in the basic act, shall be entitled to receive compensation from the participating authority responsible for the damage suffered or the authority of the jurisdiction in which the claimant is resident or, in the case of a legal person, has its registered offices.
(2) In the event that the participating authority against which an action is brought is not the participating authority responsible for the information management activity having caused the damage, the latter shall be required to reimburse, on request, the sums paid as compensation, unless the use of the data by the participating authority requesting reimbursement infringes the basic act.

(3) If any failure by a participating authority to comply with its obligations under the basic act causes damage to another participating authority, the former authority shall be held liable for such damage, unless and in so far as the other participating authority failed to take reasonable steps to prevent the damage from occurring, or to minimise its impact.
(4) The damages will be calculated and compensated in accordance with the general principles common to the laws of the Member States.

VI-41 Penalties for unlawful data processing

Participating authorities shall ensure that any data processing as part of an information management activity within the scope of this book contrary to the basic act is subject to effective, proportionate and dissuasive penalties.

C. Explanations

Chapter 1: General Provisions

VI-1 Scope of application

1 As explained in the introduction[15] and in accordance with Article I-1(3), Book VI follows a **comprehensive approach concerning the authorities** to which Book VI applies. The scope of application comprises horizontal and vertical information management activities, and therefore not only information management activities of EU authorities, but also of national authorities.

2 By contrast, the substantive scope of application does not cover all existing information management activities. Book VI is **focused on certain inter-administrative information exchange activities,** as listed in Article VI-1(1) sentence 1 and defined in Article VI-2(1) to (3), namely via a structured information mechanism, under a duty to inform without prior request, or through the establishment and use of a (shared) database. As stipulated in Article VI-1(1) sentence 2, and following the general approach of the ReNEUAL Model Rules, purely internal activities within a single Member State are not covered by the rules of Book VI. It follows from the definitions in Article VI-2(1) to (3) that neither are internal information management activities within a single EU authority.[16]

3 As Article VI-1(2) highlights, **some information management activities are regulated in other books** of these model rules, in particular Book V, dealing with information exchange under the duty to mutual assistance,[17] and Chapters 3 and 4 of Book III (Unilateral Single-Case Decision Making) regarding the gathering of information, the right to a hearing, and inter-administrative consultations.

[15] See para 3 of the introduction.
[16] See Book V, paras 6–8 of the explanations.
[17] See paras 5, 6 of the introduction.

Due to limited resources, **a number of information management activities are not regulated** by the ReNEUAL Model Rules at this stage of the ReNEUAL project. In addition, comprehensive legal provisions already exist in some cases for such activities. This is especially the case for rules on access to documents held by public authorities. Relevant legal instruments, including Regulation 1049/2001[18] and the INSPIRE Directive 2007/2,[19] therefore remain unaffected. Also, the (public) use of public sector information to inform or warn the general public[20] remains outside the scope of the ReNEUAL Model Rules. Such activities may be integrated into these model rules at a later stage. 4

VI-2 Definitions

Article VI-2 complements Article I-4 and contains definitions of terms which are especially important for Book VI. This is, for instance, the case for the definitions in paragraphs (1) to (3) which concern the sub-categories of information management activities to which Article VI-1(1) renders Book VI applicable. The definition of the term 'information system' is relevant as some rules of this book apply only to activities supported by such a system.[21] Paragraphs (5) and (6) define types of authorities which are not defined in one of the following ReNEUAL Model Rules.[22] By contrast, **some terms used in Book VI remain undefined.** This is especially the case for terms like 'personal data' or 'data processing', which are already well defined in existing EU data protection law and need no further definition.[23] The terms 5

[18] Regulation (EC) 1049/2001 of the European Parliament and of the Council of 28 May 2001 regarding public access to European Parliament, Council and Commission documents [2001] OJ L145/43.

[19] Directive 2007/2/EC of the European Parliament and the Council of 14 March 2007 establishing an Infrastructure for Spatial Information in the European Community (INSPIRE) [2007] OJ L108/1.

[20] Regulation (EC) 178/2002 of the European Parliament and of the Council of 28 January 2002 laying down the general principles and requirements of food law, establishing the European Safety Authority and laying down procedures in matters of food safety [2002] OJ L31/1 last amended by Regulation (EC) 596/2009 of the European Parliament and of the Council of 18 June 2009 adapting a number of instruments subject to the procedure referred to in Article 251 of the Treaty to Council Decision 1999/468/EC with regard to the regulatory procedure with scrutiny—Adaptation to the regulatory procedure with scrutiny—Part Four [2009] OJ L188/14, Art 10; Directive 2001/95/EC of the European Parliament and of the Council of 3 December 2001 on general product safety [2001] OJ L11/4 last amended by Regulation (EC) 596/2009 of the European Parliament and of the Council of 18 June 2009 adapting a number of instruments subject to the procedure referred to in Article 251 of the Treaty to Council Decision 1999/468/EC with regard to the regulatory procedure with scrutiny [2009] OJ L188/14, Art 5.

[21] See para 20 of the introduction.

[22] In contrast to those types of authorities as defined in Arts VI-6, VI-7, VI-8, VI-14, VI-30.

[23] For example Directive 95/46/EC of the European Parliament and of the Council of 24 October 1995 on the protection of individuals with regard to the processing of personal data and on the free movement of such data [1995] OJ L281/3 last amended by Regulation (EC) 1882/2003 of the European Parliament and of the Council of 29 September 2003 adapting to Council Decision 1999/468/EC the provisions relating to committees which assist the Commission in the exercise of its implementing powers laid down in instruments subject to the procedure referred to in Article

'data' and 'information' are not defined in accordance with existing EU law, which does not differentiate between the two.[24] This is an adequate approach also for these model rules.

6 The definition of '**structured information mechanism**' in paragraph 1 is partially inspired by existing EU law.[25] In contrast to some existing EU law, the definition in Article VI-2(1) stipulates that this specific and advanced information management activity is to be differentiated from information exchanged under the basic duties to mutual assistance as provided in Book V. The differences between 'simple' mutual assistance according to Book V and structured information mechanisms are further developed in Article III-11(1). According to the definition, information workflows within one authority are not covered and therefore Book VI does not apply to them.[26]

7 According to Article VI-2(2), a '**duty to inform**' as regulated by Book VI comprises only duties to inform another authority. The lack of a request differentiates the duty to inform from (informational) mutual assistance as defined in Article V-2. The provision of information may be horizontal from one Member State authority to another Member State authority or between separate EU authorities, as well as vertical between Member States' and EU authorities. Consequently, duties to inform another official within the same authority as well as duties to inform the public or private parties are not regulated by the ReNEUAL Model Rules.[27] The

251 of the EC Treaty [2003] OJ L284/1, Art 2(a); Commission Proposal for a Regulation of the European Parliament and of the Council on the protection of individuals with regard to the processing of personal data and on the free movement of such data (General Data Protection Regulation) COM(2012) 11 final, Art 4(2).

[24] For example Directive 95/46/EC of the European Parliament and of the Council of 24 October 1995 on the protection of individuals with regard to the processing of personal data and on the free movement of such data [1995] OJ L281/3 last amended by Regulation (EC) 1882/2003 of the European Parliament and of the Council of 29 September 2003 adapting to Council Decision 1999/468/EC the provisions relating to committees which assist the Commission in the exercise of its implementing powers laid down in instruments subject to the procedure referred to in Article 251 of the EC Treaty [2003] OJ L284/1, Art 2(a); Commission Proposal for a Regulation of the European Parliament and of the Council on the protection of individuals with regard to the processing of personal data and on the free movement of such data (General Data Protection Regulation) COM(2012) 11 final, Art 4(2).

[25] Compare Regulation (EU) 1024/2012 of the European Parliament and of the Council of 25 October 2012 on administrative cooperation through the Internal Market Information System and repealing Commission Decision 2008/49/EC ('the IMI Regulation') [2012] OJ L316/1 last amended by Directive 2014/67/EU of the European Parliament and of the Council of 15 May 2014 on the enforcement of Directive 96/71/EC concerning the posting of workers in the framework of the provision of services and amending Regulation (EU) No 1024/2012 on administrative cooperation through the Internal Market Information System ('the IMI Regulation') [2014] OJ L 159/11, Art 5(d).

[26] See also para 2 of the Explanations.

[27] See also para 2 of the Explanations.

provision of information may be regular, at specified time intervals, or triggered by a specific event.

The definition of '**database**' in paragraph 3 as the third information management activity regulated by these model rules is inspired by existing EU law defining the term 'filing system'.[28] In addition to such filing systems a database must be supported by an IT system. Similar to the two other activities regulated by Book VI, and in accordance with the focus of Book VI on composite information management, a database used by only a single authority is not covered by the definition in paragraph 3.[29] In addition, databases lawfully used only by authorities from one Member State are not regulated by Book VI according to Article VI-1(1) sentence 2. In other words, Book VI applies only to databases shared by at least two public authorities from different jurisdictions or shared by at least two EU authorities. **8**

The term '**information system**' is used in very diverse ways by different EU legal acts, as well as in the academic literature. Paragraph 4 defines it not as a specific information activity, but rather uses the term to further qualify the three activities listed in Article VI-1(1)(a) to (c). Therefore the term is not decisive for the scope of application of Book VI, but for the applicability of some more demanding provisions of Book VI.[30] In contrast to databases which are by definition supported by an IT system,[31] structured information mechanisms and duties to inform may, but will not always, be supported by an information system. **9**

Such qualified standards are justified either if an information activity is supported by an IT system, i.e. either a specific software for the exchange of information or an IT infrastructure,[32] or the activity is supported by an organizational infrastructure, **10**

[28] Compare Directive 95/46/EC of the European Parliament and of the Council of 24 October 1995 on the protection of individuals with regard to the processing of personal data and on the free movement of such data [1995] OJ L281/3 last amended by Regulation (EC) 1882/2003 of the European Parliament and of the Council of 29 September 2003 adapting to Council Decision 1999/468/EC the provisions relating to committees which assist the Commission in the exercise of its implementing powers laid down in instruments subject to the procedure referred to in Article 251 of the EC Treaty [2003] OJ L284/1, Art 2(c); also Commission Proposal for a Regulation of the European Parliament and of the Council on the protection of individuals with regard to the processing of personal data and on the free movement of such data (General Data Protection Regulation) COM(2012) 11 final, Art 4(4).

[29] See also para 2 of the explanations.

[30] See also para 20 of the introduction.

[31] See Article VI-2(3).

[32] Compare Regulation (EU) 1024/2012 of the European Parliament and of the Council of 25 October 2012 on administrative cooperation through the Internal Market Information System and repealing Commission Decision 2008/49/EC ('the IMI Regulation') [2012] OJ L316/1 last amended by Directive 2014/67/EU of the European Parliament and of the Council of 15 May 2014 on the enforcement of Directive 96/71/EC concerning the posting of workers in the framework of the provision of services and amending Regulation (EU) No 1024/2012 on administrative cooperation through the Internal Market Information System ('the IMI Regulation') [2014] OJ L 159/11, Art 8(1)(a); see also Regulation (EU) 1077/2011 of the European Parliament and of the Council of 25 October 2011 establishing a European Agency for the operational management of large-scale IT

i.e. organizational arrangements like contact points (Article VI-7), management authorities (Article VI-8) or supervisory authorities (Book VI, Chapter 4).

11 Individual rights established in the context of this book are in principle rights of '**persons concerned**', which include both natural and legal persons. The definition of the term persons concerned is made irrespective of the fact that rights to data protection might principally be enjoyed by natural persons only. The personal scope of protection of the norms contained in this book therefore needs to be interpreted in each individual situation, but taking into account that in principle persons concerned can be both natural and legal persons. The final part of the definition is inspired by data protection rules,[33] but extended to legal persons. As in data protection law, a person concerned is identifiable only by means reasonably likely to be used.

VI-3 Need for a basic act

12 Article VI-3 stipulates an **obligation to base an information management activity on a basic act** if it falls within the scope of Book VI. By contrast, other books of these model rules contain a legal basis for information management activities like mutual assistance (Book V), or basic forms of information gathering (Book III). This is not possible in Book VI as this book applies to more advanced activities which need to be specified in greater detail than the general framework of Book VI can provide. Book VI therefore determines certain transversal issues, but does not change the need for a basic act.

13 The rule of law requires that administrative actions which may infringe fundamental rights are based on a legal justification. This **principle of legality** is also stipulated in Article 52(1) sentence 1 of the CFR. This principle does not only apply to

systems in the area of freedom, security and justice [2011] OJ L286/1 last amended by Regulation (EU) 603/2013 of the European Parliament and of the Council of 26 June 2013 on the establishment of 'Eurodac' for the comparison of fingerprints for the effective application of Regulation (EU) 604/2013 establishing the criteria and mechanisms for determining the Member State responsible for examining an application for international protection lodged in one of the Member States by a third-country national or a stateless person and on requests for the comparison with Eurodac data by Member States' law enforcement authorities and Europol for law enforcement purposes, and amending Regulation (EU) 1077/2011 establishing a European Agency for the operational management of large-scale IT systems in the area of freedom, security and justice (recast) [2013] OJ L180/1.

[33] See Directive 95/46/EC of the European Parliament and of the Council of 24 October 1995 on the protection of individuals with regard to the processing of personal data and on the free movement of such data [1995] OJ L281/31 last amended by Regulation (EC) 1882/2003 of the European Parliament and of the Council of 29 September 2003 adapting to Council Decision 1999/468/EC the provisions relating to committees which assist the Commission in the exercise of its implementing powers laid down in instruments subject to the procedure referred to in Article 251 of the EC Treaty [2003] OJ L284/1, Art 2(a); Commission Proposal for a Regulation of the European Parliament and of the Council on the protection of individuals with regard to the processing of personal data and on the free movement of such data (General Data Protection Regulation) COM(2012) 11 final, Art 4(1).

legally binding acts like an administrative decision as regulated by Book III. Article 8(2) sentence 1 of the Charter provides that personal data may only be processed on the basis of the person concerned, or some other legitimate basis laid down by law.[34] Administrative information management activities will in many if not in most cases concern at least partially personal data. To establish any of the advanced forms of information management activities covered by Book VI solely on the willingness of the persons concerned to give their consent is not an adequate option. Therefore, Article VI-3 is merely reiterating a constitutional obligation with regard to the processing of personal data and to that extent is only declaratory.

Consequently, Article VI-3 establishes constitutively the obligation to base an activity on a basic act only for those information management activities which concern absolutely no personal data. This **obligation** is justified **for two principal reasons.** First, such an approach guarantees legal certainty as in many cases it might still be possible that an information management activity also comprises the processing of personal data. Second, information management activities regulated in Book VI concern the information exchange between at least two, and in most cases between a large number of, distinct public authorities from various jurisdictions.[35] Under such circumstances, a clear and stable legal basis for the interaction between those authorities provides not only for a clear allocation of responsibilities, but also for administrative effectiveness and efficiency. The derogation clause in Article VI-3(4) provides for the necessary flexibility over pilot projects. In addition, according to Article VI-3(2), the basic act need not necessarily be a legislative act. The administration is thereby empowered to choose between different levels of formalization. If feasible and lawful, the information management activity may also be based on a cascade of basic acts with different legal natures. **14**

An important source of inspiration for the wording of Article VI-3(1) and (4) has been Article 54(1) and (2)(a) of the Financial Regulation,[36] which provides for a similar obligation to base budget implementation activities on a basic act. In addition, Article VI-3(2) has been inspired by Article 2(d) of the Financial Regulation.[37] **15**

[34] See also European Parliament legislative resolution of 12 March 2014 on the proposal for a regulation of the European Parliament and of the Council on the protection of individuals with regard to the processing of personal data and on the free movement of such data (General Data Protection Regulation) P7_TA(2014)0212, Art 6(3).

[35] See paras 3, 13 of the introduction.

[36] Regulation (EU, EURATOM) 966/2012 of the European Parliament and of the Council of 25 October 2012 on the financial rules applicable to the general budget of the Union and repealing Council Regulation (EC, Euratom) 1605/2002 [2012] OJ L298/1 last amended by Regulation (EU, Euratom) 547/2014 of the European Parliament and of the Council of 15 May 2014 amending Regulation (EU, Euratom) 966/2012 on the financial rules applicable to the general budget of the Union [2014] OJ L163/18.

[37] Regulation (EU, EURATOM) 966/2012 of the European Parliament and of the Council of 25 October 2012 on the financial rules applicable to the general budget of the Union and repealing Council Regulation (EC, Euratom) 1605/2002 [2012] OJ L298/1 last amended by Regulation

16 Article VI-3(3) lists a **number of issues which must be regulated in the basic act,** but does not restrict the discretion of the relevant body concerning the concrete arrangements of these issues. These obligatory aspects define the activity in important details (a, b, f, h) and concretize the organizational architecture for its implementation within the abstract framework established by other articles of Book VI (c, d, e). The general list of Article VI-3(4) is complemented by other provisions of Book VI[38] for more specific information management activities. By contrast with Article VI-3(3), some of these provisions leave it to the discretion of the relevant body to regulate the respective issue in the basic act or not.

VI-4 Evaluation of information management activities

17 Obligations to regularly prepare **general evaluative reports** exist for most information management activities to which Book VI is applicable.[39] They allow for the relevant administrative bodies as well as for legislative bodies to reconsider the existing organizational and legal arrangements and to propose modifications to optimize them, adapt them to new circumstances, or to abolish duties to implement information management activities no longer needed, or that have proved to be dysfunctional.

(EU, Euratom) 547/2014 of the European Parliament and of the Council of 15 May 2014 amending Regulation (EU, Euratom) 966/2012 on the financial rules applicable to the general budget of the Union [2014] OJ L163/18.

[38] See Arts VI-4(1) sentence 3, VI-8(4), VI-9(2) sentence 2, VI-11(1) and (3), VI-12(1) sentence 1 and (2) sentence 2, VI-13(1) sentence 1, VI-14(1) sentence 1, (2) sentence 1, (4) sentence 1, VI-16(2), VI-17, VI-18(2), VI-19(2), VI-22, VI-23, VI-25(2) sentence 1, VI-26(1) sentence 4, VI-27(1), VI-29, and VI-30(1).

[39] Regulation (EU) 1052/2013 of the European Parliament and of the Council of 22 October 2013 establishing the European Border Surveillance System (Eurosur) [2013] OJ L295/11, Art 20(3); Regulation (EC) 767/2008 of the European Parliament and of the Council of 9 July 2008 concerning the Visa Information System (VIS) and the exchange of data between Member States on short-stay visas (VIS Regulation) [2008] OJ L218/60 last amended by Regulation (EC) 610/2013 of the European Parliament and of the Council of 26 June 2013 amending Regulation (EC) No 562/2006 of the European Parliament and of the Council establishing a Community Code on the rules governing the movement of persons across borders (Schengen Borders Code), the Convention implementing the Schengen Agreement, Council Regulations (EC) No 1683/95 and (EC) No 539/2001 and Regulations (EC) No 767/2008 and (EC) No 810/2009 of the European Parliament and of the Council [2013] OJ L182/1, Art 50; Decision 2119/98/EC of the European Parliament and of the Council of 24 September 1998 setting up a network for the epidemiological surveillance and control of communicable diseases in the Community [1998] OJ L268/1 last amended by Regulation (EC) 596/2009 of the European Parliament and of the Council of 18 June 2009 adapting a number of instruments subject to the procedure referred to in Article 251 of the Treaty to Council Decision 9/468/EC with regard to the regulatory procedure with scrutiny [2009] OJ L188/14, Art14; Directive 2001/95/EC of the European Parliament and of the Council of 3 December 2001 on general product safety [2001] OJ L11/4 last amended by Regulation (EC) 596/2009 of the European Parliament and of the Council of 18 June 2009 adapting a number of instruments subject to the procedure referred to in Article 251 of the Treaty to Council Decision 1999/468/EC with regard to the regulatory procedure with scrutiny [2009] OJ L188/14, Art 4(d); Regulation (EC) 1987/2006 of the European Parliament and of the Council of 20 December 2006 on the establishment, operation and use of the second generation Schengen Information System (SIS II) [2006] OJ L381/4, Art 50(4), (5).

The intervals specified for reports differ for the various existing activities and these differences are justified. Therefore, they shall be defined in the basic acts.

In some cases, certain information may not be directly accessible to the body which is responsible for the overall report. Where such information is needed by that body, paragraph 2 obliges relevant authorities to provide additional information in specific reports. These specific reports shall be annexed to the overall evaluation in order to allow the addressees of the overall report to double-check. **18**

While the reports mentioned so far enable an evaluation with regard to the objectives of the information management activity itself, the **data protection reports** regulated in paragraph 3 highlight data protection as an especially important aspect of information management. Data protection reports, similar to general evaluation reports are a widespread feature of the recent legal infrastructure for advanced information management activities[40] and represent best practice to be included in the model rules. Data protection reports shall support the political evaluation of information management activities and should be based on results of data protection audits according to Articles VI-36(3) and VI-37(3). The latter (in)directly serve supervisory functions and are therefore supplementary, but are not a substitute for them. **19**

VI-5 Duties of sincere cooperation with regard to information systems

Article VI-5 specifies the general duty of sincere cooperation. It serves thereby as a standard against which, for example, the supervisory authority can evaluate action by participating authorities. Such sincere cooperation is imperative for composite information management and may, *inter alia*, oblige the participating authorities to establish or comply with a set of interoperability standards. **20**

[40] Regulation (EC) 1987/2006 of the European Parliament and of the Council of 20 December 2006 on the establishment, operation and use of the second generation Schengen Information System (SIS II) [2006] OJ L381/4, Art 46(3); Council Decision 2007/533/JHA of 12 June 2007 on the establishment, operation and use of the second generation Schengen Information System (SIS II) [2007] OJ L205/63, Art 62(3); Regulation (EU) 1024/2012 of the European Parliament and of the Council of 25 October 2012 on administrative cooperation through the Internal Market Information System and repealing Commission Decision 2008/49/EC ('the IMI Regulation') [2012] OJ L316/1 last amended by Directive 2014/67/EU of the European Parliament and of the Council of 15 May 2014 on the enforcement of Directive 96/71/EC concerning the posting of workers in the framework of the provision of services and amending Regulation (EU) No 1024/2012 on administrative cooperation through the Internal Market Information System ('the IMI Regulation') [2014] OJ L 159/11, Art 21(4); Regulation (EU) 603/2013 of the European Parliament and of the Council of 26 June 2013 on the establishment of 'Eurodac' for the comparison of fingerprints for the effective application of Regulation (EU) 604/2013 establishing the criteria and mechanisms for determining the Member State responsible for examining an application for international protection lodged in one of the Member States by a third-country national or a stateless person and on requests for the comparison with Eurodac data by Member States' law enforcement authorities and Europol for law enforcement purposes, and amending Regulation (EU) 1077/2011 establishing a European Agency for the operational management of large-scale IT systems in the area of freedom, security and justice (recast) [2013] OJ L180/1, Art 32(3).

VI-6 Competent authorities

VI-7 Contact points

VI-8 Management authorities for IT systems

21 Articles VI-6, VI-7 and VI-8 establish **basic elements of a legal architecture for EU information systems**, i.e. the functions of competent authorities, contact points, and IT systems management authorities. While the establishment of competent authorities is obligatory for all information management activities, the establishment of a management authority is only obligatory if an activity is supported by an IT system. The establishment of contact points is even dependent on an obligation in the basic act.

22 These basic elements may be **supplemented** by duties to inform and for databases **by additional functional elements** regulated in Articles VI-14 (verification), VI-30 to VI-33 (general supervision) and VI-34 to VI-39 (data protection supervision).

23 A **separate authority does not need to exist for all these functions.** For instance, a contact point may also serve as a verification authority. By contrast, other functions may not be the responsibility of only one authority. For example, according to Article 8(3) of the CFR data protection supervisors have to be independent. They may neither act as competent authorities, nor as (general) supervisory authorities that are also responsible for the effective implementation of an information management activity. Such joint responsibilities would compromise effective data protection supervision. Similar dysfunctions might arise in the case of joint responsibilities as a competent authority and a verification authority, or as a general supervisory authority.

VI-6 Competent authorities

24 According to Article VI-6(1), **competent authorities bear the main and direct responsibility** for performing an information management activity. The competent authority in most cases will be the authority which is also preparing and implementing the external or final administrative action triggering or supported by the inter-administrative information exchange. In addition, other provisions of these model rules place a number of important responsibilities on the (data supplying) competent authorities.[41]

25 According to Article VI-6, the **competent authorities must be clearly designated.** In addition, Article VI-6 provides for the accessible documentation of those bodies. These requirements allow effective and efficient information exchange between

[41] Compare Art VI-12(2), VI-14(3), VI-15, VI-16, VI-18, VI-19, VI-20, VI-21, VI-22, VI-24, VI-25(2).

competent authorities and guarantee a clear allocation of responsibilities within complex information networks. The wording of this provision has been inspired by existing EU law.[42]

VI-7 Contact points

Article VI-7 regulates **contact points** as the second basic element of the legal architecture for composite information management. In contrast to competent authorities, which are an obligatory element of any information management activity, the establishment of contact points is **merely a legislative option**. Contact points, which in existing EU law are also referred to as coordinators or liaison offices, are a widely used organizational instrument to facilitate inter-administrative information exchange.[43] 26

[42] For example Decision 2119/98/EC of the European Parliament and of the Council of 24 September 1998 setting up a network for the epidemiological surveillance and control of communicable diseases in the Community [1998] OJ L268/1 last amended by Regulation (EC) 596/2009 of the European Parliament and of the Council of 18 June 2009 adapting a number of instruments subject to the procedure referred to in Article 251 of the Treaty to Council Decision 9/468/EC with regard to the regulatory procedure with scrutiny [2009] OJ L188/14, Art 9; Regulation (EC) 1987/2006 of the European Parliament and of the Council of 20 December 2006 on the establishment, operation and use of the second generation Schengen Information System (SIS II) [2006] OJ L381/4, Art 7; Regulation (EC) 767/2008 of the European Parliament and of the Council of 9 July 2008 concerning the Visa Information System (VIS) and the exchange of data between Member States on short-stay visas (VIS Regulation) [2008] OJ L218/60 last amended by Regulation (EC) 610/2013 of the European Parliament and of the Council of 26 June 2013 amending Regulation (EC) No 562/2006 of the European Parliament and of the Council establishing a Community Code on the rules governing the movement of persons across borders (Schengen Borders Code), the Convention implementing the Schengen Agreement, Council Regulations (EC) No 1683/95 and (EC) No 539/2001 and Regulations (EC) No 767/2008 and (EC) No 810/2009 of the European Parliament and of the Council [2013] OJ L182/1, Art 6(3); Council Regulation (EC) 515/97 of 13 March 1997 on mutual assistance between the administrative authorities of the Member States and the cooperation between the latter and the Commission to ensure the correct application of the law on customs and agricultural matters [1997] OJ L82/1 last amended by Regulation (EC) 766/2008 of the European Parliament and of the Council of 9 July 2008 amending Council Regulation (EC) 515/97 on mutual assistance between the administrative authorities of the Member States and cooperation between the latter and the Commission to ensure the correct application of the law on customs and agricultural matters [2008] OJ L218/48, Art 29(2); Directive 2001/95/EC of the European Parliament and of the Council of 3 December 2001 on general product safety [2001] OJ L11/4 last amended by Regulation (EC) 596/2009 of the European Parliament and of the Council of 18 June 2009 adapting a number of instruments subject to the procedure referred to in Article 251 of the Treaty to Council Decision 1999/468/EC with regard to the regulatory procedure with scrutiny [2009] OJ L188/14, Art 6; Regulation (EU) 1052/2013 of the European Parliament and of the Council of 22 October 2013 establishing the European Border Surveillance System (Eurosur) [2013] OJ L295/11, Art 5.

[43] For example, Commission Regulation (EU) 16/2011 of 10 January 2011 laying down implementing measures for the Rapid alert system for food and feed [2011] OJ L6/7, Art 2; Directive 2001/95/EC of the European Parliament and of the Council of 3 December 2001 on general product safety [2001] OJ L11/4 last amended by Regulation (EC) 596/2009 of the European Parliament and of the Council of 18 June 2009 adapting a number of instruments subject to the procedure referred to in Article 251 of the Treaty to Council Decision 1999/468/EC with regard to the regulatory procedure with scrutiny [2009] OJ L188/14, Art 6 read in conjunction with Section 9 of

27 Although competent authorities bear the main responsibility for the information exchange it may be that they have only very limited experience with multijurisdictional exchange of information or lack relevant knowledge in terms of foreign languages, relevant foreign law, or the allocation of responsibilities in another country. In such cases contact points may provide **supplementary resources** as they are regularly involved in composite information management and bundle relevant professional skills and abilities. They may also serve as mediators in case of conflicts between competent authorities.

28 Article VI-7 merely establishes contact points as an **organizational option,** since some inter-administrative information exchange schemes do not need such supplementary support. This will generally be the case with information exchange between two EU authorities,[44] or between highly specialized central authorities on the Member State level with regular interaction with their counterparts in other Member States or on the EU level.

29 As contact points serve as an organizational infrastructure supporting inter-administrative information exchange they qualify as an information system according to Article VI-2 (4). This is highlighted by the demanding obligations according to Article VI-7 (3) even if a basic act may derogate from it.

VI-8 Management authorities for IT systems

30 Article VI-8 stipulates that a basic act shall establish or identify a management authority if an information management activity is supported by an IT system as defined in Article VI-2(4). Therefore, **management authorities are a basic element of the architecture of many, more advanced, EU information systems.**[45] The basic act can set up a new management authority, or designate an existing Member State or EU authority as management authority. It might be especially effective and

Annex II; Directive 2006/123/EC of the European Parliament and of the Council of 12 December 2006 on services in the internal market [2006] OJ L376/36, Arts 6, 21(2), 28(2); Council Regulation (EC) 768/2005 of 26 April 2005 establishing a Community Fisheries Control Agency and amending Regulation (EEC) 2847/93 establishing a control system applicable to the common fisheries policy [2005] OJ L128/1 last amended by Council Regulation (EC) 1224/2009 of 20 November 2009 establishing a Community control system for ensuring compliance with the rules of the common fisheries policy, amending Regulations (EC) 847/96, (EC) 2371/2002, (EC) 811/2004, (EC) 768/2005, (EC) 2115/2005, (EC) 2166/2005, (EC) 388/2006, (EC) 509/2007, (EC) 676/2007, (EC) 1098/2007, (EC) 1300/2008, (EC) 1342/2008 and repealing Regulations (EEC) 2847/93, (EC) 1627/94 and (EC) 1966/2006 [2009] OJ L343/1, Art 13(2)(b); Regulation (EC) 1987/2006 of the European Parliament and of the Council of 20 December 2006 on the establishment, operation and use of the second generation Schengen Information System (SIS II) [2006] OJ L381/4, Art 7(2); Council Framework Decision 2009/315/JHA of 26 February 2009 on the organisation and content of the exchange of information extracted from the criminal record between Member States [2009] OJ L93/23, Art 3.

[44] But see also Commission Regulation (EC, EURATOM) 1302/2008 of 17 December 2008 on the central exclusion database [2008] OJ L344/12, Art 6.

[45] See also para 24 of the Explanations.

efficient to designate the existing European Agency for the Operational Management of Large-Scale IT Systems established by Regulation 1077/2011.[46]

Paragraph 2 lists a **number of important tasks** for such a **management authority.** This list has been inspired by existing EU law[47] and comprises operational management tasks with a technical focus. These technical tasks of the management authority are to be differentiated from the substantive administrative tasks of the competent authorities which are supported by the IT system. These different responsibilities of the competent authority and of the management authority are underlined by paragraph 3.[48] Paragraph 4 provides flexibility in this highly technical and dynamic field of law. An example of rules under this provision might be rules establishing inter- **31**

[46] Regulation (EU) 1077/2011 of the European Parliament and of the Council of 25 October 2011 establishing a European Agency for the operational management of large-scale IT systems in the area of freedom, security and justice [2011] OJ L286/1 last amended by Regulation (EU) 603/2013 of the European Parliament and of the Council of 26 June 2013 on the establishment of 'Eurodac' for the comparison of fingerprints for the effective application of Regulation (EU) 604/2013 establishing the criteria and mechanisms for determining the Member State responsible for examining an application for international protection lodged in one of the Member States by a third-country national or a stateless person and on requests for the comparison with Eurodac data by Member States' law enforcement authorities and Europol for law enforcement purposes, and amending Regulation (EU) 1077/2011 establishing a European Agency for the operational management of large-scale IT systems in the area of freedom, security and justice (recast) [2013] OJ L180/1.

[47] See Regulation (EU) 1077/2011 of the European Parliament and of the Council of 25 October 2011 establishing a European Agency for the operational management of large-scale IT systems in the area of freedom, security and justice [2011] OJ L286/1 last amended by Regulation (EU) 603/2013 of the European Parliament and of the Council of 26 June 2013 on the establishment of Eurodac for the comparison of fingerprints for the effective application of Regulation (EU) 604/2013 establishing the criteria and mechanisms for determining the Member State responsible for examining an application for international protection lodged in one of the Member States by a third-country national or a stateless person and on requests for the comparison with Eurodac data by Member States' law enforcement authorities and Europol for law enforcement purposes, and amending Regulation (EU) 1077/2011 establishing a European Agency for the operational management of large-scale IT systems in the area of freedom, security and justice (recast) [2013] OJ L180/1, Arts 1(2), 2; Regulation (EU) 1024/2012 of the European Parliament and of the Council of 25 October 2012 on administrative cooperation through the Internal Market Information System and repealing Commission Decision 2008/49/EC ('the IMI Regulation') [2012] OJ L316/1 last amended by Directive 2014/67/EU of the European Parliament and of the Council of 15 May 2014 on the enforcement of Directive 96/71/EC concerning the posting of workers in the framework of the provision of services and amending Regulation (EU) No 1024/2012 on administrative cooperation through the Internal Market Information System ('the IMI Regulation') [2014] OJ L 159/11, Art 8; Regulation (EC) 1987/2006 of the European Parliament and of the Council of 20 December 2006 on the establishment, operation and use of the second generation Schengen Information System (SIS II) [2006] OJ L381/4, Art 15.

[48] Source of inspiration for this paragraph Regulation (EU) 1024/2012 of the European Parliament and of the Council of 25 October 2012 on administrative cooperation through the Internal Market Information System and repealing Commission Decision 2008/49/EC ('the IMI Regulation') [2012] OJ L316/1 last amended by Directive 2014/67/EU of the European Parliament and of the Council of 15 May 2014 on the enforcement of Directive 96/71/EC concerning the posting of workers in the framework of the provision of services and amending Regulation (EU) No 1024/2012 on administrative cooperation through the Internal Market Information System ('the IMI Regulation') [2014] OJ L 159/11, Art 8(3).

operability standards between the joint IT system and connected systems of the participating EU and Member States' authorities.

VI-9 Principle of transparent information management

VI-10 Principle of data quality

32 Articles VI-9 and VI-10 highlight **two important principles for composite information management** and joint data processing,[49] i.e. the principles of transparency and of data quality. Both principles serve two distinct but interrelated objectives: the provision of reliable inter-administrative information exchange and the protection of the subjective rights of persons concerned.

33 Inter-administrative information exchange is only reliable if the data provided meets **high standards of data quality** as defined in Article VI-10.[50] An incentive to provide high data quality is to assign a corresponding responsibility to the data supplying authority.[51] In order to hold the data supplying authority accountable Article

---

[49] Directive 95/46/EC of the European Parliament and of the Council of 24 October 1995 on the protection of individuals with regard to the processing of personal data and on the free movement of such data [1995] OJ L281/31 amended by Regulation (EC) 1882/2003 of the European Parliament and of the Council of 29 September 2003 adapting to Council Decision 1999/468/EC the provisions relating to committees which assist the Commission in the exercise of its implementing powers laid down in instruments subject to the procedure referred to in Article 251 of the EC Treaty [2003] OJ L284/1, Art 2(b); see also Commission Proposal for a Regulation of the European Parliament and of the Council on the protection of individuals with regard to the processing of personal data and on the free movement of such data (General Data Protection Regulation) COM(2012) 11 final, Art 4(3).

[50] Compare Regulation (EC) 1987/2006 of the European Parliament and of the Council of 20 December 2006 on the establishment, operation and use of the second generation Schengen Information System (SIS II) [2006] OJ L381/4, Art 34(1); see also The Schengen acquis—Convention implementing the Schengen Agreement of 14 June 1985 between the Governments of the States of the Benelux Economic Union, the Federal Republic of Germany and the French Republic on the gradual abolition of checks at their common borders [2000] OJ L239/19, Art 105.

[51] Compare Directive 2001/95/EC of the European Parliament and of the Council of 3 December 2001 on general product safety [2001] OJ L11/4 last amended by Regulation (EC) 596/2009 of the European Parliament and of the Council of 18 June 2009 adapting a number of instruments subject to the procedure referred to in Article 251 of the Treaty to Council Decision 1999/468/EC with regard to the regulatory procedure with scrutiny [2009] OJ L188/14, Section 10 of Annex II; Commission Decision 2010/15/EU of 16 December 2009 laying down guidelines for the management of the Community Rapid Information System 'RAPEX' established under Article 12 and of the notification procedure established under Article 11 of Directive 2001/95/EC (the General Product Safety Directive) [2009] OJ L22/1, Part II.3.2.4 of the Annex; The Schengen acquis—Convention implementing the Schengen Agreement of 14 June 1985 between the Governments of the States of the Benelux Economic Union, the Federal Republic of Germany and the French Republic on the gradual abolition of checks at their common borders [2000] OJ L239/19, Art 105; see also Regulation (EC) 883/2004 of the European Parliament and of the Council of 29 April 2004 on the coordination of social security systems [2004] OJ L 166/1 last amended by Commission Regulation (EU) 1372/2013 of 19 December 2013 amending Regulation (EC) 883/2004 of the European Parliament and of the Council on the coordination of social security systems and Regulation (EC) 987/2009 of the European Parliament and of the Council laying down the procedure for implementing Regulation (EC) 883/2004 [2013] OJ L346/27, Art 78(2).

VI-9 provides for transparent and retraceable data processing. Additional instruments to enhance the quality of data are provided throughout Book VI.[52]

If data exchanged between participating authorities **concern individuals**, these persons concerned must be entitled and enabled to protect their (data protection) rights effectively. The starting point is the obligation of the data supplying authority to provide only data of high quality. **34**

This obligation will only be effective if responsibilities are clearly allocated in cases of composite information management. Consequently, an indispensable component for effective protection of such rights is the possibility of the persons concerned to identify clearly and easily the responsible authority in order to hold that authority accountable. Article VI-9 ensures that this information can be provided to the person concerned in accordance with Article VI-15(1). **35**

Chapter 2: Structured Information Mechanisms

VI-11 Standards for structured information mechanisms

Paragraph 1

The drafting team proposes a definition of 'structured information mechanism' in terms of a cooperation system in which the **cooperative obligations are structured in a pre-defined workflow**, allowing authorities to communicate and interact with one another. In particular, the authorities participating in the system are thereby aided in contacting the right competent authority in another country, and can overcome the linguistic barriers by use of pre-translated sets of standard questions and answers; the authorities can follow the progress of the information request through tracking mechanisms, and so on. The system thus involves the use of standardizing instruments, which are aimed at facilitating cooperation and the exchange of information. **36**

As a **general rule**, and, in accordance with Article VI-3, we assume that, in order to establish a structured information mechanism, a basic act has to be adopted. In this case, the basic act should indicate the standardizing instruments, which characterize the specific mechanism. A clear example of this kind of mechanism is the Internal Market Information System (IMI), regulated by Regulation 1024/2012.[53] **37**

[52] See especially Articles VI-14 (verification), VI-19 (obligations to update, correct or delete data) and VI-21 (duty to independently assess information).

[53] Regulation (EU) 1024/2012 of the European Parliament and of the Council of 25 October 2012 on administrative cooperation through the Internal Market Information System and repealing Commission Decision 2008/49/EC ('the IMI Regulation') [2012] OJ L316/1 last amended by Directive 2014/67/EU of the European Parliament and of the Council of 15 May 2014 on the enforcement of Directive 96/71/EC concerning the posting of workers in the framework of the provision of services and amending Regulation (EU) No 1024/2012 on administrative cooperation through the Internal Market Information System ('the IMI Regulation') [2014] OJ L 159/11.

Paragraph 2

38 Once the structure of the system is outlined by the basic act, at least two other aspects have to be considered: the **quality of the information** exchanged **and** the **protection of personal data**. In this sense, paragraph 2 clarifies that the information exchanged through the system has to be accurate and processed in accordance with the relevant national and European regulations. Hence, the competent authorities have to be placed under the obligation to check, and if necessary to correct and delete, the information exchanged when needed.

Paragraph 3

39 The same obligation outlined in paragraph 2 applies to the **exchange of personal data**. In this case, in order to guarantee even more effective protection, the correction or the deletion of the personal data can occur at the request of the data subject and at the suggestion of a participating authority that did not supply the data in question. In particular, the structured information mechanism has to be subject to a data protection framework to be outlined in the basic act. This must indicate, among other things, the categories of data that may be gathered, exchanged, and stored. Also, it has to indicate rules on the accessibility and blockage of data, which has to take place, as a general rule, six months after the closure of the procedure in question. Moreover, the basic act has to provide relevant technical measures to ensure the security of the exchange of information within the IT system, and has to subject all the authorities involved in the management of information to confidentiality obligations.

40 In relation to the supervision of the data exchanged through structured information mechanisms, this supervision can be assigned to the European Data Protection Board by EU law (Article VI-39).

Chapter 3: Duties to Inform Other Public Authorities Without Prior Request and Databases

41 Chapter 3 regulates duties to inform without prior request and databases. These two information management activities establish highly integrated structures of composite information management. Many issues with regard to these two activities can and should be regulated in the same way. Consequently, many of the following model rules apply to both activities and the drafting team preferred to regulate them in one chapter in order to avoid redundancy and confusion. Nevertheless, this chapter provides specific rules for each of these two actions if appropriate.[54] These specific rules are integrated systematically in this chapter.

42 The chapter comprises **two sections**, one dealing with **general standards** for both activities, and another concerning the **subsequent management** of the information

[54] See the overview in paras 21 and 22 of the introduction.

provided through these activities. The latter section is organized in four subsections, each concerning a specific issue, i.e. access to data, modification of data, use of data, and data protection including data security. Some data protection issues are not regulated in the last subsection. Instead, they are integrated into one of the previous subsections, in accordance with the general approach of this book to establish a comprehensive and data protection-friendly legal framework for inter-administrative information exchange. Therefore, rules on information to and access for persons concerned are part of the subsection on data access (Article VI-15), and the right of persons concerned to have data erased is highlighted as one especially important component for an obligation to update, correct or delete data (Article VI-19(3)). Similarly, rules guaranteeing the data protection principle of purpose limitation are included in the sub-section on the use of data and information (Article VI-24).

Section 1: General Standards for Duties to Inform and Databases

VI-12 General standards for duties to inform

Article VI-12 sets general standards for a duty to inform defined in Article VI-2(2). **43**
Exchange of information under a duty to inform without prior request may thereby be **triggered ad hoc** by predefined events, as is the case in many warning systems, **or** establish **a repetitive flow of information** through a permanent or recurring provision of information. An important limitation of the exchange of personal data arises from the data minimization principle.[55]

Duties to inform spontaneously pursue different objectives. In order to facilitate **44**
communication between the participating authorities, existing EU provisions provide for a predefined set of notifications, which indicate different levels of urgency, or oblige the recipients to undertake certain follow-up measures or administrative actions. Unfortunately, similar notifications are labelled differently in the respective legal acts. The list in paragraph 3 presents five important types of notification in order to promote a more uniform labelling of notifications and to minimize the risk of misconception.[56] If needed the basic act may provide additional types of notification. It is for the competent data supplying authority to select the appropriate

[55] Based on Commission Proposal for a Regulation of the European Parliament and of the Council on the protection of individuals with regard to the processing of personal data and on the free movement of such data (General Data Protection Regulation) COM(2012) 11 final, Art 5(c), Explanatory Memorandum, 3.4.2.

[56] A similar, but not uniform, list of notification types can be found in Commission Decision 2010/15/EU of 16 December 2009 laying down guidelines for the management of the Community Rapid Information System 'RAPEX' established under Article 12 and of the notification procedure established under Article 11 of Directive 2001/95/EC (the General Product Safety Directive) [2009] OJ L22/1, Part II.3.1.1 Alternative 1 and 2 of the Annex; Commission Regulation (EU) 16/2011 of 10 January 2011 laying down implementing measures for the Rapid alert system for food and feed [2011] OJ L6/7, Art 1 Nos 4, 5, 7, 8; Directive 2006/123/EC of the European Parliament and of the Council of 12 December 2006 on services in the internal market [2006] OJ L376/36, Art 35(2), (3).

type of notification. Paragraph 2 highlights factors which should be taken into account when making this choice.

45 Emergency notification means a notification in the case of extreme urgency; standard alert notification refers to the notification of a risk which might require rapid action. An information notification requiring action means that the information sent without prior request already implies that specific action needs to be taken, whereas a simple information notification does not require action. A follow-up notification contains additional information relating to an already existing notification, for example about actions actually taken or new information on a certain risk.

46 Information provided under a duty to inform should **in general** be exchanged in **electronic form** and only in exceptional and duly justified cases in writing or orally. The priority of electronic information exchange fosters efficiency as well as effectiveness. It also serves the principle of retraceable data processing.[57] In the rare cases that information is exchanged orally, the competent authority should nonetheless confirm the oral exchange of information in electronic or written form afterwards. This avoids misunderstandings and serves the principle of retraceable data processing.

VI-13 General standards for databases

47 According to Article VI-3(3)(b), the basic act establishes the **purpose** for which the relevant **information management activity** shall be performed. In order to reduce the amount of data entered into a database, data may only be entered for the purpose defined in the basic act. The data minimization principle requires that the limitations, as in Article VI-12(1), also apply to the entry of personal data into a database.[58] This principle also requires the deletion of stored data after a certain time limit. The relevant time limits are regulated in Articles VI-26 and VI-27.

VI-14 Verification

48 As already mentioned in the explanations to Article VI-10,[59] information exchange is reliable if the data provided meets high standards of data quality. A way in which to **enhance the quality of data** is the ex-ante verification of data through a separate verification authority. This approach is already taken in various information

---

[57] See Art VI-9.

[58] Based on Commission Proposal for a Regulation of the European Parliament and of the Council on the protection of individuals with regard to the processing of personal data and on the free movement of such data (General Data Protection Regulation) COM(2012) 11 final, Art 5(c).

[59] See para 33 of the Explanations.

systems.[60] It is up to the legislator to decide whether to establish a duty to verify data or not as the verification needs to be provided in the basic act.

The existing information systems establish different **verification authorities.** In RAPEX the Contact Points and the Commission verify the data: the Contact Point checks and validates all notifications before transmitting them to the Commission and resolves any unclear issues before a notification is transmitted through RAPEX.[61] The Commission then checks all notifications received through the RAPEX application before transmitting them to the Member States to ensure that they are correct and complete.[62] **49**

Paragraph 2 provides as a default rule that the verification should be carried out **within the shortest time possible.** It would be preferable for the basic act to provide a clear time limit for verification. **50**

Circumstances may exist in which it is **not possible to verify the data ex-ante.** According to paragraph 3, such data has to be flagged as unverified by either the verification or the data supplying authority and has to be verified after it has been distributed. The authority that is more capable of deciding if it is necessary to leave the data unverified due to time constraints in urgent or emergency situations shall flag the data. The flag indicates to the receiving authorities that they should perform independent assessments of the information in question in accordance with Article VI-21. **51**

[60] For example Commission Decision 2010/15/EU of 16 December 2009 laying down guidelines for the management of the Community Rapid Information System 'RAPEX' established under Article 12 and of the notification procedure established under Article 11 of Directive 2001/95/EC (the General Product Safety Directive) [2009] OJ L22/1, Part II.2.3.3–4, II.3.4 of the Annex; Regulation (EU) 603/2013 of the European Parliament and of the Council of 26 June 2013 on the establishment of 'Eurodac' for the comparison of fingerprints for the effective application of Regulation (EU) 604/2013 establishing the criteria and mechanisms for determining the Member State responsible for examining an application for international protection lodged in one of the Member States by a third-country national or a stateless person and on requests for the comparison with Eurodac data by Member States' law enforcement authorities and Europol for law enforcement purposes, and amending Regulation (EU) 1077/2011 establishing a European Agency for the operational management of large-scale IT systems in the area of freedom, security and justice (recast) [2013] OJ L180/1, Art 23; The Schengen acquis—Convention implementing the Schengen Agreement of 14 June 1985 between the Governments of the States of the Benelux Economic Union, the Federal Republic of Germany and the French Republic on the gradual abolition of checks at their common borders [2000] OJ L239/19, Art 105.

[61] Commission Decision 2010/15/EU of 16 December 2009 laying down guidelines for the management of the Community Rapid Information System 'RAPEX' established under Article 12 and of the notification procedure established under Article 11 of Directive 2001/95/EC (the General Product Safety Directive) [2009] OJ L22/1, Part II.2.3.3–4 of the Annex.

[62] Commission Decision 2010/15/EU of 16 December 2009 laying down guidelines for the management of the Community Rapid Information System 'RAPEX' established under Article 12 and of the notification procedure established under Article 11 of Directive 2001/95/EC (the General Product Safety Directive) [2009] OJ L22/1, Part II.3.4 of the Annex.

52 The verification standards should be defined in the basic act in order to **adapt the standards** in paragraph 4 to **the specifics of administrative tasks** supported by the respective duty to inform or to database. Paragraph 4 establishes a default standard in case the basic act does not specify the verification standards, and has been inspired by comparative analysis of existing EU law. According to the default rule of paragraph 4, the information needs to be complete, formally accurate, and not evidently false and legible. Information would be evidently false, for instance, if it does not concern matters within the scope of the duty to inform or the shared database.

53 The introduction of a **minimum standard** is necessary as the verification standards can vary quite significantly. Existing EU law uses no uniform terminology and tends to list redundant standards. Whereas the verification standard of RASFF includes completeness, legibility—that is, use of Commission dictionaries and understandable language—and correctness of data,[63] RAPEX only requires completeness and correctness of data, but not legibility.[64] In addition, while, in the case of the RASFF, correctness includes the requirement that the data fall within the scope of RASFF, or comply with other requirements of its legal basis,[65] for RAPEX, a purely formal standard of correctness seems to apply.[66] However, RAPEX provides that the 'validating' authority has to guarantee the accuracy of the data exchanged.[67] The verification rules of the Schengen Information System differ even more, as they simply stipulate that the verification authority coordinates the quality of data.[68]

54 At this stage the ReNEUAL Model Rules do not regulate the impact of verification processes on the allocation of responsibilities, and especially the impact of the potential liability of the verification authority.[69] This evolving field of law is not yet sufficiently stabilized to be codified.

[63] Commission Regulation (EU) 16/2011 of 10 January 2011 laying down implementing measures for the Rapid alert system for food and feed [2011] OJ L6/7, Art 8.

[64] Commission Decision 2010/15/EU of 16 December 2009 laying down guidelines for the management of the Community Rapid Information System 'RAPEX' established under Article 12 and of the notification procedure established under Article 11 of Directive 2001/95/EC (the General Product Safety Directive) [2009] OJ L22/1, Part II.3.4.1–2 of the Annex.

[65] Commission Regulation (EU) 16/2011 of 10 January 2011 laying down implementing measures for the Rapid alert system for food and feed [2011] OJ L6/7, Art 8.

[66] Commission Decision 2010/15/EU of 16 December 2009 laying down guidelines for the management of the Community Rapid Information System 'RAPEX' established under Article 12 and of the notification procedure established under Article 11 of Directive 2001/95/EC (the General Product Safety Directive) [2009] OJ L22/1, Part II.3.4.1 of the Annex.

[67] Commission Decision 2010/15/EU of 16 December 2009 laying down guidelines for the management of the Community Rapid Information System 'RAPEX' established under Article 12 and of the notification procedure established under Article 11 of Directive 2001/95/EC (the General Product Safety Directive) [2009] OJ L22/1, Part II.3.2.4 of the Annex.

[68] Regulation (EC) 1987/2006 of the European Parliament and of the Council of 20 December 2006 on the establishment, operation and use of the second generation Schengen Information System (SIS II) [2006] OJ L381/4, Art 7.

[69] Case T-212/06 *Bowland Dairy Products Ltd v Commission* [2009] ECR II-4073.

Section 2: Management of Information

Subsection 1: Access to Data and Information

VI-15 Information to and access for persons concerned

The obligation of data controllers to inform the person concerned[70] about data **55** processing relating to that natural or legal person, as well as their right to request access to the data relating to him or her processed by a data controller, are central instruments of **good information management as well as of data protection law** required by Article 8(2) sentence 2 of the CFR.[71] In accordance with the general approach of this Book[72] Article VI-15 integrates such rights into the subsection on access to data and information. Having regard to the extensive and detailed requirements in the existing and proposed data protection law Article VI-15(1) and (2)

---

[70] See para 11 of the explanations.

[71] More detailed obligations to inform data subjects are provided by Directive 95/46/EC of the European Parliament and of the Council of 24 October 1995 on the protection of individuals with regard to the processing of personal data and on the free movement of such data [1995] OJ L281/31 last amended by Regulation (EC) 1882/2003 of the European Parliament and of the Council of 29 September 2003 adapting to Council Decision 1999/468/EC the provisions relating to committees which assist the Commission in the exercise of its implementing powers laid down in instruments subject to the procedure referred to in Article 251 of the EC Treaty [2003] OJ L284/1, Arts 10, 11; Regulation (EC) 45/2001 of the European Parliament and of the Council of 18 December 2000 on the protection of individuals with regard to the processing of personal data by the Community institutions and bodies and on the free movement of such data [2001] OJ L8/1 last amended by Corrigendum to Regulation (EC) 45/2001 of the European Parliament and of the Council of 18 December 2000 on the protection of individuals with regard to the processing of personal data by the Community institutions and bodies and on the free movement of such data [2007] OJ L164/35, Arts 11, 12; see also European Parliament legislative resolution of 12 March 2014 on the proposal for a regulation of the European Parliament and of the Council on the protection of individuals with regard to the processing of personal data and on the free movement of such data (General Data Protection Regulation) P7_TA(2014)0212, Art 14; detailed rights to access for data subjects are established by Directive 95/46/EC of the European Parliament and of the Council of 24 October 1995 on the protection of individuals with regard to the processing of personal data and on the free movement of such data [1995] OJ L281/31 last amended by Regulation (EC) 1882/2003 of the European Parliament and of the Council of 29 September 2003 adapting to Council Decision 1999/468/EC the provisions relating to committees which assist the Commission in the exercise of its implementing powers laid down in instruments subject to the procedure referred to in Article 251 of the EC Treaty [2003] OJ L284/1, Art 12; Regulation (EC) 45/2001 of the European Parliament and of the Council of 18 December 2000 on the protection of individuals with regard to the processing of personal data by the Community institutions and bodies and on the free movement of such data [2001] OJ L8/1 last amended by Corrigendum to Regulation (EC) 45/2001 of the European Parliament and of the Council of 18 December 2000 on the protection of individuals with regard to the processing of personal data by the Community institutions and bodies and on the free movement of such data [2007] OJ L164/35, Arts 13ff; see also European Parliament legislative resolution of 12 March 2014 on the proposal for a regulation of the European Parliament and of the Council on the protection of individuals with regard to the processing of personal data and on the free movement of such data (General Data Protection Regulation) P7_TA(2014)0212, Art 15.

[72] See paras 5–9 of the introduction.

can refer to these provisions including, where applicable, to the respective national data protection law.[73]

56 In order to set clear standards with regard to composite information management, Article VI-15(1) and (2) requires as a **minimum standard the provision** of information which is especially important with regard to inter-administrative information exchange as regulated in Book VI. In addition to general data protection law, the model rules require that the person concerned should be informed about the legal basis for the respective information management activity. Another important element of Article VI-15(1) and (2) with regard to composite information management is the clear allocation of responsibility within information networks for providing such information or access to the data supplying authority. In order to provide an alternative route in complex networks the provision stipulates in conjunction with Articles VI-30 and VI-33 supplementary obligations of the Supervisory Authority.

57 In defining the persons concerned as being natural as well as legal persons (Article VI-2(7)), such rights are, where applicable, also **extended to legal persons** despite the fact that they are not covered by traditional data protection law.[74] This innovative proposal supports their rights of confidentiality as provided by Article VI-28, and highlights the relevance of composite information activities for legal persons,

[73] Sources of inspiration Regulation (EU) 1024/2012 of the European Parliament and of the Council of 25 October 2012 on administrative cooperation through the Internal Market Information System and repealing Commission Decision 2008/49/EC ('the IMI Regulation') [2012] OJ L316/1 last amended by Directive 2014/67/EU of the European Parliament and of the Council of 15 May 2014 on the enforcement of Directive 96/71/EC concerning the posting of workers in the framework of the provision of services and amending Regulation (EU) No 1024/2012 on administrative cooperation through the Internal Market Information System ('the IMI Regulation') [2014] OJ L 159/11, Art 19(1); Council Decision 2008/615/JHA of 23 June 2008 on the stepping up of cross-border cooperation, particularly in combating terrorism and cross-border crime [2008] OJ L210/1, Art 31; Regulation (EC) 767/2008 of the European Parliament and of the Council of 9 July 2008 concerning the Visa Information System (VIS) and the exchange of data between Member States on short-stay visas (VIS Regulation) [2008] OJ L218/60 last amended by Regulation (EC) 610/2013 of the European Parliament and of the Council of 26 June 2013 amending Regulation (EC) No 562/2006 of the European Parliament and of the Council establishing a Community Code on the rules governing the movement of persons across borders (Schengen Borders Code), the Convention implementing the Schengen Agreement, Council Regulations (EC) No 1683/95 and (EC) No 539/2001 and Regulations (EC) No 767/2008 and (EC) No 810/2009 of the European Parliament and of the Council [2013] OJ L182/1, Art 37; Regulation (EC) 1987/2006 of the European Parliament and of the Council of 20 December 2006 on the establishment, operation and use of the second generation Schengen Information System (SIS II) [2006] OJ L381/4, Art 41; Council Regulation (EC) 515/97 of 13 March 1997 on mutual assistance between the administrative authorities of the Member States and the cooperation between the latter and the Commission to ensure the correct application of the law on customs and agricultural matters [1997] OJ L82/1 last amended by Regulation (EC) 766/2008 of the European Parliament and of the Council of 9 July 2008 amending Council Regulation (EC) 515/97 on mutual assistance between the administrative authorities of the Member States and cooperation between the latter and the Commission to ensure the correct application of the law on customs and agricultural matters [2008] OJ L218/48, Art 36.

[74] See the definitions cited in footnote 71.

which are involved with many EU information networks such as, for example, early warning systems.

The drafting team however decided **not to include a right to be heard** for persons before information is transmitted under a duty to inform or entered into a database.[75] The drafters prefer at this stage of the project to rely on effective rights to be informed ex-post, explained in the previous paragraphs, as well as on the right to erasure as regulated in Article VI-19(3). These rights are fostered by the obligation of the data supplying authority to ensure that persons concerned can effectively exercise the right of access which is highlighted in Article VI-15(4).[76] In particular, the data supplying authority is obliged to inform the person concerned of these rights of access and erasure, as well as about the procedures applicable for exercising these rights.[77] The information about the concrete procedures to exercise the established data protection rights is especially important with regard to the complexities of multi-jurisdictional composite information management. **58**

The **subjective rights** addressed in paragraphs 1 and 2 of this article are also essential elements of effective data protection. They should therefore not be limited **59**

[75] Such a new right is discussed by the Decision of the European Ombudsman closing his own-initiative inquiry into case OI/3/2008/FOR against the European Commission (06.07.2012), para 152 concerning the Commission's Early Warning System (EWS), available at http://www.ombudsman.europa.eu/en/cases/decision.faces/en/11731/html.bookmark; see also Case C-276/12 *Jiří Sabou v Finanční ředitelství pro hlavní město Prahu* [2013] OJ C367/16, paras 46, 51(1).

[76] Sources of inspiration Regulation (EC) 767/2008 of the European Parliament and of the Council of 9 July 2008 concerning the Visa Information System (VIS) and the exchange of data between Member States on short-stay visas (VIS Regulation) [2008] OJ L218/60 last amended by Regulation (EC) 610/2013 of the European Parliament and of the Council of 26 June 2013 amending Regulation (EC) No 562/2006 of the European Parliament and of the Council establishing a Community Code on the rules governing the movement of persons across borders (Schengen Borders Code), the Convention implementing the Schengen Agreement, Council Regulations (EC) No 1683/95 and (EC) No 539/2001 and Regulations (EC) No 767/2008 and (EC) No 810/2009 of the European Parliament and of the Council [2013] OJ L182/1, Art 37(1)(f); Regulation (EU) 1024/2012 of the European Parliament and of the Council of 25 October 2012 on administrative cooperation through the Internal Market Information System and repealing Commission Decision 2008/49/EC ('the IMI Regulation') [2012] OJ L316/1 last amended by Directive 2014/67/EU of the European Parliament and of the Council of 15 May 2014 on the enforcement of Directive 96/71/EC concerning the posting of workers in the framework of the provision of services and amending Regulation (EU) No 1024/2012 on administrative cooperation through the Internal Market Information System ('the IMI Regulation') [2014] OJ L159/11, Recital (26), Art 19(1).

[77] Source of inspiration Regulation (EC) 767/2008 of the European Parliament and of the Council of 9 July 2008 concerning the Visa Information System (VIS) and the exchange of data between Member States on short-stay visas (VIS Regulation) [2008] OJ L218/60 last amended by Regulation (EC) 610/2013 of the European Parliament and of the Council of 26 June 2013 amending Regulation (EC) No 562/2006 of the European Parliament and of the Council establishing a Community Code on the rules governing the movement of persons across borders (Schengen Borders Code), the Convention implementing the Schengen Agreement, Council Regulations (EC) No 1683/95 and (EC) No 539/2001 and Regulations (EC) No 767/2008 and (EC) No 810/2009 of the European Parliament and of the Council [2013] OJ L182/1, Art 37(1)(f).

without good justification. Article 13 Data Protection Directive 95/46[78] delegates the detailed regulation of this topic to the national legislators. In order to have a clear and uniform set of rules applicable to all participating authorities on this important issue Article VI-15(5) stipulates certain possible justifications for refusal of access. Most of these justifications are inspired by Article 20 of the Data Protection Regulation 45/2001.[79] In addition, access may be denied on grounds of limitations established in the basic act. This provision provides the legislator with the flexibility required to adjust the framework to sector-specific particularities. Effective legal protection requires that the person concerned is informed about the grounds of refusal, and rights of appeal to the competent data protection supervisor either at national or EU level (Book VI, Chapter 4 Section 2).

VI-16 Access for competent authorities

VI-17 Access management rules in information systems

60 The access to information for competent authorities provided through duties to inform or shared databases is an important aspect of the concept of privacy-by-design. Therefore, it is necessary to create a **general rule** about this issue placing an obligation that the basic act and implementing provisions **designate clearly such access rights.**[80] Access rights should differentiate between different participating

[78] Directive 95/46/EC of the European Parliament and of the Council of 24 October 1995 on the protection of individuals with regard to the processing of personal data and on the free movement of such data [1995] OJ L281/31 last amended by Regulation (EC) 1882/2003 of the European Parliament and of the Council of 29 September 2003 adapting to Council Decision 1999/468/EC the provisions relating to committees which assist the Commission in the exercise of its implementing powers laid down in instruments subject to the procedure referred to in Article 251 of the EC Treaty [2003] OJ L284/1.

[79] Regulation (EC) 45/2001 of the European Parliament and of the Council of 18 December 2000 on the protection of individuals with regard to the processing of personal data by the Community institutions and bodies and on the free movement of such data [2001] OJ L8/1 last amended by Corrigendum to Regulation (EC) 45/2001 of the European Parliament and of the Council of 18 December 2000 on the protection of individuals with regard to the processing of personal data by the Community institutions and bodies and on the free movement of such data [2007] OJ L164/35, Art 20.

[80] Sources of inspiration Regulation (EC) 767/2008 of the European Parliament and of the Council of 9 July 2008 concerning the Visa Information System (VIS) and the exchange of data between Member States on short-stay visas (VIS Regulation) [2008] OJ L218/60 last amended by Regulation (EC) 610/2013 of the European Parliament and of the Council of 26 June 2013 amending Regulation (EC) No 562/2006 of the European Parliament and of the Council establishing a Community Code on the rules governing the movement of persons across borders (Schengen Borders Code), the Convention implementing the Schengen Agreement, Council Regulations (EC) No 1683/95 and (EC) No 539/2001 and Regulations (EC) No 767/2008 and (EC) No 810/2009 of the European Parliament and of the Council [2013] OJ L182/1, Art 6(2); see also Regulation (EU) 1024/2012 of the European Parliament and of the Council of 25 October 2012 on administrative cooperation through the Internal Market Information System and repealing Commission Decision 2008/49/EC ('the IMI Regulation') [2012] OJ L316/1 last amended by Directive 2014/67/EU of the European Parliament and of the Council of 15 May 2014 on the enforcement of Directive 96/71/EC concerning the posting of workers in the framework of the provision of services and

authorities. Information necessary for the fulfilment of the duties of one (category of) competent authority may not be relevant for another. Therefore, access rights must be allocated taking into account the specifics of each distinct administrative duty supported through an information management activity.

Article VI-17 supplements Article VI-16 and Article VI-3(3)(h) and states that the basic act should clearly establish any **specific requirements** concerning the **mechanism for exchanging information** including the structure and security requirements of information systems. Article VI-17 clarifies that the basic act also needs to establish clear and comprehensive access management rules if the information system is used by public authorities to exchange data gathered under a duty to inform, or if the information system establishes a database. Therefore, Article VI-17 does not only apply to shared databases, but also to duties to inform if they are performed through an information system. **61**

Subsection 2: Alteration and Deletion of Data and Information

Subsection 2 regulates the alteration, updating and deletion of data transmitted under a duty to inform or processed through a database. While Article VI-18 provides a clear allocation of competences with regard to alteration and deletion of data stored in a shared database, Article VI-19 stipulates in detail conditions under which the competent authorities are obliged to update, correct, or delete data. **62**

Article VI-18 comprises the **competences to alter and delete data**. It is only applicable to data contained in a database as defined in Article VI-2(3). Information transmitted under a duty to inform, which is solely stored in national repositories and not in such a shared database, is not covered by this provision. Consequently, national law is applicable. This approach is in line with Article VI-26(5) referring to national law with regard to storage of information provided through a duty to inform in national files. By contrast, Article VI-19 applies to all information transmitted under a duty to inform, either stored in shared databases or in national data repositories. Nevertheless, the obligation of the data supplying authority to correct data, stipulated in Article VI-19(1), means with regard to data which is not stored in a shared database where the supplying authority is obliged to inform the other authorities about the inaccuracy or illegality of the previous information. It is the respective Member State authority that is in a position to actually alter the national data repository or file. **63**

According to Article VI-18(1), the information contained in a database may be **altered or deleted** either **by the competent authority**[81] **or** the **Supervisory Authority.** Article VI-33 specifies when the Supervisory Authority has the power to **64**

amending Regulation (EU) No 1024/2012 on administrative cooperation through the Internal Market Information System ('the IMI Regulation') [2014] OJ L 159/11, Art 9.

[81] For the definition of competent authority see Art VI-6.

alter or delete data. In all other cases the data supplying authority is the only authority competent to alter and delete data.[82] Alteration and deletion of data is a form of data processing. It is therefore covered by the principle of transparent and retraceable data processing, laid down in Article VI-9. This means that the tag, made obligatory under Article VI-9(2), also includes details about the alteration and deletion of data. The derogation clause in paragraph 2 of this article provides the legislator with the necessary flexibility and is inspired by existing EU law.[83]

[82] Sources of inspiration Regulation (EC) 767/2008 of the European Parliament and of the Council of 9 July 2008 concerning the Visa Information System (VIS) and the exchange of data between Member States on short-stay visas (VIS Regulation) [2008] OJ L218/60 last amended by Regulation (EC) 610/2013 of the European Parliament and of the Council of 26 June 2013 amending Regulation (EC) No 562/2006 of the European Parliament and of the Council establishing a Community Code on the rules governing the movement of persons across borders (Schengen Borders Code), the Convention implementing the Schengen Agreement, Council Regulations (EC) No 1683/95 and (EC) No 539/2001 and Regulations (EC) No 767/2008 and (EC) No 810/2009 of the European Parliament and of the Council [2013] OJ L182/1, Art 24; Regulation (EU) 603/2013 of the European Parliament and of the Council of 26 June 2013 on the establishment of 'Eurodac' for the comparison of fingerprints for the effective application of Regulation (EU) 604/2013 establishing the criteria and mechanisms for determining the Member State responsible for examining an application for international protection lodged in one of the Member States by a third-country national or a stateless person and on requests for the comparison with Eurodac data by Member States' law enforcement authorities and Europol for law enforcement purposes, and amending Regulation (EU) 1077/2011 establishing a European Agency for the operational management of large-scale IT systems in the area of freedom, security and justice (recast) [2013] OJ L180/1, Art 27; Regulation (EC) 1987/2006 of the European Parliament and of the Council of 20 December 2006 on the establishment, operation and use of the second generation Schengen Information System (SIS II) [2006] OJ L381/4, Art 34(2); Council Regulation (EC) 515/97 of 13 March 1997 on mutual assistance between the administrative authorities of the Member States and the cooperation between the latter and the Commission to ensure the correct application of the law on customs and agricultural matters [1997] OJ L82/1 last amended by Regulation (EC) 766/2008 of the European Parliament and of the Council of 9 July 2008 amending Council Regulation (EC) 515/97 on mutual assistance between the administrative authorities of the Member States and cooperation between the latter and the Commission to ensure the correct application of the law on customs and agricultural matters [2008] OJ L218/48, Art 32; Council Decision 2007/533/JHA of 12 June 2007 on the establishment, operation and use of the second generation Schengen Information System (SIS II) [2007] OJ L205/63, Art 49(2); The Schengen acquis—Convention implementing the Schengen Agreement of 14 June 1985 between the Governments of the States of the Benelux Economic Union, the Federal Republic of Germany and the French Republic on the gradual abolition of checks at their common borders [2000] OJ L239/19, Art 106(1).

[83] For example Regulation (EU) 603/2013 of the European Parliament and of the Council of 26 June 2013 on the establishment of 'Eurodac' for the comparison of fingerprints for the effective application of Regulation (EU) 604/2013 establishing the criteria and mechanisms for determining the Member State responsible for examining an application for international protection lodged in one of the Member States by a third-country national or a stateless person and on requests for the comparison with Eurodac data by Member States' law enforcement authorities and Europol for law enforcement purposes, and amending Regulation (EU) 1077/2011 establishing a European Agency for the operational management of large-scale IT systems in the area of freedom, security and justice (recast) [2013] OJ L180/1, Art 3(3); Regulation (EC) 810/2009 of the European Parliament and of the Council of 13 July 2009 establishing a Community Code on Visas (Visa Code) [2004] OJ L243/1 last amended by Regulation (EU) 610/2013 of the European Parliament and of the Council of 26 June 2013 amending Regulation (EC) 562/2006 of the European Parliament and of the Council establishing a Community Code on the rules governing the movement of persons across

However, the competent authority needs to be one of the competent bodies designated pursuant to Article VI-6.

The **duty** for the competent authority **to update, correct, or delete outdated, incorrect, or unlawful data,**[84] stipulated in **Article VI-19**, aims at enhancing data quality. Paragraph 2 highlights that the legislator may also include an additional obligation in the basic act for the data supplying authority to update the information regularly.[85] The timing of mandatory updates should be specified in the basic act. **65**

Article VI-19(3) underlines the **right of erasure.** For natural persons such a right is already established by the applicable data protection law.[86] But for legal persons this is an innovative proposal. The concerned persons may demand, *inter alia*, that his or her data which may no longer be stored shall be blocked and finally deleted. The relevant conditions and time-limits for blocking and deletion are stipulated in Articles VI-26 and VI-27.[87] **66**

---

borders (Schengen Borders Code), the Convention implementing the Schengen Agreement, Council Regulations (EC) 1683/95 and (EC) 539/2001 and Regulations (EC) 767/2008 and (EC) 810/2009 of the European Parliament and of the Council [2013] OJ L182/1, Art 34(1); Commission Decision 2010/15/EU of 16 December 2009 laying down guidelines for the management of the Community Rapid Information System 'RAPEX' established under Article 12 and of the notification procedure established under Article 11 of Directive 2001/95/EC (the General Product Safety Directive) [2009] OJ L22/1, Part II.3.2.3 of the Annex.

84 Partially inspired by Regulation (EC) 1987/2006 of the European Parliament and of the Council of 20 December 2006 on the establishment, operation and use of the second generation Schengen Information System (SIS II) [2006] OJ L381/4, Art 34.

85 Source of inspiration Commission Proposal for a Council Framework Decision on the organization and content of the exchange of information extracted from criminal records between Member States, COM(2005) 690 final, Art 5; see also Opinion of the European Data Protection Supervisor on the Proposal for a Council Framework Decision on the organisation and content of the exchange of information extracted from criminal records between Member States (COM (2005) 690 final) [2006] OJ C313/26, Section IV.32.

86 Source of inspiration Regulation (EC) 767/2008 of the European Parliament and of the Council of 9 July 2008 concerning the Visa Information System (VIS) and the exchange of data between Member States on short-stay visas (VIS Regulation) [2008] OJ L218/60 last amended by Regulation (EC) 610/2013 of the European Parliament and of the Council of 26 June 2013 amending Regulation (EC) No 562/2006 of the European Parliament and of the Council establishing a Community Code on the rules governing the movement of persons across borders (Schengen Borders Code), the Convention implementing the Schengen Agreement, Council Regulations (EC) No 1683/95 and (EC) No 539/2001 and Regulations (EC) No 767/2008 and (EC) No 810/2009 of the European Parliament and of the Council [2013] OJ L182/1, Art 38(2). The relevant data protection provisions are Directive 95/46/EC of the European Parliament and of the Council of 24 October 1995 on the protection of individuals with regard to the processing of personal data and on the free movement of such data [1995] OJ L281/31 last amended by Regulation (EC) 1882/2003 of the European Parliament and of the Council of 29 September 2003 adapting to Council Decision 1999/468/EC the provisions relating to committees which assist the Commission in the exercise of its implementing powers laid down in instruments subject to the procedure referred to in Article 251 of the EC Treaty [2003] OJ L284/1, Art 12(b).

87 See paras 75–80 of the explanations.

67 Paragraph 4 establishes an **obligation** for any participating authority **to inform the data supplying authority** immediately if they have doubts about the accuracy or lawfulness of the data processed. The data supplying authority shall then check the information and if necessary correct or delete the data. Similar provisions exist in various EU laws[88] in order to ensure and enhance the accuracy of data. Apart from this, it is important to highlight that a follow-up notification[89] sent by another competent authority shall not be considered an amendment to a previous notification in the sense of this paragraph as both notifications will be accessible in the database. It may therefore be transmitted without the agreement of the competent authority which sent the previous notification.

68 Paragraph 5 deals with the question how to handle the situation where the accuracy of data has been contested, but the **accuracy or inaccuracy has not been established.** It resolves this issue by proposing a flag that indicates this dispute.[90] The

---

[88] Regulation (EC) 767/2008 of the European Parliament and of the Council of 9 July 2008 concerning the Visa Information System (VIS) and the exchange of data between Member States on short-stay visas (VIS Regulation) [2008] OJ L218/60 last amended by Regulation (EC) 610/2013 of the European Parliament and of the Council of 26 June 2013 amending Regulation (EC) No 562/2006 of the European Parliament and of the Council establishing a Community Code on the rules governing the movement of persons across borders (Schengen Borders Code), the Convention implementing the Schengen Agreement, Council Regulations (EC) No 1683/95 and (EC) No 539/2001 and Regulations (EC) No 767/2008 and (EC) No 810/2009 of the European Parliament and of the Council [2013] OJ L182/1, Art 24(2); Council Regulation (EC) 515/97 of 13 March 1997 on mutual assistance between the administrative authorities of the Member States and the cooperation between the latter and the Commission to ensure the correct application of the law on customs and agricultural matters [1997] OJ L82/1 last amended by Regulation (EC) 766/2008 of the European Parliament and of the Council of 9 July 2008 amending Council Regulation (EC) 515/97 on mutual assistance between the administrative authorities of the Member States and cooperation between the latter and the Commission to ensure the correct application of the law on customs and agricultural matters [2008] OJ L218/48, Art 32; Regulation (EU) 603/2013 of the European Parliament and of the Council of 26 June 2013 on the establishment of 'Eurodac' for the comparison of fingerprints for the effective application of Regulation (EU) 604/2013 establishing the criteria and mechanisms for determining the Member State responsible for examining an application for international protection lodged in one of the Member States by a third-country national or a stateless person and on requests for the comparison with Eurodac data by Member States' law enforcement authorities and Europol for law enforcement purposes, and amending Regulation (EU) 1077/2011 establishing a European Agency for the operational management of large-scale IT systems in the area of freedom, security and justice (recast) [2013] OJ L180/1, Art 25(4); Regulation (EC) 1987/2006 of the European Parliament and of the Council of 20 December 2006 on the establishment, operation and use of the second generation Schengen Information System (SIS II) [2006] OJ L381/4, Art 34(3); Council Decision 2007/533/JHA of 12 June 2007 on the establishment, operation and use of the second generation Schengen Information System (SIS II) [2007] OJ L205/63, Art 49(3); Commission Decision 2008/333/EC of 4 March 2008 adopting the SIRENE Manual and other implementing measures for the second generation Schengen Information System (SIS II) [2008] OJ L123/1, Section 2.7 of the Annex; Commission Decision 2008/334/JHA of 4 March 2008 adopting the SIRENE Manual and other implementing measures for the second generation Schengen Information System (SIS II) [2008] OJ L123/39, Section 2.7 of the Annex.

[89] Article VI-12(3)(e).

[90] Sources of inspiration Council Decision 2008/615/JHA of 23 June 2008 on the stepping up of cross-border cooperation, particularly in combating terrorism and cross-border crime [2008] OJ L210/1, Art 28; Regulation (EU) 603/2013 of the European Parliament and of the Council of 26

person concerned or another authority is therefore entitled to have the data he or she contests flagged. Consequently, the authority using the data is informed about the existing dispute and, in accordance with Article VI-21, it is obliged to assess the relevant information even more carefully. Paragraph 5 does not regulate the procedure for the final dispute resolution. Instead, this issue is regulated by Chapter 4 establishing—in conjunction with the applicable data protection law—a coordinated data protection supervision structure as well as the (general) Supervisory authority. The latter is highlighted in paragraph 6 and is especially important for the resolution of inter-administrative disputes which do not fall into the jurisdiction of data protection supervisors.

Subsection 3: Use of Data and Information

The establishment of duties to inform and databases is not an end in itself, but an instrument for the effective implementation of EU policies. Therefore, the **use of the information provided through such composite information management is crucial and cannot be taken for granted** as the use of 'foreign' information is a matter of mutual trust. Therefore, in order to guarantee that competent authorities make effective use of the relevant information, **Article VI-20** establishes a duty for the competent authority to consider the supplied information. This is a common provision that can be found in existing EU legislation.[91] The second sentence of **69**

June 2013 on the establishment of 'Eurodac' for the comparison of fingerprints for the effective application of Regulation (EU) 604/2013 establishing the criteria and mechanisms for determining the Member State responsible for examining an application for international protection lodged in one of the Member States by a third-country national or a stateless person and on requests for the comparison with Eurodac data by Member States' law enforcement authorities and Europol for law enforcement purposes, and amending Regulation (EU) 1077/2011 establishing a European Agency for the operational management of large-scale IT systems in the area of freedom, security and justice (recast) [2013] OJ L180/1, Art 29(8) stating that the Member State should give a written explanation why it is not prepared to correct or erase the data; see also Regulation (EU) 1024/2012 of the European Parliament and of the Council of 25 October 2012 on administrative cooperation through the Internal Market Information System and repealing Commission Decision 2008/49/EC ('the IMI Regulation') [2012] OJ L316/1 last amended by Directive 2014/67/EU of the European Parliament and of the Council of 15 May 2014 on the enforcement of Directive 96/71/EC concerning the posting of workers in the framework of the provision of services and amending Regulation (EU) No 1024/2012 on administrative cooperation through the Internal Market Information System ('the IMI Regulation') [2014] OJ L 159/11, Art 19(2) stating that if the data subject contests the accuracy of the data this fact should be recorded.

[91] For example Council Decision 87/600/Euratom of 14 December 1987 on Community arrangements for the early exchange of information in the event of a radiological emergency [1987] OJ L 371/76, Art 4; Council Regulation (EC) 1224/2009 of 20 November 2009 establishing a Community control system for ensuring compliance with the rules of the common fisheries policy, amending Regulations (EC) 847/96, (EC) 2371/2002, (EC) 811/2004, (EC) 768/2005, (EC) 2115/2005, (EC) 2166/2005, (EC) 388/2006, (EC) 509/2007, (EC) 676/2007, (EC) 1098/2007, (EC) 1300/2008, (EC) 1342/2008 and repealing Regulations (EEC) 2847/93, (EC) 1627/94 and (EC) 1966/2006 [2009] OJ L343/1 last amended by Regulation (EU) 508/2014 of the European Parliament and of the Council of 15 May 2014 on the European Maritime and Fisheries Fund and

Article VI-20 stresses that this obligation applies especially in relation to the search and consultation of information in databases.[92] While the transmission of new information under a duty to inform will usually attract the attention of the participating authorities, it is not self-evident that they will consult shared databases actively, especially if they are additional to existing national data repositories, or require the involvement of specially designated officers or contact points.

70 **Article VI-21** is inspired by the jurisprudence of the CJEU, which obliges users of the Schengen Information System to take advantage of the SIRENE offices in order to validate sensitive information provided through that system.[93] Consequently, information provided through information systems, as defined in Article VI-2(4) **has to be assessed by the competent authority** considering administrative action based on such information. Consequently, the acting authority may not refer solely to the information provided through the information system to justify its action. If the competent authority has doubts about the accuracy of the information it has to consult the information supplying authority in order to guarantee the accuracy of data at an early stage of processing.[94] Thereby, Article VI-21 supplements the

---

repealing Council Regulations (EC) No 2328/2003, (EC) No 861/2006, (EC) No 1198/2006 and (EC) No 791/2007 and Regulation (EU) No 1255/2011 of the European Parliament and of the Council [2014] OJ L149/1, Art 72; Regulation (EU) 1052/2013 of the European Parliament and of the Council of 22 October 2013 establishing the European Border Surveillance System (Eurosur) [2013] OJ L295/11, Art 9.

[92] Regulation (EC) 767/2008 of the European Parliament and of the Council of 9 July 2008 concerning the Visa Information System (VIS) and the exchange of data between Member States on short-stay visas (VIS Regulation) [2008] OJ L218/60 last amended by Regulation (EC) 610/2013 of the European Parliament and of the Council of 26 June 2013 amending Regulation (EC) No 562/2006 of the European Parliament and of the Council establishing a Community Code on the rules governing the movement of persons across borders (Schengen Borders Code), the Convention implementing the Schengen Agreement, Council Regulations (EC) No 1683/95 and (EC) No 539/2001 and Regulations (EC) No 767/2008 and (EC) No 810/2009 of the European Parliament and of the Council [2013] OJ L182/1, Art 15; Decision 2119/98/EC of the European Parliament and of the Council of 24 September 1998 setting up a network for the epidemiological surveillance and control of communicable diseases in the Community [1998] OJ L268/1 last amended by Regulation (EC) 596/2009 of the European Parliament and of the Council of 18 June 2009 adapting a number of instruments subject to the procedure referred to in Article 251 of the Treaty to Council Decision 9/468/EC with regard to the regulatory procedure with scrutiny [2009] OJ L188/14, Art 6; Regulation (EU) 603/2013 of the European Parliament and of the Council of 26 June 2013 on the establishment of 'Eurodac' for the comparison of fingerprints for the effective application of Regulation (EU) 604/2013 establishing the criteria and mechanisms for determining the Member State responsible for examining an application for international protection lodged in one of the Member States by a third-country national or a stateless person and on requests for the comparison with Eurodac data by Member States' law enforcement authorities and Europol for law enforcement purposes, and amending Regulation (EU) 1077/2011 establishing a European Agency for the operational management of large-scale IT systems in the area of freedom, security and justice (recast) [2013] OJ L180/1, Art 9(3).

[93] See Case C-503/03 *Commission v Kingdom of Spain* [2006] ECR I-1097.

[94] Second sentence inspired by Regulation (EC) 1987/2006 of the European Parliament and of the Council of 20 December 2006 on the establishment, operation and use of the second-generation Schengen Information System (SIS II) [2006] OJ L381/4, Art 25(2).

functions of information systems. They are both necessary for the effective discharge of public powers, as well as the effective protection of individuals' rights. In order to base its decision on correct facts the competent authority has an obligation to make full use of the relevant features of the information system.[95]

Article VI-22 supplements Article VI-12(3)(a), (b) and (d) and obliges the compe- **71**
tent authority to **take** the **action** specified in the basic act. If necessary, the acting competent authority must send a **follow-up notification**[96] to inform the other participating authorities.

According to **Article VI-23,** competent authorities may **deviate from the duties** to **72**
assess information independently[97] and to take specific actions as a result of information.[98] However, the principle of legal certainty requires that these cases are clearly specified in the basic act or the relevant implementing rules. Consequently, Article VI-23 is not directly applicable.

In line with the **principle of data minimization, Article VI-24** stipulates that an **73**
exchange of data is only permitted for purposes which are clearly defined in the relevant provisions of EU law. This rule reflects common practice in the relevant EU legislation.[99] Nevertheless, in some cases there is a need to use the information

---

[95] For example Regulation (EC) 810/2009 of the European Parliament and of the Council of 13 July 2009 establishing a Community Code on Visas (Visa Code) [2004] OJ L243/1 last amended by Regulation (EU) 610/2013 of the European Parliament and of the Council of 26 June 2013 amending Regulation (EC) 562/2006 of the European Parliament and of the Council establishing a Community Code on the rules governing the movement of persons across borders (Schengen Borders Code), the Convention implementing the Schengen Agreement, Council Regulations (EC) 1683/95 and (EC) 539/2001 and Regulations (EC) 767/2008 and (EC) 810/2009 of the European Parliament and of the Council [2013] OJ L182/1, Art 21(2); Regulation (EC) 178/2002 of the European Parliament and of the Council of 28 January 2002 laying down the general principles and requirements of food law, establishing the European Safety Authority and laying down procedures in matters of food safety [2002] OJ L31/1 last amended by Regulation (EC) 596/2009 of the European Parliament and of the Council of 18 June 2009 adapting a number of instruments subject to the procedure referred to in Article 251 of the Treaty to Council Decision 1999/468/EC with regard to the regulatory procedure with scrutiny—Adaptation to the regulatory procedure with scrutiny—Part Four [2009] OJ L188/14, Art 35; Regulation (EC) 1987/2006 of the European Parliament and of the Council of 20 December 2006 on the establishment, operation and use of the second generation Schengen Information System (SIS II) [2006] OJ L381/4, Arts 8, 25 (obligation to use the communication infrastructure SIRENE for exchange of supplementary information).

[96] See Art VI-12(3)(e).

[97] See Art VI-21.

[98] See Art VI-22.

[99] For example, Regulation (EU) 1024/2012 of the European Parliament and of the Council of 25 October 2012 on administrative cooperation through the Internal Market Information System and repealing Commission Decision 2008/49/EC ('the IMI Regulation') [2012] OJ L316/1 last amended by Directive 2014/67/EU of the European Parliament and of the Council of 15 May 2014 on the enforcement of Directive 96/71/EC concerning the posting of workers in the framework of the provision of services and amending Regulation (EU) No 1024/2012 on administrative cooperation through the Internal Market Information System ('the IMI Regulation') [2014] OJ L 159/11, Art 9(5); Council Framework Decision 2006/960/JHA of 18 December 2006 on simplifying the exchange of information and intelligence between law enforcement authorities of the Member States

for purposes different from the ones that justified the previous information exchange. Therefore, paragraph 2 provides a restrictive exemption clause for such cases.[100] According to paragraph 3, the distribution of data and information to third parties also requires specific legislative authorization.

Subsection 4: Data Protection and Information Security

74 **Article VI-25** underlines the **need to comply with existing data protection provisions**, which supplement these model rules in some cases with more specific rules. Paragraph 2 complements Article VI-3 as well as Article VI-10 by specifying the relevance of defined data categories to compliance with the principle of data minimization.[101]

---

of the European Union [2006] OJ L386/89 last amended by Corrigendum to Council Framework Decision 2006/960/JHA of 18 December 2006 on simplifying the exchange of information and intelligence between law enforcement authorities of the Member States of the European Union [2007] OJ L75/26, Art 8(3); Council Framework Decision 2009/315/JHA of 26 February 2009 on the organisation and content of the exchange of information extracted from the criminal record between Member States [2009] OJ L93/23, Art 9(1); Council Regulation (EC) 515/97 of 13 March 1997 on mutual assistance between the administrative authorities of the Member States and the cooperation between the latter and the Commission to ensure the correct application of the law on customs and agricultural matters [1997] OJ L82/1 last amended by Regulation (EC) 766/2008 of the European Parliament and of the Council of 9 July 2008 amending Council Regulation (EC) 515/97 on mutual assistance between the administrative authorities of the Member States and cooperation between the latter and the Commission to ensure the correct application of the law on customs and agricultural matters [2008] OJ L218/48, Art 26(b); Regulation (EC) 1987/2006 of the European Parliament and of the Council of 20 December 2006 on the establishment, operation and use of the second generation Schengen Information System (SIS II) [2006] OJ L381/4, Art 31; Commission Regulation (EC, EURATOM) 1302/2008 of 17 December 2008 on the central exclusion database [2008] OJ L344/12, Art 1(2).

[100] Wording based on Council Framework Decision 2006/960/JHA of 18 December 2006 on simplifying the exchange of information and intelligence between law enforcement authorities of the Member States of the European Union [2006] OJ L386/89 last amended by Corrigendum to Council Framework Decision 2006/960/JHA of 18 December 2006 on simplifying the exchange of information and intelligence between law enforcement authorities of the Member States of the European Union [2007] OJ L75/26, Art 8(3); also inspired by Council Regulation (EC) 515/97 of 13 March 1997 on mutual assistance between the administrative authorities of the Member States and the cooperation between the latter and the Commission to ensure the correct application of the law on customs and agricultural matters [1997] OJ L82/1 last amended by Regulation (EC) 766/2008 of the European Parliament and of the Council of 9 July 2008 amending Council Regulation (EC) 515/97 on mutual assistance between the administrative authorities of the Member States and cooperation between the latter and the Commission to ensure the correct application of the law on customs and agricultural matters [2008] OJ L218/48, Art 30(1).

[101] Sources of inspiration Regulation (EC) 767/2008 of the European Parliament and of the Council of 9 July 2008 concerning the Visa Information System (VIS) and the exchange of data between Member States on short-stay visas (VIS Regulation) [2008] OJ L218/60 last amended by Regulation (EC) 610/2013 of the European Parliament and of the Council of 26 June 2013 amending Regulation (EC) No 562/2006 of the European Parliament and of the Council establishing a Community Code on the rules governing the movement of persons across borders (Schengen Borders Code), the Convention implementing the Schengen Agreement, Council Regulations (EC) No 1683/95 and (EC) No 539/2001 and Regulations (EC) No 767/2008 and (EC) No 810/2009 of the European Parliament and of the Council [2013] OJ L182/1, Art 5; Council Regulation (EC)

Article VI-26 creates the **obligation to block and the right to request blocking** of data stored in a database as a result of an information exchange under a duty to inform after a specified period. In line with the approach followed in Article VI-15 the right to request blocking or deletion of data is not confined to natural persons, but is also granted to legal persons. As mentioned earlier,[102] some duties to inform are combined with a respective shared database, while others rely on de-centralized data storage in national repositories with no direct access for authorities from other Member States, or from another level in the EU multi-level-structure. Article VI-26 reflects these two options in paragraphs 1 to 4 and paragraph 5 respectively. **75**

Paragraphs 1 to 4 solely regulate **storage of data in shared databases.** In contrast to Article VI-27, accessibility of data is only justified by these paragraphs as long as the relevant data is necessary to achieve the legally justified purposes for which it was originally supplied. Storage of the data beyond that period of time requires an additional explicit legal basis as required by Article VI-27. **76**

Sentence 2 of Article VI-26(1) refers to the f**ormal closure of** the relevant **procedure** initiated by a notification as defined in Article VI-12(2) and (3). This procedure can be a (formal) administrative procedure, as defined in Article I-4(2), if it ends in a decision as defined in Article III-2(1).[103] Nevertheless, it is also possible that the applicable sector-specific law does not empower the competent authority to adopt such a (formal) decision but only to issue a warning or take another non-legally binding measure. To cover such cases, sentence 2 uses the broader term 'procedure' instead of 'administrative procedure'. In line with this reasoning, the heading of Article VI-27 refers to data storage 'beyond procedures associated with a duty to inform'. **77**

Article VI-26(1) sentence 1 and 2 use the generic term '**accessible**'. This allows for a differentiated regulation with two stages before data is finally completely deleted at the second stage. Between full accessibility for the purposes of the information exchange and its complete deletion data shall—and can—be blocked (sentence 3). Paragraphs 2 and 3 specify how the relevant authorities must deal with blocked data.[104] It is important to be clear about the limited purposes for which further data **78**

515/97 of 13 March 1997 on mutual assistance between the administrative authorities of the Member States and the cooperation between the latter and the Commission to ensure the correct application of the law on customs and agricultural matters [1997] OJ L82/1 last amended by Regulation (EC) 766/2008 of the European Parliament and of the Council of 9 July 2008 amending Council Regulation (EC) 515/97 on mutual assistance between the administrative authorities of the Member States and cooperation between the latter and the Commission to ensure the correct application of the law on customs and agricultural matters [2008] OJ L218/48, Arts 24, 25.

[102] See paras 62–68 of the explanations concerning competences and obligation to delete data.

[103] Compare Book III, para 5 of the explanations.

[104] Partially inspired by Regulation (EU) 603/2013 of the European Parliament and of the Council of 26 June 2013 on the establishment of 'Eurodac' for the comparison of fingerprints for the effective application of Regulation (EU) 604/2013 establishing the criteria and mechanisms for

processing are allowed. These are limited to legal protection,[105] ensuring data security, or overriding reasons in the public interest that have been verified. This last derogation clause must be interpreted narrowly. Paragraph 4 regulates the final stage of deletion and provides for another derogation clause. It is important to stress that any decision that entails retaining the data for a longer period needs special justification and must be reviewed regularly.

79 Article VI-26(5) is inspired by existing EU law and clarifies that the right of Member States to keep national files shall not be affected.[106]

80 As already explained, **Article VI-27** regulates **storage of data in shared databases beyond procedures associated with a duty to inform.**[107] Article VI-27(1), (2) is not confined to personal data but regulates **all kinds of data.** Nevertheless, the basic act may stipulate different storage rules between personal data on one hand and other data on the other. Paragraph 3 provides a rule on the blocking of personal data, which is adapted to the specifics of data storage beyond procedures associated with a duty to inform, while paragraph 4 refers to rules set out in Article VI-26. Paragraph 5 provides the option to delete data earlier than at the established storage time if the data supplying authority requests this explicitly and if the person concerned agrees.[108] In order to ensure that data is not deleted as long as an authority

determining the Member State responsible for examining an application for international protection lodged in one of the Member States by a third-country national or a stateless person and on requests for the comparison with Eurodac data by Member States' law enforcement authorities and Europol for law enforcement purposes, and amending Regulation (EU) 1077/2011 establishing a European Agency for the operational management of large-scale IT systems in the area of freedom, security and justice (recast) [2013] OJ L180/1, Art 18(2).

[105] Sources of inspiration: Council Regulation (EC) 515/97 of 13 March 1997 on mutual assistance between the administrative authorities of the Member States and the cooperation between the latter and the Commission to ensure the correct application of the law on customs and agricultural matters [1997] OJ L82/1 last amended by Regulation (EC) 766/2008 of the European Parliament and of the Council of 9 July 2008 amending Council Regulation (EC) 515/97 on mutual assistance between the administrative authorities of the Member States and cooperation between the latter and the Commission to ensure the correct application of the law on customs and agricultural matters [2008] OJ L218/48, Art 33(4); Regulation (EU) 1024/2012 of the European Parliament and of the Council of 25 October 2012 on administrative cooperation through the Internal Market Information System and repealing Commission Decision 2008/49/EC ('the IMI Regulation') [2012] OJ L316/1 last amended by Directive 2014/67/EU of the European Parliament and of the Council of 15 May 2014 on the enforcement of Directive 96/71/EC concerning the posting of workers in the framework of the provision of services and amending Regulation (EU) No 1024/2012 on administrative cooperation through the Internal Market Information System ('the IMI Regulation') [2014] OJ L 159/11, Recital (22).

[106] Regulation (EC) 1987/2006 of the European Parliament and of the Council of 20 December 2006 on the establishment, operation and use of the second generation Schengen Information System (SIS II) [2006] OJ L381/4, Art 38(3).

[107] See paras 76, 77 of the explanations.

[108] Based on Regulation (EU) 1024/2012 of the European Parliament and of the Council of 25 October 2012 on administrative cooperation through the Internal Market Information System and repealing Commission Decision 2008/49/EC ('the IMI Regulation') [2012] OJ L316/1 last amended by Directive 2014/67/EU of the European Parliament and of the Council of 15 May 2014

or the person concerned is interested in its storage, the data supplying authority's request is as necessary as the consent of the person concerned.

Article VI-28 is inspired by conventional provisions about **confidentiality.**[109] The confidentially should also apply after members of staff leave office or employment.[110] **81**

Article VI-29 introduces an obligation to establish proper **security standards for IT systems.** It seems appropriate to introduce such an obligation, which supplements the general rule concerning the need for a basic act, not only for shared databases, but also for duties to inform when they are performed through information systems as defined in Article VI-2.[111] The rules that are established pursuant to **82**

on the enforcement of Directive 96/71/EC concerning the posting of workers in the framework of the provision of services and amending Regulation (EU) No 1024/2012 on administrative cooperation through the Internal Market Information System ('the IMI Regulation') [2014] OJ L 159/11, Art 14(5).

[109] Compare Council Regulation (EC) 659/1999 of 22 March 1999 laying down detailed rules for the application of Article 93 of the EC Treaty [1999] OJ L83/1 last amended by Council Regulation (EU) 734/2013 of 22 July 2013 amending Regulation (EC) 659/1999 laying down detailed rules for the application of Article 93 of the EC Treaty [2013] OJ L204/15, Art 24.

[110] Based on Regulation (EC) 1987/2006 of the European Parliament and of the Council of 20 December 2006 on the establishment, operation and use of the second generation Schengen Information System (SIS II) [2006] OJ L381/4, Art 11; also similar in Directive 2001/95/EC of the European Parliament and of the Council of 3 December 2001 on general product safety [2001] OJ L11/4 last amended by Regulation (EC) 596/2009 of the European Parliament and of the Council of 18 June 2009 adapting a number of instruments subject to the procedure referred to in Article 251 of the Treaty to Council Decision 1999/468/EC with regard to the regulatory procedure with scrutiny [2009] OJ L188/14, Art 16; similar obligation on the Management Authority in Regulation (EC) 767/2008 of the European Parliament and of the Council of 9 July 2008 concerning the Visa Information System (VIS) and the exchange of data between Member States on short-stay visas (VIS Regulation) [2008] OJ L218/60 last amended by Regulation (EC) 610/2013 of the European Parliament and of the Council of 26 June 2013 amending Regulation (EC) No 562/2006 of the European Parliament and of the Council establishing a Community Code on the rules governing the movement of persons across borders (Schengen Borders Code), the Convention implementing the Schengen Agreement, Council Regulations (EC) No 1683/95 and (EC) No 539/2001 and Regulations (EC) No 767/2008 and (EC) No 810/2009 of the European Parliament and of the Council [2013] OJ L182/1, Art 26(9).

[111] For similar provisions, see Regulation (EC) 767/2008 of the European Parliament and of the Council of 9 July 2008 concerning the Visa Information System (VIS) and the exchange of data between Member States on short-stay visas (VIS Regulation) [2008] OJ L218/60 last amended by Regulation (EC) 610/2013 of the European Parliament and of the Council of 26 June 2013 amending Regulation (EC) No 562/2006 of the European Parliament and of the Council establishing a Community Code on the rules governing the movement of persons across borders (Schengen Borders Code), the Convention implementing the Schengen Agreement, Council Regulations (EC) No 1683/95 and (EC) No 539/2001 and Regulations (EC) No 767/2008 and (EC) No 810/2009 of the European Parliament and of the Council [2013] OJ L182/1, Arts 26(2)(b), 29(2), 32 where the Management Authority has the responsibilities. The Member States responsible shall ensure the security of data before and during transmission and each Member State shall ensure the security of the data which it receives from VIS. In addition each Member State shall adopt specific security measures in relation to the national system; Regulation (EC) 810/2009 of the European Parliament and of the Council of 13 July 2009 establishing a Community Code on Visas (Visa Code) [2004] OJ L243/1 last amended by Regulation (EU) 610/2013 of the European Parliament and of the Council of 26 June 2013 amending Regulation (EC) 562/2006 of the European Parliament and of

this provision must provide a level of information security equal to that established by Directive 95/46[112] and Regulation 45/2001.[113]

Chapter 4: Supervision and Dispute Resolution

83 Inter-administrative information exchange as regulated in this book affects the interests of a **great number of participating authorities** as well as **concerned persons.** In addition, the quality of this information exchange depends on the **performance and sincere cooperation** of the participating authorities. The clear allocation of responsibilities and the legal obligations of the various actors as stipulated in Chapters 1, 2, and 3 of this book willl enhance the effectiveness and efficiency as well as the lawfulness of such inter-administrative information exchange. Nevertheless, under the complex circumstances of such composite information management, additional instruments must be in place in order to support and require compliance with these rules and objectives, that is, effective accountability mechanisms.

84 Book VI regulates such **accountability mechanisms** in Chapters 4 and 5. Chapter 5 on remedies and liability provides some important mechanisms in this regard, although it does not cover all relevant instruments of judicial protection in accordance with the general approach of the ReNEUAL Model Rules.[114] Against this background, Chapter 4 establishes effective and coordinated mechanisms for supervision and dispute resolution in order to provide a comprehensive framework

the Council establishing a Community Code on the rules governing the movement of persons across borders (Schengen Borders Code), the Convention implementing the Schengen Agreement, Council Regulations (EC) 1683/95 and (EC) 539/2001 and Regulations (EC) 767/2008 and (EC) 810/2009 of the European Parliament and of the Council [2013] OJ L182/1, Art 44 on data encryption; Regulation (EC) 1987/2006 of the European Parliament and of the Council of 20 December 2006 on the establishment, operation and use of the second generation Schengen Information System (SIS II) [2006] OJ L381/4, Art 10 lists the responsibilities of Member States in the field of technical security whereas Arts 15 and 16 state that the Management Authority is responsible for the security of the communication infrastructure.

[112] Directive 95/46/EC of the European Parliament and of the Council of 24 October 1995 on the protection of individuals with regard to the processing of personal data and on the free movement of such data [1995] OJ L281/31 last amended by Regulation (EC) 1882/2003 of the European Parliament and of the Council of 29 September 2003 adapting to Council Decision 1999/468/EC the provisions relating to committees which assist the Commission in the exercise of its implementing powers laid down in instruments subject to the procedure referred to in Article 251 of the EC Treaty [2003] OJ L284/1.

[113] Regulation (EC) 45/2001 of the European Parliament and of the Council of 18 December 2000 on the protection of individuals with regard to the processing of personal data by the Community institutions and bodies and on the free movement of such data [2001] OJ L8/1 last amended by Corrigendum to Regulation (EC) 45/2001 of the European Parliament and of the Council of 18 December 2000 on the protection of individuals with regard to the processing of personal data by the Community institutions and bodies and on the free movement of such data [2007] OJ L164/35.

[114] See Book I, para 5 of the Explanations.

for inter-administrative accountability. As already highlighted, the objectives of this framework are twofold and comprise effective composite information management on the one hand and protection of individual rights on the other.

Chapter 4 sets the necessary framework rules for the supervision of information management activities supported by information systems with participating authorities from various jurisdictions within the EU. Such composite information management helps to ensure **that in the context of de-centralized but integrated administration** all relevant facts of a matter can be collected and shared prior to decision-making by a national or Union body, but often creates situations in which administrative action takes effect beyond the territorial limits of the jurisdiction of the decision-making body. **85**

Such a regulatory framework for de-centralized implementation and administration of EU law through information systems raises not only the **question of effective discharge of administrative duties,** it can also have considerable implications for the **exercise of the rights of individuals,** including rights to data protection and protection of business secrets. Such rights also include procedural rights of good administration, such as rights to a fair hearing, rights of defence, rights of access to information and—more generally but importantly—the right to an effective judicial remedy. **86**

As explained in the introduction to this book, Book VI is based on the observation that data **protection law and the general law of composite information management are interdependent** and need an integrated regulatory approach. This is also the case for the supervision of such a composite information exchange. The starting point for consideration of the administrative structure is Article 8(3) of the CFR, which establishes the obligation to create an independent supervisory authority for data protection. This independence under a widely held interpretation of Article 8(3) CFR could be compromised if the data protection supervisors were also responsible for tasks other than data protection *stricto sensu*, such as supervisory functions fostering effective inter-administrative information exchange. **87**

Therefore, a comprehensive supervisory framework unavoidably needs a **twofold structure.** The first element is a coordinated framework for the effective data protection supervision of information systems with components in the jurisdiction of various data protection supervisors (section 2). **88**

The **objective of the general supervisory authority**—as the second element—is described in Section 1 (Article VI-30(2)). It is designed to ensure several objectives. First, individuals will be able to turn to a single interlocutor for the protection of their rights. This is especially important with regard to rights that are not protected by data protection law, for instance business secrets. Individuals would have more effective protection and benefit from access to EU courts in case of non-satisfaction with the decisions of such an authority. Also, the instrument of a single supervisory authority **89** allows for using it as an administrative appeals body against decisions of participating authorities. Second, the general supervisory authority is an effective instrument to enforce compliance with the numerous objective obligations associated with inter-administrative information exchange. In this regard the general supervisory authority can also serve as arbiter in case of conflicts between the participating authorities, or can resolve such conflicts through binding inter-administrative decisions.

Section 1: General Supervision and Dispute Resolution

90 The **supervisory authority** of each information system must be designated or created in the basic act. It will have the right to take binding decisions in the sense of Book III.

91 Its **functions** include to manage the relations within the participating authorities by supervising the activities within the network (Article VI-30(2)(a)) and resolving conflicts between the participating authorities in the context of their work in the system (Article VI-30(2)(b)).

92 This **mediating activity** is further developed in Article VI-31. This process is modelled on a similar feature in the European food safety network in which the Commission is in charge of mediating in case of disputes between participating authorities.[115]

93 **Supervisory tasks** (Article VI-30(2)(c)) and **verification tasks** (Article VI-30(2)(d)) conferred on the supervisory authority in the basic act will require that authority to be able to oblige other participating authorities in the information system (Article VI-32) to conform with its interpretation. The supervisory authority will be authorized to review the legality of information management activities for compliance with all sources of EU law including general principles of EU law. The supervisory authority will have the power to direct orders at the participating authorities to ensure compliance with EU law. Such controlling activity can take place, under Article VI-32(2), (3) upon

- the supervisory authority's own initiative.
- a request lodged by another participating authority.[116]
- complaints lodged by concerned persons.

[115] See Regulation (EC) 178/2002 of the European Parliament and of the Council of 28 January 2002 laying down the general principles and requirements of food law, establishing the European Safety Authority and laying down procedures in matters of food safety [2002] OJ L31/1 last amended by Regulation (EC) 596/2009 of the European Parliament and of the Council of 18 June 2009 adapting a number of instruments subject to the procedure referred to in Article 251 of the Treaty to Council Decision 1999/468/EC with regard to the regulatory procedure with scrutiny—Adaptation to the regulatory procedure with scrutiny—Part Four [2009] OJ L188/14, Art 60(2).

[116] See Regulation (EC) 1829/2003 of the European Parliament and of the Council of 22 September 2003 on genetically modified food and feed [2003] OJ L268/1 last amended by Regulation (EC) 298/2008 of the European Parliament and of the Council of 11 March 2008 amending Regulation (EC) 1829/2003 on genetically modified food and feed, as regards the implementing powers conferred on the Commission [2008] OJ L97/64, Art 36.

The supervisory authority will also have the obligation to **protect individual data protection and access to information rights** (Article VI-30(2)(e),(f)) in cooperation with the EDPS and the national data protection authorities. 94

In order to be able to effectively protect these fundamental rights of individuals, the supervisory authority will have the **power to grant access to, alter, or delete data** in the information system (Article VI-33). This is a key provision establishing a centralized 'one-stop-shop' style remedy for individuals. It is an essential element to ensure individual protection in the de-centralized implementation of EU law. 95

Granting individuals the opportunity to inquire about existing data and requesting the correction or deletion of incorrect or illegally obtained and held data is necessary in order to **ensure** that—depending on the technical design of the information system—an individual would not have to make **several simultaneous requests for correction** in various jurisdictions in order to have an effective remedy against violations of their rights, or risk addressing the wrong participating authority. A single supervisory authority with the powers to grant remedies therefore not only allows individuals an effective remedy against the wrong, it also opens the way, in case of a negative decision of the supervising authority, to allow access to the EU courts to bring an action for annulment against a decision refusing to act, or an action for failure to act, in case of inaction. 96

Other specific tasks can be added in the basic act for an information system. 97

Section 2: Data Protection Supervision of Databases

Section 2 is based on **two alternative solutions,** which are models from which the legislature in specific policy areas can choose. One is the model for the cooperation of data protection supervisors provided for in Articles VI-36—VI-38. The other is the model of the draft EU General Data Protection Regulation to establish a European Data Protection Board (Article VI-39). The choice between these two alternatives will allow the legislator to find solutions that are adapted to the specific design of individual information systems. 98

In addition to this external data protection supervision, Article VI-34 provides for the mandatory appointment of one **data protection officer** per database. Data protection officers serve as central contact points for the Data Protection Authorities. The obligation to appoint a Data Protection Officer for Union institutions, bodies, offices, and agencies dealing with data already arises from Article 24 of Regulation 45/2001.[117] In addition to this existing obligation, Article VI-34(1) obliges Member 99

[117] Regulation (EC) 45/2001 of the European Parliament and of the Council of 18 December 2000 on the protection of individuals with regard to the processing of personal data by the Community institutions and bodies and on the free movement of such data [2001] OJ L8/1 last

State authorities also to appoint a Data Protection Officer when acting in the context of EU databases.[118]

100 Article VI-34(2) clarifies that the **appointment and tasks of data protection officers** are governed by Article 24 of Regulation 45/2001[119] as *lex generalis*,[120] as long as the

amended by Corrigendum to Regulation (EC) 45/2001 of the European Parliament and of the Council of 18 December 2000 on the protection of individuals with regard to the processing of personal data by the Community institutions and bodies and on the free movement of such data [2007] OJ L164/35; see also Regulation (EU) 1077/2011 of the European Parliament and of the Council of 25 October 2011 establishing a European Agency for the operational management of large-scale IT systems in the area of freedom, security and justice [2011] OJ L286/1 last amended by Regulation (EU) 603/2013 of the European Parliament and of the Council of 26 June 2013 on the establishment of 'Eurodac' for the comparison of fingerprints for the effective application of Regulation (EU) 604/2013 establishing the criteria and mechanisms for determining the Member State responsible for examining an application for international protection lodged in one of the Member States by a third-country national or a stateless person and on requests for the comparison with Eurodac data by Member States' law enforcement authorities and Europol for law enforcement purposes, and amending Regulation (EU) 1077/2011 establishing a European Agency for the operational management of large-scale IT systems in the area of freedom, security and justice (recast) [2013] OJ L180/1, Art 28(2); Council Decision 2009/371/JHA of 6 April 2009 establishing the European Police Office (Europol) [2009] OJ L121/37, Art 28; Council Decision 2002/187/JHA of 28 February 2002 setting up Eurojust with a view to reinforcing the fight against serious crime [2002] OJ L 63/1 last amended by Council Decision 2009/426/JHA of 16 December 2008 on the strengthening of Eurojust and amending Decision 2002/187/JHA setting up Eurojust with a view to reinforcing the fight against serious crime [2009] OJ L138/14, Art 17.

[118] The existing Data Protection Directive does not oblige data processing bodies to establish Data Protection Officers, but provides this as an option for them. The proposed obligation is in line with Commission Proposal for a Regulation of the European Parliament and of the Council on the protection of individuals with regard to the processing of personal data and on the free movement of such data (General Data Protection Regulation) COM(2012) 11 final, Art 35.

[119] Regulation (EC) 45/2001 of the European Parliament and of the Council of 18 December 2000 on the protection of individuals with regard to the processing of personal data by the Community institutions and bodies and on the free movement of such data [2001] OJ L8/1 last amended by Corrigendum to Regulation (EC) 45/2001 of the European Parliament and of the Council of 18 December 2000 on the protection of individuals with regard to the processing of personal data by the Community institutions and bodies and on the free movement of such data [2007] OJ L164/35.

[120] For example Regulation (EU) 1077/2011 of the European Parliament and of the Council of 25 October 2011 establishing a European Agency for the operational management of large-scale IT systems in the area of freedom, security and justice [2011] OJ L286/1 last amended by Regulation (EU) 603/2013 of the European Parliament and of the Council of 26 June 2013 on the establishment of 'Eurodac' for the comparison of fingerprints for the effective application of Regulation (EU) 604/2013 establishing the criteria and mechanisms for determining the Member State responsible for examining an application for international protection lodged in one of the Member States by a third-country national or a stateless person and on requests for the comparison with Eurodac data by Member States' law enforcement authorities and Europol for law enforcement purposes, and amending Regulation (EU) 1077/2011 establishing a European Agency for the operational management of large-scale IT systems in the area of freedom, security and justice (recast) [2013] OJ L180/1, Art 28(2).

basic act establishing the database does not contain specific rules.[121] As Regulation 45/2001[122] applies per se to institutions, bodies, offices, and agencies of the Union, Member State authorities are only bound *mutatis mutandis*. Data protection officers of Member State authorities collaborate with their respective National Data Protection Authority and the European Data Protection Board, where applicable, under Article VI-39[123] and they must be registered with their respective National Data Protection Authority.

Option One: cooperative supervision under Articles VI-36 to VI-38

The first of the two options mentioned above, the **default option** formulated in Article VI-36 to VI-38, is in line with several newer legal acts establishing databases. Under this model, the supervisory competences can be split between the **EDPS and the National Supervisory Authorities**, which must cooperate to fulfil their task in an effective way.[124] Such a **cooperative supervision** is concretized by Articles VI-36 to VI-38 as the general rules of external data protection supervision of databases. In most of the recently adopted basic acts concerning shared databases 101

[121] For example Council Decision 2009/371/JHA of 6 April 2009 establishing the European Police Office (Europol) [2009] OJ L121/37, Art 28; Council Decision 2002/187/JHA of 28 February 2002 setting up Eurojust with a view to reinforcing the fight against serious crime [2002] OJ L 63/1 last amended by Council Decision 2009/426/JHA of 16 December 2008 on the strengthening of Eurojust and amending Decision 2002/187/JHA setting up Eurojust with a view to reinforcing the fight against serious crime [2009] OJ L138/14, Art 17.

[122] Regulation (EC) 45/2001 of the European Parliament and of the Council of 18 December 2000 on the protection of individuals with regard to the processing of personal data by the Community institutions and bodies and on the free movement of such data [2001] OJ L8/1 last amended by Corrigendum to Regulation (EC) 45/2001 of the European Parliament and of the Council of 18 December 2000 on the protection of individuals with regard to the processing of personal data by the Community institutions and bodies and on the free movement of such data [2007] OJ L164/35.

[123] The Data Protection Officers of EU institutions and bodies collaborate with the EDPS.

[124] See Regulation (EC) 1987/2006 of the European Parliament and of the Council of 20 December 2006 on the establishment, operation and use of the second generation Schengen Information System (SIS II) [2006] OJ L381/4, Arts 44–46; Regulation (EU) 1024/2012 of the European Parliament and of the Council of 25 October 2012 on administrative cooperation through the Internal Market Information System and repealing Commission Decision 2008/49/EC ('the IMI Regulation') [2012] OJ L316/1 last amended by Directive 2014/67/EU of the European Parliament and of the Council of 15 May 2014 on the enforcement of Directive 96/71/EC concerning the posting of workers in the framework of the provision of services and amending Regulation (EU) No 1024/2012 on administrative cooperation through the Internal Market Information System ('the IMI Regulation') [2014] OJ L 159/11, Art 21; Regulation (EU) 603/2013 of the European Parliament and of the Council of 26 June 2013 on the establishment of 'Eurodac' for the comparison of fingerprints for the effective application of Regulation (EU) 604/2013 establishing the criteria and mechanisms for determining the Member State responsible for examining an application for international protection lodged in one of the Member States by a third-country national or a stateless person and on requests for the comparison with Eurodac data by Member States' law enforcement authorities and Europol for law enforcement purposes, and amending Regulation (EU) 1077/2011 establishing a European Agency for the operational management of large-scale IT systems in the area of freedom, security and justice (recast) [2013] OJ L180/1, Arts 30–32.

the external supervision is organized in a cooperative structure similar to the model under option one described in Articles VI-36 to VI-38. Examples are Regulation 1024/2012[125] and Regulation 603/2013.[126]

102 Article VI-36 concretizes the **tasks, duties, and competences** of the **EDPS,** who is competent to monitor the lawfulness of the **processing** of personal data **by EU authorities** and—if a Management Authority is set up pursuant to Article VI-8—**by the Management Authority.**[127] Paragraphs 1, 2 and 4 of Article VI-36 essentially

---

[125] Regulation (EU) 1024/2012 of the European Parliament and of the Council of 25 October 2012 on administrative cooperation through the Internal Market Information System and repealing Commission Decision 2008/49/EC ('the IMI Regulation') [2012] OJ L316/1 last amended by Directive 2014/67/EU of the European Parliament and of the Council of 15 May 2014 on the enforcement of Directive 96/71/EC concerning the posting of workers in the framework of the provision of services and amending Regulation (EU) No 1024/2012 on administrative cooperation through the Internal Market Information System ('the IMI Regulation') [2014] OJ L 159/11.

[126] Regulation (EU) 603/2013 of the European Parliament and of the Council of 26 June 2013 on the establishment of 'Eurodac' for the comparison of fingerprints for the effective application of Regulation (EU) 604/2013 establishing the criteria and mechanisms for determining the Member State responsible for examining an application for international protection lodged in one of the Member States by a third-country national or a stateless person and on requests for the comparison with Eurodac data by Member States' law enforcement authorities and Europol for law enforcement purposes, and amending Regulation (EU) 1077/2011 establishing a European Agency for the operational management of large-scale IT systems in the area of freedom, security and justice (recast) [2013] OJ L180/1.

[127] Regulation (EC) 1987/2006 of the European Parliament and of the Council of 20 December 2006 on the establishment, operation and use of the second generation Schengen Information System (SIS II) [2006] OJ L381/4, Art 45(1); Council Decision 2007/533/JHA of 12 June 2007 on the establishment, operation and use of the second generation Schengen Information System (SIS II) [2007] OJ L205/63, Art 61(1); Regulation (EC) 767/2008 of the European Parliament and of the Council of 9 July 2008 concerning the Visa Information System (VIS) and the exchange of data between Member States on short-stay visas (VIS Regulation) [2008] OJ L218/60 last amended by Regulation (EC) 610/2013 of the European Parliament and of the Council of 26 June 2013 amending Regulation (EC) No 562/2006 of the European Parliament and of the Council establishing a Community Code on the rules governing the movement of persons across borders (Schengen Borders Code), the Convention implementing the Schengen Agreement, Council Regulations (EC) No 1683/95 and (EC) No 539/2001 and Regulations (EC) No 767/2008 and (EC) No 810/2009 of the European Parliament and of the Council [2013] OJ L182/1 VIS Management Authority has responsibilities and Member States have obligations concerning data security, Art 42(1); Regulation (EU) 603/2013 of the European Parliament and of the Council of 26 June 2013 on the establishment of 'Eurodac' for the comparison of fingerprints for the effective application of Regulation (EU) 604/2013 establishing the criteria and mechanisms for determining the Member State responsible for examining an application for international protection lodged in one of the Member States by a third-country national or a stateless person and on requests for the comparison with Eurodac data by Member States' law enforcement authorities and Europol for law enforcement purposes, and amending Regulation (EU) 1077/2011 establishing a European Agency for the operational management of large-scale IT systems in the area of freedom, security and justice (recast) [2013] OJ L180/1, Art 31(1); Council Regulation (EC) 515/97 of 13 March 1997 on mutual assistance between the administrative authorities of the Member States and the cooperation between the latter and the Commission to ensure the correct application of the law on customs and agricultural matters [1997] OJ L82/1 amended by Regulation 766/2008 of the European Parliament and of the Council of 9 July 2008 amending Council Regulation (EC) 515/97 on mutual assistance between the administrative authorities of the Member States and cooperation between the latter and the Commission to

consist of a slightly updated adaptation of Article 41(2) of Regulation 45/2001[128] to this system of cooperative supervision between the EDPS and the national supervisory authorities. Further, the EDPS will be in charge of auditing the data processing on a regular basis. Such an auditing is foreseen by several basic acts establishing databases[129] and is generalized by Article VI-36(3). The auditing competence of the EDPS in a system of cooperative supervision is restricted to the data processing of EU authorities and the data processing of a Management Authority.

On the other hand, the supervision of data processing by Member State authorities is undertaken by the **National Supervisory Authorities** (Article VI-37(1)) designated in Article 28 of Directive 95/46,[130] or Article 25 of Council Framework Decision 103

ensure the correct application of the law on customs and agricultural matters [2008] OJ L218/48, Art 37(3).

[128] Regulation (EC) 45/2001 of the European Parliament and of the Council of 18 December 2000 on the protection of individuals with regard to the processing of personal data by the Community institutions and bodies and on the free movement of such data [2001] OJ L8/1 last amended by Corrigendum to Regulation (EC) 45/2001 of the European Parliament and of the Council of 18 December 2000 on the protection of individuals with regard to the processing of personal data by the Community institutions and bodies and on the free movement of such data [2007] OJ L164/35.

[129] Regulation (EC) 1987/2006 of the European Parliament and of the Council of 20 December 2006 on the establishment, operation and use of the second generation Schengen Information System (SIS II) [2006] OJ L381/4, Art 45(2); Council Decision 2007/533/JHA of 12 June 2007 on the establishment, operation and use of the second generation Schengen Information System (SIS II) [2007] OJ L205/63, Art 61(2); Regulation (EC) 767/2008 of the European Parliament and of the Council of 9 July 2008 concerning the Visa Information System (VIS) and the exchange of data between Member States on short-stay visas (VIS Regulation) [2008] OJ L218/60 last amended by Regulation (EC) 610/2013 of the European Parliament and of the Council of 26 June 2013 amending Regulation (EC) No 562/2006 of the European Parliament and of the Council establishing a Community Code on the rules governing the movement of persons across borders (Schengen Borders Code), the Convention implementing the Schengen Agreement, Council Regulations (EC) No 1683/95 and (EC) No 539/2001 and Regulations (EC) No 767/2008 and (EC) No 810/2009 of the European Parliament and of the Council [2013] OJ L182/1 VIS Management Authority has responsibilities and Member States have obligations concerning data security, Art 42(2), (3); Regulation (EU) 603/2013 of the European Parliament and of the Council of 26 June 2013 on the establishment of 'Eurodac' for the comparison of fingerprints for the effective application of Regulation (EU) 604/2013 establishing the criteria and mechanisms for determining the Member State responsible for examining an application for international protection lodged in one of the Member States by a third-country national or a stateless person and on requests for the comparison with Eurodac data by Member States' law enforcement authorities and Europol for law enforcement purposes, and amending Regulation (EU) 1077/2011 establishing a European Agency for the operational management of large-scale IT systems in the area of freedom, security and justice (recast) [2013] OJ L180/1, Art 31(2).

[130] Directive 95/46/EC of the European Parliament and of the Council of 24 October 1995 on the protection of individuals with regard to the processing of personal data and on the free movement of such data [1995] OJ L281/31 last amended by Regulation (EC) 1882/2003 of the European Parliament and of the Council of 29 September 2003 adapting to Council Decision 1999/468/EC the provisions relating to committees which assist the Commission in the exercise of its implementing powers laid down in instruments subject to the procedure referred to in Article 251 of the EC Treaty [2003] OJ L284/1.

2008/977/JHA,[131] depending on which of the two rules is applicable to the specific data processing. For the fulfilment of this task, the National Supervisory Authorities are endowed with the powers referred to in Directive 95/46,[132] respectively the Council Framework Decision 2008/977/JHA.

104 Given that data processing in databases often suffers from a lack of transparency for the data subject, he or she can hardly be expected to be able to identify the responsible data processing authority. It will therefore be the general task of Data Supervisory Authorities to **assist the data subject in the exercise of such rights**. In order to assure an effective assistance both the Supervisory Authority of the Member State in which the data subject is located, and the Supervisory Authority of the Member State which transmitted the data, are competent to advise the data subject; the two Authorities shall cooperate to this end. In order to facilitate the exercise of his rights, the data subject may only lodge a request with the Supervisory Authority of the Member State where he is located, which has to communicate the request to the authority of the Member State which transmitted the data (Article VI-37(2)).[133] National Supervisory authorities are also required to audit data processing of the Member State authorities. This is complementary to the auditing task of the EDPS (Article VI-36(3)).[134]

---

[131] Council Framework Decision 2008/977/JHA of 27 November 2008 on the protection of personal data processed in the framework of police and judicial cooperation in criminal matters [2008] OJ L350/60.

[132] Directive 95/46/EC of the European Parliament and of the Council of 24 October 1995 on the protection of individuals with regard to the processing of personal data and on the free movement of such data [1995] OJ L281/31 last amended by Regulation (EC) 1882/2003 of the European Parliament and of the Council of 29 September 2003 adapting to Council Decision 1999/468/EC the provisions relating to committees which assist the Commission in the exercise of its implementing powers laid down in instruments subject to the procedure referred to in Article 251 of the EC Treaty [2003] OJ L284/1.

[133] Regulation (EU) 603/2013 of the European Parliament and of the Council of 26 June 2013 on the establishment of 'Eurodac' for the comparison of fingerprints for the effective application of Regulation (EU) 604/2013 establishing the criteria and mechanisms for determining the Member State responsible for examining an application for international protection lodged in one of the Member States by a third-country national or a stateless person and on requests for the comparison with Eurodac data by Member States' law enforcement authorities and Europol for law enforcement purposes, and amending Regulation (EU) 1077/2011 establishing a European Agency for the operational management of large-scale IT systems in the area of freedom, security and justice (recast) [2013] OJ L180/1, Art 29(13).

[134] See Regulation (EC) 1987/2006 of the European Parliament and of the Council of 20 December 2006 on the establishment, operation and use of the second generation Schengen Information System (SIS II) [2006] OJ L381/4, Art 44(2); Regulation (EC) 767/2008 of the European Parliament and of the Council of 9 July 2008 concerning the Visa Information System (VIS) and the exchange of data between Member States on short-stay visas (VIS Regulation) [2008] OJ L218/60 last amended by Regulation (EC) 610/2013 of the European Parliament and of the Council of 26 June 2013 amending Regulation (EC) No 562/2006 of the European Parliament and of the Council establishing a Community Code on the rules governing the movement of persons across borders (Schengen Borders Code), the Convention implementing the Schengen Agreement, Council Regulations (EC) No 1683/95 and (EC) No 539/2001 and Regulations (EC) No 767/2008 and (EC) No 810/2009 of the European Parliament and of the Council [2013] OJ L182/1, Art 41(2); Council Decision

The system of **cooperation between the national supervisory authorities and the EDPS** is addressed in Article VI-38. They are under a duty to cooperate which is a concretization of the general obligation of loyal cooperation arising from Article 4 TEU modelled on specific provisions of EU law.[135] Article VI-38(1) and (2) concretize this cooperation by imposing specific duties and time limits.[136] These obligations 105

2007/533/JHA of 12 June 2007 on the establishment, operation and use of the second generation Schengen Information System (SIS II) [2007] OJ L205/63, Art 60(2).

[135] Compare Regulation (EC) 1987/2006 of the European Parliament and of the Council of 20 December 2006 on the establishment, operation and use of the second generation Schengen Information System (SIS II) [2006] OJ L381/4, Art 46(1); Council Decision 2007/533/JHA of 12 June 2007 on the establishment, operation and use of the second generation Schengen Information System (SIS II) [2007] OJ L205/63, Art 62(1); Regulation (EC) 767/2008 of the European Parliament and of the Council of 9 July 2008 concerning the Visa Information System (VIS) and the exchange of data between Member States on short-stay visas (VIS Regulation) [2008] OJ L218/60 last amended by Regulation (EC) 610/2013 of the European Parliament and of the Council of 26 June 2013 amending Regulation (EC) No 562/2006 of the European Parliament and of the Council establishing a Community Code on the rules governing the movement of persons across borders (Schengen Borders Code), the Convention implementing the Schengen Agreement, Council Regulations (EC) No 1683/95 and (EC) No 539/2001 and Regulations (EC) No 767/2008 and (EC) No 810/2009 of the European Parliament and of the Council [2013] OJ L182/1, Art 43(1); Regulation (EU) 1024/2012 of the European Parliament and of the Council of 25 October 2012 on administrative cooperation through the Internal Market Information System and repealing Commission Decision 2008/49/EC ('the IMI Regulation') [2012] OJ L316/1 last amended by Directive 2014/67/EU of the European Parliament and of the Council of 15 May 2014 on the enforcement of Directive 96/71/EC concerning the posting of workers in the framework of the provision of services and amending Regulation (EU) No 1024/2012 on administrative cooperation through the Internal Market Information System ('the IMI Regulation') [2014] OJ L 159/11, Art 21(3); Regulation (EU) 603/2013 of the European Parliament and of the Council of 26 June 2013 on the establishment of 'Eurodac' for the comparison of fingerprints for the effective application of Regulation (EU) 604/2013 establishing the criteria and mechanisms for determining the Member State responsible for examining an application for international protection lodged in one of the Member States by a third-country national or a stateless person and on requests for the comparison with Eurodac data by Member States' law enforcement authorities and Europol for law enforcement purposes, and amending Regulation (EU) 1077/2011 establishing a European Agency for the operational management of large-scale IT systems in the area of freedom, security and justice (recast) [2013] OJ L180/1, Art 32(1).

[136] Compare Regulation (EC) 1987/2006 of the European Parliament and of the Council of 20 December 2006 on the establishment, operation and use of the second generation Schengen Information System (SIS II) [2006] OJ L381/4, Art 46(2), (3); Council Decision 2007/533/JHA of 12 June 2007 on the establishment, operation and use of the second generation Schengen Information System (SIS II) [2007] OJ L205/63, Art 62(2); Regulation (EC) 767/2008 of the European Parliament and of the Council of 9 July 2008 concerning the Visa Information System (VIS) and the exchange of data between Member States on short-stay visas (VIS Regulation) [2008] OJ L218/60 last amended by Regulation (EC) 610/2013 of the European Parliament and of the Council of 26 June 2013 amending Regulation (EC) No 562/2006 of the European Parliament and of the Council establishing a Community Code on the rules governing the movement of persons across borders (Schengen Borders Code), the Convention implementing the Schengen Agreement, Council Regulations (EC) No 1683/95 and (EC) No 539/2001 and Regulations (EC) No 767/2008 and (EC) No 810/2009 of the European Parliament and of the Council [2013] OJ L182/1, Art 43(2), (3); Regulation (EU) 603/2013 of the European Parliament and of the Council of 26 June 2013 on the establishment of 'Eurodac' for the comparison of fingerprints for the effective application of Regulation (EU) 604/2013 establishing the criteria and mechanisms for determining the Member State responsible for examining an application for international protection lodged in one

exist irrespective of general rules and obligations about mutual assistance as described in Book V.

106 The basic act can also assign the supervision of the data processing within a database to a **single authority**—either the EDPS or one of the National Supervisory Authority—**or** a **group of Supervisory Authorities**. Such a representative supervision allows a holistic approach to supervision similar to the Supervision by a European Data Protection Board under Article VI-39. However, the representative supervision only concerns the data processing *within* the database, but not the entry into the database and the retrieval from the database, which—in a system of cooperative supervision—remain within the competence of either the EDPS or the National Supervisory Authorities under Articles VI-36 and VI-37. The supervision of the whole database, including the entry into and the retrieval from the database can only be assigned to the European Data Protection Board under Article VI-39.

Option Two: integrated supervision under Article VI-39

107 Article VI-39 allows for assigning the external supervision completely to a **European Data Protection Board**. As the data processing in shared databases represents a particularly integrated form of composite administrative procedures, there might be good reason in practice to assign the entire external supervision to one body integrating the supervisory authorities from the European as well as from the national level. This is the basis of the model contained in Article VI-39.

108 A **similar integrated model** was essentially developed in the pre-Lisbon period. Before the entry into force of the Treaty of Lisbon, Directive 95/46 and Regulation 45/2001[137] were only applicable to the former 'first pillar' Community law. These

of the Member States by a third-country national or a stateless person and on requests for the comparison with Eurodac data by Member States' law enforcement authorities and Europol for law enforcement purposes, and amending Regulation (EU) 1077/2011 establishing a European Agency for the operational management of large-scale IT systems in the area of freedom, security and justice (recast) [2013] OJ L180/1, Art 32(3), (4); Commission Proposal for a Regulation of the European Parliament and of the Council on the protection of individuals with regard to the processing of personal data and on the free movement of such data (General Data Protection Regulation) COM(2012) 11 final, Art 55(2).

[137] Directive 95/46/EC of the European Parliament and of the Council of 24 October 1995 on the protection of individuals with regard to the processing of personal data and on the free movement of such data [1995] OJ L281/31 last amended by Regulation (EC) 1882/2003 of the European Parliament and of the Council of 29 September 2003 adapting to Council Decision 1999/468/EC the provisions relating to committees which assist the Commission in the exercise of its implementing powers laid down in instruments subject to the procedure referred to in Article 251 of the EC Treaty [2003] OJ L284/1; Regulation (EC) 45/2001 of the European Parliament and of the Council of 18 December 2000 on the protection of individuals with regard to the processing of personal data by the Community institutions and bodies and on the free movement of such data [2001] OJ L8/1 last amended by Corrigendum to Regulation (EC) 45/2001 of the European Parliament and of the Council of 18 December 2000 on the protection of individuals with regard to the processing of personal data by the Community institutions and bodies and on the free movement of such data [2007] OJ L164/35.

acts did not apply to former 'third pillar' matters. In view of this, especially in the field of the 'third pillar' Justice and Home Affairs, the European legislator established several Joint Supervisory Bodies with the competence for several shared data resources like the VIS or agencies like Europol. These Joint Supervisory Bodies were normally composed of one or two representatives of the National Supervisory Authorities and they monitored the application of the data protection provisions of the basic legal act and/or the Framework Decision 2008/977/JHA.[138]

Some newer legal instruments, like the Regulation and the Council Decision regarding the SIS II, abandoned the concept of Joint Supervisory Bodies and instead established a system of cooperation between the EDPS and the National Supervisory Authorities similar to the model under Articles VI-36 to VI-38.[139] **109**

Other legal instruments maintained the concept of Joint Supervisory Bodies.[140] The draft General Data Protection Regulation further developed this integrated model of composite data protection under the label of a European Data Protection Board as an **organizational structure for enhancing the coherence of the implementation of data protection law.** In contrast to the draft regulation, these model rules develop the European Data Protection Board under the second option not only as a preparatory or advisory body, but as a body with powers to take binding decisions **110**

[138] See Council Decision 2009/371/JHA of 6 April 2009 establishing the European Police Office (Europol) [2009] OJ L121/37, Art 34(1); Council Decision 2009/917/JHA of 30 November 2009 on the use of information technology for customs purposes [2009] OJ L323/20, Art 25(1).

[139] See Regulation (EC) 1987/2006 of the European Parliament and of the Council of 20 December 2006 on the establishment, operation and use of the second generation Schengen Information System (SIS II) [2006] OJ L381/4, Arts 44–46; Regulation (EU) 1024/2012 of the European Parliament and of the Council of 25 October 2012 on administrative cooperation through the Internal Market Information System and repealing Commission Decision 2008/49/EC ('the IMI Regulation') [2012] OJ L316/1 last amended by Directive 2014/67/EU of the European Parliament and of the Council of 15 May 2014 on the enforcement of Directive 96/71/EC concerning the posting of workers in the framework of the provision of services and amending Regulation (EU) No 1024/2012 on administrative cooperation through the Internal Market Information System ('the IMI Regulation') [2014] OJ L 159/11, Art 21(3); Regulation (EU) 603/2013 of the European Parliament and of the Council of 26 June 2013 on the establishment of 'Eurodac' for the comparison of fingerprints for the effective application of Regulation (EU) 604/2013 establishing the criteria and mechanisms for determining the Member State responsible for examining an application for international protection lodged in one of the Member States by a third-country national or a stateless person and on requests for the comparison with Eurodac data by Member States' law enforcement authorities and Europol for law enforcement purposes, and amending Regulation (EU) 1077/2011 establishing a European Agency for the operational management of large-scale IT systems in the area of freedom, security and justice (recast) [2013] OJ L180/1, Arts 30–32.

[140] Council Decision 2009/371/JHA of 6 April 2009 establishing the European Police Office (Europol) [2009] OJ L121/37, Art 34; Council Decision 2009/917/JHA of 30 November 2009 on the use of information technology for customs purposes [2009] OJ L323/20, Art 25—both adopted one day before the entry into force of the Lisbon Treaty in order to maintain for a transitionary period the initial inter-governmental structure in this field.

on data protection problems arising from composite information management. This board is developed here for cases where the legislator opts for more integrative supervision. When assigning the external data protection supervision of databases to the European Data Protection Board (Article VI-39), this has to be enshrined in the basic act establishing the database.

111 Under the model proposed by Article VI-39, the **legislator may assign** the supervision of the processing of personal data in databases to a European Data Protection Board. The rules concerning the composition and the decision-making of the Board are strongly influenced by the Proposal for a General Data Protection Regulation.[141] If the Proposal is adopted or if Directive 95/46[142] is amended in the sense that the Article 29 Working Party becomes a Data Protection Board, the assignment has to be made to the Board after the General Data Protection Regulation[143] or after the modified Directive 95/46.[144] However, the Commission is not allowed to participate in the Data Protection Board, as it is acting as a participating authority or even as a Management Authority in several databases. For that reason, participation of the Commission in a Data Protection Board has to be regarded as incompatible with Article 16(2) TFEU and Article 8(3) CFR, which state that the Data Protection Supervision has to be carried out by an independent body.

112 If the legislator has assigned the supervision to the Data Protection Board, the Board is granted the powers set out in Articles IV-36 and IV-37. To structure the

[141] See Commission Proposal for a Regulation of the European Parliament and of the Council on the protection of individuals with regard to the processing of personal data and on the free movement of such data (General Data Protection Regulation) COM(2012) 11 final, Arts 64(2), 68(1).

[142] Directive 95/46/EC of the European Parliament and of the Council of 24 October 1995 on the protection of individuals with regard to the processing of personal data and on the free movement of such data [1995] OJ L281/31 last amended by Regulation (EC) 1882/2003 of the European Parliament and of the Council of 29 September 2003 adapting to Council Decision 1999/468/EC the provisions relating to committees which assist the Commission in the exercise of its implementing powers laid down in instruments subject to the procedure referred to in Article 251 of the EC Treaty [2003] OJ L284/1.

[143] See Commission Proposal for a Regulation of the European Parliament and of the Council on the protection of individuals with regard to the processing of personal data and on the free movement of such data (General Data Protection Regulation) COM(2012) 11 final; European Parliament legislative resolution of 12 March 2014 on the proposal for a regulation of the European Parliament and of the Council on the protection of individuals with regard to the processing of personal data and on the free movement of such data (General Data Protection Regulation) P7_TA(2014)0212.

[144] Directive 95/46/EC of the European Parliament and of the Council of 24 October 1995 on the protection of individuals with regard to the processing of personal data and on the free movement of such data [1995] OJ L281/31 last amended by Regulation (EC) 1882/2003 of the European Parliament and of the Council of 29 September 2003 adapting to Council Decision 1999/468/EC the provisions relating to committees which assist the Commission in the exercise of its implementing powers laid down in instruments subject to the procedure referred to in Article 251 of the EC Treaty [2003] OJ L284/1.

supervision of databases, the Board shall adopt a supervision plan for each database every year. A revocable delegation of parts of the supervision tasks to the EDPS, or to one or a group of Supervisory Authorities, can be made in these plans. They will be binding upon the EDPS and the National Supervisory Authorities. A duty to cooperate with other supervisory authorities is enshrined in Article VI-39(4).

Chapter 5: Remedies and Liability

VI-40 Right to compensation in relation to composite information management activities

Compensation rights under the first paragraph of Article VI-40 are designed to protect individuals. It is **based on a system of choice.** Under the first alternative, an individual can seek damages directly from the authority, which was responsible for the unlawful act leading to the damage. This is the model currently provided for in several EU policy fields, such as in the area of Visas, Schengen or the EURODAC system.[145] **113**

The alternative under Article VI-40(2) provides for an individual to **seek damages** in the jurisdiction of residence or of registration. This is a measure protecting individuals against the potential disadvantages of de-centralized administration of EU law through information systems with participants from various jurisdictions in the EU whose Court systems, law, and language may not be familiar to the person suffering damage. Such a system of representative liability has been developed **114**

[145] See Regulation (EC) 767/2008 of the European Parliament and of the Council of 9 July 2008 concerning the Visa Information System (VIS) and the exchange of data between Member States on short-stay visas (VIS Regulation) [2008] OJ L218/60 last amended by Regulation (EC) 610/2013 of the European Parliament and of the Council of 26 June 2013 amending Regulation (EC) No 562/2006 of the European Parliament and of the Council establishing a Community Code on the rules governing the movement of persons across borders (Schengen Borders Code), the Convention implementing the Schengen Agreement, Council Regulations (EC) No 1683/95 and (EC) No 539/2001 and Regulations (EC) No 767/2008 and (EC) No 810/2009 of the European Parliament and of the Council [2013] OJ L182/1, Art 33(1); Regulation (EU) 603/2013 of the European Parliament and of the Council of 26 June 2013 on the establishment of 'Eurodac' for the comparison of fingerprints for the effective application of Regulation (EU) 604/2013 establishing the criteria and mechanisms for determining the Member State responsible for examining an application for international protection lodged in one of the Member States by a third-country national or a stateless person and on requests for the comparison with Eurodac data by Member States' law enforcement authorities and Europol for law enforcement purposes, and amending Regulation (EU) 1077/2011 establishing a European Agency for the operational management of large-scale IT systems in the area of freedom, security and justice (recast) [2013] OJ L180/1, Art 37(1); Regulation (EC) 1987/2006 of the European Parliament and of the Council of 20 December 2006 on the establishment, operation and use of the second generation Schengen Information System (SIS II) [2006] OJ L381/4, Art 48(1); See Council Decision 2007/533/JHA of 12 June 2007 on the establishment, operation and use of the second generation Schengen Information System (SIS II) [2007] OJ L205/63, Art 64(1).

on the basis of these specific considerations in, for example, the context of the Schengen area.[146]

115 Provisions allowing for **inter-administrative damage claims** are common in EU policies. They are included in Article VI-40 (3).[147]

116 Article VI-40(4) takes up the example of the existing rules for the European Food Safety Authority, referring to the **General Principles of EU law on damages as the criteria for the award.**[148] This is included in order to limit possibilities of so called 'forum shopping' under which individuals could seek out the jurisdiction offering the highest levels of damage payments to the detriment of the authorities which would need to internally reimburse the paying authority.

VI-41 Penalties for unlawful data processing

117 The **principle of loyal cooperation** (Article 4(3) TEU) requires Member States of the EU not only to ensure that they afford equal means of enforcement to rights and obligations arising out of EU law as they would to those arising under national law (the principle of equivalence). It also requires that the Member States ensure

[146] See Regulation (EC) 1987/2006 of the European Parliament and of the Council of 20 December 2006 on the establishment, operation and use of the second generation Schengen Information System (SIS II) [2006] OJ L381/4, Art 48(2); See Council Decision 2007/533/JHA of 12 June 2007 on the establishment, operation and use of the second generation Schengen Information System (SIS II) [2007] OJ L205/63, Art 64(2); The Schengen acquis—Convention implementing the Schengen Agreement of 14 June 1985 between the Governments of the States of the Benelux Economic Union, the Federal Republic of Germany and the French Republic on the gradual abolition of checks at their common borders [2000] OJ L239/19, Art 116(2).

[147] See Regulation (EC) 1987/2006 of the European Parliament and of the Council of 20 December 2006 on the establishment, operation and use of the second generation Schengen Information System (SIS II) [2006] OJ L381/4, Art 48(3); See Council Decision 2007/533/JHA of 12 June 2007 on the establishment, operation and use of the second generation Schengen Information System (SIS II) [2007] OJ L205/63, Art 64(3); Regulation (EC) 767/2008 of the European Parliament and of the Council of 9 July 2008 concerning the Visa Information System (VIS) and the exchange of data between Member States on short-stay visas (VIS Regulation) [2008] OJ L218/60 last amended by Regulation (EC) 610/2013 of the European Parliament and of the Council of 26 June 2013 amending Regulation (EC) No 562/2006 of the European Parliament and of the Council establishing a Community Code on the rules governing the movement of persons across borders (Schengen Borders Code), the Convention implementing the Schengen Agreement, Council Regulations (EC) No 1683/95 and (EC) No 539/2001 and Regulations (EC) No 767/2008 and (EC) No 810/2009 of the European Parliament and of the Council [2013] OJ L182/1, Art 33(2).

[148] See Regulation (EC) 178/2002 of the European Parliament and of the Council of 28 January 2002 laying down the general principles and requirements of food law, establishing the European Safety Authority and laying down procedures in matters of food safety [2002] OJ L31/1 last amended by Regulation (EC) 596/2009 of the European Parliament and of the Council of 18 June 2009 adapting a number of instruments subject to the procedure referred to in Article 251 of the Treaty to Council Decision 1999/468/EC with regard to the regulatory procedure with scrutiny—Adaptation to the regulatory procedure with scrutiny—Part Four [2009] OJ L188/14, Art 47(2).

effective enforcement of rights and obligations arising from EU law (the principle of effectiveness). Article VI-41 is a provision ensuring that these general principles of EU law are specifically enforced with regard to data processing. The specific requirement of requiring 'effective, proportionate and dissuasive penalties' stems from provisions in the Schengen, Visa and EURODAC (cooperation in the context of granting the right of Asylum).[149]

[149] See Regulation (EC) 1987/2006 of the European Parliament and of the Council of 20 December 2006 on the establishment, operation and use of the second generation Schengen Information System (SIS II) [2006] OJ L381/4, Art 49; see Council Decision 2007/533/JHA of 12 June 2007 on the establishment, operation and use of the second generation Schengen Information System (SIS II) [2007] OJ L205/63, Art 65; Regulation (EC) 767/2008 of the European Parliament and of the Council of 9 July 2008 concerning the Visa Information System (VIS) and the exchange of data between Member States on short-stay visas (VIS Regulation) [2008] OJ L218/60 last amended by Regulation (EC) 610/2013 of the European Parliament and of the Council of 26 June 2013 amending Regulation (EC) No 562/2006 of the European Parliament and of the Council establishing a Community Code on the rules governing the movement of persons across borders (Schengen Borders Code), the Convention implementing the Schengen Agreement, Council Regulations (EC) No 1683/95 and (EC) No 539/2001 and Regulations (EC) No 767/2008 and (EC) No 810/2009 of the European Parliament and of the Council [2013] OJ L182/1, Art 36; Regulation (EU) 603/2013 of the European Parliament and of the Council of 26 June 2013 on the establishment of 'Eurodac' for the comparison of fingerprints for the effective application of Regulation (EU) 604/2013 establishing the criteria and mechanisms for determining the Member State responsible for examining an application for international protection lodged in one of the Member States by a third-country national or a stateless person and on requests for the comparison with Eurodac data by Member States' law enforcement authorities and Europol for law enforcement purposes, and amending Regulation (EU) 1077/2011 establishing a European Agency for the operational management of large-scale IT systems in the area of freedom, security and justice (recast) [2013] OJ L180/1, Art 41.

INDEX

The manufacturer's authorised representative in the EU for product safety is Oxford University Press España S.A. of el Parque Empresarial San Fernando de Henares, Avenida de Castilla, 2 – 28830 Madrid (www.oup.es/en or product.safety@oup.com). OUP España S.A. also acts as importer into Spain of products made by the manufacturer.

www.ingramcontent.com/pod-product-compliance
Lightning Source LLC
LaVergne TN
LVHW011820200926
848484LV00005B/1261
9780198795308